Community Resources for Older Adults

Programs and Services in an Era of Change

Robbyn R. Wacker
Karen A. Roberto
Linda E. Piper

Pine Forge Press

Thousand Oaks, California ■ London ■ New Delhi

The Authors' Purpose

Students preparing for careers in gerontology and related areas need more than a description of existing community resources available for older adults. They need to understand how programs come to exist through federal legislation, who uses these resources, how they are delivered, and the challenges service providers face meeting the needs of the aging baby boom cohort.

We have developed a text that gives students a basic understanding of aging policy that created the "aging network" and of theories that can be used to explain help-seeking behavior. Each chapter provides the reader with an in-depth review of the programs and services provided by the "aging network," and the private sector, current scholarship in each topic area, and national and Internet resources. Students will learn to identify the challenges inherent in providing services to older adult through case studies, learning activities and best practice models. Instructors can use these learning activities to stimulate critical thinking about service delivery and what changes might be needed in the future. We hope that *Community Resources for Older Adults* is a text that both you and your students enjoy.

Robbyn R. Wacker
University of Northern Colorado

Karen A. Roberto
Virginia Polytechnic Institute and State University

Linda E. Piper
Weld County Area Agency on Aging

Community Resources for Older Adults

Programs and Services in an Era of Change

by Robbyn R. Wacker, Karen A. Roberto, and Linda E. Piper

In this book you will find:

- An overview of legislation that provides the foundation for the aging network

- A discussion of theories that help predict service use thus offering readers a framework to understanding use and non-use of services by older adults

- Chapters that contain descriptions of the programs and services—both public and private—available to older adults, in-depth reviews of the current body of empirical literature in each program area and discussions of the challenges programs and services will face in the future

- Best practice examples of community programs from around the country that illustrates unique ways of meeting the needs of older adults

- National organizations and Internet resources for each topic area

- Case studies that encourage critical thinking about the delivery and use of community resources

- Learning activities that challenge students to explore the community resources that exist in the reader's locale

Also available with this book:

- Instructor's Manual written by the authors that provides test materials, handouts/overheads highlighting the lecture materials and teaching resources

- The Internet address to an innovative *Community Resources for Older Adults* Webpage providing readers with up-to-date information about aging policy, new programs and services, best practice models, and other resources of interest

  http://www.hhs.unco.edu/geron.htm

THE PINE FORGE PRESS TITLES OF RELATED INTEREST

Adventures in Social Research: Data Analysis Using SPSS® with Windows®
  by Earl Babbie and Fred Halley
Aging: Concepts and Controversies, 2nd edition, by Harry R. Moody Jr.
Aging: Social Inequality and Public Policy by Fred Pampel
Building Community: Social Science in Action edited
  by Philip Nyden, Anne Figert, Mark Shibley, and Darryl Burrows
Shifts in the Social Contract: Understanding Change in American Society
  by Beth A. Rubin
Social Work in the 21st Century by Eileen Gambrill and Michael Reisch
Worlds of Difference: Inequality in the Aging Experience, 2nd ed.,
  by Eleanor Palo Stoller and Rose Campbell Gibson

The Pine Forge Press Series in Research Methods and Statistics

Edited by Kathleen S. Crittenden

Regression: A Primer by Paul Allison
A Guide to Field Research by Carol A. Bailey
Designing Surveys: A Guide to Decisions and Procedures
  by Ronald Czaja and Johnny Blair
Social Statistics for a Diverse Society by Chava Frankfort-Nachmias
Experimental Design and the Analysis of Variance by Robert Leik
How Sampling Works by Richard Maisel and Caroline Hodges Persell
Program Evaluation by George McCall
Investigating the Social World: The Process and Practice of Research
  by Russell K. Schutt

COMMUNITY RESOURCES FOR OLDER ADULTS

Programs and Services in an Era of Change

Robbyn R. Wacker · Karen A. Roberto · Linda E. Piper

PINE FORGE PRESS
Thousand Oaks   London   New Delhi

Be sure to stop by the Community Resources
for Older Adults Web site for up-to-date information
regarding community resources for older adults

http://www.hhs.unco.edu/geron.htm

For information:

 Pine Forge Press
A Sage Publications Company
2455 Teller Road
Thousand Oaks, California 91320
E-mail: sales@pfp.sagepub.com

SAGE Publications Ltd.
6 Bonhill Street
London EC2A 4PU
United Kingdom

SAGE Publications India Pvt. Ltd.
M-32 Market
Greater Kailash I
New Delhi 110 048 India

Printed in the United States of America

Library of Congress Cataloging-in-Publication Data

Wacker, Robbyn R.
    Community resources for older adults: Programs and services in an era of change / by Robbyn R. Wacker, Karen A. Roberto, and Linda E. Piper.
        p.   cm.
    Includes bibliographical references (p.) and index.
    ISBN 0-8039-9089-8 (pbk.: acid-free paper)
    1. Aged—Services for—United States. 2. Community health services for the aged—United States. 3. Old age assistance—United States. 4. Aged volunteers in social service—United States.
    I. Roberto, Karen A. II. Piper, Linda E. III. Title.
    HV1461.W32 1997
    362.6'3'0973—dc21   97-33796

98 99 00 01 02 03 10 9 8 7 6 5 4 3 2 1

Production Editor:	Diana E. Axelsen
Production Assistant:	Lynn Miyata
Typesetter/Designer:	Rebecca Evans
Indexer:	Virgil Diodato
Cover Designer:	Ravi Balasuriya
Print Buyer:	Anna Chin

About the Authors

Robbyn R. Wacker, Ph.D., is Assistant Dean of the College of Health and Human Sciences and Associate Professor of Gerontology at the University of Northern Colorado. Her research interests include legal issues of older adults, including guardianships of older adults and grandparent visitation. She is coauthor (with Pat Keith) of *Older Wards and Their Guardians*. Currently, she is conducting research on nurse aide turnover in long-term care facilities and home health agencies. She teaches courses at the graduate and undergraduate levels in community resources, social policy, and research methods. Prior to obtaining her doctorate, she provided legal assistance to older adults through the Title III Legal Services program.

Karen A. Roberto, Ph.D., is Director of the Center for Gerontology and Professor of Adult Development and Aging at Virginia Polytechnic Institute and State University. Her research examines the psychosocial aspects of aging. Within this realm, her primary focus is on older women's adaptation to life with osteoporosis and its accompanying problems (e.g., chronic pain); relationships between family members in later life (e.g., caregivers and care recipients, parents and children, and grandparents and grandchildren); friendships of older men and women; and the interactions between older adults, their families, and community services. She has published numerous articles and book chapters in each of these areas. She also has edited three books, the most recent of which is *Relationships Between Women in Later Life* (1996). She is a fellow of the Gerontological Society of America and the Association for Gerontology in Higher Education.

Linda E. Piper, M.Ed., has been Director for the Weld County Area Agency on Aging for 17 years. Prior to that, she served as the Director of the Weld County Senior Meals Program for 2 years. She has a wide range of experience developing, coordinating, and implementing community-based programs. She served on the statewide advisory committee to implement the Home and Community-Based Long-Term Care Program for the state of Colorado and has been active with numerous other state and local policy planning committees. Under her leadership, the Weld County Area Agency on Aging was one of four pilot projects through a federal Long-Term Care Systems Development Grant to determine a home and community-based services model for Colorado. Since 1988, she has been an adjunct instructor with the University of Northern Colorado Gerontology Program, teaching graduate-level management and personnel management courses, as well as classes in planning and community resources.

About the Publisher

Pine Forge press is a new educational publisher, dedicated to publishing innovative books and software throughout the social sciences. On this and any other of our publications, we welcome your comments and suggestions.

Please call or write us at:

Pine Forge Press
A Sage Publications Company
2455 Teller Road
Thousand Oaks, California 91320
(805) 499-4224
E-mail: sales@pfp.sagepub.com

Brief Contents

Detailed Contents

Acknowledgments

As is typical of a project of this magnitude, many people have helped us along the way. Some did so willingly, others by default because they were in the right (or maybe wrong) place at a time that we needed help. We would like to take this opportunity to acknowledge those persons who made this undertaking a pleasant and manageable experience. First, we thank former and current graduate students at the University of Northern Colorado (UNC) and at Virginia Tech for all their help in collecting articles, tracking down references, and offering feedback on early drafts of each chapter and on the development of some of the learning activities presented at the end of the chapters. They include Peggy Haller, Conny Seay, Flora Robison, and Tia Jones from UNC and Phyllis Greenberg and Paula Usita from Virginia Tech. Our secretarial staff, Sherry Yost, Laurie Guthmann, Linda King, and Renee Chandler, supported us in many ways. The Interlibrary Loan department at UNC's Michener Library also deserves recognition for helping us get the information we needed within record time of our asking.

A special thanks goes to a number of our colleagues who helped us obtain up-to-date information and gave us valuable feedback on our work. They are Eva Jewell, Mindy Rickard, Dorothy Escamilla, Pete Archuleta, Donna Liess, Lu Horner, Jerry Kearney, Cornelia Dietz, Crystal Day, Jim Sheehan, Mary Margaret Cox, Felicity Spring, Lois Onorato, Jan Meyers, Tom Mauser, Patsy Drewer, Elizabeth Borden, Joan Miller, Ellen Kirsten, Juliet Fried, Jeanne Erickson, and Virginia Fraser. We also appreciate the assistance of Sharon Larson, Region VIII Administration on Aging, for providing so much information on the Older Americans Act and its history.

We are indebted to the reviewers who offered their insights on earlier drafts of the manuscript:

Jane Cloutterbuck, University of Massachusetts, Boston

Shirley Lockery, University of Michigan, Ann Arbor

Linda Breytspraak, University of Missouri, Kansas City

Karen Connor, Drake University

Benjamin Dickerson, Baylor University

Lynne Hodgson, Quinnipiac College

Joanne Grabinski, Eastern Michigan University

William Lane, SUNY, Cortland

Georgia Anetzberger, The Benjamin Rose Institute

Enid Cox, University of Denver

John Pynoos, University of Southern California

Tonya Parrott, Quinnipiac College

We would like to acknowledge that many of the resources listed at the end of each chapter were selected from the *Resource Directory for Older People,* published by the National Institute on Aging. This is a wonderful compilation of a wide variety of national social service organizations that offer information or assistance. Copies may be purchased by calling 202-512-1800.

Of course, a big thank-you goes to Steve Rutter and his staff at Pine Forge Press. Steve's continued encouragement and enthusiasm made sitting down to write another chapter easier to do. It was a pleasure to work with someone with such insight and vision. We are also grateful to Alison Binder, copy editor, and Diana Axelsen, production editor, for their expertise and hard work during this project.

Robbyn R. Wacker

Robbyn R. Wacker

Karen A. Roberto

Karen A. Roberto

Linda E. Piper

Linda E. Piper

I would like to thank Jani Malkiewicz for her encouragement and support on a daily basis during the long course of this project. I would also like to acknowledge my parents, Reinhart and Alta, for their continued love and support, and my niece, Kisha Wacker, who has taught me lessons about personal courage and perseverance. Finally, I have been fortunate to have had, at various stages of my life, some wonderful educators and mentors: Pat Keith, Kathi Hutchison, Sharron Johnson, and Sharon Peterson. Thanks!

RRW

I would like to thank my husband, Steven Sheetz, for his support, thoughtful words, and much needed hugs during the entire process.

KAR

Thanks to Will Piper, my husband, for his editing assistance, patience, and support, and to all my staff at the Area Agency on Aging and close friends who have encouraged me and provided me with case study material.

LEP

Part I

The Social Context of Community Resource Delivery

1

On the Threshold of a New Era

What will society in the United States be like in the year 2030? It is hard to know exactly how different our daily lives will be, but we do know that by the year 2030, our society will be experiencing something that none other has experienced. As we rapidly approach the 21st century, more Americans than ever before will be living in their sixth, seventh, and eighth decades of life. By the year 2030, the first members of the baby boom generation, born in 1946, will be 84 years of age, and the youngest members, born in 1964, will be 65. By the year 2030, there will be 65 million people aged 65 and older—35 million more than in 1990 (Bouvier & De Vita, 1991). Demographically, the baby boom cohort is sandwiched between two smaller cohorts, and as a result of its enormous size, it has commanded attention at every stage of its life course. Just like school systems in the 1960s that were forced to react to the soaring enrollments of the baby boom cohort, social institutions that serve older baby boomers will be challenged once again.

Will this graying of our population dramatically change our society? As demographers, economists, gerontologists, and sociologists debate this question, we can be relatively safe in predicting that because of their unique characteristics, the aging baby boomers will cause a reexamination of current aging policies and services. Unlike generations before them, collectively they will be better educated, will be better off financially, will be living in the suburbs, and will be beneficiaries of the programs that were put in place for their grandparents. On the other hand, this giant cohort is tremendously diverse. Although as a group, boomers will have higher levels of education compared with generations before them, more than 3 million will not have advanced beyond the eighth grade (Siegel, 1989). Although boomers' earnings are comparable with their parents' at a similar stage in life, the distribution of wealth in the United States has become more unequal in the last two decades; it is projected that 4 million boomers in the year 2030 will have incomes below 150% of the poverty line (Lewin-VHI, Inc., cited in Kingston, 1996). In addition, the poverty gap between whites and people of color was just as wide in 1994 as it was in 1959—a rate of 3 to 1 (O'Hare, 1996)—a statistic that will no doubt have implications for the financial well-being and quality of life for ethnic minorities in later life.

Another unique characteristic of the boomer cohort is the marriage and family patterns compared with those of their parents and grandparents. Boomers tended to marry later, have higher rates of divorce, and have smaller families than their parents (Bouvier & De Vita, 1991). Many will live in blended families, increasing the complexity of kin networks. Boomers also are living within more nontraditional forms of "family," including single-parent families, cohabitating heterosexual and same-gender couples, and intergenerational families. These unique family characteristics might reduce the number of potential family caregivers and increase role ambiguity of adult children within divorced and blended families. Will these adult children feel an obligation to care for both biological and stepparents? Because families play a key role in providing instrumental and emotional support, as well as long-term care, to their older family members, it is uncertain whether these differences will negatively influence family support patterns and thus create a greater demand for formal services. The families who choose not to have children will also be at risk of having fewer informal resources.

Collectively, these demographic characteristics will shape the type, amount, and nature of community resources in the future. They will increase the demand for home health care and retirement housing options. Many baby boomers will move into third, fourth, and even fifth careers and seek educational opportunities and greater flexibility in work and retirement options. The social safety net may need to be expanded for the underclass and lower class. The sheer numbers of aged boomers will challenge policymakers to rethink health care, retirement programs, and pension plans. Even now, projections, both dire and not so dire, are being made about Social Security and Medicare. Thus, demographic characteristics of the next generation of older adults will have direct implications on social policies that, in turn, support programs and services for older adults. In this next section, we discuss a few more of the salient demographic characteristics of the boomer cohort.

Growth of the Older Population

The projected growth in the older population is depicted in Exhibit 1.1. According the U.S. Bureau of the Census (1993), persons aged 65 and older constituted 8.1% of the population in 1950. By the year 2050, that percentage will increase to 22.9%. The percentage of older adults in each age group will increase as well. For example, in 1990, the percentage of older adults aged

Exhibit 1.1   **Actual and Projected Growth of the Older Population**

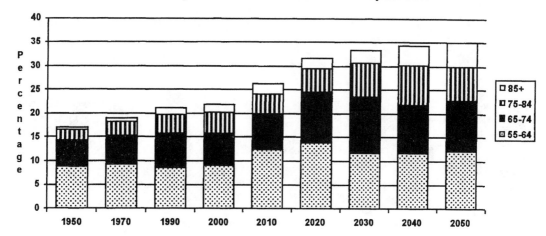

SOURCE: Compiled from data from U.S. Senate Special Committee on Aging (1991a).

55 to 64 was 8.5% and is expected to increase to 12.3% by the year 2050. Similarly, older adults aged 75 to 84 years constituted 4% of the population in 1990; by the year 2050, that percentage will jump to 7.2%. Because of the increase in life expectancy, demographic projections call for a substantial increase in the percentage of older adults aged 85 or more. Moreover, persons 85 years of age and older represent the fastest-growing part of the older adult population. The population aged 85 and older will more than double from 3 million in 1990 to 7 million in 2020 and increase to 14 million by 2040.

What are the social implications of such an increase in the older adult population? Many writers in the popular press suggest that the increase in the number of older adults signals an impending social and fiscal crisis and that aged persons will become a financial burden to society (e.g., Smith, 1992). Others (Gerber, Wolff, Klores, & Brown, 1989; McDaniel, 1986) argue that a "crisis mentality" overlooks other important demographic factors. Although it is true that the United States, along with other developed nations, will experience an increase in the older adult population, the number of older adults has steadily increased during the last 130 years. This steady increase has allowed society to adapt to the changes of an aging population. Many scholars believe society will be able to adapt to this new cohort of older adults as well.

The assumption that older adults will place a burden on society is often based on the old age dependency ratio. The old age dependency ratio, the ratio of persons aged 65 and older to persons aged 20 to 64, will increase from 20:100 in 1990 to 38:100 in 2030. On the other hand, the *overall dependency ratio,* which includes "dependent" persons aged 0 to 19 along with

Exhibit 1.2 **Percentage of Older Adults by Race: 1990 and 2050**

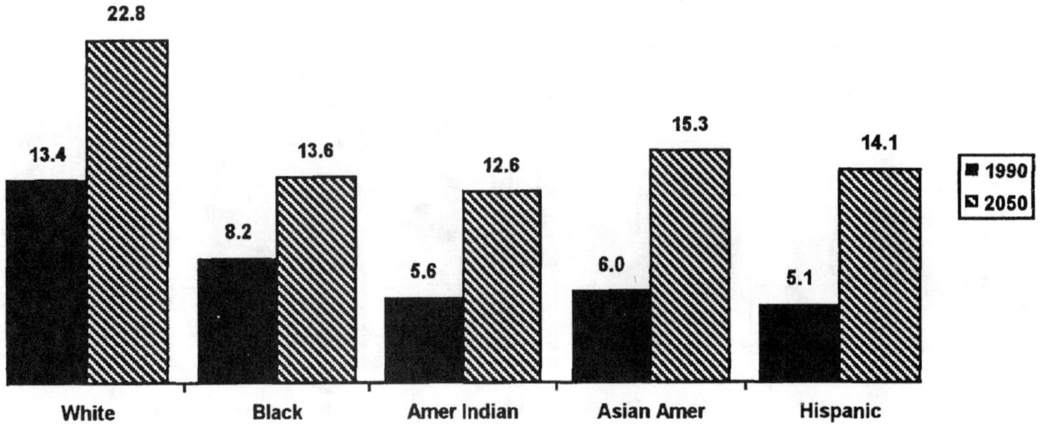

SOURCE: U.S. Bureau of the Census (1996a).

persons aged 65 and older, will be approximately the same in the year 2030 as it was in 1920 (74:100 and 76:100, respectively) and lower than it was in 1965 because of a decline in the youth dependency ratio (U.S. Senate Special Committee on Aging, 1991a). Thus, the increase in the number of older adults does not automatically result in greater social burden because the increasing demand on public programs by older adults might be offset by declining demands on public funds for supporting children. As Kingston (1996) points out, the increase in the number of older adults in the next century does not mean that society will be overwhelmed with caring for the older adult population, but it does suggest that we must begin to plan for the needs of the aging boomers.

Growth of the Minority Older Adult Population

In addition to the increase in the number of older adults, the percentage of older adults of color is expected to increase. In 1990, the nonwhite older adult population composed 14% of the total 65+ population; that percentage is expected to increase to 32% by the year 2050 (U.S. Senate Special Committee on Aging, 1991a). Exhibit 1.2 illustrates the percentage of older adults by race for the years 1990 and 2050. Although white older adults will still represent a greater percentage of those over age 65 in the year 2050, the

Exhibit 1.3   **Projected Increase in the Number of Older Adults Living Alone by Age**

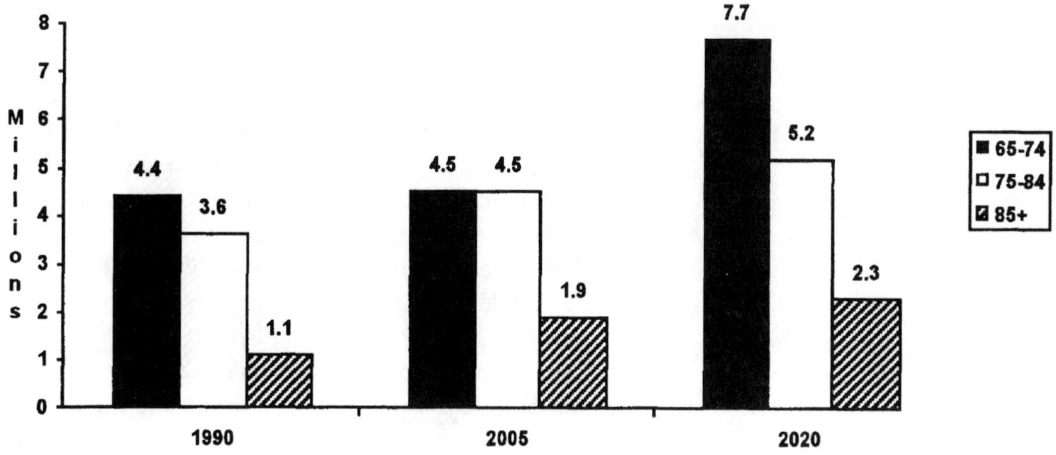

SOURCE: U.S. Senate Special Committee on Aging (1991a).

percentages of blacks, American Indian, Asian Americans, and Hispanics will increase dramatically.

Growth in the Number of Older Adults Living Alone

A final demographic characteristic having social service implications is the increase in the number of older adults who will be living alone. The percentage of older adults who live alone is expected to increase from 9.2% in 1990 to 10.9% in 2005 and to 15.2%, or 15.2 million, in 2020. Moreover, the percentage of older adults living alone increases with age (see Exhibit 1.3). By the year 2020, the number of older adults aged 85 and older who live alone is projected to double to 2.3 million persons. Older adults who live alone are more likely to live in poverty and are less likely to receive help with activity limitations than are older adult couples who co-reside (U.S. Senate Special Committee on Aging, 1991a).

Implications of Demographic Characteristics for Community Resources

These selected demographic projections and unique characteristics have a number of implications for the delivery of community resources to older adults. The growth in the older adult population will increase the demand for all types of services. Professionals working to deliver the programs and services designed to improve the quality of life of older adults will thus be challenged to do even more with less. Because of the diverse nature of the boomer population with regard to ethnicity, income, family history, and life experience, professionals will be expected to be knowledgeable about a wide range of services and programs that serve both mainstream and disenfranchised individuals. Community programmers also must recognize and accommodate cultural diversity and remove the social and cultural barriers to service accessibility. In the near future, professionals will be called on to be visionaries in planning and developing services and programs to meet the needs of this new cohort with its diverse characteristics.

Now that we have had a chance to consider the challenges that lie ahead for services and programs that assist older adults, let's return to the present and consider more immediate issues. In every community, community resources are designed to assist older adults in a variety of ways. Therefore, individuals working with older adults need to have a good understanding of these resources as well as the patterns of service use by older adults and their families. Anyone who has ever worked with older adults knows that more often than not, the problems that they confront are complex and multifaceted.

Consider the case of Mrs. Duran, who confides that she is about to be evicted from her apartment. Further questioning reveals that she has not received her Social Security check for 2 months. She has limited resources for food, has received a utility shutoff notice, and has been unable to renew her insulin prescription for her diabetes. Or consider Mr. Jackson, who does not know what to do with himself since he retired. He has played golf or fished almost every day but is getting bored and disillusioned with retirement life. What community resources can be accessed to help Mrs. Duran and Mr. Jackson? Advocates who have an understanding of various programs and services assisting older adults can recommend appropriate options for both Mrs. Duran and Mr. Jackson.

A Text About Programs and Services in an Era of Change

Because of the multiple challenges that older adults can experience and the changing demographics of the older adult population, we have created a text that provides a broad-based discussion of community resources. We believe that to effectively meet the needs of older adults who can benefit from using services and programs, professionals must understand the social and psychological dynamics of help-seeking behavior. It is not enough to know what services are available and appropriate; practitioners must also be armed with theoretical knowledge to understand *why* a daughter, despite her exhaustion, refuses to bring her father to the local adult day program and *why* an older adult, who barely survives on a small pension, refuses to apply for additional income support that would make life a bit more bearable. In addition, we believe that practitioners also must understand the service use patterns and how families interact with the formal network when they need assistance in caring for their older family members. Greater understanding of these patterns can better prepare students and practitioners for understanding the dynamics of when and how families choose to use the formal network.

We also believe that simply describing the existing programs and services that assist older adults provides an incomplete picture. Practitioners and students should also benefit from the interplay that exists between research and practice because research results have practical applications for the delivery of services and programs. In each chapter, we draw from empirical research to describe who uses and provides such programs. We also include information about program outcomes when available.

Next, professionals need to be alerted to the infinite number of programs and services in communities that exist outside those funded through the Older Americans Act (OAA) of 1965 and subsequent amendments. Thus, we attempt to introduce readers to many programs that are both publicly and privately funded. Moreover, we discuss the different ways in which aging programs have successfully networked with one another to develop public and private partnerships in an attempt to reach more older adults.

Organization of the Book

This book consists of three parts. In addition to this chapter, Part I has two other chapters. Chapter 2 presents a brief review of major aging policies, including Social Security, Medicare, and the Older Americans Act, the basis for the existence of many older adult programs. Chapter 3 explains the patterns of service use by older adults and the theories that can predict help-seeking behavior.

Part II of the book is based on the concept of the *continuum of care.* Conceptually, the continuum of care is a system of social, personal, financial, and medical services that supports the well-being of any older adult, regardless of the person's level of functioning. The goal, of course, is to have the appropriate services available to match the presenting needs.

Exhibit 1.4 **Continuum of Services**

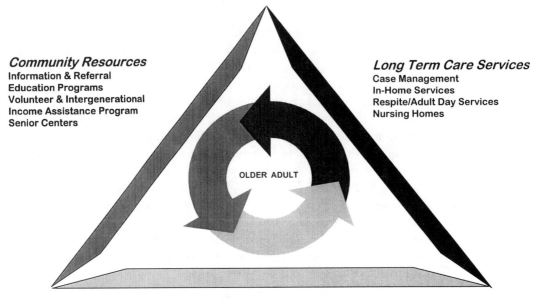

Community Resources
Information & Referral
Education Programs
Volunteer & Intergenerational
Income Assistance Program
Senior Centers

Long Term Care Services
Case Management
In-Home Services
Respite/Adult Day Services
Nursing Homes

OLDER ADULT

Support Services
Nutrition   Health & Wellness
Mental Health   Transportation
Housing   Legal

The continuum is often thought of in a linear way—older adults move from one end of the continuum (independence) to the other (dependence), and services exist at every point along the continuum to meet their social, medical, and personal needs. In addition, services impinge differently on the personal autonomy of its participants. For example, those who attend senior centers come and go as they please and make choices about their level of participation. In contrast, a nursing home is the most restrictive environment and impinges a great deal on personal autonomy and choice.

We have opted to depict the continuum of care as a more dynamic and interactive system (see Exhibit 1.4). Rather than moving in a linear fashion from independence to dependence, older adults move in and out of areas of service need as they experience changing levels of independence and dependence, health and illness, and financial stability and instability. For example, older adults just discharged from the hospital may need in-home services as well as home-delivered meals. Yet as they become less dependent, they might access services offered at the senior center. Those who are striving to maintain their independence can access services that exist within the continuum.

Therefore, Part II presents the variety of community resources available for older adults and is divided into three sections, based on our depiction of the continuum of care. The first section presents information about *community services*. These are services that benefit older adults with low levels of dependency and impinge little on their personal autonomy. These services offer participants opportunities to enhance personal and social well-being. Specifically, we address information and referral services (Chapter 4), volunteer and intergenerational programs (Chapter 5), education (Chapter 6), senior centers (Chapter 7), employment programs (Chapter 8), and income assistance programs (Chapter 9).

Support services are discussed in the second section of Part II. These services help older adults who need assistance in maintaining their level of functioning. Support services include nutrition programs (Chapter 10), health and wellness programs (Chapter 11), mental health services (Chapter 12), legal services (Chapter 13), transportation (Chapter 14), and housing (Chapter 15).

The final chapters in Part II provide information about community-based and institutional long-term care services. These services represent those that exist to assist individuals who have greater dependency needs. Chapters included in this section are case management (Chapter 16), home care (Chapter 17), respite care (Chapter 18), and nursing homes (Chapter 19).

We have organized each chapter in Part II to include policy background, a description of users and programs, and future concerns. Each chapter includes case studies to help readers think critically about the service delivery issues. These cases were developed on the basis of actual experiences we have encountered (names and situations were altered to protect individuals' identity). In addition, best practice models that highlight creative and unique programs and sources for additional information are presented. The best practice models are representative of the programs and services that exist in various communities. Learning activities designed to expand understanding of the issues are also included. Additional resources, including the names and addresses of professional organizations and Internet resources, are located at the end of each chapter.

Part III contains the final chapter on programs and services for the future (Chapter 20). This chapter presents an in-depth look at the challenges that lie ahead for the aging network.

Accessing Updated Information

Because Congress frequently enacts legislation that affects the existence of community resources and programs, information presented in texts such as this can become quickly outdated. Professionals often do not have access to information about the new and creative ways communities are delivering services to older adults. To address these two concerns, we have created a Web site that provides legislative and programmatic updates. The *Community Resources for Older Adults* Web site will have updated information on aging policy, best practice models, and information about additional resources. Readers can access our Web site at

http://www.hhs.unco.edu/geron.htm

Please stop by for a visit.

2

Legislative Foundations for Programs, Services, and Benefits Supporting Older Adults

---

It had been a busy week at the area agency on aging office. Dorothy, the administrative assistant, was tidying up her desk on Friday afternoon and thinking about all the people the office had helped that week. Mrs. Wright, in her early 80s, came first to her mind. Mrs. Wright's husband had just had surgery for throat cancer. For the next couple of months, he would be restricted to a liquid diet for most of his meals. Low income but not poverty level, the Wrights could not afford the full cost of a nutritional food supplement at their local grocery store. The Wrights found out about the area agency on aging's food supplement program from their doctor. It has saved them nearly half the cost on the two cases a week required for Mr. Wright while he recovers. With her many years' experience working at the agency's front desk, Dorothy knew that this couple would not have qualified for welfare assistance. She realized, again, how important the Older Americans Act (OAA) programs are to many people.

In countless communities across the country, local area agencies on aging (AAAs) work to help older adults such as the Wrights. All older Americans 60 and older can benefit from services provided by the "aging network" because of legislation enacted more than 25 years ago. On July 14, 1965, President Lyndon B. Johnson signed into law the OAA, thus launching milestone legislation in the evolution of the nation's public policy for older adults.

The OAA is one of many laws that have been enacted to assist older adults in maintaining their physical, social, psychological, and financial well-being. This chapter will discuss of some of the important laws that laid the foundation for the creation of programs, services, and benefits for older adults. We begin with a review of some of the more notable aging legislation enacted.

Legislative Foundations of Social Programs and Services

Long before the enactment of the OAA, policies designed to protect older adults from the vicissitudes of old age were slowly put into place (see Exhibit 2.1). For example, in 1920, the Civil Service Retirement Act, a federal pension program, was enacted for government employees, members of Congress, and people in the uniformed and civil service. Some 15 years later, the Social Security Act (1935) was passed. Social Security—Old-Age, Survivor, and Disability Insurance (OASDI)—was created to ensure that working American families had a measure of economic security. Social Security is one of the best known legislative policies enacted for the benefit of retirees, and later for survivors, dependents, and persons with disabilities. It was the first legislation to represent a "social contract" that was "to provide protection as a matter of right for the American worker in retirement" (Ficke, 1985, p. 115). It has proved to be one of the most popular, as well as adaptable, pieces of legislation in existence.

The Social Security Act was signed into law by President Franklin D. Roosevelt on August 14, 1935. The main provision of the act was to provide a social insurance program designed to pay retired workers age 65 or older a continuing income after retirement. The first payments began in 1937 and were made as lump sum payments averaging $58.06. Monthly payments began in January 1940. The first monthly retirement check was issued to Ida May Fuller of Ludlow, Vermont, in the amount of $22.54. Miss Fuller died in January 1975 at the age of 100. During her 35 years as a beneficiary, she received more than $20,000 in benefits (Social Security Administration, 1997a). Originally, the amount received by Miss Fuller, $22.54, would be the amount she would receive for the rest of her life. Not until 1952 did Congress legislate increases in the monthly benefit. From that point, increases came only when legislated by Congress until 1972, when Congress enacted a law providing for annual cost of living increases, the amount to be determined by the annual increase in consumer prices.

There have been hundreds of amendments to the Social Security Act. Most have made minor adjustments to the act; several of these amendments, however, have profoundly increased the responsibility of the act to extend benefits to previously uncovered groups (see Exhibit 2.1). One such amendment, passed by Congress in 1950, extended benefits to permanently and

Exhibit 2.1 **A National Policy on Aging: Selected Historical Highlights**

1920   The Civil Service Retirement Act was enacted to provide a retirement system for many government employees, including members of the U.S. Congress and those in the uniformed aid civil services.

1927   American Association for Old Age Security organized to further national interest in old age legislation.

1935   Social Security Act was passed and signed into law by President Roosevelt "to provide protection as a matter of right for the American worker in retirement."

1937   Railroad Retirement Act was enacted to provide annuities and pensions for retired railroad employees and their families.

1937   U.S. Housing Act stimulated passage of enabling legislation in majority of states to provide low-rent public housing.

1950   The first National Conference on Aging held in Washington, D.C., was sponsored by the Federal Security Agency.

1950   Social Security Act amended to establish program of aid to permanently and totally disabled persons and to broaden aid to dependent children to include relative with whom the child is living.

1956   Special Staff on Aging was assigned coordinating responsibilities for aging within the Office of the Secretary of Health, Education, and Welfare.

1959   Housing Act was amended authorizing a direct loan program of nonprofit rental projects for older adults at low interest rates. Provisions also reduced the eligible age for public low-rent housing for low-income older persons to age 62 for women and age 50 for disabled individuals.

1961   First White House Conference on Aging convened in Washington, D.C.

1961   Social Security amendments lowered retirement age for men from age 65 to 62, increased minimum benefits paid, broadened program to include additional categories of retired persons, increased benefits to aged widows, and liberalized the retirement test.

1962   More than 160 bills were introduced in Congress related to aged persons and aging. Eight were enacted.

1964   Food Stamp Act provided for improved levels of nutrition among low-income households through a cooperative federal-state program of food assistance.

1964   National Association of State Units on Aging is officially established, formalizing a loose confederation of state administrators of aging programs.

1965   Older Americans Act was passed and signed into law. Major provisions included establishment of the Administration on Aging within the Department of Health, Education, and Welfare and grants to states for community planning, services, and training. The act also stipulated that state agencies on aging be established to administer the program.

1965   Medicare health insurance program for older adults was legislated and financed through the Social Security system.

1965   Social Security amendments established Title XIX, "Grants to States for Medical Assistance," commonly known as Medicaid.

1967   Amendments to the Older Americans Act extended its provisions for 2 years and directed AoA to undertake a study of personnel needs in the aging field.

1967   Age Discrimination Act was passed and signed into law by President Johnson.

1967   Amendments to the Older Americans Act extended its provisions for 3 years and authorized the use of Title III funds to support areawide model projects.

1971   Second White House Conference on Aging convened in Washington, D.C.

1972   Nutrition Program for the Elderly Act was passed and signed into law by President Nixon (redesignated Title VII of the Older Americans Act, as amended in 1973).

1972   Supplemental Security Income was passed as a part of the Social Security Act.

1973   Older Americans comprehensive service amendments established area agencies on aging under an expanded Title III and also authorized grants for model projects, senior centers, and multidisciplinary centers of gerontology, adding a new Title IX.

continued

Exhibit 2.1

1973 Older Americans Community Service Employment Act authorized funding for Title VII nutrition projects and extended the act's provisions for 2 years.

1973 Domestic Volunteer Service Act was passed and signed into law. Major provisions included the RSVP and Foster Grandparent programs. Title VI of the Older Americans Act, as a result, was later repealed.

1974 Amendments to the Older Americans Act added a special transportation program under Title III "model projects."

1974 Social Security amendments authorized Title XX, Grants to States for Social Services. Among the programs that could be supported under this provision were protective services, homemaker services, adult day care service transportation services, training, employment opportunities, information and referral, nutrition assistance, and health support.

1975 Amendments to the Older Americans Act added new language authorizing the commissioner on aging to make grants under Title III to Indian tribal organizations. Priority services were mandated (transportation, home care, legal services, and home renovation and repair). Amendments also made minor changes in Title IX, Community Service Employment for Older Americans.

1977 Amendments to the Older Americans Act authorized changes in the Title VII nutrition services program, primarily relating to the availability of surplus commodities through the U.S. Department of Agriculture.

1978 Comprehensive Older Americans Act Amendments of 1978 consolidated Title III, V, and VII (social services, multipurpose centers, and nutrition services, respectively) into one Title III; redesignated the previous Title IX (Community Service Employment Act) as Title V, and added a new Title VI, Grants for Indian Tribes.

1978 Amendments to the Older Americans Act extended the act's programs through September 30, 1984.

1984 Older Americans Act Amendments of 1984 clarified the roles of state and area agencies on aging in coordinating community-based services and in maintaining accountability for the funding of national priority services (legal, access, and in-home services), provided for greater flexibility in administering programs by providing for increased transfer authority between Parts B and C of Title III, and added a new Title VII, Older Americans Personal Health Education and Training Program, for funding grants to institutions of higher education to develop standardized programs of health education and training for older persons to be provided in multipurpose senior centers.

1987 Amendments to the Older Americans Act required coordination of in-home, access, and legal services with activities of agencies working with persons with Alzheimer's disease.

1987 In-home support services for frail elders and disease prevention and health promotion services are now supported under Title III.

1991 Administration on Aging becomes an independent agency that reports to the DHHS.

1992 Title III-C authorizes school-based meals for older school volunteers and assistance in paying the costs of meals of older adults who volunteer in intergenerational programs.

1992 Amendments to the OAA added Part D to Title III, authorizing support for frail elders.

1992 Amendments to the Older Americans Act added Part F to Title III, Disease Prevention and Health Promotion Services.

1992 Office of Long-Term Care Ombudsman Programs is established within the Administration on Aging.

1992 Title VII, Vulnerable Elder Rights Protection, is enacted, combining many of the provisions under Title III.

1996 Amendments to the Older Americans Act were debated.

SOURCE: Compiled from Ficke (1985) and the Older Americans Act of 1965, as amended.

a. For the latest update on changes to the OAA, see the *Community Resources for Older Adults* Web site (http://www.hhs.unco.edu/geron.htm).

totally disabled workers. This was eventually broadened to cover workers under age 50 and their dependents. By 1960, 559,000 people were receiving disability benefits, with an average benefit of $80 per month. In 1995, 1.1 million disabled workers received an average benefit of $682 per month (Social Security Administration, 1997b).

Another significant amendment to the Social Security Act occurred in 1972 when at the request of President Richard M. Nixon, the federal-state programs of Old-Age Assistance, Aid to the Blind, and Aid to the Permanently and Totally Disabled were streamlined to create the Supplemental Security Income (SSI) program. Under the SSI program, each eligible person living in his or her own household and having no other income is provided, as of January 1995, a monthly cash payment of $458, or $687 for a couple if both members are eligible (Social Security Administration, 1997b). Both Social Security and SSI are discussed in greater detail in Chapter 9.

Other early legislation benefiting older adults enacted soon after the Social Security Act included the Railroad Retirement Act of 1937 (providing pensions for railroad retirees) and the U.S. Housing Act of 1937 (enabling legislation for states to provide low-rent housing). Between 1940 and 1964, a number of other legislative and political activities occurred. In addition to the amendments added to the Social Security Act mentioned above, the Housing Act was amended and expanded, and the Food Stamp Act of 1964 was enacted.

The 1950s marked the emergence of another important influence on the evolution of aging policy—the White House Conferences on Aging. The first National Conference on Aging was held in Washington, D.C., in 1950, and the first White House Conference on Aging was held in 1961 (Ficke, 1985) and, more recently, in 1995. The conference delegates, representatives of federal, state, and local governments as well as professionals in the field of gerontology and older adults, convened to develop specific recommendations for executive or legislative action on aging policy.

The next significant date in the history of aging policy is 1965, when two major laws were enacted—Medicare and the OAA. Sixteen days after President Johnson signed the OAA, he signed Medicare, the national health insurance program for older adults, into law on July 30, 1965, through amendments to the Social Security Act. The passage of both the OAA and Medicare in the same year has marked the mid-1960s as the most politically friendly period for older Americans' programs in history. The passage of Medicare was historic not only for the health benefits that it would afford millions of older Americans but also for the sheer significance of overcoming more than 30 years of political opposition, largely from the American Medical Association, to government-funded health coverage. All along, most proponents had intended for government-funded health coverage to be universal.

After years of debate, a compromise was offered that adopted an incremental approach whereby older adults would be covered first, thereby pushing universal coverage into the distant future (Rich & Baum, 1984). Today, Medicare provides partial health coverage for 37 million Americans 65 years of age and older as well as people of any age with permanent kidney failure and certain people with disabilities under 65 years of age (Health Care Finance Administration [HCFA], 1996a). Specific benefits of Medicare are discussed in Chapter 11.

Although not the first major legislation addressing the needs of America's older adults, the OAA has become a landmark in the evolution of the nation's public policy for older adults (Bechill, 1992). Social Security represents greater than 150 times the expenditures of the OAA, but the OAA is largely responsible for the development of what is frequently referred to as the "aging network." The advocacy and coordination mandates of the act, as we will discuss later, have played a significant role in encouraging our nation's systems of human services to come together to do a better job of meeting the needs of older Americans.

In the remainder of this chapter, we discuss the history of the passage of the OAA, followed by a review of each of the act's titles and a discussion of the impact of the OAA on the lives of older adults. We conclude by presenting some of the controversial issues surrounding the OAA.

Emergence of the Aging Network

The origin of the OAA can be traced to the 1961 White House Conference on Aging. Health care coverage was the key issue that emerged from the many state aging conferences that were held prior to the White House Conference. After the White House Conference in 1961, a special committee drafted resolutions that eventually led to the 1965 enactment of both Medicare and the OAA. The OAA was the first program to focus on community-based services for older adults and the first legislation mandated to bring together a fragmented and uncoordinated public and private service delivery system to meet the basic needs of elders at the community level (Lee, 1991). This visionary nature of the OAA sets it apart from other previous and subsequent legislative initiatives.

The passage of the OAA created a network of services that is unique to social programming. Much more than a collection of agencies, the aging network is a formidable structure, made up of a well-defined system that links the Administration on Aging (AoA), the U.S. Department of Health and Human Services (DHHS), 57 state units on aging (SUAs), 670 area agencies on aging (AAAs), Title VI grants to more than 200 Indian tribes, and more than 20,000 providers delivering services to older Americans (see Exhibit 2.2). This network is bonded together around a central role—to support the federal role in transforming a patchwork of programs for the older population into a locally coordinated service system. Relying on partnerships among the three levels of government, education and research institutions, and a wide range of voluntary organizations working with older people, the aging network's emphasis on planning, coordination, and advocacy has provided an infrastructure and point of entry for other public and private initiatives that supplement OAA funding. These public-private initiatives represent an extraordinary record of achievement in making a small amount of federal money go a long way to help hundreds of thousands of older people avoid nursing home placement and remain independent in the community. Today, aging network programs are supported by an array of sources in conjunction with the AoA, including Medicaid, social service block grants, state and local governments, the private sector, and individual contributions. With this combination of resources, more than 8 million older adults received services or participated in programs funded under the OAA in 1992 (AoA, 1994b).

Another notable aspect of the OAA and the network of services that has evolved from the act is that this service network is a universal program. This universal emphasis recognizes that all older persons have needs and that programs and services should be available, as a result, to all older persons (Bechill, 1992). Therefore, there is no means test cutoff for programs and services funded under the act; persons are eligible for services regardless of income or assets. Using an age-based criteria, all older persons 60 years of age or older are eligible for services. Language in the act, however, places emphasis on helping older persons with the greatest social and economic need, particularly low-income minority persons. More recent amendments to the OAA emphasize services to older adults who are frail in addition to low-income and minority elders (see Exhibit 2.1). The act strongly encourages providers of services to give participants the "opportunity" to donate toward the cost of a service, but the law strictly forbids charging for the service or denying access to a service because of the inability to donate. The dilemma arising from the emphasis on universality, targeting, and cost sharing all in the same legislation will be discussed in more detail later in the chapter and in Chapter 20.

Older Americans Act Titles

Currently, the OAA contains seven titles. *Title I* sets forth 10 broad policy objectives aimed at improving the lives of older people not only regarding income (the principal objective of Social Security) but also in physical and

Exhibit 2.2 **The Older Americans Act Network**

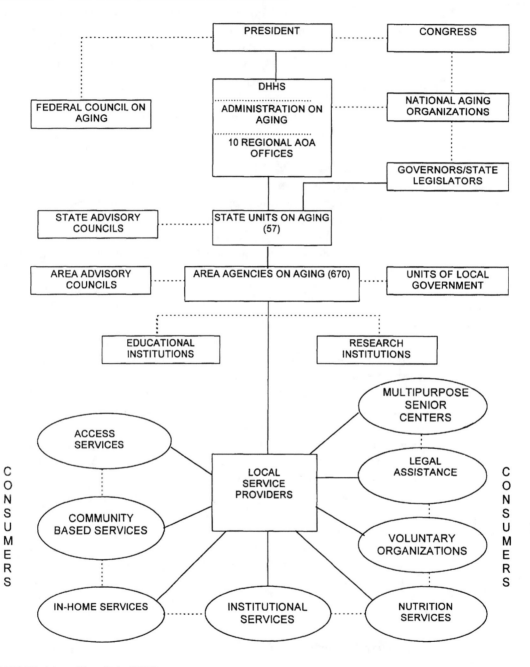

SOURCE: Adapted from Ficke (1985).

Best Practice **Linking Public and Private Partnerships**

Many local area agencies on aging have worked to develop partnerships with the private sector to meet the needs of older adults in their communities. Here are a few examples.

The New York City Department for the Aging/AAA organizes the "Ability Is Ageless" 55+ Job Fair, co-sponsored by WNBC-TV. Approximately seven other companies, such as Chase Manhattan Bank, provide printing, posters, and giveaway prizes. Other businesses rent booths for $500. The State Department of Labor staff assist with the fair as well. In 1991, more than 100 companies and more than 3,500 older adults attended. Follow-up data found that in a year, at least 350 older job seekers were hired as a result of the fair. For more information, contact the Bureau of Program and Resource Development, NYC Department for the Aging, 202-577-7349.

The Colorado Aging and Adult Services/State Unit on Aging is a part of the Governor's Older Worker Task Force, created as an interagency group of state-level government organizations providing employment services or funding to older adults. Shortly after the group was formed, members realized that they needed private sector input and created the Private Sector Advisory Council. The council provides the Colorado State Unit on Aging with knowledge, viewpoints, and information about older workers issues. The council has developed a public education project, including a brochure about the impact of Colorado's aging workforce, conference for employers, and an award to honor employers who do an exemplary job of hiring and retaining older employees. For more information, contact Colorado Aging and Adult Services, 303-866-5911.

The Clearfield Area Agency on Aging's "Blizzard Box Program" is a collaborative effort of the Clearfield Rotary Club and Dairy Queen Stores of Clearfield and DuBois, Pennsylvania. Volunteers deliver Blizzard Boxes—emergency food kits—along with regular home-delivered meals during the fall. The Blizzard Boxes are to be used when bad weather prevents the delivery of regular meals. The program was initially funded by the Rotary Club, but to meet increasing demand for Blizzard Boxes, local Dairy Queens donate $0.30 for every Blizzard sold during Labor Day. For more information, contact Clearfield County Area Agency on Aging, 814-765-2696.

SOURCE: Chicago Department on Aging, National Council on the Aging, & Washington Business Group on Health (1992).

mental health, housing, employment, and community service. These broad objectives, listed below, continue to be the philosophical cornerstone of this act.

■ An adequate income in retirement in accordance with the American standard of living

■ The best possible physical and mental health which science can make available and without regard to economic status

■ Obtaining and maintaining suitable housing, independently selected, designed and located with reference to special needs and available at costs which older citizens can afford

■ Full restorative services for those who require institutional care; and a comprehensive array of community-based long-term care services adequate to appropriately sustain older people in their communities and in their homes, including support to family members and other persons providing voluntary care to older individuals needing long-term care services

■ Opportunity for employment with no discriminatory personnel practices because of age

■ Retirement in health, honor and dignity after years of contribution to the economy

■ Participating in and contributing to meaningful activity within the widest range of civic, cultural and recreational opportunities

■ Efficient community services, including access to low-cost transportation, which provide a choice in supported living arrangements and social assistance in a coordinated manner and which are readily available when needed with emphasis on maintaining a continuum of care for vulnerable older individuals; which provide social assistance in a coordinated manner and which are readily available when needed

■ Immediate benefit from proven research knowledge which can sustain and improve health and happiness

■ Freedom, independence and the free exercise of individual initiative in planning and managing their own lives, full participation in the planning and operation of community-based services and programs provided for their benefit, and protection against abuse, neglect, and exploitation (OAA, 1965, Title I, p. 1)

These far-reaching goals are to be carried out jointly by federal, state, tribal, and local governments to achieve an adequate offering of community-based services for older adults. With a $1.3 billion budget in 1995, the programs and services funded through OAA are more limited than this vision might imply (National Academy on Aging, 1995).

Title II created the AoA within the Office of the Secretary of the DHHS. AoA is headed by a commissioner on aging appointed by the president. Through the years, there has been considerable debate about the placement of AoA within the executive branch of government. The debate has centered on whether AoA should be an independent office at the White House level, be an office of the DHHS, or be placed under a department of DHHS. In 1992, President Clinton placed the AoA commissioner directly under the DHHS secretary—a move applauded by aging advocates because the commissioner has the direct ear of the DHHS secretary and even the president when necessary.

The AoA is the federal focal point for aging issues and program planning. It has two principal roles. First, AoA is at the top of the federal-state-local hierarchy, or aging services network, that carries out the planning, coordinating, and provision of services to older adults (see Exhibit 2.2). AoA promotes training, technical assistance, and regulatory direction to help the states and local AAAs carry out their mandates. Essentially, every time the act is reauthorized and amended, AoA must interpret congressional intent through rule making and rule interpretation. States, local AAAs, and other interested parties may comment on the rules and frequently influence the way a particular rule is written. This is often a long and drawn-out process.

Another important role of AoA is to provide leadership on national policies affecting older adults. This is done by encouraging cooperation and coordination among the major federal agencies on federal aging policies. AoA, thus, is a major advocate for older adults throughout the federal government. For example, the Department of Housing and Urban Development (HUD) plans and implements programs to address the housing needs of *all* low-income population groups. The Federal Transit Administration (FTA) helps develop policy and funding initiatives to respond to a wide range of transit issues including transit infrastructure. AoA is the only federal agency that has the authority to cross over agency boundaries to provide overall leadership on singularly aging issues and programs. When AoA was first established, Congress adamantly voiced its expectation that AoA have high visibility in the executive branch for developing and sponsoring a nationwide program to achieve the objectives set forth in the act (Ficke, 1985).

The Federal Council on Aging is also established under Title II of the act. This 15-member council is appointed by the president, the president pro tempore of the Senate, and the Speaker of the House. The council is intended to be representative of rural and urban older persons, national organizations, business, labor, minorities, and the general public. Two of the members must be older persons. Functions of the council include advising the president on the special needs of older Americans; monitoring the impact of aging policies; and making recommendations to the president, the secretary of DHHS, and Congress. The Federal Council on Aging prepares an annual report on its work and the status of elders in America for the president. This report is widely distributed to Congress, other governmental agencies, and interested citizens.

Title III, the largest program under the act, authorizes the development of local services to help older persons. It has been described as the heart and soul of the OAA. Title III gives authority for the development of programs to assist older persons through grants to states. States, in turn, award funds to local planning and service areas (PSAs) whose boundaries have been designated by the state. State units on aging administer the AoA grants at the state level, and the AAAs administer the AoA grants for the PSAs (a list of state units on aging appears in Appendix 1). An allocation formula based on the number of persons aged 60 and older residing in the state as of the most recent census determines the amount of funding each state receives. It follows then, that Florida and California, which have large numbers of older adults 60 years of age and older, will receive larger federal allocations than states with fewer older adults, such as Colorado or Vermont. States must provide a minimum 5% cash match to the federal AoA grant. These matching funds vary greatly by state from the minimum 5% to a dollar-for-dollar match and help to increase the overall resources available under the OAA. SUAs keep 10% of their federal allocation for administration of the SUA. The balance is allocated to the PSAs by a more complex formula devised by the SUA using federal guidelines. The allocation formulas typically are based on census data numbers for persons 60 plus, 60 plus low income, 60 plus minority, 60 plus rural, and 60 plus frail residing in each PSA. AAAs must also provide local match, which may be either cash or in-kind support such as the value of volunteer hours or value of donated space and equipment to carry out a particular program.

The local AAA is responsible for (a) developing the area plan for a comprehensive and coordinated system of services to meet the needs of older persons, (b) funding service provider agencies to fill gaps in priority service areas, and (c) serving as the advocate and focal point for older people within its PSA. Throughout the country, AAAs exhibit many organizational designs and structures based on local needs and preferences. The AAA office within a PSA may be a unit of general purpose local government, such as a county, city, or regional council of government, or a public or nonprofit private agency. In any given location, AAAs can be a part of a council of governments or regional planning commission, part of a county unit of government or city government, part of educational institutions, or freestanding private nonprofits.

Under Part A of Title III, both SUAs and AAAs must develop multiyear plans describing in detail how a coordinated, comprehensive service delivery system will be provided. AAAs must also designate, where feasible, a focal point for service delivery in each community, giving strong consideration to multipurpose senior centers. The act requires that the AAA establish a council to advise the agency on the development of multiyear plans, funding and administration, and programs and services. The local councils may conduct public hearings and review and comment on all community policies, programs, and actions that affect older persons in their regions. Advisory council membership must be made up of more than 50% older persons, including older persons with greatest economic or social need, older individuals of color, and persons eligible to participate in programs assisted under the act. Other members may represent older individuals, local elected officials, and the general public. This mandate for grassroots participation in the planning and administration of local AoA programs has given a voice to thousands of older adults on services that affect their daily lives.

Title III, Part B, of the act is the supportive services component (see Exhibit 2.3). The mission of Part B is to develop a continuum of community-based services to assist older persons in remaining independent in the community for as long as is reasonably possible. To that end, AoA regulations state that AAAs must provide assurances that an adequate proportion of funds are allotted to service providers in their PSAs for services that provide access (transportation, outreach, and information and referral); in-home services (homemaker and home health aide, visiting and telephone reassurance, chore maintenance, and services for families of Alzheimer's disease); and legal assistance. In most cases, AAAs do not provide direct services. Instead, they subcontract with other organizations to facilitate the provision of a full range of services.

Title III, Part C, allows for a separate federal allocation from Title III to the states and then downward to AAAs for the operation of congregate and home-delivered nutrition programs. The national nutrition program for older adults (described in more detail in Chapter 10), a result of 1972 amendments to OAA, is a major service component under Part C. It allows AAAs to fund both congregate (group) and home-delivered meals for older adults 60 years of age and older and their spouses. In response to the dramatic increase in numbers of frail older adults, the OAA was amended in 1992 to allow AAAs to transfer (up to 30%) funds from the congregate meals budget to the home-delivered meals budget. In addition, the 1992 amendments authorized school-based meals for older school volunteers and assistance in paying the cost of meals of older adults who volunteer in intergenerational programs. The outline of the Title III service categories listed in Exhibit 2.3 speaks to

Exhibit 2.3 **Older Americans Act Community-Based Services Under Title III and Title VII**

Services to facilitate access

- Transportation
- Outreach
- Information and referral
- Client assessment and case management

Services provided in the community

- Congregate meals
- Multipurpose senior centers
- Casework, counseling, and emergency services
- Legal assistance and financial counseling
- Adult day services, protective services, and health screening
- Housing and residential repair and renovation
- Physical fitness and recreation
- Preretirement and second-career counseling
- Employment
- Crime prevention and victim assistance
- Volunteer services
- Health and nutrition education
- Transportation
- Elder abuse prevention education and training

Services provided in the home

- Home health, homemaker, and home repairs
- Home delivered meals and nutrition education
- Chore maintenance, visiting, shopping, letter writing, escort services, and reader services
- Telephone reassurance
- Supportive services for families of older adults with Alzheimer's disease and similar disorders

Services to residents of care-providing facilities

- Casework, counseling, and placement and relocation assistance
- Group services and complaint and grievance resolution
- Visiting and escort services
- Long-term care ombudsman program

SOURCE: Ficke (1985).

the wide range of flexible options AAAs have locally to develop a comprehensive offering of services to meet the particular needs of their PSA.

Title III, Part D, was added to the act in the 1992 amendments. Part D is a relatively small program that was intended to address home care needs but was never adequately funded. Title III, Part D, provides funding for such services as homemaker, personal care and home health services, visiting and telephone reassurance, chore maintenance, in-home respite, adult day services, and minor home repair. Recipients of this service must be 60 years of age and older, have an impairment level that limits the individual's capacity to perform activities of daily living, and not have the social support systems that allow the individual to perform the activities of daily living.

Title III, Part F, Disease Prevention and Health Promotion Services, was incorporated into the OAA in 1987. It was funded in the 1992 amendments to the act and encompasses 12 broad categories of disease prevention and health promotion services. Services under Part F must be prioritized to serve those older persons who are medically underserved and those who have the greatest economic need for such services. According to the act, disease prevention and health promotion services include

- Health risk assessments
- Routine health screening
- Nutritional counseling
- Health promotion programs
- Physical fitness
- Home injury control services
- Mental health promotion
- Education concerning Medicare benefits
- Medication management screening and education
- Information on age-related diseases and chronic disabling conditions
- Gerontological counseling and counseling regarding other social services

In addition to service programs, AoA, under *Title IV,* awards funds to support research, demonstration, and training programs. Research projects collect information about the status and needs of various subgroups of older adults in the population that is used to plan services and opportunities that will assist them. Demonstration projects test new program initiatives that better serve older adults, especially those who are vulnerable. AoA also provides funds to educational institutions to develop curricula and training programs for professionals and paraprofessionals in the field of aging (AoA, 1995a). This title makes the OAA unique among federal programs in its ability

---

For Your Files **Demonstration Projects
Funded Under Title IV**

The goal of the Neighborhood Elders Support Team project is to build
neighborhood capacity to identify and address the needs of frail and
homebound elders through formal and informal networks of care. NEST
will coordinate volunteer teams to provide in-home safety, preventive
health education and screening, professional care, and social and practical support as needed to maintain independent living. Program objectives include establishing multidisciplinary case conference teams, using
volunteer health and other professionals from the neighborhood, engaging student interns in care coordination and monitoring, and providing
training for citywide dissemination. For more information, contact Bernal
Heights Senior Services, 415-206-2142.

The Legal Services of Northern California expanded its Senior Legal Hotline in Sacramento to cover the 39 northern counties in California. The
expanded hotline serves low-income minority older adults and those with
social and economic needs. The hotline is capable of processing more
than 8,000 calls each year and relies on more than 120 private attorneys
who provide pro bono or low-fee representation. For more information,
contact the Legal Services of Northern California, 916-444-6760.

---

to be a catalyst for new approaches to meeting the local needs of older
persons and their families (Region VIII Office, Administration on Aging, n.d.).

As of 1996, literally hundreds of projects have been funded through Title
IV. Initially, funding concentrated on the development of education and
training programs to increase the number of qualified personnel in gerontology. It is difficult to believe that 30 years ago, nearly all service programs
faced critical shortages in trained personnel and that fewer than 10% to 20%
of workers in the field of aging had any formal preparation for work with
older people (Ficke, 1985).

Research and development projects were first directed to programs of
practical action. For example, in 1968, 29 grants for more than $2 million
were made by AoA to fund projects designed to gain new knowledge on the
nutritional needs of older persons. This demonstration project laid the
groundwork for the national nutrition program for older adults (mentioned
earlier) funded under Title III, Part C, since 1977. Between 1973 and 1977,
approximately 25 new research and demonstration grants were funded to
research ways to maintain vulnerable older persons (e.g., those in poorer

health) in their own homes or in appropriate community settings. Later, beginning in 1984, discretionary funds under Title IV were directed to social integration of older persons, strengthening family supports, systems improvement, reaching out to minorities, and improving capacity through the application of knowledge (Ficke, 1985).

Multidisciplinary centers of gerontology also have benefited significantly from Title IV grants. Among the first and more prominent centers were the Institute of Gerontology at the University of Michigan, Wayne State University, the Andrus Gerontology Center at the University of Southern California, and the Center for Aging and Human Development at Duke University. These centers were specifically mandated to recruit and train personnel in the field of aging, conduct basic and applied research, provide consultation to state and area agencies on aging, serve as a repository of information on aging, and help develop training programs on aging (Ficke, 1985). Between 1978 and 1984, AoA expanded the multidisciplinary center grant program to include support for "special emphasis" centers. Six centers were funded initially to concentrate on the concerns of income maintenance; health; employment; housing; older women; and education and leisure. The purpose of these centers was to help AoA fulfill its role as advocate for the nation's older adults and to bridge the gap between research and practice. A list of support centers is presented in Exhibit 2.4. Presently, funding for support centers appears to be headed for a sizable decrease. As a result, many of the centers might be eliminated or their activities seriously curtailed. Updates on the status of the centers will be posted on the *Community Resources for Older Adults* Web page at

http://www.hhs.unco.edu/geron.htm

Since 1985, Title IV research and development accomplishments have been in the areas of long-term care, home and community-based services, elder abuse, legal services hotlines, and disaster assistance. For long-term care and home and community-based services, one of the most visible examples of Title IV support is the Eldercare Locator, an effort to help local and long distance caregivers find the information they need by calling a toll-free number (more details on the Eldercare Locator can be found in Chapter 4). The Long-Term Care Channeling Program, described in Chapter 16, is also a significant development from Title IV grants. Title IV was virtually the only source of funding for the initial planning stages for states wanting to develop home and community-based programs for older adults needing long-term care. For elder abuse prevention, Title IV demonstration projects have brought together the aging and domestic violence communities to more

Exhibit 2.4 **Resources Centers Supported by the Administration on Aging**

National Resource Center on Long Term Care, National Association of State Units on Aging, 1225 I Street NW, Suite 725, Washington, DC 20005, 202-898-2578

National Rural Long Term Care Resource Center, University of Kansas Medical Center, Center on Aging, 3901 Rainbow Boulevard, Kansas City, KS 66167-7117, 913-588-1636

National Resource Center: Diversity and Long Term Care, Brandeis University, Heller School-Institute for Health Policy, P.O. Box 9110, Waltham, MA 02254, 617-736-3930

National Center for Long Term Care, University of Minnesota School of Public Health, Institute of Health Services Research, 420 Delaware SE, Box 197, Minneapolis, MN 55455, 612-624-5171

National Policy & Resource Center on Housing and Long Term Care, University of Southern California, Andrus Gerontology Center, Los Angeles, CA 90089, 213-740-1364

National Long Term Care Ombudsman Resource Center, National Citizens Coalition for Nursing Home Reform, 1224 M Street NW, Washington, DC 20005-5183, 202-393-2018

National Center on Elder Abuse, American Public Welfare Association, Research and Demonstration Department, 810 First Street NE, Suite 500, Washington, DC 20002, 202-682-0100

National Policy and Resource Center on Nutrition and Aging, Department of Dietetics and Nutrition, 200 Florida International University, Miami, FL 33199, 305-348-1517

National Policy and Resource Center on Women and Aging, Brandeis University, Heller School-Institute for Health Policy, P.O. Box 9110, Waltham, MA 02254, 617-736-3863

National Eldercare Legal Assistance Project, National Senior Citizens Law Center, 1815 H Street NW, Suite 700, Washington, DC 20006, 202-887-5280

National Legal Assistance Support, American Bar Association, Commission on Legal Problems of the Elderly, 1800 M Street NW, Washington, DC 20036, 202-331-2630

Legal Counsel for the Elderly, American Association of Retired Persons, 601 E Street NW, Washington, DC 20049, 202-434-2120

Black Elderly Legal Assistance Support Project, National Bar Association, 1225 11th Street NW, Washington, DC 20001, 202-842-3900

National Legal Assistance Support and Information, National Clearinghouse for Legal Services, Inc., 205 W. Monroe Street, 2nd Floor, Chicago, IL 60606-5013, 312-263-3830

Eldercare Initiative in Consumer Law Project, National Consumer Law Center, Inc., 11 Beacon Street, Boston, MA 02108, 617-523-8010

Strengthening Legal Assistance Project, The Center for Social Gerontology, 2307 Shelby Avenue, Ann Arbor, MI 48103-3895, 313-665-1126

Pension Rights Center, 918 16th Street NW, Suite 704, Washington, DC 20006, 202-296-3776

National Legal Support for Elderly People With Mental Disabilities Project, Bazelon Center for Mental Health Law, 1101 15th Street NW, Suite 1212, Washington, DC 20005-5002, 202-467-5730

National Minority Aging Organizations, Project Aliento, Asociación Nacional Pro Personas Mayores, 3325 Wilshire Blvd., Suite 800, Los Angeles, CA 90010, 213-487-1922

Responding to the Needs of the Minority Elderly Project, National Caucus and Center on the Black Aged, Inc., 1424 K Street NW, Suite 500, Washington, DC 20005, 202-637-8400

Public Policy and Indian Elders in the Media, National Indian Council on Aging, 6400 Uptown Boulevard NE, Suite 510W, Albuquerque, NM 87110, 505-888-3302

Meeting the Special Concerns of Hispanic Older Women Project, National Hispanic Council on Aging, 2713 Ontario Road NW, Washington, DC 20009, 202-265-1288

Native Elder Health Care Resource Center, University of Colorado at Denver, National Center for American & Alaskan Native Mental Health Research, 4455 East 12 Avenue, Room 308, Denver, CO 80220, 303-372-3232

University of North Dakota Resource Center on Native Americans, Office of Native American Programs, P.O. Box 7134, Grand Forks, ND 58202, 701-777-4291

SOURCE: Administration on Aging (1997b).

effectively address domestic violence that affects older women. With Title IV assistance, statewide legal hotlines have been established in 11 states, and, most recently, Title IV funding has supported disaster relief programs to victims of hurricanes, earthquakes, floods, and the Oklahoma City bombing. Whatever disagreement may exist about the viability of the OAA, most agree that Title IV has represented an atypical but largely successful effort by the federal government to advance the cause of aging through applied research, training, and demonstration projects.

Title V establishes authority for development of community service employment programs for unemployed, low-income persons 55 years of age and older. Initially administered from the Office of Economic Opportunity and later from the Department of Labor, the program was added to the OAA in 1973 but continues to be administered by the Department of Labor. In 1995, 65,000 older adults were enrolled in Title V Programs. Participants work part-time, typically in service areas such as education, health and hospitals, recreation and parks, and senior centers. A majority of the funds are administered through national organizations such as Green Thumb (an affiliate of the National Farmers Union), the American Association of Retired Persons (AARP), the National Council on the Aging, the National Center on Black Aged, the National Council on Senior Citizens, the Asociación Nacional Pro Personas Mayores, and the National Urban League. Title V projects contribute to the general welfare of communities through public service to local entities such as hospitals, senior centers, libraries, and historical sites while increasing employment opportunities for low-income older adults.

Title VI establishes authority for grants to Indian tribes to develop social and nutritional programs for older Indians. Title VI was amended in 1978 to allow grants to be made directly to federally recognized tribal organizations. Tribes must represent at least 60 persons 60 years of age or older. In 1981, in an attempt to give more flexibility to the tribes, another amendment stipulated that the organizations may not be required, as under Title III, Part B, to provide ombudsman and legal services. In 1993, grants were awarded to 215 tribal organizations, which served 91,500 people not including Native Hawaiians (National Academy on Aging, 1995).

Title VII, on vulnerable elder rights protection, was enacted as part of the OAA in 1992. The purpose of Title VII is to promote advocacy designed to protect the basic rights and benefits of vulnerable elders, especially those older adults with great economic needs. According to the OAA, Title VII has a dual focus. The first is to bring together long-term ombudsman programs; programs for the prevention of abuse, neglect, and exploitation; state elder rights and legal assistance development programs; and insurance/benefits outreach, counseling, and assistance programs. The second is to facilitate the coordination and linkage between the four programs in each state.

The purpose of the long-term care ombudsman program is to identify, investigate, and resolve complaints concerning the residents of nursing homes and board and care homes. The ombudsman program is discussed in greater detail in Chapter 19. Programs for the prevention of elder abuse, neglect, and exploitation are designed to provide public education about elder abuse and conduct outreach to help identify cases of abuse, neglect, or exploitation. Programs are also responsible for offering training and technical assistance about elder abuse to professionals working with older adults. The state elder rights and legal assistance development program requires that SUAs establish programs to provide leadership in improving the quality and quantity of legal assistance programs. Finally, the state outreach, counseling, and assistance programs are to offer older adults assistance and counseling in applying for public benefits such as SSI and Medicaid and in comparing various types of health and medical insurance policies. Each of these will be discussed in greater detail in Chapter 11. Activities under Title VII have been funded out of Title III and have not been funded as a separate title since 1996.

Currently, Congress has yet to finalize appropriations for the OAA for 1998. For updates on changes in the OAA, check the *Community Resources for Older Adults* Web site at

http://www.hhs.unco.edu/geron.htm

In the next section, we present the past, current, and proposed funding levels for the OAA.

Funding for the Older Americans Act

Exhibit 2.5 lists 1997 funding levels for the OAA (our Web site provides a comparison of funding levels beginning in 1995). Many activities received less funding in fiscal year 1996 compared with funding levels of fiscal year 1995. Title III-B supportive services, III-C congregate meal programs, and III-F preventive health services all experienced a decline in funding. Funding for ombudsman services and elder abuse programs funded previously under Title VII are now included under Title III-B. Funds for research/training/demonstration projects funded under Title IV were significantly reduced in fiscal year 1996. Although Title V is administered through the Department of Labor, the funding levels are also listed in Exhibit 2.5. The increase in Title V funds from fiscal year 1996 to proposed fiscal year 1997 reflects the increase in the minimum wage recently enacted by Congress. Overall, funding for the OAA has decreased from fiscal year 1995 levels.

Exhibit 2.5 **Older Americans Act Appropriations for Fiscal Years 1996 and 1997 (Dollars in Thousands)**

Title	Activity	Fiscal Year 1996 Enacted	Fiscal Year 1997 President's Budget	House	Senate	Final
III-B	Supportive services and centers	300,556	294,787[1]	300,556	300,556	300,556
	Nutrition services					
III-C1	Congregate meals	364,535	357,019	364,535	364,535	364,535
III-C2	Home delivered meals	105,339	94,191	105,339	105,339	105,339
III-D	In-home services-frail elders	9,263	9,263	9,263	9,263	9,263
III-F	Preventive health services	15,623	16,982	0	15,623	15,623
IV	Research/training/demonstration	2,850	11,666	0	4,000	4,000
V	Senior community service employment[2]	373,000	350,000	373,000	373,000	463,000[3]
VI	Grants to Indian tribes	16,057	16,057	16,057	16,057	16,057
VII	Grants to states for protection of vulnerable elders					
	Ombudsman services	0	4,449	0	0	0
	Prevention of elder abuse	0	4,732	0	0	0
	Insurance and benefits counseling	0	1,976	0	0	0
	Federal Council on Aging	0	226	0	0	0
	Program direction	15,097	16,789	14,795	14,795	14,795
	Total AOA (excludes Title V)	829,320	828,137	810,137	810,545	830,168

SOURCE: Administration on Aging (1997a).

NOTES: 1. Title III-B includes earmarks of $4.449 million for ombudsman services and $4.732 million for elder abuse.

2. Title V is administered by the Department of Labor.

3. Fiscal year 1997 increase of $90 million in Title V covers the minimum wage increase.

Outcomes of the Older Americans Act

The OAA has been law for more than three decades. Its grandiose objectives spelled out in Title I of the act have remained intact. The governmental structures at the federal, state, and local levels have reached mature and stable plateaus, and a wide variety of programs have been put into place nationwide. Has the OAA, then, accomplished its original goals? Little comprehensive research exists to support either a positive or negative claim.

Some say that the OAA has failed because it has not adequately served minorities. For example, a study by the U.S. Commission on Civil Rights in 1982 showed that the number of older adults of color receiving services was a small percentage of the total number of eligible persons in six American cities. A study conducted by the Public Policy Institute of the AARP (Hasler, 1990) concluded that minority participation in AoA programs fluctuated greatly from year to year and that there was a clear problem with the reliability and validity of data being collected to report minority participation.

Another charge that has been leveled against the OAA is that those who are poor and isolated are underserved. For example, senior centers and group meals (both widely funded by local AAAs) attract primarily the healthy and active among the aged (Rich & Baum, 1984).

Other critics of the aging network hold that not enough of the federal funds intended for services to older adults ever reach them. They contend that the federal, state, and local aging network bureaucracies are self-serving and that too much of the funding is channeled into supporting these bureaucracies (Estes, 1979).

Finally, in her landmark book, *The Aging Enterprise,* Estes (1979) identified a number of shortcomings associated with the passage of the OAA. Although her comments were made nearly 20 years ago, they are still being debated today. First, Estes states that the OAA does nothing to alleviate the economic and social conditions that determine the quality of life of older Americans. Indeed, securing a "brown bag" of groceries for older adults who have limited food does nothing to help them escape the poverty that causes daily worry about obtaining food. Moreover, the social structures that have led some older adults into marginal economic status are not addressed—such as providing mechanisms for ensuring adequate retirement income for lifelong homemakers. Estes contends that existing social policy for aged persons simply preserves the existing social class distinctions. Second, Estes argues that the insistence on age-segregated programs creates tension between social groups and makes older adults targets of blame for the country's economic hardships. The rise in groups such as Americans for Generational Equity and the current discussion about rising health care costs associated with Medicare seem to offer support for this concern. Finally, Estes notes that funding the OAA reassures the public that aged persons are adequately being cared for while nothing is being done to change the functioning of social class. She recommends that structural changes be made in income, retirement, and employment policies that accentuate class differences; that universalist policies be adopted that among other things, would facilitate intergenerational bonding; and that universal health care be enacted.

Those who support the OAA point to hundreds of thousands of older adults who receive services through OAA programs. These services are important for maintaining current levels of well-being as well as for assisting those who have low levels of functioning. Thus, the programs and services supported by the OAA help elders with better levels of well-being maintain their physical and social vitality as well as assist those at risk of physical decline and social isolation. Services available under the OAA help people such as the Wrights, described at the beginning of the chapter—to whom would they turn if the aging network ceased to exist? Moreover, locally based AAAs must be responsive to the needs of the people they are directed to serve. For example, as the population has aged and there are more and more frail elders, local AAA funding has shifted to concentrate more on programs that help meet the needs of these individuals. One example of a program that has improved the lives of frail elders is the nutrition program. A study of the national nutrition program for older adults conducted in 1994 showed that the nutritional well-being of participants has measurably improved (Ponza, Ohls, & Millen, 1996). Others point to the success of many AAAs in leveraging other resources, both public and private, to support needed services.

Should the success of the OAA be measured against the degree to which it accomplishes its goals stated in Title I? Such lofty philosophical underpinnings are laudable, but they are impossible to reach, given the act's limited resources. We will revisit the OAA in Chapter 20 and consider the future of the act. In the next chapter, we examine some of the factors associated with service use by older adults and some theoretical models that can be used to explain why some older adults choose not to seek services.

 **3**

Patterns of Service Use and Theories of Help-Seeking Behavior

---

Katherine Hahn is an 80-year-old retired physician who lives alone with her two dogs in a condominium in Phoenix. She never married, and her only living relative is her brother who lives in Germany. As of late, she has not been well, and dirty laundry, trash, and old newspapers have begun to accumulate in the entryway into her apartment, where there is a terrible stench. She has become increasingly frail and unable to descend her stairway safely to get outside. As a result, she is unable to take her dogs outside, so the dogs wear diapers. The neighbors are starting to complain to the management. She refuses all attempts to help her.

Most older adults enjoy good health, are active well into later life, and are content with retirement; the role changes that accompany later life, however, have the potential to be quite disruptive unless adequate support is available. For example, widowhood is often associated with a decrease in income, a loss of emotional support, and a decline in physical health that can complicate simple daily tasks, such as shopping and preparing meals. Most communities offer a number of community and social support services to help older adults cope with their changing social, personal, and financial circumstances.

Community and support services can improve the well-being of recipients, but how many older adults use the services available to them? A review of the literature about the use of community service programs reveals a common theme—only a small percentage of older adults report using services (Krout, 1983b; Mitchell, 1995; Spense, 1992; Starret, Wright, Mindle, & Van Tran, 1989). Consider Katherine Hahn's situation. She could use the assistance of a home health aide or homemaker. Certainly, she could use a volunteer to walk her dogs. But she refuses any assistance. How can we explain this paradox? Moreover, many older adults in our communities need assistance. But whom do they rely on most often to meet those needs? In this chapter, we present information about the social care older adults receive from informal and formal networks and how the informal and formal networks interact to assist older adults. Next, we examine possible reasons why older adults might not be inclined to use community services and present some social psychological theories that help explain help-seeking behavior. We end this chapter with a discussion about how social theory can be used to help understand patterns of service use among older adults.

Social Care for Older Adults

When we encounter a problem, need help getting something done, or just need someone to talk to, what do we do? Most of us probably first seek help or advice from someone we know in our *informal network*—a friend or family member—rather than from a resource in the *formal network*. Older adults also show a preference for turning to the people with whom they are familiar and who are involved in their daily lives. Researchers have discovered that older adults turn to their informal network of family and friends for help before they turn to the formal network (Cantor, 1983, 1991; Horowitz, 1985; Litwak, 1985; Suitor & Pillemer, 1990). When seeking help from members of the informal network, older adults exhibit a hierarchical preference for assistance from spouses and children first, and then friends and neighbors (Cantor, 1979; Horowitz, 1985; Palley & Oktay, 1983). The care given by persons in the informal network is generally long-term, is motivated by a desire to reciprocate for past assistance, is offered free of charge, and generally requires a low level of knowledge or training (Doty, 1986; Travis, 1995). Spouses, children, siblings, and other family members provide older adults with personal care, emotional support, and social support services such as meal preparation, transportation, and mediation with bureaucracies (Brody, 1981; Matthews & Rosner, 1988; Sangl, 1985; Shanas, 1979; Stone, Cafferata, & Sangl, 1987). A voluminous amount of research exists documenting that family caregivers of older adults assume this significant role at great expense to their financial, psychological, and physical well-being (e.g., Biegel, Sales, & Schultz, 1991; Montgomery & Kamo, 1989; Scharlach & Boyd, 1989; Strawbridge & Wallhagen, 1991). Siblings, as well as friends, also provide support to one another in later life, but their help is more likely to be emotional support and companionship rather than assistance with the tasks of daily living (Bedford, 1989; Jones & Vaughan, 1990; Wellman & Wortley, 1989).

In contrast to the informal network, the *formal network* consists of agencies that operate within a bureaucratic structure, generally have no prior emotional relationship with their clients, and provide care for a limited or specified amount of time (Lipman & Longino, 1982; Litwak & Misseri, 1989). The community resources that we discuss later in this book represent the formal network that exists to enhance the well-being of older adults. As Travis (1995) pointed out, the formal network also consists of agencies that are nonservice in nature and include religious, ethnic, and social groups. When families become caregivers to frail older adults, they in essence become gatekeepers to the use of formal services. There has been considerable interest regarding when and how the informal network interacts with the formal network.

Informal and Formal Interaction

Although families offer a tremendous amount of care to older family members, there are occasions when older adults and their families turn to the formal network for assistance. Because the informal network plays such an important role in delivering and securing assistance for older adults, researchers have been interested in creating conceptual approaches to aid in understanding the interaction between the informal and formal network.

Litwak (1985) proposed the *dual specialization model,* suggesting that informal and formal networks carry out responsibilities that are best suited to each. For example, the informal network can respond to unscheduled or unplanned needs, and the formal network can offer scheduled, structured care provided by trained professionals. Being available to assist a frail older adult with frequent trips to the bathroom in the middle of the night is best provided by a caregiving spouse or child; checking on vital signs once a day is a task better suited for a trained individual in the formal network. According to Litwak's model, both the informal and formal networks work best when they perform the tasks to which they are most suited.

The *supplemental model* (Stoller, 1989; Stoller & Pugliesi, 1988) acknowledges that the informal network is the primary source of social care but that formal services are used to supplement assistance provided by the informal network when its resources are not able to meet the caregiving needs. The informal network relies on formal services to augment, rather than replace, its caregiving activities.

To date, the research on the interplay between the formal and informal network has been sparse. Clearly, more longitudinal research is needed to determine the patterns of formal network use during the course of the caregiving career. The conceptual models discussed here can alert the practitioner to be cognizant of the different ways in which the informal network reaches out to the formal network and to realize that the formal network frequently assists both the older adults and their informal network. We turn next to a review of the factors associated with service use.

Service Use by Older Adults

Researchers have identified a number of factors that are related to service use, but studies often report conflicting results regarding which factors predict service use. These differences are in part due to the use of dissimilar independent variables when predicting service use and the different community resources studied. Despite these methodological limitations, we can make some generalizations about the variables associated with service use. Characteristics such as age, transportation, gender, marital status, living arrangement, geographical location, and ethnicity have all been found to be associated with the use of community services. Specifically, as age increases, so does service use (Chappell & Blandford, 1987; Krout, 1985b; McCaslin, 1989; Webber, Fox, & Burnette, 1994). Older women are more likely to use services than are older men (Coulton & Frost, 1982; McCaslin, 1989). Those with access to transportation are more likely to use services (Krout, 1983b; McCaslin, 1989; Mitchell, 1995). Older adults living in rural communities are less likely to use community resources than are their urban counterparts (Krout, 1983b; Spense, 1992). Older adults who are married are less likely to use services than are older adults who live alone (Krout, 1983b; Spense, 1992). Finally, persons of color are significantly less likely to use community services than are their white counterparts (Carlton-LaNey, 1991; Fellin & Powell, 1988; Guttman, 1980; Spense, 1992).

Presently, much of the research investigating service use by older adults has focused on the relationship between demographic and social characteristics and service use. More research is needed to indicate the reasons *why* older adults do or do not use community services.

Psychosocial Barriers to Service Use

Studies of help-seeking behavior have identified several social-psychological barriers that might explain why older people do not use programs that could help them. Some years ago, Lipman and Sterne (1962) suggested that older adults are reluctant to use services because they wish to maintain an image of self-reliance and competency. A person's image of self-reliance might be compromised when he or she experiences a decline in physical health and is unable to continue some activities. When the perception of self-reliance and competency is compromised, asking for formal assistance only verifies this personal shortcoming. Moen (1978) found that respondents in her study were reluctant to admit needs and did not want to use services that they associated with "welfare" programs. Furthermore, American culture puts a high value on independence and self-reliance, and, as a result, people feel uncomfortable when they "impose" on others for assistance.

Along with the cultural norms and values people hold about self-reliance, their self-perceptions and social comparisons with others can influence the act of seeking assistance. For example, many older adults do not see themselves as old. At age 93, one of our grandfathers stated that he did not want to go to the senior center to socialize with those "old" people. Perhaps, like many other older adults, his view of himself did not fit his image of who uses services or attends programs designed for older adults. Similarly, Powers and Bultena (1974) suggested that older respondents in their study might have been reluctant to use services because they perceived that programs were meant for older adults who were worse off than themselves.

Another barrier to seeking help is the desire to avoid embarrassment (Shapiro, 1983). The act of asking someone for assistance implies that a person has problems that cannot be resolved on his or her own. For the current cohort of older adults, who survived such hardships as the Depression, this admission might be difficult. Moreover, when recipients seek formal services, they are forced to make their personal problems public (Williamson, 1974).

These psychosocial variables (e.g., independence, self-reliance, and embarrassment), although perceptive, are somewhat limited because they do not explore the help-seeking context in greater detail. Below we discuss theoretical models that can help explain service use among older adults.

Psychosocial Theories of Service Use

Within the fields of gerontology, sociology, and psychology, several theories or models can be used to help explain who is likely to use services and the reasons why some older adults might not be willing to seek assistance. Although researchers have not specifically applied some of these models and theories to older adult populations, they offer a way to think about the factors that might be associated with service use. These theories are psychosocial in nature in that they draw on social as well as psychological dimensions.

Continuity Theory

Continuity theory (Atchley, 1971, 1989, 1997) is a theory of adult development based on the premise that as adults develop, they become invested in mental pictures that organize their ideas about themselves and their external environment. Moreover, these ideas are actively constructed as people age. As adults reach middle age, they have a good idea of their strengths and weaknesses and use these ideas to make choices that take advantage of their strengths. Thus, Atchley (1997) states that when making choices in life,

> people will be attracted to past views of self, . . . the coping strategies that have been successful, ways of thinking that have been effective, people that have been supportive and helpful, and environments that have met the need for security and predictability. (p. 272)

Application of continuity theory to help-seeking behaviors suggests that the coping strategies used by older adults throughout their lives will likely predict under what circumstances they will seek or accept help. Remember the story of Katherine at the beginning of the chapter? She refused all attempts to help improve her health and living arrangements. No doubt, spending her life as a doctor, especially in a time when there were few women physicians, fashioned her self-perception and ways of contending with difficulties. She was probably an independent, self-sufficient woman and found that she could successfully cope with most of life's challenges primarily by herself. On the basis of this assumption about her past ways of handling difficult situations, the application of continuity theory to her situation leads to no surprise at her reluctance to accept assistance. Longitudinal research on help-seeking behavior and the use of formal services employing the continuity theory would help to better understand how past views of self and coping strategies developed throughout the life course can influence help-seeking behavior in later life.

Social Behavior Model

Anderson and Newman (1973) developed the social behavior model in an attempt to explain why individuals use health services. More recently, researchers have relied heavily on this model for guidance when investigating the use of social services. The model (shown in Exhibit 3.1) suggests that using services is a function of older adults' predisposition to use the service, enabling factors that either facilitate or impede use of a service, and the need for the service (Anderson, 1995; Anderson & Newman, 1973).

According to the social behavior model, certain individuals are more inclined than others to use services because of personal characteristics that are present before the need for a service arises. These predisposing characteristics include the demographic factors of age and gender. They also include social structure characteristics of marital status; education; occupation;

Exhibit 3.1 **Social Behavior Model**

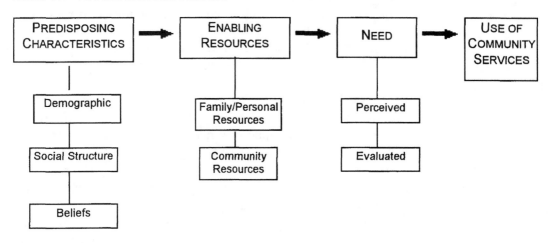

SOURCE: Adapted from Anderson (1995). Used with permission.

ethnicity; and social networks that are thought to determine the status of a person in the community, his or her ability to cope with the problem at hand, and the resources available to deal with the problem. General beliefs about support services might also predict service use.

Even those who are predisposed to using services will not unless they can access those services. Enabling characteristics that facilitate the use of services include personal and family characteristics of income level, insurance coverage, access to transportation, and awareness of service. At the community level, enabling characteristics include the availability of the service and the distance to the service. Finally, service need can be either an individual's subjective assessment of need or an evaluated need provided by a professional.

Anderson and Newman (1973) conceptualized the social behavior model as sequential in nature. Researchers have found that predicting service use cannot be influenced by need alone, unless the person is predisposed to use the service and then has the necessary enabling resources.

Let us illustrate how we can use this model to predict whether an older adult would attend a congregate meal site. Walter is 78 years old and has lived alone since his spouse of 45 years died 2 years ago. His monthly income is $850 a month, and he lives in a small one-bedroom apartment. Although he is in good health and is able to drive, he does not go out much and easily becomes despondent when thinking of his spouse. Walter has found that he is uncomfortable with shopping and cooking because his wife was responsible for most of those duties. As a result, he often skips breakfast and lunch.

After learning about his plight, a friend tells him about the congregate meal program offered three times per week at the senior center and invites Walter to go with him. Walter steadfastly refuses and states, "I do not need to eat like I used to, and I am getting along just fine." How can we explain Walter's reluctance to attend the congregate meal program? At first glance, he has many characteristics presented in the social behavior model that should be related to attending the program. He has the resources that would enable him to pay the suggested donation for the meal, he has transportation to the site, and he is aware of the service. Walter does not, however, perceive that he has an unmet nutritional need. In his mind, he can do without going to the congregate meal program, and he does not see how he could benefit from attending. Unless there is a change in Walter's perceived need for the program, he probably will not attend.

The social behavior model has had varying success in predicting actual community service use. Researchers using this model have found that predisposing characteristics of older age, being female, not being married, and higher levels of education and the enabling characteristic of income are associated with increased likelihood of service use (Krout, 1983b; Peterson, 1989). But these characteristics do not explain use as well as awareness and need. Although awareness of services is strongly related to service use, it is often not sufficient to predict use. Researchers have reported that even when respondents were aware of community programs, their use of programs continued to be low (Krout, 1984; Mitchell, 1995; Powers & Bultena, 1974). Overall, perceived need is most often the best predictor of service use. In this next section, we describe some theories designed to predict help-seeking behavior developed primarily from the field of psychology.

The Psychology of Help-Seeking Behavior

People probably can remember a time when they were sick enough to see a doctor but did not until a friend or family member cajoled them into going. Or perhaps they can recall a time when they drove around hopelessly lost but refused to stop and ask for directions. Why do individuals refuse to ask for help when clearly they would be better off if they did? According to the psychology of help-seeking behavior, seeking assistance is more complicated than might be expected.

Decisions about whether to seek help involve weighing the psychological costs of asking for assistance against the benefits that might occur. In contrast to the social behavioral model, the help-seeking theories we will be discussing take into account the psychological processes of a person who is considering seeking assistance. In this next section, we present a summary of the reactance theory, the attribution theory, the equity theory, and the threat to self-esteem model. We base this summary on the work of Fisher, Nadler, and Whitcher-Alagna (1983), who provided an in-depth review of how each of these theories can be used to predict help-seeking behavior.

Reactance Theory

The reactance theory (Brehm, 1966) suggests that people value certain states such as freedom of choice and autonomy. When these states are threatened, a negative psychological state (reactance) occurs, and people respond in ways that attempt to restore the valued states. The degree of reactance experienced by an individual depends on how important the freedom is to the individual, the number of freedoms lost or threatened, and the strength of the threat (Brehm, 1966; Brehm & Brehm, 1981). Thus, when recipients perceive that the aid or assistance will threaten their freedom or autonomy, they are likely to react negatively (Fisher et al., 1983). Some researchers have shown that reactance can occur even if there is no direct personal threat to freedom. For example, Fisher and his colleagues suggest that individuals might refuse aid if they think there are "strings attached" that could compromise freedom. Furthermore, as recipients seek to reestablish their freedom or autonomy, they may also form a negative impression of the person who is trying to provide the assistance (Gergen, Morse, & Kristeller, 1973).

How we can use reactance theory to explain why an older adult might choose not to seek assistance? Consider the case of Lydia, an 82-year-old widow living alone in a mobile home that she and her husband bought some years ago. Her monthly income consists of a Social Security check of $225 that she receives as a surviving spouse. An outreach worker informs Lydia that she is probably eligible for SSI, which would provide her with additional income as well as Medicaid coverage for her health care needs. She refuses and states that she does not want to give any information about her personal affairs to a government worker. She fears that once she gives them any personal information and begins to receive SSI, the government could invade other aspects of her personal life or restrict what she does with her money. According to the reactance theory, even though a direct threat to Lydia's autonomy does not exist, she does not want to go through a process that she perceives will indirectly cause harm to her autonomy. As a result, she chooses not to accept any financial assistance.

Attribution Theory

Think about the last time someone helped you out of a difficult situation. Do you recall asking yourself why that person decided to help you? When contemplating whether to ask for help, did you wonder why you needed help with that problem? Attribution theory states that individuals formulate attributions to understand, predict, and control their environment and help explain why certain events occur (Kelley, 1967). Attributions are assigned to both internal (self) and external (environment) factors to help understand the occurrence of events or behaviors.

Let us examine the first question—why did that person help you? If you have been on the receiving end of some assistance recently, you might have pondered for a moment *why* the person helping you chose to do so. What was the person's real motivation for helping you fix your flat tire or helping you solve a computer problem? How we formulate an answer to this question plays an important role in whether we will allow someone to help us.

According to the attribution theory, a recipient of assistance will want to know what motivated the helper's behavior (Fisher et al., 1983). In deciding what the helper's motive is, the recipient can attribute the helping person's behavior to three possible motives. Fisher et al. suggested that the recipient might think that (a) the person providing the assistance acted from genuine concern; (b) the person might have acted for ulterior motives; or (c) the person performed the action because his or her role demanded it. These possible inferences readily apply to seeking assistance from helpers in the older person's formal network. If the older adult believes that the person providing assistance does so because that person's role requires it or that the helper acts from genuine concern, chances are that the older adult will be less hesitant about seeking assistance from a formal source.

Another application of the attribution theory is its use in answering another important question linked to seeking help when people need it—why do we need help? Remember, the basic premise of the attribution theory is that individuals scan their environment to explain some of their behaviors or actions. If individuals cannot explain their behaviors by external (environmental) factors, then they will look inward for internal factors (personal disposition). In the process of trying to determine why they need help, the attribution theory states that individuals will look for three types of information. One is the *distinctiveness* of the behavior (does the behavior always occur), the second is *consensus* (are others responding similarly), and the third is *consistency* (how often the behavior occurs).

The recipient assesses each of these dimensions in any help-seeking situation. An internal or external attribution depends on the combination of different levels of distinctiveness, consensus, and consistency (Fiske & Taylor, 1991). For example, if you decide that you *always* have trouble with computers (low distinctiveness), that you have had difficulty using computers ever since you first started working on them (high consistency), and that other people do not seem to have the same trouble you do with computers (low consensus), then you are likely to attribute your computer trouble to an internal attribute (you cannot learn new things). In contrast, if you have experienced difficulty with only one particular computer in the computer lab (high distinctiveness), you infrequently have trouble using computers (low consistency), and you notice others in the computer lab having the same difficulty (high consensus), then you will probably attribute your troubles to an external factor (the computer is a lemon).

This reasoning process is an important determinant in the decision to seek assistance. For example, if recipients feel that they need assistance because of a personal inadequacy (internal attribution), then self-perception is low and help seeking might not occur (Fisher et al., 1983). On the other hand, if individuals perceive that many people need help for a similar condition (high consensus), they will make an external attribution and will be more likely to accept assistance (Gerber, 1969; Tessler & Schwartz, 1972).

How can the attribution theory be used to understand why a caregiver might not use the services of an adult day program? Consider the situation of Jacque, an adult daughter. Her mother, Olivia, is 82 and has lived alone since her spouse died 11 years ago. In the last 6 months, Jacque has seen her mother's physical condition steadily worsen—she is becoming more forgetful, and her unsteady gait causes her to fall frequently. Jacque has helped with shopping, meals, and other errands along with working and caring for her own two children. Her work and family obligations make it impossible to constantly supervise her mother during the day, and she is becoming increasingly worried about Olivia's well-being. A friend tells Jacque about the local adult day program and suggests she take Olivia. What are the chances that Jacque will use the services of the adult day program?

If we apply the attribution theory to this situation, we can expect that when Jacque is deciding whether to take her mother to the program, she will think about why she would need to use the services of an adult day program. She might come to the conclusion that taking her mother to the program demonstrates that she does not have the personal fortitude to take care of her (an internal attribution). She may, on the other hand, attribute the need for assistance to her mother's condition (external attribution). If her reasoning follows this latter line of thinking, she will probably be more likely to use the adult day program. If she formulates an internal attribution, she will be less inclined to use the service.

Equity Theory

Social exchange theories suggest that individuals interact with one another through the exchange of valued objects or sentiments. Several similar versions of exchange theories exist, including Walster, Berscheid, and Walster's (1973) equity theory. This theory is based on the premise that individuals strive to maintain equity within their relationships (Adams, 1965). Individuals who feel they are getting more than they should and who feel indebted to others react negatively to these situations in which equity is compromised (Rook, 1987). When inequities occur, individuals experience a certain degree of distress and attempt to rectify the imbalance either by altering the tangible elements of the interaction process or by psychologically reformulating the interaction context. Furthermore, equity theory states that the greater the degree of inequity, the greater the degree of stress experienced because of the inequity (Hatfield & Sprecher, 1983). In a help-seeking situation, recipients will feel inequality when they have a higher ratio of outcomes to inputs (Walster et al., 1973).

A number of researchers reported that individuals on the receiving end of assistance who were unable to reciprocate were less likely to seek or ask for assistance (DePaulo, 1978; Greenberg & Shapiro, 1971; Manton, 1987). When researchers introduced reciprocity into an inequitable situation, recipients reported feeling better about the assistance they were receiving (Wilke & Lazette, 1970). In situations in which introducing reciprocity is not possible, changing a recipient's perception of the helping context can be just as useful in restoring a sense of equity (Greenberg & Westcott, 1983; Roberto & Scott, 1986). If we apply this idea to receiving assistance from the formal network, older adults may avoid feeling indebted by differentiating between programs in which they are entitled (i.e., Social Security) and those that are needs based (i.e., food stamps; Lipman & Sterne, 1962). There is a sense of equity in programs such as Social Security because older adults have *paid* into the program—and they are receiving financial benefits to which they are entitled. In contrast, the number of older adults who participate in programs in which recipients are always on the receiving end and provide nothing in return for those benefits may be low.

Equity theory also can be used to explain help-seeking behavior. Consider the situation of Hanna, 72, who suffers from rheumatoid arthritis that severely limits her ability to attend activities outside her home. Before her arthritis limited her activities, she worked part-time and was a volunteer at the local hospital. Although she enjoyed working, she always remarked how much satisfaction she experienced when helping patients. She describes herself as an independent person, having always provided for her needs. Because her arthritis keeps her from volunteering and getting out as much as she would like, she finds herself becoming more and more isolated. She reads in the newspaper about a friendly visiting program, a service in which a volunteer provides social companionship and assistance with errands. She wonders how she could ever compensate someone for coming and spending

Best Practice **Equity Theory in Action**

New programs are under way in nine states and the District of Columbia that are based on the principle of equity. These programs offer persons of all ages the opportunity to earn and spend service credits. Allowing service credits to be earned while doing community work or personal assistance enables communities to harness the energy, talent, and wisdom of people of all ages—especially older adults. Service credit volunteers earn credits guaranteed by a local community organization each time they help someone. The volunteers can use the credits to get help for themselves when they need it or donate their credits to a friend or general fund to help others. There are more than 3,000 service credit volunteers providing about 15,000 hours of service a month. Service credit volunteers do all types of things for others, including at-home personal care, household chores, and service outside the home such as shopping and escort services. Program directors report that volunteers like knowing that the work they do will enable them to get help when they need it and that the program allows people to participate in a mutual help program (Cahn, n.d.).

For more information about service credit programs, contact the Service Credit Banking Projects, Office for Technical Assistance and Direction, 301-405-2532.

time with her—she feels that she has nothing in return to give the volunteer. If Hanna feels she will be unable to reciprocate the help she receives, it might be difficult for her to accept the assistance of the volunteer.

Threats to Self-Esteem Model

The threats to self-esteem model (Fisher et al., 1983) is based on the assumption that most help-seeking situations contain a mixture of both positive and negative elements (Exhibit 3.2). Whether the helping situation is perceived as positive or negative depends on the characteristics of the (a) aid, (b) helper, (c) recipient, and (d) context. If recipients perceive the aid as highlighting their inferiority or dependency, recipients will view the aid as *self-threatening*. In contrast, if the recipients see the aid as positive, the recipients will perceive the assistance as *self-supportive*. If the helper is similar in age or status to the recipients or has a higher status than that of the recipients, the recipients are likely to see the aid as highlighting their inferiority, and the helping situation becomes self-threatening (Fisher & Nadler, 1976; Nadler, Fisher, & Streufest, 1976). Recipient characteristics also can influence

Exhibit 3.2   **Formalized Threat to Self-Esteem Model**

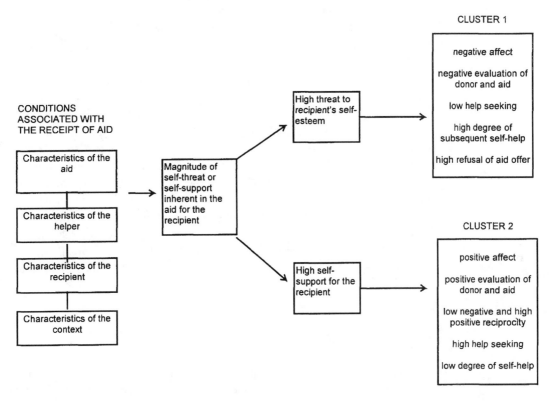

SOURCE: From "Four Conceptualizations of Reaction to Aid" (p. 75), by J. D. Fisher, A. Nadler, and S. Whitcher-Alagna, 1983, in J. D. Fisher, A. Nadler, B. M. DePaulo (Eds.), *New Directions in Helping* (Vol. 1), New York: Academic Press. Used with permission.

how the help-seeking episode can influence the perception of the help-seeking behavior. Researchers have found that recipients who were ego-involved in the task and who valued autonomy were more threatened by receiving the assistance (DePaulo & Fisher, 1980; Nadler, Sheinberg, & Jaffe, 1981). Evidence suggests that those with high self-esteem are more reluctant to receive help than those with low self-esteem (Nadler & Mayseless, 1983).

Accordingly, the recipient will perceive the characteristics associated with the receipt of aid as either self-threatening or self-supporting. This in turn will influence the recipient's decision to seek assistance. If the recipient perceives the help as predominantly self-threatening, the recipient's reaction will be negative (Cluster 1 in the model). On the other hand, if the recipient views the assistance as primarily self-supportive, the recipient's reaction will be positive (Cluster 2 in the model).

Let us look at how the threats to self-esteem model can help predict help-seeking behavior. Consider Mabel and John, who have lived in a small rural community for 25 years. Mabel is 75 and still works at the local school district as a secretary. She is quite proud of the many years she has worked and is well known in the community. John, 84, retired 15 years ago and has remained healthy until recently. John has begun to experience back problems, high blood pressure, and arthritis that limits his mobility. He has successfully recovered from angioplasty for clogged arteries in his heart and neck. Because of John's health problems, Mabel thinks it is time to look into additional insurance that will supplement their Medicare coverage. Mabel has collected information from various insurance companies but is having trouble determining which policy is best. The local area agency on aging has trained a number of older adults who live in the community to be insurance counselors and assist other older adults in comparing Medigap policies. Mabel refuses to use the service because she does not want to "look stupid" in front of the people she knows. In this situation, Mabel perceives that both the situation and the characteristics of the donor are self-threatening and most likely will not seek the assistance of the insurance counselor.

Application of Theory in Practice

Theories can be powerful tools in understanding and predicting the patterns and behaviors of others. The theories and models described in this chapter can give practitioners and students a better understanding of why older adults may or may not use the services and programs that would enhance their well-being. If service providers are aware of the different models and theories of help-seeking behavior, they can work to deliver their services in such a way that addresses issues of equity or self-esteem. Using attribution theory, adult day program directors can convey a message to overworked caregivers that can help them reformulate the attributions they construct about using the services of an adult day program. Changing caregivers' internal attribution that using adult day care services is an indication that they are personal failures to an external attribution will increase the likelihood of program use. Simply informing older adults of the services that exist in communities will not guarantee that they will use the services. Understanding and acknowledging the psychosocial barriers to accepting help will increase the use of community-based services by older adults in times of need.

Part II

Community, Support, and Long-Term Care Services

4

Information and Referral

Gary was panicked. His mother, Ruth, was coming home from the hospital in 2 days. Ruth, 81, had suffered her third stroke. She was confused and weakened on her right side but not paralyzed. He knew that his mother could not return to her apartment at this time. He could not imagine Ruth living with him. With his bachelor's lifestyle and two jobs, he simply could not provide the care and attention she needed. His girlfriend suggested that he look in the community services section of the phone book for help. There he found Carelink listed under senior services. He didn't know what to expect, but he knew he had to start somewhere. Pete, the Carelink information and referral specialist, spent 20 minutes suggesting several options for Gary. When Gary talked with his girlfriend that evening, he told her that he still felt overwhelmed but that he had no idea there were so many services for seniors with problems such as his mother's.

It is easy to see why Gary was overwhelmed with the idea of caring for his mother. Who will supervise her during the day? Who will cook her meals and administer her medications when he is at work? What about rehabilitation therapy? Although people such as Gary know that there must be services and programs in their community that can help, they often do not know where to begin to look. Not knowing who to call for assistance can result in leaving a personal or familial crisis unresolved; finding help, however, can be extremely difficult. As Levinson (1988) pointed out, the volume of services that exists is so great that the result is a complex and fragmented network that makes finding information problematic for the average person. Information and referral (I&R) services are designed to help older adults and their families access the services they need. Chelimsky (1991) defined I&R as "the active process of linking someone who has a need or problem with an agency that provides services meeting that need or solving that problem"

(p. 2). In this chapter, we review the policies that helped create I&R services, describe the different types of programs and the people they serve, and look at the challenges that lie ahead for I&R services.

Policy Background

Information and referral services trace their origins to a social support agency created in the 1870s called the social service exchange. Social service exchanges were created to prevent duplication of relief giving and increase the efficiency of screening "worthy" from "unworthy" applicants (McCaslin, 1981). By 1946, there were 320 exchanges, but the number of exchanges dropped to 97 by 1963 (Long, Anderson, Burd, Mathis, & Todd, 1971).

During this period, the social service exchanges were being replaced by different I&R systems. In the 1940s, Britain and the United States set up information centers to assist World War II veterans in finding appropriate resources. By 1949, however, the majority of these centers had shut down as well (Long et al., 1971). Also during this time, the United Community Funds and Councils of America, the predecessor to the United Way, began to provide information about social welfare resources and, with the creation of the Public Health Service, began to expand I&R efforts into health and aging resources (Levinson, 1988; Long et al., 1971).

A boost to the concept of I&R services emerged in the 1960s with the increase in public and private sector programs, which included legislation promoting the creation of I&R services to persons who were chronically ill, mentally ill, and aged (Levinson, 1988). In addition, the OAA of 1965 instructed the AoA to create a network of I&R services. Amendments to the OAA in 1978 provided that the AoA act as a clearinghouse for all information related to the needs and interests of older persons and provide access to services that included transportation, outreach, and I&R (Lowy, 1980). I&R services are currently funded along with other programs under Title III-B (Support Services and Senior Centers) of the OAA. Because I&R services are funded in this manner, the amount of Title III dollars spent in delivering I&R services to older adults is unknown.

The OAA defines I&R as a service for older adults that (a) provides individuals with current information on opportunities and services available to the individuals within their communities, including information relating to assistive technology; (b) assesses the problems and capacities of the individuals; (c) links the individuals to the opportunities and services that are available; and (d) to the maximum extent practicable, ensures that the individuals receive the services they need and that they are aware of the opportunities available by establishing adequate follow-up procedures.

In part because of 1992 amendments in the OAA requiring the AoA to establish I&R as a priority service, the AoA has been actively involved in promoting and enhancing I&R services. For example, the National Association of State Units on Aging received a grant from the AoA to establish the National Information and Referral Support Center to strengthen the capacity of I&R activities under the OAA. The support center has served as the focal point for education and training of I&R providers across the country. During the first 3 years of the project, the support center developed a variety of products designed to promote consistency and improve the quality of I&R services. To meet these goals, the support center developed three guides— the *Assessment Guide for Older Americans Act Information and Referral Services,* the *Implementation Guide for Older Americans Act Information and Referral Services,* and the *National Standards for Older Americans Act Information and Referral Services* (Whaley & Hutchinson, 1993a, 1993b, 1993c; see also Quirk, Whaley, & Hutchinson, 1994). In addition, the support center is encouraging the exchange of information about I&R services through the compilation of existing I&R materials, the publication of the *Information and Referral Reporter,* which is circulated to 3,000 subscribers nationwide, and the promotion of the Annual National Aging I&R Symposium to discuss aging and I&R issues.

Another national initiative to enhance I&R services is the AoA's creation of the National Eldercare Locator. This nationwide I&R service, created in 1991, is administered by the National Association of Area Agencies on Aging and the National Association of State Units on Aging. The service links callers with I&R networks of state and local organizations that assist older adults and their families. These policy initiatives have been instrumental in providing technical support to I&R services. In this next section, we examine the I&R program structure and services as well as provide a profile of users of I&R services.

Users and Programs

Although I&R services play an important role in linking older adults with needed services, few scholarly evaluations of I&R services have been conducted during the last 25 years. Moreover, local studies that have evaluated I&R services are unpublished and not readily accessible (McCaslin, 1981). As a result, the picture of who uses I&R services and the outcomes of such use remain unclear. The few studies that have been conducted on I&R programs are reported below.

In 1975, the AoA embarked on a 6-year research and demonstration project to develop a more useful and comprehensive system of I&R centers

---

For Your Files   **Eldercare Locator**

The Eldercare Locator is sponsored by the Administration on Aging, the National Association of Area Agencies on Aging, and the National Association of State Units on Aging. Fully operational since November 1992, the Eldercare Locator is a nationwide directory assistance service designed to help older persons and caregivers locate local support resources for aging Americans. This service links callers with the I&R networks of state and local AAAs. During the first month of operation, 2,150 calls were received. Three years later, the number of calls jumped to 4,906, a 128% increase.

When contacting the Eldercare Locator, callers speak to a friendly, trained professional who has access to an extensive list of I&R services. The Eldercare Locator will provide the names and phone numbers of organizations within a desired location, anywhere in the country. Anyone may call the toll-free number, 800-677-1116, Monday through Friday, 9 a.m. to 11 p.m., Eastern Time. Callers should have the following information ready: (a) county and city name or zip code and (b) a brief description of the problem.

SOURCE: "Eldercare Locator Gets High Marks" (1996).

(Long, 1975). An evaluation of services provided by a demonstration project—the Wisconsin Information Service (WIS)—was conducted. Thirteen I&R sites were created and evaluated throughout Wisconsin from 1972 to 1974. Researchers found that 90% of inquiries were made by telephone and that slightly less than half (40%) of the respondents said that they found out about the service through word of mouth. More than 75% of respondents who were informed about WIS through outreach efforts followed through with a contact to a recommended agency. A similar percentage of callers followed through with a call to a recommended agency; when referral appointments were made, however, 82% followed through with the recommended contact. All the WIS centers in the study served a high proportion of older adults. In addition, a higher percentage of older adults (55.6%) received escort and/or transportation services than did those callers who were younger (18.8%).

Two years later, Mark Battle Associates (1977) provided additional information about I&R services for the AoA by conducting a national study of 62 I&R programs across the country. The researchers collected data from I&R directors and staff, state or area agencies on aging, and users about the organizational structure, type of services offered, and client satisfaction. They reported that I&R services that were age segregated were more likely to provide a more comprehensive array of services than those I&R services that were age integrated. The average number of calls about or from older adults was 179 per month, and the range of callers was from 2 to 11,000. Of the users, 75% indicated that the I&R staff had fully or partially resolved their problems, and almost all users (97%) indicated that they were pleased with the way in which their interviews were conducted. A similar percentage (92%) indicated that the I&R service did a good job in assisting them. The most common problems of older callers were related to financial matters and Social Security, transportation, health problems and care, and home health care. Housing maintenance and repair, food and nutrition, and homemaker services were also frequently mentioned.

The different nuances of I&R programs with regard to data collection make it difficult to identify consistencies across programs. In addition, simply collecting the data can be problematic. For example, to protect the caller's identity, some I&R agencies do not collect information about the caller's race, income, or other demographic information (U.S. General Accounting Office [GAO], 1991b). This makes it hard to generalize about the type of older adults who use I&R systems and the problems for which they are seeking assistance. The studies that have been conducted, however, can inform us about the types of older adults seeking services and serve as a starting point for more rigorous empirical investigations.

Coyne (1991) examined the demographic characteristics and use patterns of 257 callers to a statewide I&R service specializing in Alzheimer's disease and related dementia. Results indicated that the average age of respondents was 50 years and that the majority were women (78%). In addition, the majority were married and working full-time (71% and 58%, respectively). Slightly less than half the callers were direct caregivers (44%), and 31% were family members of caregivers. The majority of callers also indicated that they were pleased with the services they received. For example, 96% reported that they received the information they requested and thought the information was helpful. Of callers who received referrals to specific community agencies, 65% reported that they contacted or used the referral.

Researchers have also investigated the effectiveness of various outreach efforts by I&Rs, such as direct mailings of resource directories and door-to-door canvassing in targeted neighborhoods. For example, Cherry, Prebis, and Pick (1995) examined the effects of a mass-mailed *Senior Access Directory* to 35,000 older adults over the age of 60 living in northwest Indiana. To evaluate the effectiveness of the mailing in increasing service awareness and use, staff asked all callers 9 days before the mailing and 10 days after the mailing how they found out about the agency and whether they had used the directory. More than 80% of the respondents indicated that the directory had increased awareness of services. Moreover, 44% reported that receiving the directory prompted some action, such as talking to family members or calling an agency listed in the directory. Finally, calls to the United Way more than doubled, increasing from 52 before to 122 after the distribution.

Characteristics of Programs

Where and how do older adults and their families access I&R services? The location of the agency responsible for providing I&R services, the target population served, and the scope of information and services provided all vary by community. For example, I&R programs can be located in government offices, public or private agencies, voluntary associations, public libraries, or community centers (McCaslin, 1981). Local AAAs may directly deliver I&R services or contract with other agencies to deliver I&R services to older adults. Moreover, I&Rs might target services to the general population or to a specific population, such as older adults, families with children, or persons with disabilities or chronic conditions. They might provide information about all types of community resources and services or specialize in one information area, such as services for persons with Alzheimer's disease. I&R services may have information about national, state, or local services (Levinson, 1988). Despite these myriad differences, all I&R programs have the same goal—to link individuals to appropriate services. A well-designed I&R will:

■ Increase the awareness of older persons and their caregivers about beneficial and necessary services and opportunities in the community

■ Provide information and referral about the agencies and organizations that provide the services

■ Help older persons and their caregivers by advocating for them and linking them to the agencies providing the services

■ Follow up to ensure that an adequate linkage between the older person or their caregiver and the appropriate service was made (Whaley & Hutchinson, 1993c, p. 5)

Developing and Maintaining a Resource File. The foundation of a good I&R service is its resource database. It must be accurate, be up-to-date, and include detailed information about community agencies. According to the guidelines established by the National Information and Referral Support Center, the database should include the following information about community agencies:

Legal name
Common name

Acronym

Address

Telephone

Hours and days of service

Service(s) provided

Eligibility requirements

Intake procedures

Area served

Branch offices

Accessibility

Auspices

Fee structures

Date of last update

Documents required by the organization for application

Cost of service

Length of time on organization's waiting list

Name of the organization's administrator

Other (Whaley & Hutchinson, 1993a, p. 5)

In addition, Whaley and Hutchinson (1993c) recommend that I&R services should also collect information about the characteristics of the inquirer. Collecting information about the inquirer's socioeconomic status, demographic characteristics, the nature and extent of the problem, and level of assistance needed can assist in problem-solving activities as well as provide valuable information about gaps in community resources.

Promotion of Information and Referral Services

The functions of an I&R program are useless unless older adults and their families know how to access I&R services. Unfortunately, studies of awareness of community resources consistently identify I&R services as the least known by older adults (Krout, 1983b). Clearly, if I&R programs want to empower persons who are "information poor," older adults and their families must be made aware of I&R services and benefits (Levinson, 1988). The *National Standards* document (Whaley & Hutchinson, 1993c) recommends that I&R services promote their agencies through personal contact, public service announcements, news stories, printed materials, telephone directories, and displays. In addition, I&R systems should network with other com-

Exhibit 4.1 **Extent of Provider Intervention in Information and Referral Services**

	Extent of I&R Intervention		
I&R Function	Less Intervention		More Intervention
Basic I&R components	Information giving	→ Referral giving	→ Follow-up
Support services	Translation services	→ Transportation	→ Escort services
Advocacy	Individual advocacy	→ Family advocacy	→ Group advocacy

SOURCE: Adapted from *Information and Referral Networks* (p. 44), by R. W. Levinson, 1988, New York: Springer. Copyright © by Springer Publishing Company, Inc., New York 10012. Used by permission.

munity agencies to encourage interagency linkages and target subpopulations of older adults such as foreign language groups, low-income persons, minorities, persons who are socially isolated, and persons with hearing or vision impairments. Canvassing targeted neighborhoods is another strategy often used to inform older adults about I&R services. When canvassing neighborhoods, outreach workers can make contact with older adults who may be unaware of the help community services can provide (Cushing & Long, 1974).

Functions of Information and Referrals

As shown in Exhibit 4.1, I&R programs can provide a range of services within each different I&R function. The functions of an I&R include basic I&R activities, support services that facilitate use of needed services, and advocacy (Levinson, 1988; Whaley & Hutchinson, 1993b). Within each function, a range of services is provided to older adults. Ideally, all I&Rs should offer services along the I&R continuum to inquirers, and the I&R specialists should conduct interviews to determine the extent of I&R assistance that inquirers need.

Information and Referral Process

Exhibit 4.2 illustrates the I&R process. When inquirers contact the I&R service, an I&R specialist determines the needs of the caller, the appropriate resources needed to address the identified needs, and whether referral giving or simply information giving is necessary. The specialist also provides follow-up and assesses the need for advocacy. Each of these steps is discussed below.

Exhibit 4.2 **Delivery Process of Information and Referral Services**

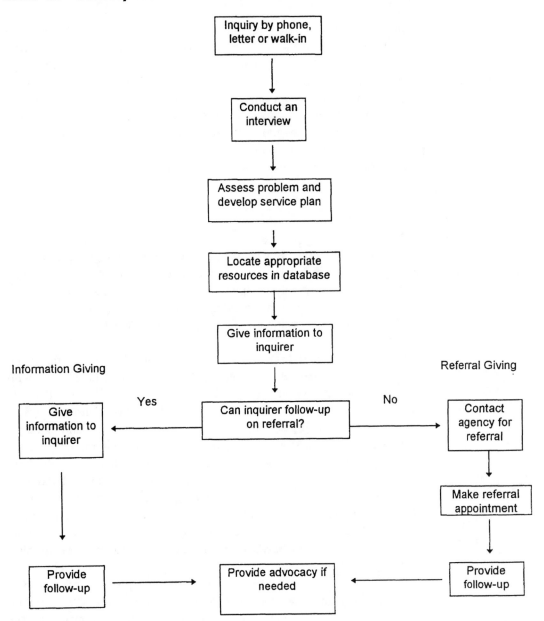

SOURCE: Adapted from *Information and Referral Networks* (pp. 147-149), by R. W. Levinson, 1988, New York: Springer. Copyright © by Springer Publishing Company, Inc., New York 10012. Used by permission.

Information Giving

At the least, an I&R service responds to the request of an inquirer about a particular agency or service by providing basic information about the appropriate agency. The I&R staff member gives the inquirer the agency's name, address, and phone number, or an explanation of the agency's application process (Whaley & Hutchinson, 1993b). For example, if a caregiver calls and requests information about local adult day programs, the I&R service would give the caller the name, address, and phone number of all local adult day programs. Other information that could be helpful to the caller, such as hours of operation or type of service provided, would also be given.

Referral Giving

Referral giving is a more involved process than information giving. In referral giving, the I&R staff is actively involved in assessing the needs of the caller, matching those needs with the appropriate agency, and linking them to the appropriate agency either by providing the caller with agency information or by calling the agency and arranging for services (Whaley & Hutchinson, 1993b).

Let's use Gary and his mother as an example of how referral giving works. When Gary calls the I&R service, he explains that his mother, who has suffered a series of strokes, will be coming to live with him. Because Gary has no idea what services could help him, the I&R specialist must assess the needs of Gary and his mother. After assessing the nature and extent of their problem, the I&R specialist can give Gary options for keeping his mother at home. He may be able to care for his mother with help from in-home health services, meals on wheels, and the use of an adult day program. The I&R specialist may also determine whether Gary's mother qualifies for help in paying for community-based long-term care services. Finally, the I&R specialist determines if it would be appropriate to contact these agencies directly to notify them of Gary's forthcoming contact or to make an appointment on his behalf.

Contacting the agency on behalf of the caller is especially critical in situations in which the caller does not speak English, is hesitant or uncertain about dealing with bureaucracies, or does not have the personal resources needed to negotiate through the process. The complexity of the problems that the inquirer has might require that the I&R specialist make multiple referrals, repeated contacts with the inquirer, and numerous contacts with appropriate agencies (Levinson, 1988). I&R programs that help inquirers access the services they recommend are commonly referred to as *Information and Assistance* (I&A) or *Enhanced I&R* programs, rather than I&R programs.

For Your Files **Alliance of Information and Referral Systems**

The Alliance of Information and Referral Systems (AIRS) is an agency that was formed to improve the access to services through the use of I&R systems. AIRS provides publications about I&R, conducts national training conferences, and acts as a clearinghouse for I&R. AIRS publications include a newsletter, the *Journal of the Alliance of Information and Referral Systems,* and the *National Directory of I&R Services* in the United States and Canada. Inquirers can reach AIRS by calling 206-632-0855 (or e-mail pkaairs@aol.com). Its home page is located at the Information and Referral Resource Network home page (http://www.ir-net.com/airs), an I&R Web site developed by CDIS, Inc. The Web site also provides links to other I&R sites.

Follow-Up

All I&R programs should follow up on referral cases, including those who received only information, to determine whether inquirers contacted the recommended community service, and if not, why they did not; what assistance was given; and any additional needs that may have arisen (Whaley & Hutchinson, 1993b). Follow-up allows the I&R specialist an opportunity to provide additional assistance securing other services, if needed. Moreover, follow-up can provide the I&R with valuable information about waiting lists or other problems (e.g., eligibility requirements) inquirers encountered trying to access recommended services (Huttman, 1985).

Advocacy and Intervention

In some instances, the I&R specialist will need to act as an advocate on behalf of an individual or groups of clients. The I&R specialist may need to act as an advocate when clients have difficulty receiving services for which they are eligible, when they have been mistreated, or when they are unable to effectively represent themselves (Whaley & Hutchinson, 1993b). The I&R specialist also can act as an advocate on behalf of a group of older adults by articulating service gaps and needed policy changes to community and government leaders.

Information and Referral Services With a National Scope

As previously mentioned, the Eldercare Locator is an I&R service funded by the AoA and sponsored by the National Association of State Units on Aging and the National Association of Area Agencies on Aging. The Eldercare Locator is a nationwide directory service designed to help older persons and caregivers locate services. Inquirers can call a toll-free number to receive assistance. Callers are asked to provide the information specialist with the county and city name or zip code and the type of problem or service desired. The Eldercare Locator also can be obtained from the National Aging Information Center's Web site (http://www.ageinfo.org). Publications such as the *Resource Directory for Older People* (National Institute on Aging and Administration on Aging, 1996) are available from the National Aging Information Center.

Challenges for Information and Referral Services

As the number of private and public programs and services for older adults continues to grow, the more difficult it will be to locate the appropriate service in a time of need. I&R services will need to respond to a variety of challenges.

Enhancing Information and Referral Services

At the request of the Special Committee on Aging, the U.S. GAO (1991b) examined 12 I&R programs that experts believed were illustrative of the promising ways in which I&R systems served older adults. GAO's research revealed effective methods of delivering I&R services used by the programs. On the basis of these findings, the GAO made four recommendations for I&R programming. The first was locating I&R services where older populations live or frequently visit, such as grocery stores, drugstores, and shopping centers. For example, the Waxter Center for Senior Citizens in Baltimore, Maryland, has located 14 I&R offices in neighborhood senior centers; of those, 6 are located in minority neighborhoods. The second recommendation was to hire professional staff, including minorities, to service diverse cultural populations. The Area 7 Area Agency on Aging in Billings, Montana, uses Native American I&R workers to make home visits to isolated older adults at six Indian reservations. The effectiveness of using minority I&R staff to work with communities of color was documented by the Office of Senior Information, Referral, and Health Promotion in San Francisco. They found that in the year after hiring a black outreach worker, the program served 405 more black clients. Employing a Chinese American outreach worker also increased the number of Chinese clients served by the program.

Best Practice   **Information and Referral Services**

The National Information and Referral Support Center identified a number of state and local agencies on aging that used unique strategies to promote the use of I&R services. Here are three examples of best practice I&R activities.

White River Area Agency on Aging, Batesville, Arkansas

The White River Area Agency in Aging promoted the concept of "one-stop shopping" to older persons and their caregivers in a 10-county rural area by developing a colorful, attention-getting flyer mailed to each of 69,900 households in the service area. The flyer explained services available; directed persons to call the I&R for service information; featured a peel-off label containing the agency's name and toll-free telephone number; and contained information to target low-income and minority older persons on benefits such as SSI, food stamps, qualified Medicare beneficiary, and person care services. The objectives of this project were to improve access to information and to increase visibility and use of the I&R service. For more information, contact White River Area Agency on Aging, 501-793-4433.

Oklahoma Aging Services Division, Oklahoma City, Oklahoma

Working with national, state, and local agencies, the state of Oklahoma developed a training manual featuring techniques for conducting outreach to black older adults. Increasing outreach efforts and service use among blacks was the primary goal of the proposal. Demographic data and proceedings from the 7th Annual State of Oklahoma Minority Outreach and I&R Conference were digested and compiled into a comprehensive outreach manual. The benefits of the project are the collaboration with other groups, meeting an I&R systems improvement plan objective, and creating an outreach manual that can be replicated. For more information, contact Aging Services Division at 405-521-2281.

Bucks County Area Agency on Aging, Pennsylvania

The Bucks County Area Agency on Aging conducted a cable television project to offer an alternative way for TV viewers to think about when to call the I&R. The project was an effort to improve existing I&R services by using new strategies for outreach and building a new relationship with cable TV in Bucks County. Volunteers produced three 30-second informational videos for cable TV and a how-to manual for replication. Benefits of the project include the enhancement of current I&R capabilities, increased visibility of the I&R, and opportunities for older volunteers to develop new skills that are on the cutting edge of the communications industry. For more information, call Bucks County Area Agency on Aging, 215-348-0510.

SOURCE: Quirk, Whaley, & Hutchinson (1994).

Exhibit 4.3 **First Call for Help: Web Page of Southwestern Indiana Regional Council on Aging**

Agency:	Southwestern Indiana Regional Council on Aging
Common Name:	SWIRCA / Council on Aging
Director:	Robert J. "Steve" Patrow, Executive Director
Address:	16 West Virginia P.O. Box 3938 Evansville, IN
Phone:	464-7800
Hours/Days:	8:00am - 4:30pm M-F 1-800-253-2188 FAX:464-7811
Programs Offered:	Job Training Special Financial Assistance for Health Needs Congregate Meals Subsidized or Free Apparel Service Home Improvements and Repairs Assistance Special Residential Placement Subsidized Transportation For the Aging Match-Up Day Care-Adults Respite Care Telephone Reassurance Citizen-Client Liaison and/or Advocacy Outreach - Special Groups Service Eligibility Determination Information and Referral - Specific Group Participatory Recreation - Sports Participatory Recreation - Social

For additional information on resources, call First Call For Help at (812) 421-2800

For comments or suggestions about the United Way of Southwestern Indiana Community Resource Guide, send email to firstcall@evansville.net

SOURCE: Southwestern Indiana Regional Council on Aging (1997). Website:
http://www.accessevansville.org/crg/A32500.htm

The third recommendation was the use of automated information resources and telephone technology to effectively provide information. Strategies included the use of automated information booths at sites throughout the community, multilingual telephone message lines, and computer bulletin boards. Indeed, I&R services have begun to appear on the World Wide Web. For example, Exhibit 4.3 shows the I&R home page of the Southwestern Indiana Regional Council on Aging (`http://www.accessevansville.org/A32500.htm`). Posting information on the Web provides an additional avenue for older adults and their caregivers to access information. Inquirers can access information any time and anywhere they have access to the necessary computer technology. Currently, such access is limited to a small percentage of the population with Internet technology.

Publicizing I&R services to older adults and their caregivers through active outreach methods was the fourth recommendation. Suggestions for active outreach included publicizing services in locations such as convenience and video rental stores. Many programs distribute printed materials publicizing I&R services throughout their communities. Examples of such efforts include monthly agency newsletters mailed to 19,000 older adults in Manhattan, Kansas, and the distribution of a senior magazine called *Lifetimes* to local doctors' offices, nutrition sites, service providers in Indianapolis, and seniors in an eight-county area.

Future efforts of increasing access to information must include locating I&R services in nontraditional places and providing options for multiple entry points to information. Nontraditional places include the workplace, restaurants, and schools. Multiple entry points would assist clients because service providers not associated with I&R programs are often the first point of contact for older adults. Hence, staff must be familiar with I&R programs as well as services available in communities. It should not matter where older adults start their inquiry for assistance; persons working with older adults must know where to send their clients for more assistance.

Enhancing Information and Referral Databases

Additional empirical evaluations are needed to provide a profile of I&R programs and services. Such an evaluation would be timely in light of the recent guidelines provided by AoA to promote consistency of I&R services and data collection processes. Studies could examine the problems that inquirers have, the short- and long-term outcomes of I&R intervention, and training needs of staff. In addition, if most people receive information outside a formal I&R service, such pathways to service access need to be identified.

Supporting the Future of Information and Referral

Although none of the 45 resolutions put forth by the delegates of the 1995 White House Conference on Aging specifically identified I&R, many included

I&R services as a means of achieving the proposed actions. For example, the delegates proposed supporting policies that mandate the dissemination of information regarding all health care providers who accept Medicare and Medicaid, that assist older persons and their families in choosing creative alternatives to institutional care, that provide I&R services for caregivers that are sensitive to disability and difference in language and culture, and that improve and expand I&Rs to ensure the availability of appropriate care, services, and treatment.

 ## CASE STUDY

FINDING AND ASKING FOR HELP

Frank is an 83-year-old Hispanic man who has had several small strokes during the last 3 years. The strokes have weakened him, and, on occasions, he is mildly confused. He and his wife, Maria, have been married for 35 years. Maria is Frank's second wife and is 26 years younger than Frank.

When Frank retired, they moved to a large urban community in which both have relatives. Although Frank and Maria do not have children, Frank has three daughters from his first marriage, whom he rarely sees. Maria attends her neighborhood church regularly and does some volunteer work for the parish. Otherwise, they lead a quiet life.

Since Frank's retirement, Maria has worked at a nursing home as a laundry assistant. Eventually, the many years of hard field work and an injury from lifting laundry culminated in a serious lower back condition. She had two back surgeries; neither surgery was successful. The arrangements for the second surgery were bungled because the surgery was not approved by her health maintenance organization (HMO). The HMO refused to pay for the surgery, and Frank and Maria are now responsible for a $20,000 medical bill that they are unable to pay.

Maria is no longer able to work. She would like to take over the payments of the HMO insurance that the nursing home gave her as a benefit. These payments are $326 per month. The local hospital charity fund has made the payments for a couple of months but cannot continue the assistance much longer. Fortunately, Frank is covered by Medicaid. A detailed examination of their financial condition shows that they are barely able to make ends meet. They have expenses of $625 per month and income of $623 per month, derived from the $494 per month Social Security received by Frank and $129 per month received by Maria. Now that Frank is no longer able to drive, transportation is a serious problem for the couple. At Frank's insistence, Maria never learned to drive. With her own health in jeopardy, no health insurance coverage, and little income of her own, Maria worries constantly about how she will take care of Frank and what she will do if something happens to him. Maria's good friend from church decides to take matters in her own hands and call a senior I&R number that she heard about on the radio.

CASE STUDY QUESTIONS

1. Would you agree that Maria's friend is calling an appropriate resource in regard to Frank and Maria's situation? Why or why not?

2. List and describe each factor that has a role in justifying Maria's concern about Frank's future and her own.

3. Suppose you are the I&R specialist assigned to this case. What additional information about Frank and Maria's situation would you want to know?

4. What do you think is Maria's greatest concern? What do you believe is her greatest problem? If not the same, which problem should be addressed first? Defend your answer.

5. What community resources would you recommend for Frank and Maria? List at least five.

6. How comfortable would you be as an I&R specialist that Maria and her friend could follow through on their own with the information that you have provided them? If concerned, what might you do to ensure that some of the suggested resource agencies are contacted?

LEARNING ACTIVITIES

1. Watch your daily local newspaper for a week. How many aging network agencies advertise their programs or services during that time? What are the pros and cons of using newspapers as a source of information about aging services and programs? Call the newspaper to determine how much it would cost programs to advertise.

2. Using the case study in this chapter about Frank and Maria, identify the resources you think they need. Go to the library and select two phone books—one of an urban city and one of a rural community in your state. If possible, select unfamiliar cities, and try to identify the community resources you would call that could assist them. What problems did you encounter in

locating those services in the phone book? Were there noticeable differences between the rural and urban locations?

3. See if you can locate a senior resource book in your community. How many calls did you have to make before you located a copy? Examine the resource book closely. How is it organized? How much detailed information does the resource book provide about each service or program? What changes would you recommend?

4. Log on to the Internet. What type of community resources does your community have online? (If your community does not have any information online, select a city in your state.) How easy or hard was it to find information and services for older adults? Do you think the Internet will become a viable resource for older adults and their family to find out about services and programs?

FOR MORE INFORMATION

National Resources

1. Aging Network Services, 4400 East-West Highway, Suite 907, Bethesda, MD 20814, 301-657-4329 (http://www.ageis.com).

   The network provides comprehensive assessment of older adults in their own settings with recommendations for appropriate services.

2. B'nai B'rith, 1640 Rhode Island Avenue NW, Washington, DC 20036, 202-857-1099 (e-mail: seniors@bnaibrith.org).

   B'nai B'rith is the world's oldest and largest Jewish service organization. The CaringNetwork is a fee-for-service program that offers information, referrals, and advice to older persons and their families throughout the United States.

3. National Asian Pacific Center on Aging, Melbourne Tower, 1511 3rd Avenue, Suite 914, Seattle, WA 98101, 206-624-1221.

   This private organization works to improve the delivery of health and social services to Asian Pacific older adults and maintains a national network of service agencies.

4. National Information and Referral Support Center, 1225 I Street NW, Suite 725, Washington, DC 20005-3914, 202-898-2578.

   The support center provides technical assistance to those who deliver I&R and I&A under the OAA. It publishes the *Information and Referral Reporter* quarterly.

Web Resources

1. Boulder County: Human Services Center, Boulder, CO
   http://bcn.boulder.co.us/human-social/center.html

   This site has extensive information about and links to local, state, federal, and international human service agencies.

2. Michigan Aging Services: Michigan Senior Resource Directory
   http://mass.iog.wayne.edu/OSAMSRD/msrdhome.html

   Those who access this home page will be able to obtain information about 25 directories of governmental, human service, and legal agencies and associations located in Michigan.

3. Long Beach Community Medical Center and Older Adult Health Services, Long Beach, CA
   http://www.lbcommunity.com/senior/ssinf.html

   This site is an example of I&R for health care services and includes information about adult day programs, memory disorder testing, transportation, and support groups.

4. Community Information and Referral, Phoenix, AZ
   http://aztec.asu.edu/cirs/cirs.html

   Visitors can search this community I&R home page by selecting either an alphabetical listing of community service agencies or by community service categories.

5. Administration on Aging, Washington, DC
   http://www.aoa.dhhs.gov

   The AoA's home page has an extensive number of links to other national organizations and programs of interest to older adults and their families.

6. Senior Link Online
   http://www.seniorlink.com

   Senior Link is an elder care resource Web site that offers referral and consultation for older adults, their families, and providers. Visitors can access elder care professionals, programs, providers, facilities, and agencies that are involved in caring for older adults.

7. Alliance of Information and Referral Systems (AIRS)
   http://www.ir-net.com/airs

   AIRS functions as a clearinghouse for issues related to managing and using I&R services. Its Web site provides visitors with access to information about professional development opportunities, an information resources library, and calendar of events.

8. National Aging Information Center
   http://www.ageinfo.org

   The Eldercare Locator can be obtained from this Web site. The information center also has publications available such as the *Resource Directory for Older People.*

5

Volunteer and Intergenerational Programs

Twice a week, 88-year-old Hazel volunteers at a local adult day care center. She helps with the hands-on care of participants. Her volunteer duties include helping people to eat, walking with them to the bathroom, and just sitting and talking with them. She also does what the director calls "tender loving pushing." Hazel enjoys volunteer work. When interviewed by a local newspaper, Hazel said, "I hope if something happens to me, there will always be someone to care."

With the growth of the older population and the decline in resources, community agencies often seek assistance from seniors in delivering their programs and services. In many communities, senior volunteerism has developed into a highly organized and often large-scale activity. Approximately 40% of all older adults formally volunteer their time to help meet the needs of the communities in which they live (Fischer, 1993). It is not uncommon to find older volunteers, such as Hazel, working within their local churches, civic or religious groups, hospitals, nursing homes, schools, and human service agencies. According to national estimates, older volunteers contribute about 3.6 billion hours of service to organizations every year (Marriott Senior Living Services, 1991).

Most individuals give multiple reasons when asked why they volunteer. As with younger volunteers, the responses of older individuals frequently focus on altruistic motivations. They say they volunteer to help others or to do something useful (Independent Sector, 1988). But older adults also differ from their younger counterparts in their reasons for volunteering. Fischer and Schaffer (1993) report that older individuals are more likely than younger adults to volunteer because of their desire for personal growth, their availability of free time, and their religious beliefs. They are much less likely than younger volunteers to be motivated by material rewards to themselves or their families, to report the importance of status and reward motivations, and to volunteer for the sake of career development. Despite the need for volunteers and the willingness of many seniors to volunteer, older adults are often an untapped resource for volunteer positions. A nationwide study of older adults estimated that approximately 14 million Americans over the age of 65, or 37.4% of the senior population, are willing to volunteer if asked (Marriott Senior Living Services, 1991). Organizations need to consider a variety of factors when recruiting older volunteers, including the individuals' experience and personal interests. Older adults who have volunteered before are easier to recruit than inexperienced volunteers. Situations most attractive to both experienced and inexperienced older volunteers are those in which they perceive that (a) there is pressing need, (b) the program needs their help because there is almost no one else to help, and (c) their work will have an immediate and beneficial impact (Fischer & Schaffer, 1993).

In this chapter, we begin by examining federal support for volunteer programs. Next, we profile senior volunteers and describe the various volunteer programs designed specifically for older adults, including those with an intergenerational focus. We conclude with a discussion of the current and future issues facing senior volunteer programs.

Policy Background

The idea of structured programs to promote senior volunteerism first emerged in 1963 when President Kennedy pushed for the establishment of a National Service Corps.[1] This organization was to "provide opportunities for service for those aged persons who can assume active roles in community volunteer efforts" (Special Committee on Aging, 1963, p. 14). Although Congress defeated the proposal for the corps, there was strong pressure from the Senate to include senior participation in programs (e.g., VISTA) sponsored by the newly created Office of Economic Opportunity.

President Johnson supported his predecessor's idea of using the experiences and talents of older adults within their local community but with a new focus on engaging poor people in service endeavors. His vision was to create new roles and functions for older people while providing them with income support via employment and providing services to local communities. In 1965, the first service program targeting low-income seniors emerged, the Foster Grandparent Program. Seniors who enroll in this program provide one-on-one assistance to children with special and exceptional needs

(ACTION, 1992). The program was first administered by the Office of Economic Opportunity. In 1968, the Foster Grandparent Program moved to the Department of Health, Education, and Welfare, where it stayed for 3 years until it was incorporated into the then newly created agency, ACTION (the federal domestic volunteer agency).

In 1971, ACTION became the new administrative home of the Foster Grandparent Program and several other service-orientated programs, including the largest and most versatile program for older adults, the Retired Senior and Volunteer Program (RSVP). This program differs from the Foster Grandparent Program in that older adults have the opportunity to volunteer in a variety of community projects, they are not limited in their participation by income guidelines, they do not receive a stipend, and participation does not require a minimum time commitment. A third senior-specific service program, the Senior Companion Program, began in 1974. Modeled structurally after the Foster Grandparent Program, this program recruits low-income seniors to serve frail and homebound elders. We will discuss each of these programs in greater detail later in the chapter.

Through the early 1990s, ACTION funded, monitored, and supported local public and private nonprofit organizations that sponsored these service projects. In 1993, President Clinton worked with Congress to pass the National and Community Service Trust Act. This act created the Americorps initiative and established its administrative entity, the Corporation for National and Community Service. ACTION programs became part of this umbrella organization now managed by the National Senior Service Corps.

Although the federal government provides primary funding sources for these larger-scale senior volunteer programs, foundations, the private sector, and private donations also offer financial support for program development. They also support volunteer programs specifically designed to meet the needs of local communities (Wilson & Simson, 1993). For example, funds from the Elvirita Lewis Foundation created the first intergenerational child care center and other intergenerational programs (Struntz & Reville, 1985).

Users and Programs

Characteristics of Older Volunteers

Several background characteristics distinguish older volunteers from nonvolunteers. For example, the likelihood of volunteering declines with advancing old age. Approximately 40% of persons 65 to 74, compared with 27% of persons over age 80, participate in volunteer activities (Marriott Senior Living

Services, 1991). As individuals age, they also decrease the amount of time they spend volunteering. On average, older persons under the age of 75 volunteer 6 hours per week, whereas individuals 75 years of age and older average 4.4 volunteer hours per week (Independent Sector, 1988).

Although it appears that women are more likely to volunteer than are men, the existing research does not substantiate this perception. We do know, however, that gender plays an important role in understanding the experiences of volunteers in later life. For many women, their experience as volunteers seems to parallel their experience in the paid workforce. Compared with their male counterparts, older women volunteers are more likely to occupy the lower-skilled volunteer positions and less likely to be in leadership volunteer roles (Fischer, Rapkin, & Rappaport, 1991). Older men and women volunteer for different reasons. Men are more likely to give altruistic reasons for volunteering, whereas women are more likely to give social reasons for volunteering (Morrow-Howell & Mui, 1989). Thus, for many women, volunteer satisfaction and retention relates to interaction on the job, recognition for their work, and meeting their own expectations (Stevens, 1993).

A person's race does not affect volunteer helping behavior; it appears, however, to have significant effects on the helping relationship. The helping tradition is strong in minority communities, but volunteers often provide help informally rather than as members of formal volunteer programs (Fischer & Schaffer, 1993). It also seems that when individuals participate in formal volunteer programs, they provide more effective service to individuals who are similar to themselves. For example, in a study of volunteer behavior, black volunteers serving black clients committed more time and clients viewed them as more helpful than black volunteers serving white clients; similar findings were found for white volunteers (Morrow-Howell, Lott, & Ozawa, 1990).

Social class is strongly associated with volunteerism in later life. Individuals with higher incomes and more education are more likely to volunteer (Fischer, Mueller, & Cooper, 1991; Lemke & Moos, 1989). These individuals tend to be the most active volunteers, giving more of their time than those with less education and lower incomes.

Other personal characteristics associated with volunteerism in later life include health, martial status, and previous volunteer experience. Older individuals who perceive themselves in good health are more likely to volunteer than those in poorer health (Fischer & Schaffer, 1993). Researchers also report that married older people are more likely to volunteer than elders who are not married (Fischer, Rapkin, et al., 1991; Independent Sector, 1988). Persons who volunteer throughout their adult lives are more likely to volunteer in their later years. They are also more likely to stay with their volunteer

Exhibit 5.1 **Type of Organization for Which Volunteer Work Was Performed for Persons Aged 65+: 1989**

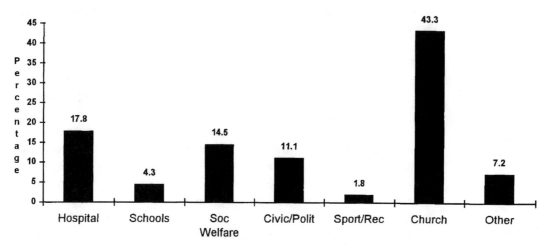

SOURCE: Compiled from data from U.S. Department of Labor (1990b).

assignments and report more satisfaction with the volunteer experience than do individuals who have less volunteer experience (Stevens, 1991).

The most common organizations for which older volunteers work are churches and other religious organizations, hospitals, and civic or political groups (see Exhibit 5.1). The types of responsibilities they assume within these organizations vary from working hands-on with individuals in need to assisting behind the scenes to ensure that the programs operate efficiently and effectively.

Federal Senior and Volunteer Programs

As previously discussed, several volunteer programs receiving federal support can be found throughout cities and towns nationwide. In this section, we describe the activities of four well-known programs: RSVP, Senior Companions, the Foster Grandparent Program, and the Senior Corps of Retired Executives (SCORE).

Retired Senior and Volunteer Program

The RSVP offers older men and women the opportunity to put their talents and experience to work in community-defined, community-supported projects (ACTION, 1992). Although RSVP is the largest federally funded volunteer organization in the country (Kelley, 1991), the programs represent a true partnership between federal, state, and local government and the private sector in each community. The federal government awards grants to community sponsors of RSVP for program operation. This support may amount up to 70% of a program's total budget. The average RSVP project receives about 50% of its support from federal resources (ACTION, 1992). Individual RSVP project sponsors are public agencies, private nonprofit organizations, and institutions that promote vital local interests and offer financial support to the project. The sponsor has full responsibility for the development and management of the project.

RSVP projects respond to community needs by matching the interests and abilities of seniors with rewarding part-time opportunities. The volunteers choose their assignments from a broad list of possibilities provided by the local RSVP office. They serve without compensation but may receive transportation or reimbursement for program-related out-of-pocket expenses. RSVP provides all volunteers with appropriate accident and liability insurance when on assignment at their host stations. Examples of organizations that serve as host agencies for the volunteers include hospitals, schools, libraries, crisis centers, nursing homes, public offices, universities, and community service programs. Among the many community-based services provided by RSVP are tax aid, Medicare counseling services, home repair programs, telephone reassurance, shopping assistance, tutoring programs, home visitation, and respite care (National Senior Service Corps, 1994b). In 1995, there were more than 750 RSVP projects located in all 50 states, the District of Columbia, Puerto Rico, and the Virgin Islands. The projects use nearly 450,000 volunteers who contribute 80,000,000 hours annually and serve through more than 60,000 public and nonprofit community organizations. The Corporation for National Service (1995) estimates the value of their service to be about $1 billion.

In 1984, RSVP went international (RSVPI), receiving sponsorship from organizations such as the Rotary and the Red Cross (Garson, 1994). Since its inception, RSVPI has carried out projects in 30 countries including Australia, Colombia, Ireland, Italy, Japan, and West Africa.

Senior Companion Program

The guiding premise of the Senior Companion Program is that the best way to help people is to help them help each other (ACTION, 1990b). Senior companions provide emotional support and assistance to older adults with a variety of needs. They serve 20 hours a week, often as members of a comprehensive care team, helping homebound older adults live independently. For example, senior companions may provide physical and emotional assistance to individuals with physical disabilities or cognitive

---

Best Practice   **Toddys Shopping Service**

The Toddys Home Shopping Program for persons who are older or disabled in Greeley, Colorado, is an excellent example of how community volunteers can have a positive impact on a community need. Access to everyday activities such as shopping is difficult for persons who are homebound. The RSVP approached a locally owned grocery, Toddys, to find out if Toddys would be interested in working with RSVP volunteers to deliver groceries to homebound individuals. After some weeks of working out the details of the process, the Toddys Shopping Service was initiated on July 28, 1978.

A homebound person within the city limits of Greeley may call Toddys on Thursdays any week of the year to place an order. Any item in the store including prescription drugs, magazines, and greeting cards are all acceptable phone orders. The only restriction on the caller is that a minimum of seven items must make up the order.

RSVP volunteers take orders by telephones made available by Toddys. This is not an easy task because shopping is a personal experience. Volunteer order takers must have good listening and questioning skills to obtain accurate descriptions of the items requested. A detailed order form helps the order takers itemize the requests. Size, color, brand, and acceptable substitutes are noted. They then pass the orders along to another group of RSVP volunteers who are the shoppers. Any Thursday morning, patrons of Toddys will find RSVP shoppers (as many as 15) busily pushing carts up and down the aisles shopping for their homebound "neighbors." Orders average 75 per week or approximately 4,000 per year. Toddys assigns one employee to spend the day bagging the groceries, delivering the groceries to the homes, and collecting the money. Toddys never charges extra for deliveries.

The long friendships made with other volunteers have become invaluable to the volunteers. On shopping days, the volunteers gather early in the morning at Toddys and meet in the small adjoining cafe for coffee and rolls. The original shopper stayed with the program for 18 years. The volunteers and the community also take pride in that the program was honored in July 1987 with a Presidential Award and again in 1992 with the J. C. Penney Golden Rule Award.

For more information, contact Retired Senior and Volunteer Program, University of Northern Colorado, Greeley, CO 80639, 970-351-2588.

---

limitations, those recovering from substance abuse problems or major medical interventions, and older adults who are frail.

Senior companions are low-income individuals, 60 years of age and older. They receive a modest allowance or stipend, reimbursement for transportation and meals, on-duty insurance, and an annual physical exam. Senior companions receive 40 hours of preservice training. Volunteer stations provide 4 hours of in-service training monthly for the senior companions. Senior companions are recognized for their work at award luncheons and other special recognition events (National Senior Service Corps, 1994a).

Local communities sponsor the Senior Companion Programs; project directors must raise at least 10% of their project funds from nonfederal sources. Most of the nonfederal funding comes from state and local governments and private social service agencies, United Way, private businesses, and fundraising campaigns. Each project has an advisory council whose members act as liaisons between projects and their communities. In 1995, there were 185 senior companion projects located in all 50 states, the District of Columbia, Puerto Rico, and the Virgin Islands. The projects employ 12,380 volunteers who contribute 12,000,000 hours of service annually helping more than 32,000 frail older adults live independently. The estimated value of saved nursing home costs and services is $150 million (Corporation for National Service, 1995).

Since 1975, researchers have conducted 35 studies of the Senior Companion Program (Freedman, 1994). The findings of these studies consistently suggest that the effort addresses a real community need and is doing so effectively. Most programs publish their evaluations as final reports submitted to the administration of the national program or the individual projects. Unfortunately, evaluators and researchers publish few outcome studies in the academic literature.

Foster Grandparent Program

The Foster Grandparent Program initiated its first 21 demonstration projects in 1965 (ACTION, 1990a). The first Foster Grandparent Program served very young children in institutions such as pediatric hospital wards and public homes for children with mental retardation, orphans, and other children without families. Today, foster grandparents help a broader array of children who experience academic or personal problems. Depending on the needs of the community and the skills and interests of the foster grandparents, these volunteers may be found in a variety of settings, including reading and literacy programs, teen pregnancy and parenting programs, juvenile correctional centers, homeless shelters, and drug treatment centers. In 1995, there were 276 projects established throughout the United States, Puerto Rico, and the Virgin Islands. Nearly 24,000 members who contribute approximately 21,600,000 hours annually carry out the projects. The government estimates the value of their service at $262 million (Corporation for National Service, 1995).

As with the Senior Companion Program, sponsors of Foster Grandparent Programs must provide at least 10% of the project's funding themselves or through other nonfederal sources. An independent advisory council, consisting of professional and lay members of the immediate community, assists each project. Project directors assign volunteers to a volunteer station. Each volunteer station formally agrees to supervise and assist foster grandparents serving under its direction.

To be eligible for the Foster Grandparent Program, volunteers must be at least 60 years old, low income (eligibility guidelines vary from state to state), no longer in the regular workforce, and capable of serving children with exceptional or special needs without detriment to themselves or the children served. Individuals must commit to serving the program 20 hours per week. Before beginning their volunteer work, all foster grandparents receive a minimum of 40 hours of training; they also receive 4 hours of in-service training per month that builds on and enhances their skills and knowledge relative to their volunteer assignments.

Foster grandparents receive several benefits because of their participation in the program. For example, they receive a small nontaxable stipend; transportation or reimbursement for transportation to and from their assigned station and other official project activities when needed; a meal or assistance with the cost of meals taken while on assignment; accident, personal liability, and excess auto coverage (for those driving their own cars); and an annual physical examination. In addition, each foster grandparent annually receives recognition of his or her services to the community at a formal public recognition event—acknowledgment perhaps as important as the monetary rewards.

During the past three decades, researchers have conducted 31 studies of the Foster Grandparent Program (Freedman, 1994). The authors of these studies suggest that participation in the program had a positive impact on the children's intellectual and social development and on the life satisfaction and morale of the older adults.

Senior Corps of Retired Executives

Established in 1964 under the auspices of the Small Business Administration, SCORE provides intensive, short-term counseling to small businesses. Besides providing free, individual counseling to persons wishing to go into business, SCORE volunteers also help people whose businesses are ailing and whose businesses are growing. For a nominal fee, SCORE also offers business and management training workshops. The primary purpose of this program is to reduce the number of companies who default on their loans (Freedman, 1994). In 1995, approximately 13,000 retired business executives in 390 local chapters served as counselors and consultants to 300,000 small businesses in approximately 800 locations throughout the United States (U.S. Small Business Administration, 1995). Members of SCORE include former CEOs of large corporations, former small-business owners, computer consultants, doctors, lawyers, government officials, and university professors.

Public and Private Volunteer Programs

In addition to volunteer programs funded by the federal government, many public and privately sponsored programs involve older adults in service to their communities. Although less is written about the participants and outcomes of these programs, they provide seniors the opportunity to give back to their professions and/or communities. Programs such as the Senior Attorney Project (Edelstein & May, 1993), the Banker Calling on Banker Program ("House Calls," 1989), and the Volunteer Patrol (Corder, 1991) are but a few examples of programs that rely on the assistance of senior volunteers in meeting the needs of their communities.

Intergenerational Programs

Many senior volunteer programs are intergenerational programs. These programs bring together two or more independent agencies or organizations that serve different client populations. Persons served by intergenerational programs come from diverse economic, ethnic, and cultural backgrounds. The children represent mainstream, special needs, or at-risk individuals from infancy through college age. The older adults are well or frail; they may be living independently or in a supportive environment such as retirement communities and long-term care facilities (Bedient, Snyder, & Simon, 1992; Courson & Heward, 1989; Farkas & Milligan, 1991; Henkin & Weinstein-Shr, 1989; Lowenthal & Egan, 1991). Most intergenerational programs focus on bringing the generations together to promote the development of relationships and to provide support and services. Although intergenerational programs are structured so that all age groups benefit from the interactions, in the vast majority of programs, one age group is the provider of services or support and another age group is the recipient of services (AARP, 1994b).

The establishment of the Foster Grandparent Program formally introduced intergenerational programming to the American public. Since its origination, the number of intergenerational programs continues to grow exponentially throughout the United States. In this section, we will highlight

---

Best Practice **Aetna Life and Casualty Senior Volunteer Program**

In the past 10 years, the business sector has emerged as a valuable source of volunteers. Through public-private partnerships, alliances have been created between business and the aging network to solve problems jointly in more efficient and effective ways. Aetna Life and Casualty, based in Hartford, Connecticut, is an excellent example of how a large corporation can connect with a community to serve the needs of older adults. Beginning in 1980, Aetna started using corporate attorneys, paralegals, and support staff to assist older adults in a wide range of cases. The program was initiated in response to publicity about the legal needs of older adults regarding public benefits, wills, probate, age discrimination, landlord-tenant rights, consumer credit, divorce, and victim assistance.

Aetna is recognized as one of the first to use corporate lawyers to provide pro bono service to individuals. This program serves a definite need for clients who do not meet the guidelines of other legal programs funded through federal and state governments. Aetna reports that lawyers who donate time for this program experience a high level of satisfaction because they are greatly appreciated by their clients.

For more information, contact Aetna Life and Casualty, One Tower Square, Hartford, CT 06183, 860-273-0123.

---

intergenerational programs and opportunities in the areas of education, recreational activities, and support programs.

Educational Programs

From preschool through college, students and older adults are working together to enhance their learning opportunities. In Chicago, for example, seniors work in preschool programs, helping young children prepare for reading (Lowenthal & Egan, 1991), whereas elementary students in Ohio provide one-on-one computer instruction to older adults (Drenning & Getz, 1992). Through the University of Pittsburgh intergenerational studies program, Intergenerations Together, older low-income adults and African American college students who are the first generation of their families to attend college participate as co-learners in a one-credit seminar that examines community services and housing options for older adults (Manheimer, Snodgrass, & Moskow-McKenzie, 1995). Southern Illinois University at Carbondale sponsors a mentoring program that pairs retired faculty members with first-term students who do not meet the criteria of high school rank and admission

For Your Files   **Illinois Intergenerational Initiative**

The Illinois Intergenerational Initiative is a coalition of individuals and organizations committed to enhancing education through intergenerational efforts, involving young and old in solving public problems and promoting vital communities through service and learning. The initiative is a Higher Education Cooperation Act partnership composed of statewide education and aging organizations such as the AARP, Illinois Retired Teachers Association, University of Illinois and Southern Illinois University systems, and the Illinois Association of School Boards. Accessing the initiative's Web site (http://www.siu.edu/offices/iii) allows individuals to download publications on starting intergenerational programs, aging across the curriculum, and ideas for intergenerational projects. Individuals can also access the quarterly intergenerational newsletter, *Continuance,* online. For more information, contact III, Mailcode 4341, Anthony Hall, Room 110, Carbondale, IL 62901, 618-453-5351.

test scores but have instead been admitted to the university on the basis of their academic potential (Bedient et al., 1992). The mentors help the students identify their academic deficiencies and guide them through appropriate exercises to enhance their skills. The situation is reversed in Philadelphia, where area college students tutor older Hispanic and Asian immigrants in English (Henkin & Weinstein-Shr, 1989).

Recreational Activities

Parks and recreation centers, senior centers, and fitness clubs are but a few organizations offering joint recreational activities and programs for younger and older adults. For example, as a result of society's focus on exercise, intergenerational fitness programs link college students with older adults (Angelis, 1992; Colston, Harper, & Mitchener-Colston, 1995). These programs allow older adults to participate in leisure and fitness programs while providing the opportunity for students to learn about the aging process. Gardening is another recreational activity easily shared between older adults of all functional levels (e.g., nursing home residents, homebound elders with physical disabilities, and healthy elders) and children or young individuals (McKee, 1995).

Support Programs

Probably the most popular model of intergenerational support programs is having older adults providing formal care for young children (Newman & Riess, 1992; Smith & Newman, 1992, 1993). The Friendly Listener Intergenerational Program (FLIP) pairs third, fourth, and fifth graders with older active and homebound volunteers who call the children home alone after school at preappointed times to check in and to talk (National Eldercare Institute on Health Promotion, 1995). Seniors, however, are not the only ones providing care and support. Teens in the Adopt an Elder Program (Waggoner, 1995) serve as junior interns in facilities that serve older adults (e.g., senior independent living, adult day services, skilled nursing homes, and Alzheimer's centers). Participants provide companionship and some minimal physical support to their assigned elder. A unique program in Honolulu trains volunteers to provide spiritual, emotional, and physical support to older adults who are frail and homebound (Takamura, 1991). Project Dana (which means "selfless giving" in the Buddhist religion) volunteers are of all ages; they are drawn primarily from within the Buddhist community and from the Moiliili Hongwanji Mission. Volunteers in the Respite Care Corps are 18 years of age or older (Pearson & Deitrick, 1989). They provide relief time for caregivers; promote social interactions for the older care receivers; and provide support, information, and contact for caregivers and the community.

Challenges for Senior Volunteer Programs

Many successful volunteer programs provide thousands of hours of volunteer services; without these volunteers, many nonprofit community organizations would not be able to maintain their current level of services. Because senior volunteers are critical to the delivery of services, programs need effective strategies to recruit and retain volunteers. Volunteer coordinators face many challenges as they attempt to staff and carry out their programs (Caro & Bass, 1995; Fischer & Schaffer, 1993).

Tapping Untapped Potential

Many older people currently do not participate in any formal volunteer program. Barriers to volunteering include employment and family obligations, health, lack of knowledge of volunteer programs, perceived lack of skills, lack of transportation, and a belief that programs should pay people for their work. Agencies must implement aggressive and systematic recruitment efforts to recruit older individuals. Programs must also make a greater effort to recruit older adults from diverse ethnic and cultural backgrounds.

In addition, the current corps of senior volunteers is aging. Greater efforts need to focus on the recruitment of young-old individuals to supplement and, at some point, replace older volunteers. Programs must develop new positions and opportunities for those elders who may be growing older but who still wish to give their time to support community programs and initiatives.

Retaining Volunteers

The first 3 to 6 months are crucial in the life cycle of a volunteer. During this time, agencies are most likely to lose senior volunteers. To enhance retention of volunteers, agencies must be selective in their recruitment efforts. Once volunteers are recruited, retention is higher when programs match their interests and skills with appropriate assignments. Volunteer positions should offer intrinsic rewards, and the volunteers should perceive their experiences as successful.

Long-term volunteers who experience feelings of burnout also may leave their volunteer positions. These feelings result from grief (especially for individuals working with persons who are seriously ill or who are dying), frustration, intrusion on their private lives, and the time demands of their assignments. Volunteer leaders need to protect their volunteers by setting limits on both the type and amount of service asked of them.

Funding Volunteer Programs

Some federally sponsored programs have experienced cutbacks in funding in the last several years. Volunteers are not free. They require investments in training and supervision. The amount of time that paid staff invests in each volunteer varies, with some estimates ranging from a low of 1 hour paid for every 1.4 hours for each volunteer to 33.5 hours for each volunteer (Baker & Murowski, 1986). Thus, the effective use of volunteers is a necessity for operating a cost-effective volunteer program. A lack of adequate resources also limits the scope and effectiveness of many volunteer programs for older adults. Financial and technical support that enhances the recruitment and retention of volunteers would greatly expand the scope of services offered by many programs.

Evaluating Volunteer Programs

Most volunteer programs put only minimal efforts into evaluating their programs (Fischer & Schaffer, 1993). Regular, systemwide evaluations are necessary to identify both the strengths and weaknesses of existing programs and the effectiveness of the services that the volunteers provide. Often, when evaluations are conducted, they are published as final reports submitted to the administration of the national program or to the individual projects. Evaluation information needs to be made more available and accessible to increase public knowledge about volunteer and intergenerational programs, garner community support for intergenerational programs, and secure funding for expansion and/or maintenance of these programs (Bocian & Newman, 1989).

Supporting the Future of Senior Volunteer Programs

The 1995 White House Conference on Aging gave specific support for volunteer programs by passing a resolution that supported policies that expand and enhance opportunities for older volunteers. Specific resolutions included (a) facilitating collaboration at the national, state, and local levels of organizations involving senior volunteers and encouraging intergenerational involvement; (b) encouraging the federal government to provide education on the value of volunteering for people's well-being and self-esteem; and (c) creating incentives for older volunteers including full-time, part-time, and episodic service opportunities, stipends, and the flexibility these provide. In addition, delegates resolved to support policies to promote intergenerational programs. Clearly, when policies support the use of older volunteers and intergenerational programs, everyone benefits.

CASE STUDY

RECONNECTING WITH THE COMMUNITY

Maggie is a 79-year-old woman whose husband, Warren, died of cancer 3 years ago. Maggie and Warren were a close couple. They had many interests in common and were known in their neighborhood for their activities with the local Audubon chapter. A county wetland area was preserved largely because of their efforts. Warren was the advocate, and Helen quietly helped with the organizing and details. This was the way they approached everything in which they were involved. When Warren died, Maggie was completely devastated. It was as if she had lost her right arm. Warren had been the outgoing person in their relationship, and she felt lost.

Maggie is a bright woman and would have gone to college if finances had permitted. Her daughters, Kathy and Michelle, did further their education and currently teach in nearby communities. For the last year, the daughters have watched their mother become ever more detached and isolated from the community. She stopped attending the Audubon chapter meetings, which she had always enjoyed. She dropped out of her bridge club and even stopped going to church. Maggie was literally pining away. Nothing seemed to get through to Maggie, no matter how many conversations her daughters had with her about the importance of getting on with her life. It seemed that the normal grieving process had continued for too long and was having a dramatic impact on their mother. Kathy and Michelle regarded their mother as a healthy, vital woman whose quality of life was deteriorating needlessly.

CASE STUDY QUESTIONS

1. Maggie's daughters are urging her "to get on with her life." On the basis of your reading of the chapter, what benefit would volunteering bring to Maggie's situation?

2. What personal characteristics of Maggie's would be important to consider when proposing volunteer opportunities to her? Why?

3. Think about the volunteer programs discussed in this chapter and any others of which you are aware. What volunteer situations might appeal most to Maggie?

4. Ultimately, it will be Maggie's decision whether she will become reinvolved in her community as a volunteer. What role could her daughters play in helping to direct their mother toward an interest in a volunteer program or activity?

5. Drawing on your own personal experiences and observations, discuss with the class examples of older adults as volunteers who impressed you. Why?

6. The chapter pointed out that recruiting and retaining older volunteers is a great challenge. What suggestions do you have that could increase recruitment and retention of older volunteers?

LEARNING ACTIVITIES

1. Interview the director of a senior volunteer program. Find out who volunteers, in what type of programs, and in what type of activities.

2. Meet with one or a group of older adult volunteers. Find out what they do, why they do it, and how volunteering has affected their lives. What are the benefits of volunteering? What did you learn about their programs, experiences, and the impact of senior volunteers? After this experience, do you see yourself volunteering when you are older? What types of volunteer activities interest you?

3. Interview staff members at a program that has older adult volunteers. What type of benefits do they realize in having the volunteers? What types of activities or duties are assigned to volunteers? What would be the effect on their program if they did not have the volunteers?

4. Attend an in-service training that is designed for older volunteers and/or those working with them. What was the emphasis of the training?

5. Observe or volunteer for an intergenerational program. Was one age group the focus of service more than the other? What types of activities or services were there? Did the participants seem to enjoy themselves? Were there problems or issues that arose? What was your overall impression?

 ## FOR MORE INFORMATION

National Resources

1. Corporation for National and Community Service, 1201 New York Avenue NW, 9th Floor, Washington, DC 20575, 800-424-8867.

   The corporation oversees AmeriCorps, the National Senior Service Corps, Foster Grandparent Program, Retired Senior and Volunteer Program, and Senior Companion Program. Information about each of the programs is available on request.

2. National Caucus and Center on Black Aged, 1424 K Street NW, Suite 500, Washington, DC 20005, 202-637-8400.

   The National Caucus and Center on Black Aged is a nonprofit organization that works to improve the quality of life for older black Americans. One of its programs includes the Living Legacy Program, which promotes intergenerational dialogue between older and younger blacks.

3. Volunteers of America, 3939 North Causeway Blvd., Suite 400, Metairie, LA 70002, 504-837-2652.

   Volunteers of America is a national nonprofit organization that offers programs and services to meet the needs of local communities. The organization offers services that assist the young and old, persons with disabilities, and persons with alcoholism. It sponsors foster grandparent and senior volunteer programs and publishes a quarterly newsletter, *Volunteers Gazette*.

Web Resources

1. Illinois Intergenerational Initiative
   http://www.siu.edu/offices/iii

   The home page of the Illinois Intergenerational Initiative offers information on how to begin intergenerational programs or service learning experiences, intergenerational conferences and workshops, intergenerational ideas and resources (that can be downloaded), and fund-raising strategies for intergenerational programming. Visitors can also access its newsletter, *Continuance*.

2. Generations Together: An Intergenerational Studies Program
   http://www3.pitt.edu/gti

   Generations Together: An Intergenerational Studies Program is an intergenerational program in the University of Pittsburgh's Center for Social and Urban Research. The home page offers information about the development and evaluation of intergenerational programs, as well as information about the development of intergenerational studies as an academic discipline.

3. Center for Intergenerational Learning
   http://www.temple.edu/departments/CIL/

   The home page of Temple University's Center for Intergenerational Learning offers information about cross-age programs, training and technical assistance, and other resources for intergenerational programming. The site also has links to other resources for intergenerational programmers.

4. Retirement and Intergenerational Studies Laboratory's Intergenerational Entrepreneurship Demonstration Project
   http://www.strom.clemson.edu/risl/aarp.html

   This home page explains the Intergenerational Entrepreneurship Demonstration Project, a pilot program that uses new retirees as volunteer mentors to at-risk youth. The retirees help the young people operate their own country market in a renovated dairy barn. Web site visitors can access the newsletter and barn catalog online.

Visit the *Community Resources for Older Adults* Web site for updates on the volunteer programs described in this chapter:
http://www.hhs.unco.edu/geron.htm

NOTE

1. Unless otherwise noted, the information in this section comes from a discussion of the origins of senior service by Freedman (1994).

6

Education Programs

Jim and Donna Wagner retired to a small rural community of 3,000. They chose the community for its geographical location, climate, and proximity to relatives. Although they enjoy small-town living, they miss the many educational and cultural opportunities that larger communities offered. Six months after they settled into their new home, Donna decided to visit the tiny senior center on Main Street. After lunch, she remained with a group of seniors for a class on famous women of the World War II era. The other seniors told Donna that the local community college brought many classes to their center through the years. They liked that the classes were noncredit and affordable. They also mentioned that the county extension agent frequently came to town and offered classes on health, self-care, and financial management for retirees.

Educators recognize now more than ever before that learning does not stop when adults enter the later stages of life. Although the process of learning changes during the life course (e.g., older adults take longer to assimilate information and are less likely to use memory schemes), study after study confirms that humans maintain the capacity for learning throughout their lives (Schaie, 1994). Like Donna and her new friends at the senior center, many seniors find participating in educational programs to be an enriching experience. Most older adults, however, prefer attending classes outside traditional academia. They want the opportunity to actively participate in classes that are of interest to them and relevant to their lives now and in the future.

The idea of lifelong education first appeared in the research literature in the 1930s. By definition, lifelong education implies a cradle-to-grave approach to learning and recognizes that people can be learners at 18 or 80 (Manheimer, Snodgrass, & Moskow-McKenzie, 1995). It differs from the

Exhibit 6.1   **Educational Attainment of Older Adults by Sex in 1990 (Percentage)**

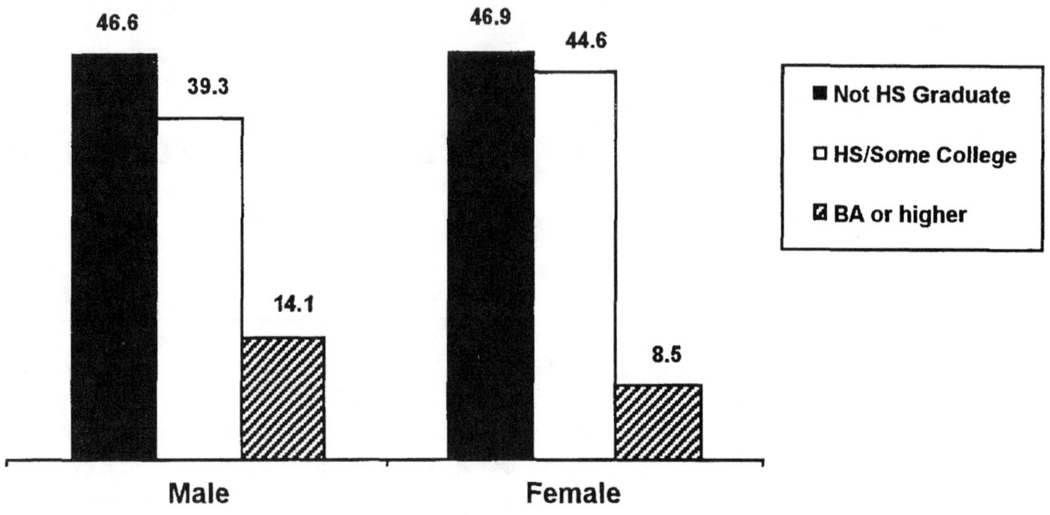

■	Not HS Graduate
☐	HS/Some College
▨	BA or higher

Male   **Female**

SOURCE: U.S. Bureau of the Census (1994b), Table 1.

traditional lockstep model of education that assumes that one's life's path unfolds in a straight line. A lifelong education model provides a more fluid perspective that considers individuals as learners and, often simultaneously, as teachers who have a broad range of needs throughout their life course (Feldman, 1991).

Educational Level of Older Adults

Contributing to the lifelong learning phenomenon is the substantial increase in the overall level of formal education achieved by Americans. Exhibits 6.1 and 6.2 show the educational attainment of older men and women in 1990 and 2030, respectively. In 1990, almost half of all older men and women did not have a high school education; 14% of older men and 8% of older women reported having a bachelor's degree or higher. The educational status of future cohorts of older adults will be dramatically different. There will be more older adults who have college degrees than those who have less than a high school education. By the year 2030, more than half of older men and women will have at least a high school education (57% and 62%, respectively), and approximately 25% of older men and women will have attained a bachelor's degree (U.S. Bureau of Census, 1994b).

Exhibit 6.2 **Educational Attainment of Older Adults by Sex in 2030 (Percentage)**

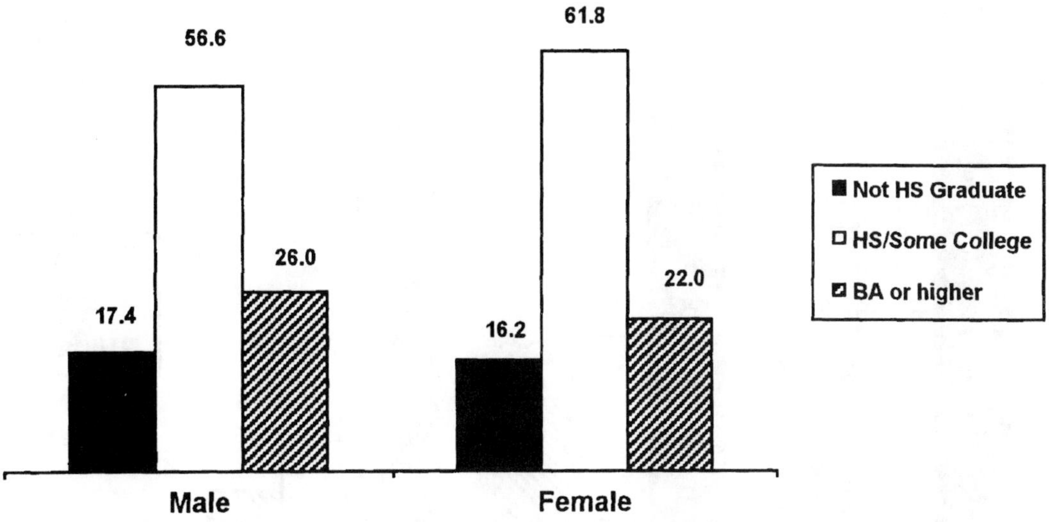

SOURCE: U.S. Bureau of the Census (1994b,) Table 1.

Education levels also differ between subgroups of older adults. For example, at every age group, older whites are more likely to be high school graduates than are older blacks or Hispanics (see Exhibit 6.3). According to census data, the portion of black and Hispanic older adults who have a high school education increases in younger age cohorts. The percentage of Hispanic elders with a high school degree increases from 17% for those over age 75 to 33% for those aged 65 to 69 years. A similar increase is found for older blacks.

In addition, the differences in the percentage of white and black older adults with a high school education will grow smaller. Presently, 87% of whites and 83% of blacks aged 25 to 29 have graduated from high school; only 61% of Hispanics aged 25 to 29 have graduated from high school. These future improvements in levels of educational attainment, however, will not be as great for black and Hispanics with a bachelor's degree. For example, presently 13% of whites, 6% of blacks, and 6% of Hispanics over age 65 have a bachelor's degree. For persons aged 25 to 29, 24% of whites, 13% of blacks, and 8% of Hispanics have a bachelor's degree (U.S. Bureau of the Census, 1996a).

These differences in educational levels will no doubt influence the types of educational programs offered to older adults. Not only will basic education programs be needed, but in addition, there will be a renewed interest in the concept of lifelong education.

Exhibit 6.3   **Percentage of High School Graduates by Age and Race: 1993**

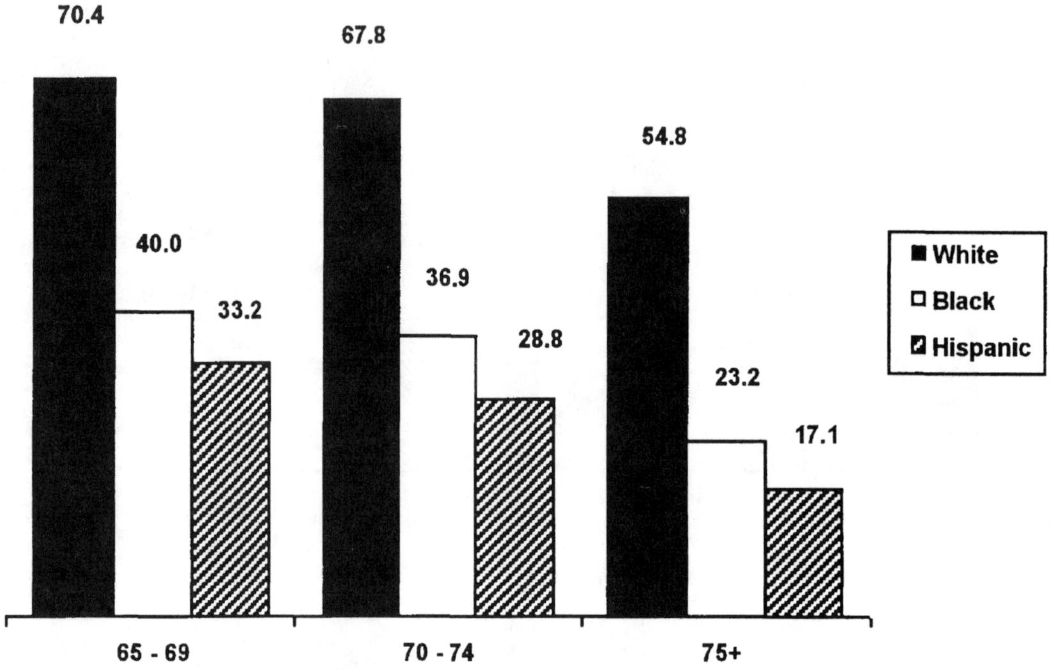

SOURCE: U.S. Bureau of the Census (1994a), Tables 1 and 2.

Lifelong Education

Moody (1976, 1988) contends that society's focus on lifelong education has emerged through five chronological stages indicative of changes in attitudes toward later life. In the late 19th and early 20th centuries, education for older adults was in the *rejection stage,* in which the prevailing belief was that older adults neither needed nor deserved more learning opportunities. Society viewed education as preparation of children and youth for the future, an investment not justifiable for older adults. From the late 1950s through the mid-1970s, beliefs about education moved through the *social services stage.* During this time, society viewed education for older adults as worthwhile if it had a special therapeutic value. Education programs focused primarily on the problem areas of growing older and the responsibility of social institutions to meet elders' needs through service programs (Peterson, 1985). By the mid-1970s, a shift began from the segregationist "social problem" perspective to an assumption that older adults should remain active and involved in their communities and in society. In this *normalization stage,* educators and practitioners minimized the differences between older and younger adults. Older adults seeking educational opportunities were placed into existing educational pathways. A decade later, the *self-actualization stage* emerged, in which learning in later life held special transformative possibilities for personal growth. Practitioners emphasized psychological and spiritual concerns as part of the educational milieu for older adults. Most recent is the *emancipation stage,* in which personal growth is inextricably bound up with the social relationship of community issues. The focus is on the empowerment of older adults to actively participate in all realms of life.

In this chapter, we explore the opportunities for lifelong learning for individuals living throughout the United States. We begin by examining the federal government's support for education programs for older adults. Next, we present a description of the types of educational programs available for seniors and a profile of older adults who attend these programs. In the final section of this chapter, we discuss the challenges facing education programs currently and in the future.

Policy Background

Historically, support specifically for the education of older adults represents only a small fraction of the total federal expenditures for education. Provisions made under Title I of the Higher Education Act of 1965 provided colleges and universities the opportunity to direct some of their resources and staff to program development for older people. Most of the support for educational programs for older adults during the late 1960s through the mid-1970s, however, came from demonstration projects funded by federal agencies such as the National Endowment for the Arts and the National Endowment for the Humanities (Manheimer, 1992). Despite enthusiastic claims of success, these projects usually terminated at the end of their grants. Without outside money, most institutions closed older adult education programs because attending to the education needs of older adults was not high on the priority list of traditional colleges and universities.

Following the gradual recovery from the post-Vietnam War recession, an increasing number of nontraditional-aged adults began to go back to school. Continuing education and lifelong learning became popular concepts. In 1976, Congress passed the Lifelong Learning Act. Hailed as "a landmark of social legislation" (Weinstock, 1978), its goal was to have lifelong learning opportunities for all citizens "without regard to restrictions of previous education or training, sex, age, handicapping condition, social or ethnic background, or economic circumstances" (p. 16). The act was the first legislation to specially mention older adults and retired persons as potential recipients of educational resources. Unfortunately, Congress did not provide funding for the act.

Although state and local governments have the responsibility for developing public and continuing education, the federal government has been instrumental in setting national priorities for education opportunities for persons of all ages. For example, one goal of *National Education Goals 2000* (U.S. Department of Education, 1990) is achieving adult literacy and lifelong learning. Within the Department of Education, the Office of Vocational and Adult Education is responsible for the administration of educational programs for older adults. The office is authorized under the Adult Education Act of 1988 to establish adult education programs to help persons aged 16 years and older acquire basic literacy skills needed to function in society. Participation in literacy programs by older adults, however, is low. Although approximately 35% of older adults are believed to be illiterate, only about 5% of participants in adult literacy programs—called adult basic education programs—are over 60 years of age (U.S. Senate Special Committee on Aging, 1991c). In addition to adult literacy programs, a variety of federal programs have supported informal educational activities of interest to older adults, including consumer education, older reader services, community schools, continuing education, and health education.

The Administration on Aging, under provisions of the Older Americans Act, also plays an important role in encouraging older adults to seek educational opportunities and in developing educational programs for older adults. The 1987 amendments to the OAA instructed local AAAs to identify the postsecondary schools in their area that offered tuition-free education to older adults and to distribute the findings to senior centers and other locations (U.S. Senate Special Committee on Aging, 1991c). Local and state AAAs also are involved in a number of grassroots education programs aimed at providing older adults with the knowledge they need to enable them to lead more productive lives by broadening their occupational, cultural, and social awareness. For example, AAAs sponsor educational programs in health and nutrition, injury prevention, preretirement and legal concerns, employment, and consumer education.

Users and Programs

There is great diversity among "learners" within the older adult population. Like any age group, older adults are heterogeneous and multidimensional in learning needs and abilities. They come from all educational levels and have interests in a variety of subjects from the liberal arts to programs more fo-

---

For Your Files **The Leadership Enhancement Program**

Many older adults wish to remain vitally involved in their communities. One such education program in Colorado trains older adults to fill leadership roles within their communities. The Leadership Enhancement Training Program, developed by Linda Piper, director of the Weld County Area Agency on Aging, is a 6-week program that examined different aspects of leadership. Topics discussed during the course included the different views of leadership, skills for problem analyses, effective communication, teamwork and leadership, public policy and community concerns, and opportunities for involvement. Class sessions included hands-on projects and guest speakers from the community.

For more information, contact the Weld County Area Agency on Aging at 970-353-3816.

---

cused on issues of aging (e.g., health care and finances). Variation also exists in the educational programs designed to meet the needs of the aging population. In this section, we examine three primary settings for formal education programs for older adults: (a) institutions of higher education, (b) community-based organizations, and (c) at-home programs. For each setting, we describe the types of programs available and the older adults who participate in them.

Institutions of Higher Education

In 1987, 94,875 Americans 65 years of age and older were enrolled in undergraduate credit programs at institutions of higher education throughout the United States (National Center for Educational Statistics, 1991). Women constituted almost 65% of the "older" undergraduate population. The institutions classified 93% of the older students as part-time students. In addition, 7,494 older adults were enrolled in graduate programs. Men made up 59% of this population of graduate students. Of older students, 66% were pursuing their graduate degrees on a part-time basis.

Thirty-eight states have established guidelines within their statutes for tuition waiver programs for older adults (U.S. Senate Special Committee on Aging, 1991c). State requirements vary with respect to minimum age, number of credits for which a person may enroll, the type of course (i.e., credit or noncredit), and the availability of space. In some states, policies for tuition waiver programs also vary by institution. Few older adults, however, take advantage of the tuition waiver policy. Many older adults are unaware of the program, whereas others find the campus environment intimidating and are not really interested in the type of learning offered by conventional higher education departments (Moody, 1988). Finally, some colleges encourage older adults to return to school by offering credit for life or work experience. For example, the Assessment of Prior Experiential Learning program at American University in Washington, D.C., allows older students to translate their work or life experience into as many as 30 credit hours toward a bachelor's degree (U.S. Senate Special Committee on Aging, 1991c).

Community Colleges

Community colleges are major providers of educational programs for older adults. In 1970, community colleges became the focus of the expanding instructional network on aging. The AoA awarded a grant to the American Association of Community and Junior Colleges to encourage the organization "to develop an awareness of the needs of older Americans and to explore ways in which these community-oriented institutions might contribute to an improvement in the quality of life in the nation's elderly population" (Korim, 1974, p. 5). Because of this project, many new programs for older people were developed by community and junior colleges in the mid-1970s. Today, nearly 25% of all community colleges offer programs designed specifically for older learners (Feldman, 1991).

A nationwide study of 388 community college administrators examined the programs and services provided for older adults within their institutions (Ventura-Merkel, 1991). A single office coordinated more than two thirds of the programs for older adults; typically, it was the office of continuing education and community services. Programs most often provided for older adults fell into three categories: financial management skills, health and cultural enrichment, and contemporary civic issues. Most of these courses were noncredit, were taught in person and on campus, were in group settings, and consisted of multiple sessions. The delivery formats judged to be the most effective were multiple-session courses and seminars and single-session workshops and presentations. The least effective modes of delivery were telecourses and credit courses.

Learning in Retirement Programs

Learning in Retirement (LIR) programs have emerged on more than 200 campuses of U.S. universities and colleges to meet the needs of older retirement-age adults. Under the generic heading of LIR programs, some 40 million older individuals have participated in the creative, self-directed learning environment (Miller, 1992).

There are two general types of LIR programs: institution-driven and member-driven (Young, 1992). Designed, controlled, and run by the college or university, *institution-driven* programs are usually overseen by continuing education divisions. A paid college staff coordinator typically manages the program, drawing on other institutional personnel as needed. College faculty members ordinarily teach the courses. Colleges and universities also sponsor *member-driven* programs, in which members develop the curriculum and teach courses themselves. The courses are almost always noncredit. These programs depend on the quality and commitment of their volunteer leaders. This arrangement offers participants an opportunity to become involved in a beneficial activity, makes it much easier to develop a social network, and can build strong commitment to both the program and the institution. It also helps ensure that the program responds to the members' wants and needs because they design it themselves. In addition, because volunteers do much of the work of the organization, the program can be cost-effective.

Overall, LIR programs offer members intellectual stimulation, structure, friendship, purpose, and challenge (Craven, 1992). Each of the existing LIR programs is unique, with the most successful programs sharing several common characteristics. These programs (a) are designed to serve the learning needs and interests of older adults located within commuting distance of the program; (b) offer a broad-ranging educational program, a substantial part of which consists of college-level learning experiences; (c) are sponsored by an accredited college or university; (d) are nonprofit, charge a modest tuition or membership fee, and have a need-based scholarship program; (e) publicly commit themselves to affirmative action goals; (f) use volunteer teachers or course leaders who are members of LIR; (g) offer social, cultural, and physical experiences that complement the curriculum and are appropriate for the program participants; and (h) provide for participant involvement in planning, evaluating, teaching, and, where appropriate, administering the program (Young, 1992).

Elderhostel

Conceived as a means of getting older adults directly involved with stimulating activities and with each other, Elderhostel combines the excitement and challenge of travel with the enrichment of academic courses on substantive subjects.[1] The founders offered the first program during the summer of 1975. Throughout that summer, 220 older individuals came to one of five New Hampshire colleges to participate. By 1980, all 50 states and several foreign countries offered Elderhostel programs. Today, programs take place in every American state, Canada, and 45 other countries with more than 300,000 participants per year.

Elderhostel is a nonprofit educational organization with 135 full-time employees in the national office in Boston. Almost every state has an Elderhostel office. Each office is responsible for the recruitment of new Elderhostel institutions, the training of personnel to administer programs at the campus level, the general support of existing programs, and maintenance of program quality in the state. A network of 1,900 participating institutions, mostly colleges and universities, plans and runs the programs. Coordinators at each site design and operate individual Elderhostel programs. They must decide what courses to offer, select the instructors, develop the weekly schedule, and determine where to house and serve meals to the hostelers. Most institutes of higher education offer their programs during the off-seasons and vacations, thereby taking advantage of the low-cost room, board, and classroom use.

The standard Elderhostel program brings together a group of 15 to 45 persons over the age of 55 to a college campus, conference center, or retreat. During their 5- or 6-night stay, they take noncredit courses accompanied by field trips and extracurricular events. The courses do not carry college credit, and there are no tests. The intent is that students delve into the subject matter for the sheer joy of learning. The typical charge for a 6-night program in 1996 was $340, which includes registration fees, accommodations, meals, 5 days of classes, and a variety of extracurricular activities.

Although most program sites offer varied programs from year to year, they typically include at least one course about the cultural or historical significance of their geographic location. In recent years, "full immersion" programs have developed in which students spend their whole time studying one topic. For example, Elderhostelers enrolled at Yavapai College in Prescott, Arizona, spend a week living on the Hopi reservation where the instructors are all Hopi (Pierce, 1993).

For individuals wishing to expand their educational horizons, Elderhostel offers international programs in more than 45 countries. Course-related field trips and excursions providing a variety of opportunities for learning about and experiencing the culture and traditions of the country and its people complement the classroom studies. International programs usually are 2 or 3 weeks long with hostelers spending a week at each site. Depending on the location, the all-inclusive cost of a 3-week program at three universities ranges from $2,600 to $5,640 (plus travel expenses to the U.S. city from which the trip departs).

Older adults attend Elderhostel because they want to expand their knowledge. They are a self-selecting group of highly motivated individuals. Most hostelers are single women. In general, they are a privileged group. Primarily Americans and Canadians, almost two thirds of the participants report an annual income of $30,000 or more and substantial prior education. More than 80% of Elderhostelers have attended college. Fewer than 1% of participants are members of minority groups.

For Your Files   **Women Work!**

Women Work! educates displaced homemakers—women who have lost their principal means of self-support through events such as widowhood or divorce—to assist them in achieving economic self-sufficiency. Local programs based in community organizations (e.g., community colleges and employment centers) offer vocational testing, employment training, tuition assistance, and job referral services. The program also produces *Network News*, a quarterly newsletter for displaced homemaker advocates; *Women Work!* a biannual newsletter for displaced homemakers; and *Women Work! Program Directory*, a listing of job training and education programs nationwide. For more information, contact Women Work! at the National Network for Women's Employment, 1625 K Street, Suite 300, Washington, DC 20006, 202-467-6346.

Community-Based Organizations

Many community-based agencies and organizations also provide educational programs for older adults. Several favorable characteristics account for the popularity of community-based education programs with older students, including their location, the schedule of program offerings, and the format of the offerings (Courtenay, 1990). Because the primary mission of the sponsoring organization is to be responsive to all the residents, these educational programs generally are dispersed throughout the community. Senior centers, hospitals, community centers, churches, and libraries often provide educational programs and/or the physical space for such programs. Almost without exception, older adults prefer educational programs offered from late morning to midafternoon during the week. The availability of alternative scheduling makes the community-based organization especially accommodating of the needs of the older learner. They also have an advantage over colleges and universities in that they are not under educational accreditation/standards requirements, do not need extensive registration procedures, and have nearby parking or free transportation. Although they typically do not have the resources to offer every type of educational experience, community-based organizations do have the flexibility to provide a wide range of subject matter.

Libraries have established a variety of on-site education programs specifically for older adults (Manheimer et al., 1995). Participants take part in learning activities such as minicourses, book and film discussions, forums on consumer and health issues, and life enrichment programs. For example, the Queens Borough Public Library offers programs on topics related to disabilities and aging, including information about community resources for older adults and health and wellness programs.

The Older Adult Service and Information System (OASIS; 1991) is a consortium between business and not-for-profit organizations that provides educational, cultural, health, and volunteer outreach programs for adults age 55 and older. Sponsored by the May Department Stores Company, OASIS centers provide participants an opportunity to remain independent and active in community affairs. The program, administered nationally from St. Louis, has centers operating in 22 cities with more than 129,000 members (Manheimer et al., 1995). Membership is free, and older adults from all socioeconomic, cultural, and educational backgrounds participate in the programs. Courses in areas such as visual arts, music, drama, creative writing, contemporary issues, history, science, exercise, and health occur usually once a week for 1 to 12 weeks.

The Shepherd's Center, a nonprofit community organization sponsored by a coalition of religious congregations, provides services and programs to more than 175,000 older adults in 25 states (Manheimer et al., 1995). One program, Adventures in Learning, provides an environment in which older adults share their knowledge, talents, skills, and interests with peers. They are the teachers, students, planners, and participants of the program. The centers charge a small registration fee (maximum of $15 for a full quarter of classes). All classes are once a week for an hour and cover a wide range of topics including current events, history, literature, religion, painting, yoga, health, and travel (Maves & Bock, 1990).

The Cooperative Extension System also provides community-based education programs for older adults. This nationwide educational network established through legislation is a partnership of the U.S. Department of Agriculture, the 74 state land grant universities, and 3,150 county administrative units throughout the United States and its territories. Guided by the cooperative extension mission, extension educators "help people improve their lives through an educational process that uses scientific knowledge focused on issues and needs" (Rasmussen, 1989, p. 4). The extension system offers older adults, particularly those living in rural areas, a vast array of educational workshops, seminars, radio and television broadcasts, and written materials on topics such as family caregiving, physical health, nutrition, mental health, and resource management. For example, the extension service at the University of Missouri provides a publication accessible through the Internet called *Retirement: A Place to Live, Choices and Options,* which describes housing options and alternatives as well as a checklist to help older adults and their families compare living alternatives (Eubank & Snodgrass, 1993). The University of Illinois Cooperative Extension Service provides an aging awareness project for 4-H youth. The *Walk in My Shoes* program teaches youth how to communicate more effectively with older adults and to learn what it is like to face the world as an aging person. More than 500

Best Practice **The Close Up Foundation**

The Close Up Foundation, in cooperation with the AARP, is a nonprofit, nonpartisan civic education organization dedicated to helping citizens better understand the important role they play in U.S. democracy. One of the program's activities is the Close Up Program for Older Americans. This program provides a unique learning experience for people over 50. It provides groups of older adults opportunities to witness legislative proceedings on the House floor, meet with Washington leaders and decision makers, and attend Capitol Hill committee hearings.

Usually 20 participants from across the nation participate as a group in the program. Experienced instructors lead the groups, and sessions are informal to promote the exchange of ideas. During this Washington learning adventure, older adults explore critical issues with policy analysts, media representatives, members of the administration, and other Washington experts. They examine topics covering the presidency, domestic issues, international relations, and the media. Included in the program are tours of historical sites and opportunities for cultural activities, such as an evening at the theater. A sample offering for a week could include a study visit to Mount Vernon, home of George Washington; a seminar on the media; a foreign policy seminar; a diplomatic visit to a foreign embassy; attendance at a legislative committee hearing; and a twilight tour of the Washington monuments.

The Close Up Foundation programs are for citizens from all areas of the nation and from all walks of life. The program cost provides for a generous package of services including accommodations and meals. Program funding is derived primarily from registration fees paid by participants; community, corporate, and philanthropic contributions; and an appropriation from Congress.

For more information, contact Program for Older Americans, Close Up Foundation, 44 Canal Center Plaza, Alexandria, VA 22314, 800-363-4762.

youths and adults in the Chicago area have received the training. The program is also available on the World Wide Web at

```
http://www.aces.uiuc.edu/uplink/Programs/wims.html
```

Although people may think of community-based education as occurring primarily in a classroom setting, outdoor programs also present older adults with learning opportunities. For example, adventure programs provide older adults with physical and psychological challenges within a framework of safety and skills development while increasing personal, social, and environmental awareness. During these programs, older adults learn the importance of good physical and mental health and develop new skills such as camping, canoeing, and working in a group situation. As a result of the successful completion of challenging activities, participants show increases in self-confidence and self-esteem, self-discovery, leadership development, creativity, and decision making (Sugerman, 1989).

At-Home Educational Experiences

With the advance of technology, both well and frail older adults can take part in new educational ventures from the convenience of their own homes. These programs reduce structural barriers (e.g., inconvenient timing and hard-to-reach locations) that often discourage older adults from attending university or community-based courses and programs.

For many years, special programs from public and state libraries have provided educational services to older adults via bookmobiles, cable television, and books by mail (Manheimer et al., 1995). In addition, librarians and volunteers provide reading programs and materials to persons who are homebound and residents of nursing homes and other institutional settings.

SeniorNet, a nonprofit membership organization that began in 1986, offers computer training and networking capabilities to older adults. Community organizations (e.g., banks, senior health organizations, financial service companies, and private foundations) sponsor local SeniorNets by furnishing computer equipment and contributing to the cost of establishing and maintaining the sites. Senior volunteers who have computer skills and are willing to share them by training new members to use computers operate the sites (SeniorNet, 1997). In 1997, more than 100 learning centers were located throughout the United States and Canada, housed in a variety of settings including senior centers, community centers, public libraries, schools and colleges, and clinics and hospitals. A typical center contains 5 to 10 computers. In addition, a nationwide on-line "electronic community" fosters long-distance information sharing among the program's 22,000 members. It provides members, particularly those not living near a site, with the opportunity to interact with one another, participate in network forums, and seek and give information through databases and special interest groups. Members also receive newsletters and can purchase the organization's publications written specifically for the older computer user.

Some older adults find self-directed learning opportunities such as correspondence study and telecourses appealing. These courses, offered through the continuing education division of many colleges and universities, were

---

For Your Files   **Computer Learning Through SeniorNet**

SeniorNet provides adults 55 and older with information and instruction on computer technologies so they can use their new skills for their own benefit and to benefit society. More than 80,000 older adults have been introduced to computers at SeniorNet learning centers.

All centers share common goals and objectives, but each has its own activities. Here are some examples:

- The center in Bakersfield, California, has joined with the Senior Aid Program at the Mexican-American Opportunity Foundation to prepare Spanish speakers to go back into the workforce.

- In Honolulu, a group of members produced a 10-minute video about Hawaii, the college (Honolulu Community College), and SeniorNet, using both video and computer technology.

- The Chicago Department of Aging established a learning center on the south side to serve its predominantly African American population. It is open 7 days a week and has about 20 seniors stopping by daily.

- The instructors of the Peoria, Illinois, center help set up computers in nursing homes and retirement homes and go online with the residents.

SeniorNet also has a publication titled *Young@Heart* that describes the SeniorNet program and introduces readers to computer technology. Visit the SeniorNet Web site (http://www.seniornet.org).

---

among the early innovations in long-distance learning. Although not marketed specifically for older adults, the independent structure of these programs may be attractive to some older adults (Brubaker & Roberto, 1993). In particular, older individuals who are self-disciplined and internally motivated to learn, live in rural or more remote areas, and/or have limited mobility or transportation can participate in courses of personal interest without leaving their homes.

Developed in Canada, the Homebound Learning Opportunities program provides health promotion and education outreach services for homebound adults over the age of 50 and their caregivers on a permanent, temporary, or seasonal basis (Penning & Wasyliw, 1992). The program offers participants more than 125 topics from which to choose for an individualized one-on-one or small-group learning experience delivered in their homes. The program also provides a lending library and an educational television show to complement the in-home offerings. Courses meet weekly for an average of 6 weeks. Sometimes, the program offers courses by telephone. This allows for greater flexibility in the timing of classes and better accommodates those whose health status may fluctuate. Retired volunteer facilitators deliver the vast majority of courses, although some paid facilitators are associated with the program. Enrollment figures for 1989-1990 revealed that 525 individuals participated in in-home educational programs; between 300 and 500 viewed the televised programs.

Challenges for Educational Programs

As we previously noted, future cohorts of older adults will have higher levels of formal education, and, as a result, participation by older adults in formal and informal learning situations is likely to continue to increase. The demand for increased opportunities for lifelong learning will no doubt challenge people to rethink the role of education as well as where and how such educational experiences are delivered. We end this chapter by addressing several current and future challenges facing education programs for older adults.

Increasing Participation of Older Adults

The growth in the number of older learners is not necessarily reflected in increasing enrollments within most traditional postsecondary institutions. Only about 5% to 7% of older Americans participate in credit-bearing and noncredit educational programs (Manheimer et al., 1995). The main focus of higher education has always been on collegiate and postcollegiate students. The current pedagogical norm at most colleges and universities does not suit the androgynous needs of older adults (Mills, 1993). Most older adults are not attracted to lengthy course commitments nor to lecture halls in which traditional college-age students listen passively. Thus, to attract more older adults, institutions of higher education may need to rethink their curricula, course content, and didactic delivery style.

For older adults who do chose to enroll in educational programs and courses at college and universities, the cost of attending usually is not a primary concern. The problems concern access. Older adults are far more dependent on a skillfully and sensitively planned environment than are younger students, who can overcome barriers (Regnier, 1988). Inconvenient parking facilities, concern for physical safety when walking to and from the classroom (e.g., poor lighting), and lack of physical comfort (e.g., uncomfortable chairs, lack of climate control, and unpleasant and unattractive classrooms) discourage them from enrolling in classes (Moore & Piland, 1994). Moore and Piland suggest that colleges conduct a "physical environment audit" (p. 316), with active involvement from older adults, to illustrate appropriate areas of the campus for older adult learner activities and to suggest realistic alterations in others that could house senior educational services. In addition, colleges and universities may need to make several significant administrative changes to meet the needs of older students. For example, they must consider the schedule/time of course offerings, the support services available to the older students, and the relevance of the learning to real-world issues facing older adults (Bass, 1992).

In addition to physical barriers, older adults face psychological and social barriers when contemplating entering the higher education arena (Dickerson, Myers, Seelbach, & Johnson-Dietz, 1990). A pervasive obstacle to participation in lifelong education by today's older adults is their lower level of educational experiences compared with younger adults. Older adults often hold negative self-images about their ability to learn that make them apprehensive about mixing with younger students. Although society expects adults to fulfill many roles in their later years (e.g., retiree and grandparent), the role of student is not commonly encouraged.

Institutions of higher education sponsoring senior educational courses and programs must address the inclusion of participants from all races, cultures, and socioeconomic groups. Today, the majority of the older learners attending traditional classroom courses or participating in nontraditional programs (i.e., LIR programs and Elderhostel) are those with the highest levels of education, income, and employment. Although LIR programs and Elderhostel provide "scholarships" or "hostelships" to encourage attendance by individuals from all economic strata, their attempts to recruit a more diverse group of older individuals have not been very successful.

Expanding the Content of Education Programs

In addition to making formal educational opportunities more accessible to older adults, attention must also be directed toward the content of educational experiences. According to Fischer (1992), colleges and universities have at least four major responsibilities to older adult learners. First, they need to help them understand the values, culture, and technology of today. Second, higher education must act as a catalyst for mobilizing young-old adults for productive roles in society for the 20 to 30 years of life after retirement. Third, colleges and universities have a responsibility to foster diversity in intellectual, cultural, and social life by educating students of all ages about aging and ageism. Finally, higher education has the responsibility of enhancing the effective use of society's limited resources by reducing older adults' needs for health and social services.

Ensuring the Quality of Educational Programs

Quality control is an issue of concern for all educational programs. Community-based educational offerings for older people have diverse sponsors, program types, audiences, and content. There is no central system of support for monitoring of these activities, so their patterns depend on the preferences of administrators and the needs of local communities. This often makes them responsive to the wishes of the older learner but does not facilitate development of easily described categories of programs, nor does it provide much assistance in predicating a program's success with other sites and sponsors (Peterson, 1990).

Financing Education Programs

A concern for institutions of higher education is the method of financing educational activities for older people. Federal and foundation funds are not nearly sufficient for the number of programs currently operating or planned. Peterson (1990) suggests that long-range funding must come from the states or from the sponsoring institutions themselves. Public institutions will need state support in revising program priorities to meet the needs of the aging population. Typically, state support is primarily for credit students, with noncredit enrollees paying most of their program costs. Because older people generally are not willing to pay high tuition for noncredit courses, colleges and universities must either find new support mechanisms or pursue new definitions of credit courses.

Yet another concern is the limited funding that directly supports the availability of educational opportunities. With decreases in federal dollars for educational programs, community-based programs will need to further develop private sponsorships. Although many foundations have given local awards, only a few have devoted large amounts of money to this area and have continued support of educational programs through several years (Peterson, 1990).

Addressing the Future of Senior Education Programs

The role and purpose of education for future cohorts of older adults will no doubt be as varied as the older population itself. Educational opportunities for older adults will need to address their different needs. According to McClusky (1974), older adults have five needs that educational programs can address. Education programs can help older adults address *coping needs*—those that help individuals deal with the social, psychological, and physiological changes brought about by aging. Courses in health education, physical exercise, adjustment to retirement, and learning how to live with losses are examples of coping needs addressed through education. *Expressive needs* are those activities in which older adults derive satisfaction, pleasure, or meaning. Given that much of learning during the life course is related to skill acquisition, there may be a greater demand for these types of educational opportunities by future cohorts of older adults. *Contribution needs* of feeling wanted and needed and fulfilling a useful role can be addressed through educational opportunities that allow older adults to act as mentors or peer counselors. Educational programs that empower older adults so they can have influence and control over their quality of life deal with *influence needs*. Courses that address these needs teach older adults about their legal rights or how they can assume leadership roles within their communities. Finally, individuals' needs to feel better off in later life compared with an earlier time in life are *transcendence needs*. Any educational experience that allows older adults to advance artistically, occupationally, educationally, or physically has the potential of addressing transcendence needs (Crandall, 1991).

In summary, future educational opportunities will need to be available at every stage of the life course and will need to offer content that fulfills the varied social and emotional needs of older adults. The resolutions made by delegates to the 1995 White House Conference on Aging are replete with references to the importance of lifelong education. For example, delegates voted to support policies to educate all persons in the community about the diversity of the aging process, to enhance the importance of education as one element of health promotion for all older persons, and to expand professional and continuing education programs for both older adults and all providers of services to older people.

 ## CASE STUDY

CAN FURTHER EDUCATION HELP A DOWNSIZED WORKER?

Martin, 45, entered the workforce shortly after graduation from high school. His first job was with a state highway department, in which he worked as a construction supervisor for 7 years. He was caught up in a reorganization and was laid off from that job. For the past 21 years, he has been employed with a major private sector highway construction firm for which he has performed many duties including materials tester, safety officer, office manager, and highway construction supervisor. Martin and his wife, Nancy, who is an administrative assistant with the U.S. Forest Service, have been earning excellent wages and benefits for more than 20 years. They have two children, a daughter in her second year of college and a son employed in a successful position with a major insurance company.

Two months ago, Martin was officially informed by his company that his job would be eliminated by the new owners. Once again, Martin found himself in a downsizing situation in which the higher-salaried positions were being eliminated to cut the operating expenses of the company. As a dislocated worker, Martin thought that this time around he would have considerably more difficulty finding a job, especially without the benefit of more education.

Martin had always wanted to pursue educational opportunities beyond high school, and, for that reason, he and Nancy had stressed the benefits of higher education with their children. Fortunately, Martin and Nancy have been careful with their finances. Even with a daughter in college, they were not panicked about Martin's losing his job. Their finances were such that Martin was thinking that this might be a good time for him to reevaluate his educational opportunities.

CASE STUDY QUESTIONS

1. This chapter discusses three philosophical perspectives about lifelong learning. Which of those perspectives most closely pertains to Martin's situation? Why?

2. What statistics and studies described in the chapter could you cite to Martin that would reassure him that a decision to return to a higher education learning environment need not be threatening because of his age?

3. What differences in attitudes might Martin encounter as a middle-aged learner in the 1950s and the 1990s?

4. If you were counseling Martin on his options, which options described in the chapter might best meet Martin's educational goals? Which generic educational programs and services might not meet Martin's needs at this time in his life?

5. If Martin decides to enroll at a local college, what problems, barriers, and frustrations might he have to overcome as an older learner? Cite chapter discussion to support your answer.

LEARNING ACTIVITIES

1. Investigate what educational opportunities are available to older adults in your community, at your college, or at other institutions. Find out about the older adults who are involved in these classes.

2. Interview an older participant in Elderhostel or other educational programs about the experience. What did the participant gain from it, what did he or she like and dislike, and why is he or she involved?

3. Sit in on a class that is geared toward older adults. How is it similar to or different from classes you attend? Interview students or the teacher of the course. What type of experiences have they had? What do they like, and what would they change? Is this something they do or plan to do on a continuing basis?

4. Interview someone involved in arranging Elderhostel or other types of educational opportunities for older adults. How did he or she decide what to offer? To whom are the classes marketed? How successful has the program been?

5. Check local newspapers, television ads, and magazines to see how education opportunities are marketed to older adults. Check the Web to see what information is provided on Elderhostel and other education programs.

6. Interview people in their 40s and 50s and those 60 and older. In what type of educational opportunities would they be interested, if any? What are their reasons for being interested in taking these classes?

FOR MORE INFORMATION

National Resources

1. American Library Association (ALA), Adult Services Division, 50 Huron Street, Chicago, IL 60611, 800-545-2433.
   http://www.ala.org

   The American Library Association's activities are focused in many areas, including developing innovative programs that support libraries in acquiring new information technology and training people in its use; and supporting libraries as centers for culture, literacy, and lifetime learning.

2. Elderhostel, 75 Federal Street, Boston, MA 02110-1941, 617-426-7788.
   http://www.elderhostel.org

   Elderhostel is a non-profit educational organization that offers academic programs hosted by educational institutions in the United States and around the world. Individuals 55 years of age and older are eligible and a spouse or an adult companion may attend with an age-eligible participant. Students live on college and university campuses, in marine biology field stations and environmental study centers and enjoy the cultural and recreational resources that host institutions and communitites have to offer. We can hardly wait!

Web Resources

1. National Institute for Literacy
    http://novel.nifl.gov/

    The home page of the National Institute for Literacy offers information about literacy forms and *listservs* (e-mail discussion groups), regional and state literacy resources, and links to other Internet resources.

2. SeniorNet, One Kearny Street, Third Floor, San Francisco, CA 94108, 415-352-1210
    SeniorNet, http://www.seniornet.org

    Don't forget to drop by the SeniorNet site. Find out more about the program, the members, and the activities at various sites.

NOTE

1. Unless otherwise noted, the background information about Elderhostel comes from Mills (1993). Elderhostel's national office provided current statistical data about the program.

7

Senior Centers and Recreation

Evelyn smiled to herself as she listened to her mother's voice on the answering machine saying that she was unavailable to take her call. Mrs. Bergen, Evelyn's mother, had moved to Lake City a year ago after Evelyn's father died. Evelyn was worried that her mother would not adjust well to living alone and living in a new community. She thought her mother would have too much time on her hands. She had no idea there were so many interesting things for her mother to do at the local senior center. She supposed that this time her mother was on the 2-day water rafting trip that the senior center offers every August. She recalled that in the last month her mother had coordinated the annual fund-raising dinner for the center. The biggest problem Evelyn has with her mother's adjustment to her new surroundings is finding her at home!

Stop for a moment and think about the activities you participate in during your free time away from work or school. Do you read a good book? Garden or fix things around the house? Jump in the car and take a short day trip? Play golf or tennis? Go fishing? Attend a concert or a movie? According to researchers, most of our leisure patterns are highly individualized and stable across our life course. So chances are that you will be enjoying the same leisure activities in later life until an intervening variable, such as health status, forces a change (Kelly, Steinkamp, & Kelly, 1986; Stanley & Freysinger, 1995). Now think about *why* you participate in your favorite leisure activity. Does it help you unwind? Make you feel connected with others? Do you gain a sense of accomplishment? Feel productive?

Researchers have identified numerous benefits associated with participation in leisure and recreational activities. According to Dumazadier (1967), leisure has three main functions—relaxation, entertainment, and personal development—and as such, acts as a buffer against major life stresses. Although these functions are important at each stage of the life course, engaging in leisure and recreational activities provides a number of benefits for older adults. Leisure activities can replace a work role, expand on preretirement skills and interests, assist in maintaining positive self-concept, and enhance mental well-being (Hooyman & Kiyak, 1996; Kelly, Steinkamp, & Kelly, 1987; Lawton, Moss, & Fulcomer, 1982; Riddick & Stewart, 1994). In addition, participating in leisure activities can help older adults such as Mrs. Bergen deal more effectively with stressful life events through shared companionship, can reduce feelings of loneliness, and can increase the ability to cope with significant life changes such as widowhood and retirement (Atchley, 1997; Coleman & Iso-Ahola, 1993).

Smale and Dupuis (1993) studied the relationship between leisure participation and psychological well-being of a national sample of 4,345 Canadians ages 11 and older. Three types of leisure activities were included in the analyses: (a) *passive activities*—television viewing and hobbies and crafts, (b) *social activities*—visiting with friends and participation in social clubs and organizations, and (c) *physical activities*—swimming and walking. Participating in hobbies and crafts, social clubs, and organizations and visiting with friends all positively contributed to respondents' well-being. In contrast, television watching detracted from feelings of well-being. When researchers examined the relationship between leisure activities and well-being by age, they found that television viewing detracted from feelings of well-being at all ages. For older adults (age 65+), higher levels of participation in hobbies and crafts, social clubs, and organizations and visiting with friends were significantly related to higher levels of psychological well-being. The relationship between physical activities and well-being was less pronounced. Smale and Dupuis concluded that leisure activities are important to psychological well-being throughout the life course.

One source of leisure activities for older adults is the senior center. According to Krout (1989b), a senior center is a designated place with a broad array of services and activities targeted to older people. It offers opportunities for social interaction, development of strong friendships, and promotion of feelings of self-worth and community belonging. In this chapter, we begin by reviewing the federal policies that have contributed to the growth of senior centers. This is followed by a discussion of who attends senior centers, the various models of senior centers, and the type of programs offered. In the final section, we present the challenges that lie ahead for senior centers.

Policy Background

The first senior center was established in 1943 in New York City (Leanse, Tiven, & Robb, 1977). The founders established the William Hodson Community Center to help alleviate loneliness among older adults observed by social workers in the city's welfare department. According to the center's first director, the center needed to offer older adults a meeting place but, more important, needed to offer services that would help participants remain in the community (Perspective on Aging, 1993). California was the location of the next two senior centers, which offered a variety of recreational and educational services (Kent, 1978; Maxwell, 1962). By 1966, there were 340 centers; today, between 12,000 and 14,000 senior centers are located across the country (Wagner, 1995a). According to the National Institute of Senior Centers (1978), senior centers are based on the philosophy that

> aging is a normal developmental process; that human beings need peers with whom they can interact and who are available as a source of encouragement and support; and that adults have the right to have a voice in determining matters in which they have a vital interest. As such, the center is a major community institution that is geared to maintain good mental health and to prevent breakdown and deterioration of mental, emotional and social functioning of the older person. (p. 5)

As senior centers emerged as a significant community resource for older adults, the Older Americans Act played an important role in the creation and support of more facilities. In the original act (1965), funds were available for senior center operations under Title IV, and dollars under Title III supported many of the programs offered at these sites.[1] The 1973 amendments of the OAA created a new Title V under which senior centers became the focal point of providing services to older adults. These amendments introduced the term *multipurpose senior center* and provided funding for renovation or acquisition of facilities to be used as multipurpose centers—community organizations designed to be the center for developing and delivering a range of services. Amendments in 1978 eliminated Title V and placed support for senior centers under Title III. In addition, the amendments required that when feasible, AAAs designate a central point for the delivery of services and give special consideration to senior centers. In part because of this increased support of senior centers under the OAA, the number of senior centers increased dramatically. By the end of the 1970s, there were an estimated 6,000 to 7,000. As funding for OAA programs in the 1980s flattened and declined, few additional legislative changes affected senior centers. In Title III under the current version of the OAA (1992), multipurpose centers are defined as "a community facility for the organization and provision of a broad spectrum of services, which shall include, but are not limited to provision of health (including mental health), social, nutritional and educational services and the provision of facilities for recreational activities for older persons" (§ 102 [35]).

Best Practice   **Serving Rural Seniors**

Weld County encompasses 4,004 square miles in north central Colorado—an area larger than Rhode Island, Delaware, and the District of Columbia combined. The challenge was how to set up and support senior programs in the county's 28 smaller communities, which range from 150 to 10,000 in population. The solution began in March 1975 after a VISTA volunteer had spent 3 months assessing both the needs of the rural Weld seniors and the barriers to providing services to them. Without exception, the response from the agencies was the same: "Weld County is so large we simply do not have the staff to do outreach work in the rural communities. Everything is concentrated in Greeley; we have nothing in the small towns."

With this information in hand, a plan was developed and approved by the county commissioners to bring the services and the seniors in the rural areas together. Small-town governments were encouraged to hire a senior aide for 20 hours per week with the promise that the county would pay the aide's salary through an employment and training program for the first year. At the end of the first year, 11 senior aide sites were in place. Today, 21 sites are active, most fully supported by their towns.

Through the years, the senior aide program has grown not only in numbers of sites in place but also in program offerings. Originally, most senior aides worked out of their homes, offering simple information and referral activities. Today, nearly all the aides work in viable senior centers, some aides have become full-time town employees, and all use volunteers in their centers. Many have new, modern centers and offer a respectable range of recreational outings, educational classes, regular senior meals, and intergenerational programs.

A unique and successful aspect of this program is the monthly daylong training meetings that provide a forum for training and information exchange. The meetings continue to this day and rotate among the participating towns, giving each aide a better understanding of the similarities and differences among the communities. A technical adviser, provided by the area agency on aging, helps the senior aides develop their monthly agendas. These meetings include a wide range of informative programs designed to help the aides provide up-to-date information and quality senior services to their communities. The senior aging network uses the monthly meetings to get the word out about their services and how to access them. The adviser also travels to each town to provide one-on-one technical assistance when needed.

In 1980, the senior aides incorporated under the name WELDCOS, Inc. They applied for general fund dollars from the county commissioners and have received a yearly allocation that they divide among themselves. Aides use the funds to help pay utilities, buy craft materials, pay for a fund-raising event, purchase equipment, and take seniors on outings. Records show that the program generates more than 50,000 volunteer hours annually for the senior centers and their communities. Community volunteers, coordinated by the aides, also assist with the overwhelming transportation needs generated in this large, rural county. The program continues to grow and thrive, providing valuable assistance and opportunities for seniors in small towns.

For more information, contact Weld County Area Agency on Aging, P.O. Box 1805, Greeley, CO 80632, 970-353-3816.

Although Title III monies fund senior centers, those dollars must also support the other programs designated under Title III. Most centers, however, rely on nonfederal money, and the average percentage of federal contributions to senior centers has fallen from 29% in 1982 to 19% in 1989 (Krout, 1990).

Users and Programs

Most of the research on senior centers during the last 25 years has focused on identifying organizational characteristics of senior centers, characteristics of participants, and types of programs and services offered. As Wagner (1995a) pointed out, much of the research on demographic characteristics of senior center participants and the role these characteristics play in predicting senior center participation paints a somewhat contradictory picture. This is no doubt reflective of the diverse communities in which centers are located. Krout (1989b) estimates that between 5 and 8 million older adults attend senior centers. As we will see below, Mrs. Bergen is in many ways representative of the many older adults who attend activities at a senior center.

Characteristics of Senior Center Participants

Early studies of senior center participants report equal percentages of female and male participants (Silvey, 1962; Storey, 1962), whereas more recent studies reveal that the majority of participants are women and live alone or with a nonrelative (Krout, 1983b; Krout, Cutler, & Coward, 1990). More than 20 years ago, researchers found that senior center participants were primarily in their 60s (Harris & Associates, 1975; Storey, 1962). More recently, researchers have found that senior center use increases with age, up to age 85,

For Your Files   **Gay and Lesbian Outreach
to Elders Senior Center**

A unique senior center in San Francisco, the Gay and Lesbian Outreach to Elders (GLOE), seeks to serve older gay men and lesbians. The mission of GLOE is to provide community-based social services to persons age 60 and older to maintain independent living and to prevent unnecessary or premature institutionalization. GLOE provides a range of senior social services including information and referral on matters of health care, housing, legal and other related services; support and discussion groups; social and recreational events; activities groups including oral history project; support services whereby a social worker conducts assessment for at-risk elders and links them to needed services; friendly visiting; and community outreach and advocacy. Fee for services is prohibited, and social-recreational activities are subsidized by suggested donations and fund-raising activities. No one is turned away for lack of funds. A recent summer activity included a nature day trip to Pescadero Marsh for bird-watching and on to Butano State Park for a picnic barbecue and a walk through the redwoods.

For more information, contact GLOE at 1853 Market Street, San Francisco, CA 94103, 415-626-7000.

when attendance declines. This suggests that the young-old adults who attended in the 1960s and 1970s are "aging in place" and that a new cohort of younger participants are not being recruited into senior centers (Krout, 1989a; Krout et al., 1990; Miner, Logan, & Spitz, 1993). Miner et al. found that *frequency* of attendance, similar to the findings on attendance, was related to age. Older participants were more likely to report that they attended the senior center frequently than were their younger counterparts, who were more likely to report rarely attending. There was no discernible pattern between age and attending senior centers "sometimes." Miner et al. concluded that observations by senior center directors that younger participants were interested only in occasional trips and special events appear to be supported by these findings. Indeed, the results on both attendance and frequency support the notion that senior center participants are aging in place and that younger cohorts are not frequent users of senior center activities.

Are older adults of color less likely to be senior center participants? At least one study reported that older blacks were more likely than whites to indicate a willingness to attend (Ralston, 1985). Yet overall, national data reveal that older adults of color are less likely than their white counterparts to attend senior centers (Harris & Associates, 1975; Krout, 1987b, 1988;

Leanse & Wagner, 1975). A national sample of recreation and senior center directors were asked to estimate the percentage of their participants by ethnic group (Wacker & Blanding, 1994). Overall, older blacks constituted an average of 8% of the participants, older Hispanics 5%, and Asian and Native Americans 2% each. The percentage of minority participants, however, varied across programs. For example, the percentage of older black and Hispanic participants ranged from 0% to 95%, and 0% to 98%, respectively. Similar percentages were noted for older Asian Americans and Native Americans. These variations in participant characteristics may reflect the location of the center; senior centers located in neighborhoods having high numbers of older adults of color probably report higher percentages of minority users. Overall, older adults of color are underrepresented at most senior centers except at those centers primarily serving them.

Health and functional status appear to differentiate users of senior centers from nonusers and act as a barrier to participation. Early studies by Hanssen et al. (1978) and Harris and Associates (1975) found that those with poor functional ability and poor health were less likely to attend. More recent studies report similar findings. In their study of 282 senior centers in New York, Cox and Monk (1990) found that only 10% of participants were classified by directors as frail. Similarly, in another study, only a small percentage of participants had a disability that required special programming accommodations (Wacker & Blanding, 1994). For example, an average of less than 9% of participants had physical disabilities or hearing impairments, 6% had visual impairments, and only 3% had cognitive impairments. Krout et al. (1990) also reported that older adults with fewer activities of daily living problems were more likely to attend a senior center than were their less well counterparts. One exception to these findings was a study by Miner et al. (1993), who found that frequency of attendance did not differ by functional ability; seniors with disabilities who ever attended a senior center participated as frequently as did their healthier counterparts. They concluded that although functional disability may make a difference in whether older adults *ever* attend a senior center, it does not influence *how often* they attend.

Socioeconomic status measures of education and income also appear to be predictors of senior center attendance. Attendees are more likely than nonattendees to have low incomes and lower levels of formal education. Miner et al. (1993) also found that those with more economic resources and higher levels of education were more likely to report "rarely" attending senior centers. They concluded that those with higher incomes and education levels have other, more expensive, alternatives for leisure activities and supportive services. Data suggest that senior centers serve neither the very rich nor very poor but are attracting older adults whose incomes are lower than the older adult population in general (Wagner, 1995a).

In summary, although findings from national and local data are somewhat contradictory, we can make some generalizations about the typical senior center participant. The typical senior center participant is generally a female, in her late 60s to middle 70s, of lower to middle economic status, living alone, white, in good physical health, and with slightly less than a high school education.

Barriers to Senior Center Participation

What factors prevent some older adults from attending senior centers? Some evidence suggests that many older adults are simply unaware of the different activities and services offered at senior centers. Indeed, Krout (1981, 1982, 1984) found that although a high percentage of respondents were aware of the existence of senior centers, nonparticipants knew little about senior center programming.

A number of barriers deter use of senior centers by minority elders. Ralston (1982) found that lack of transportation and lack of culturally appropriate programs were obstacles to attendance for blacks. History of racial segregation no doubt makes it difficult for many older persons of color to feel comfortable attending predominantly white senior centers. Moreover, in many communities, both large and small, neighborhoods are segregated by socioeconomic class and race, thus making attending senior centers in other neighborhoods difficult.

Although lack of transportation seems to be an important factor in keeping older adults from attending senior centers, studies have found that availability of transportation was not significantly related to attendance (Hanssen et al., 1978; Krout, 1983a; Leanse & Wagner, 1975). Others have found, however, that transportation problems acted as a hindrance to senior center attendance (Harris & Associates, 1975; Jirovec, Erich, & Sanders, 1989).

Researchers have identified other personal factors that inhibit senior center participation. For example, Leanse and Wagner (1975) found that younger seniors reported feeling too young to attend the center and gave poor health as the reason for nonattendance. In a study of former senior center participants, Krout (1988) found that more than half cited health problems as the reasons for nonattendance. Finally, lack of attendance may also reflect lifelong patterns of nonparticipation in voluntary associations (Krout, 1989b).

Models of Senior Centers

As senior centers sprang up across the nation in different social contexts and locations, they developed different organizational structures. Taietz (1976) was the first to identify the different models of senior centers. On the basis

---

For Your Files   ***Orgullo Communal:* The Land Grant Hall in Chilili**

Chilili, New Mexico, began as an Indian pueblo in 1614 and today is a small rural community with a strong sense of *orgullo communal* (community pride) among the present-day Hispanic citizens. The citizens of Chilili worked together to bring home-delivered meals for older Hispanics who were frail and isolated. Soon after the home-delivered meal program was developed, the community joined to transform the Land Grant Hall into a nutrition site and senior center. The center became a focal point for the delivery of such services as a clinic on wheels from Albuquerque's University Hospital. A geriatric outreach clinic was organized and sponsored by the University of New Mexico's Department of Family Medicine and the Albuquerque-Bernalillo County Office of Senior Affairs. The First Annual Chilili Center Bazaar turned out to be an intergenerational celebration with traditional Hispanic arts, food, and music.

For more information about the center's activities, contact Albuquerque-Bernalillo County Office of Senior Affairs, Albuquerque, NM 87102, 505-768-2000.

SOURCE: Miko & Sanchez (1993).

---

of his study of senior centers across the country, he suggested that centers could be categorized as either a *social agency model* or a *voluntary organizational model*. Senior centers classified as a social agency model have programs designed to meet the needs of older adults, with those who are poor and disengaged the likely participants. In contrast, the voluntary organization model assumes that older adults who are more active in voluntary organizations and who have strong attachments to the community are the ones who will participate in senior centers. Krout (1989b), however, argues that such a dichotomous distinction might not accurately reflect the wide variation of senior centers and their participants. For example, although some participants attend senior centers for recreational and educational opportunities, they may have other unmet nutritional and health needs.

Moreover, the model a senior center adopts may be linked to its geographical location. For example, rural senior centers differ from urban centers in several organizational characteristics. Rural centers are more likely to have smaller budgets, fewer paid staff, and fewer resources (Krout, 1987a). Thus, community size makes a significant difference in program planning activities, interagency networking, and the types of services and activities senior centers offer. Centers located in smaller communities were less likely to create new programs, work with other aging and nonaging organizations in joint projects, and make referrals to other agencies (Wacker & Blanding,

---

For Your Files **National Recreation and Park Association**

The National Recreation and Park Association (NRPA) is a national non-profit service organization dedicated to promoting the importance of recreation and parks and to ensuring that all people have an opportunity to find the best and most satisfying use of their leisure time. The Leisure and Aging Section of the NRPA represents and assists professionals who are involved with helping older adults remain healthy and active through participation in recreational pursuits. It also provides leadership and advocacy to ensure the availability of leisure and recreation opportunities for older adults.

NRPA has a number of publications available, such as *Best Practice Programs in Leisure and Aging; Leisure and Aging: A Selected, Annotated Bibliography,* and *Dynamic Leisure Programming With Older Adults.* For more information, contact NRPA at 2775 South Quincy Street, Suite 300, Arlington, VA 22206, 703-820-4940. Or check out their Web site (http://www.nrpa.org).

1994). Not surprisingly, programs in larger communities were able to offer a wider range of services including support groups, outreach, and job and employment counseling. The same pattern held true with activities; rural centers were less likely than centers located in more urban areas to offer many of the cultural, educational, social, recreational, and outdoor activities.

Programs Offered at Senior Centers

The variety of services and activities offered by senior centers can be classified in several ways. The National Institute of Senior Centers classified senior center activities on the basis of the participant characteristics. For example, senior centers can provide services to community institutions, group services such as education and group social work, and individual services such as health maintenance and counseling (Lowy & Doolin, 1985). In contrast, Krout (1985a) has distinguished between activities and services offered through senior centers. Activities are those programs offered by the center that are for personal enrichment and enjoyment, whereas services are designed to relieve or prevent problems for at-risk older adults. Although the type and number of services and activities offered by senior centers have expanded through the years, centers have always offered creative activities such as arts and crafts; recreation activities such as cards, bingo, parties, and dances; and services such as information and referral and meals (Krout, 1985a; Leanse & Wagner, 1975; Wacker & Blanding, 1994). Although the

Exhibit 7.1 **Types of Services and Activities Offered at Senior Centers**

Recreational opportunities

Health and wellness

Educational opportunities

Meals and nutritional education

Transportation

Arts and humanities

Employment assistance

Intergenerational programming

Information and referral

Support groups and counseling

Social and community action opportunities

Employment assistance

Volunteer activities

SOURCE: Adapted from Wagner (1995a).

availability of services and activities offered at senior centers will vary by location and size of the center, the services and activities likely to be available at local centers are listed in Exhibit 7.1.

In Krout's (1985a) national survey of senior centers, he reported that more than 75% of centers offered information and referral, outreach and transportation services, meals, health education, and screening. More than half of the centers offered home-delivered meals, friendly visiting, telephone reassurance, consumer information, crime prevention, financial/tax services, housing information, legal assistance, and assistance with Social Security and Medicare. Less than one quarter offered adult day care services, job training and placement, protective services, and peer counseling.

A comparison of Krout's (1985a) data with an early study conducted in 1975 by Leanse and Wagner revealed that the types of services offered by senior centers have increased, especially services such as home-delivered meals, classes and lectures, and active recreational activities (Krout, 1989b). Findings from a national sample of both senior centers and recreation programs serving older adults were similar to Krout's (1985a) findings in that the majority of senior centers offered health services such as fitness classes, blood pressure checks, vision and hearing tests, and health education and provided meals, transportation, and outreach (Wacker & Blanding, 1994). Less than half offered housing support/assistance, employment counseling, crisis counseling, or adult day care. Although senior centers were providing the usual craft and social activities, few were providing outdoor recreation activities or activities that were more physical in nature such as swimming, golf, and tennis. This study also revealed a more recent trend in the type of activities offered at senior centers—the inclusion of intergenerational programs. Seventy percent of senior centers offered some type of intergenerational activity. Examples of intergenerational programming included lunch buddies, whereby older adults are paired with schoolchildren to eat lunch together twice a month, pen-pal programs, and a gift shop for kids at the senior center. Programmatic characteristics were also examined by age of participant. Programs with a higher percentage of older adults over 70 years of age compared with the percentage of participants under age 70 had significantly different types of programs offered. For example, of the 22 services listed in Exhibit 7.2, programs with older participants were significantly more likely to offer those services than were programs with younger participants. Programs with older participants were more likely to offer more health-related services (e.g., health education, blood pressure checks, and vision and hearing tests) and support services (e.g., nutrition, outreach, transportation, and legal aid) than were programs with a younger clientele. More research is needed to determine whether the participant profile influenced programmatic differences or if the programs offered drew a particular type of participant.

Not surprisingly, differences in programming exist among centers with varying budgets and locations. Centers with larger budgets and more staff are more likely to offer a higher number of services and activities (Krout, 1987a; Wacker & Blanding, 1994), and there appears to be a relationship between budget size and location. Two studies by Krout (1984, 1987a) found that senior center budgets in rural communities are smaller than budgets of centers located in more urbanized areas.

Finally, senior centers also serve as a focal point for services and, in many cases, as a source of information and referral for participants. A handful of studies reported that those attending senior centers believed that their center was a source of information about other community services and played an important intermediary role between themselves and other service providers (Delisle, Boucher, & Roy, cited in West, Delisle, Simard, & Drouin, 1996).

As shown in Exhibit 7.3, programs with predominantly older participants referred their participants to support services and long-term care services more often than did those programs with predominantly younger participants. For example, more referrals were made to legal aid and nutrition programs, as well as case management services, nursing homes, home health agencies, and adult day care programs. Thus, as a source of information and referral, senior centers must be aware of a wide range of community services and respond to changing needs as participants age in place in their programs.

Exhibit 7.2 **Percentage of Services Provided by Senior Centers and Recreation Programs by Age of Participants**

Services/Activities	Programs With Older Participants (n = 218)	Programs With Younger Participants (n = 336)	χ^2
Fitness class/opportunities	95.0	91.0	NS
Information and referral	93.3	73.3	.00
Health education	91.2	71.4	.00
Blood pressure check	90.0	73.4	.00
Vision-hearing tests	81.9	61.8	.00
Nutrition site	81.0	58.2	.00
Transportation	80.0	61.4	.00
Financial education	79.4	56.9	.00
Leisure education	78.4	68.7	.02
Intergenerational activities	78.2	58.9	.00
Outreach	76.3	47.4	.00
Adult education	73.3	54.4	.00
Legal aid	70.1	48.3	.00
Cholesterol testing	56.9	52.7	NS
Support groups	56.4	45.1	.01
Recycling	52.0	50.0	NS
Housing support/assistance	49.0	31.0	.00
Job/employment counseling	41.1	30.0	.01
Gov. commodities	37.2	31.0	NS
Gift shop or store	33.3	22.9	.00
Hotline/crisis counseling	17.0	19.0	NS
Adult day care	16.4	11.1	NS

SOURCE: From *Comprehensive Leisure and Aging Study: Final Report,* p. 91, by R. R. Wacker and C. Blanding, 1994, Washington, DC: National Recreation and Park Association. Reprinted with permission from the National Recreation and Park Association. Used with permission.

Challenges for Senior Centers

Senior centers provide older adults with a place to pursue leisure activities, to socialize with others, and to receive important social services and information. As the United States experiences social and demographic changes, senior centers will face a number of challenges.

Exhibit 7.3 **Percentage of Referrals Made to Selected Agencies by Senior Center and Recreation Programs by Age of Participant**

Agency/Organization	Programs With Older Participants (n = 218)	Programs With Younger Participants (n = 336)	χ^2
Other senior centers	86.1	69.8	.00
Area Agency on Aging	86.1	68.3	.00
Nutrition sites	84.7	63.3	.00
City/County Social Service Department	83.1	58.1	.00
Local health departments	76.0	56.2	.00
Home Health	73.4	42.7	.00
Legal Aid	73.1	47.2	.00
Local Social Security Office	69.3	41.0	.00
Human service organizations (Salvation Army, etc.)	69.0	46.6	.00
Special disability groups	67.0	50.9	.00
Adult day care facility	66.6	43.4	.00
Recreation centers	66.5	70.4	NS
Case management	66.2	37.1	.00
Libraries	66.1	56.8	NS
Service clubs	60.0	52.6	NS
Schools/universities	59.4	50.8	NS
Nursing homes	57.9	40.5	.00
Local hospitals	53.1	37.8	.00
Travel agencies	49.3	43.2	NS
Religious organizations	42.2	36.2	NS
Private physicians	40.0	23.3	.00
State Office on Aging	39.1	33.0	NS
Financial planning services	37.0	31.2	NS
Youth groups	36.3	33.9	NS
YMCA/YWCA/Jewish Community Centers	35.0	34.0	NS
Health maintenance organizations	32.0	26.4	NS
Outdoor organizations	30.0	28.4	NS

SOURCE: From *Comprehensive Leisure and Aging Study: Final Report*, p. 90, by R. R. Wacker and C. Blanding, 1994, Washington, DC: National Recreation and Park Association. Reprinted with permission from the National Recreation and Park Association.

Attracting Younger Participants

The current cohort of older participants is aging in place at senior centers. Therefore, senior centers must successfully recruit younger participants and adjust programmatic offerings to match their recreation and leisure interests. Younger cohorts who will be recruited to attend senior center activities will carry with them leisure and recreation norms and interests that will no doubt differ from the current cohort of older participants. Thus, senior center directors will have to identify activities that match the different interests of the baby boomer cohort. Some possible programmatic changes might include the incorporation of computer technology in on-site activities and the delivery of information and activities through the Internet, in addition to acting as brokers for arranging individual leisure pursuits. To attract a more active, more health-conscious cohort of older adults, senior centers must become "vital aging" centers that foster personal growth and health education and wellness (Wagner, 1995b). Wagner's specific recommended programmatic changes for attracting younger members include extending hours of operation to include evening and weekend hours, changing food programs to accommodate more discernible tastes, and including more intergenerational and multigenerational programming designed to promote intergenerational family and nonfamily relationships.

With the increase in the number of oldest-old adults, senior centers also will have to come to grips with their role in serving persons who are more frail. Unfortunately, there is a dearth of information about how senior centers currently serve at-risk older adults, the impact of involving at-risk older persons with the well participants, and how at-risk older adults can be successfully recruited in senior center activities (Krout, 1993b). Cox and Monk (1990) found that senior center directors perceived that the well participants would be resistant to including impaired older persons into their programs. Several directors in their study reported being concerned about becoming "baby-sitters" for nursing home residents and felt that they did not have the staff to meet the needs of impaired older adults. Cox and Monk also point out that if senior centers are going to include frail elders in their programs, they must receive assistance from other agencies in obtaining diagnostic, program, and service resources. As Krout (1995) observed, senior centers must carefully examine the advantages and disadvantages that serving older adults who are frail will have on its operational, programmatic, and budgetary functions.

The Need for Senior Centers

In addition to these specific challenges brought about by an aging population, a larger question about the need for senior centers must be addressed. More recently, as services and programs for older adults have come under closer scrutiny and as public financial support of programs for older adults has declined, some question the need for a separate community facility for older adults. Why not have community centers that would offer programs and services for persons of all ages? Indeed, Estes (1979) argued some years ago that programmatic segregation of older adults has many negative societal and personal outcomes. On the other hand, the needs of older adults might be overlooked in another delivery context. For example, a study compared the type of programs and activities offered by senior centers and the type offered by recreation programs that served all age groups (Wacker & Blanding (1994). Senior centers were more likely to offer a wider range of services including health and preventive services, and they had more interagency referrals to other social support services such as adult day services, home health care, and legal assistance than did recreation programs that served all ages. These results suggest that because senior centers serve a particular clientele, they are able to more effectively address the varied needs of older adults. If senior centers continue to primarily serve older adults, they must, as Schoeffler (1995) points out, "overcome the perception that they are nice, but not necessary" (p. 36).

The Senior Center of the Future

So what will senior centers look like in the future? In addition to the programmatic changes mentioned above, Schoeffler (1995) argues that at a minimum, every senior center must provide information and referral services and be used as common intake locations for delivering other community services. He suggests that senior centers must become

> brokers of home and community-based long term care . . . [and] facilitate the planning, arranging, coordinating and evaluating of service delivery to ensure that the most appropriate services are provided either on-site or through referral in the most efficient, effective, and accountable manner. (p. 37)

The senior center of the future might also consider different ways of delivering its services to reach a more diverse population. Because many older adults pursue leisure activities in an informal setting or at home, neighborhood senior centers could develop ways to support in-home recreation activities (Wilhite, Sheldon, & Jekubovich-Fenton, 1994). Moreover, senior center programming might change to include social support and outreach programs for older adults and caregivers including those in rural areas (White House Conference on Aging, 1995).

Senior centers of the future must reflect the diversity that will exist in the United States. The increase in the number of older persons of color will highlight the need for senior center programming to be culturally sensitive to the diverse racial and ethnic groups of older adults. Senior centers must consider offering culturally diverse meals and activities, increasing staff sensitivity, and dealing with issues of inclusion by the majority group (Ralston, 1991). Just as U.S. society continues to struggle with racial segregation and racism within many of its cities, senior centers will no doubt be confronted with these same issues as they strive to be more inclusive of minority elders.

As the 21st century approaches, senior centers will be challenged to respond to the needs and demands of a new generation of older adults. Perhaps as a result, senior centers of the future will bear little resemblance to senior centers that presently exist.

 ## CASE STUDY

THE LONELINESS OF A CAREGIVER

Alex, 77, laid down the natural science journal he was reading and thought for a moment about the turn of events in his life since his wife, Susan, was diagnosed with Alzheimer's disease 5 years ago. When he retired from the university and she from public school teaching, they had literally catapulted into a new life of worldwide travels and volunteer work with the local Friends of the Library and several conservation groups. Their life contained all the excitement and stimulation they had hoped it would when they began planning for their retirement. Hardly a day passed when they were not socializing with friends and other volunteers. Even Alex's lifelong lapses into depression had virtually disappeared.

At first, after Susan's diagnosis, they kept up a good front. Few of their social contacts realized what was happening to Susan. Now, he thought, everything has changed. Susan needs constant supervision. Other than their two daughters who visit once a month, a couple of neighbors who drop in to say hello, and the home health aide, Alex has few contacts with the outside world. It embarrasses him to think that twice in the last year he has checked into emergency care at the hospital on orders from his doctor to have a psychiatric evaluation. Once he was released, the other time he was admitted for 3 days of psychiatric tests and counseling.

On his worst days, Alex wonders why he is alive. On better days, he's gratified that he is still able to take care of his wife. He also, at the same time, wonders how much longer he can tolerate the isolation and loneliness. His psychiatrist and the home health aide are advising him to hire a respite worker to come in and sit with Susan a couple of afternoons a week so that he can attend the downtown senior center.

CASE STUDY QUESTIONS

1. Why do you believe Alex's psychiatrist and his wife's home health aide are recommending that he connect with the local senior center? Cite research in this chapter that supports your response.

2. On the basis of what you know about Alex, what the literature says about the typical senior center participant, and theories of service use, what are the chances that Alex will follow the advice of his psychiatrist?

3. Describe a typical senior center offering of activities and services. Which of these offerings might be most beneficial to Alex? Why?

4. What barriers to becoming involved in the senior center do caregivers like Alex face? What other community support services could be helpful at this time?

5. Why do you think Alex and his wife did not join the senior center at the time of their retirement? What research supports your answer?

6. Describe a senior center program that would be most appealing to Alex.

7. What are the benefits to Alex, Susan, and society in helping Alex reconnect with his community?

⌖ LEARNING ACTIVITIES

1. Interview two or more people who are in their 50s about their leisure and recreational activities. Do they participate in passive, social, or physical activities? How do they think the pattern of their leisure activity will change as they become older or retire? Would they be interested in joining a senior center when they get older? Why or why not? What type of activities do they think senior centers should provide to people in their generation? If possible, interview a group with diversity based on gender, income, and race.

2. Visit the local senior center. What activities are available there? What percentage of programmatic offerings are for recreation? What percentage are social support services? On the basis of your review, do you think this center acts as a focal point for older adults in your community?

3. Interview the director of a local senior center. What percentage of the participants are aging in place? What strategies has the center used to attract younger participants? What, in the director's opinion, is the most innovative program the center offers? If money were no object, what program or service would the center provide?

FOR MORE INFORMATION

National Resources

1. National Eldercare Institute on Multipurpose Senior Centers and Community Focal Points, 409 Third Street SW, Suite 200, Washington, DC 20024, 202-479-1200.

    The National Eldercare Institute is funded under a cooperative agreement between the Administration on Aging and the National Council on the Aging. The institute is a resource for older Americans through multipurpose senior centers and community focal points. The institute offers training, technical assistance, and materials and sponsors research initiatives.

2. National Council of Senior Centers, 1511 K Street NW, Washington, DC 20005, 202-624-9500.

    The National Council of Senior Centers provides support and assistance to persons interested in and supporting senior centers.

3. National Senior Sports Association, 301 North Harrison Street, Suite 204, Princeton, NJ 08540, 609-466-9366.

    The National Senior Sports Association is a membership organization for men and women over 50 who enjoy travel and golf. The association promotes activities that offer seniors a chance to golf, travel, and meet others. Members receive *Senior Sport News*, which is distributed monthly.

4. National Recreation and Park Association, 2775 South Quincy Street, Suite 300, Arlington, VA 22206, 703-820-4940 (http://www.nrpa.org).

    The Leisure and Aging Section of the NRPA represents and assists professionals who are involved with helping older adults remain healthy and active through participation in recreational pursuits. NRPA's publications include *Best Practice Programs in Leisure and Aging; Leisure and Aging: A Selected, Annotated Bibliography,* and *Dynamic Leisure Programming With Older Adults.*

Web Resources

1. Senior World, Roanoke, VA
    http://www.infi.net/dthorne/index.html

    Senior World is the home page for activities, events, and services for and about seniors. Visitors can access information about recreation and leisure activities, community news, and other community services for older adults.

2. Seniors' Center, Boulder, CO
   http://bcn.boulder.co.us/community/senior-citizens/center.html

   This site is a "senior center" on the Web. Visitors will find information about all types of services and programs for older adults, from a list of local grocers and senior discounts to information about health matters and travel.

3. Shepherd's Centers of America
   http://www.qni.com/shepherd/index.html

   Shepherd's Centers of America is an interfaith, nonprofit organization whose primary purpose is to enrich the lives of older adults. The home page explains the philosophy behind the centers and provides a list of centers across the country.

4. Northshore Senior Center, Bothell, WA
   http://www.oz.net/sanford

   The home page of the Northshore Senior Center provides information about how to join the center, volunteer opportunities, and the computer learning center; visitors can access their newsletter and catalog.

5. Administration on Aging: Links to Senior Centers
   http://www.aoa.dhhs.gov/AOA/webres/senior.htm

   The AoA has provided selected links to various senior centers around the country. Expect this site to have more listings because more senior centers will be creating their own home pages.

NOTE

1. Unless noted otherwise, the history of senior centers comes from Krout (1989b).

8

Employment Programs

At 57 years of age, John suddenly found himself unemployed when his company was sold. He had worked in almost every area of the lumber business and had expected to work for the same company until he retired. The new owners offered him a position at half the salary he had been earning. With at least 8 years until retirement and his youngest child still in college, John simply could not accept the offer. He was frightened about his financial future. Through a friend, he heard that the local employment service operated a federally funded program for adults 55 and older. John qualified for the program as a displaced worker and because of his age. His employment specialist helped him regain his self-confidence and set new employment goals. The program enrolled him in a correspondence course and an on-the-job training program with a local appraisal company. After successfully completing his training, the employment counselor helped John establish himself as a self-employed appraiser.

In 1986, the first of the baby boomers turned 40 and became "older workers." By 2006, many of these individuals will be seriously contemplating the date of their retirement. In the interim, some individuals, like John, will find that their age works against them in maintaining their current positions, seeking new jobs, or requesting training—although most employers rate older workers high on such traits as loyalty, dependability, and attitude toward work. For a variety of reasons, including industry's need for workers and the economic needs of some older adults, employers can no longer ignore this growing segment of the workforce.

We begin this chapter by examining work-related policies that protect older workers. We then profile older workers and their employers with particular focus on federally supported employment training programs designed specifically for older adults. We conclude the chapter with a discussion of the challenges facing older worker and employment programs.

Policy Background

The Age Discrimination in Employment Act (ADEA), first passed in 1967, is the single most important law protecting the rights of older workers. It provides that workers over the age of 40 cannot be arbitrarily discriminated against because of age in any employment decision including hiring, discharges, layoffs, promotion, wages, and health care coverage (Brown, 1989). The 1986 amendments to the ADEA prohibit most employers from setting a mandatory retirement age. There are, however, a few exceptions to the ADEA. For example, the ADEA does not protect workers who are employed by companies that have less than 20 employees, and the ADEA permits the mandatory retirement of "executives or persons in high policy-making positions" (p. 186) at age 65 if their annual retirement pension benefits equal or exceed $44,000. In addition to the ADEA, more than 40 states have their own laws against age discrimination in employment that often provide greater protection than the federal law.

Congress also enacted the Older Workers Benefit Protection Act in 1990 to make clear that discrimination based on age in virtually all forms of employee benefits is unlawful. Specifically, it applies to employee benefits and benefit plans established or modified on or after its enactment (October 16, 1990; April 14, 1991, for private employers). The major goal of the act is to establish regulations prohibiting age discrimination for most employee fringe benefits (Wiencek, 1991). It provides statutory recognition of early retirement programs and enacts into law the "equal benefit" or "equal cost" principle, requiring employers to provide older workers with benefits at least equal to those provided for younger workers, unless the employers can prove that the cost of providing an equal benefit is greater for an older worker than for a younger worker.

The Americans With Disabilities Act (ADA) of 1990 also provides additional protection for older workers. Although disabilities are not a result of normal aging, the ADA classifies many ailments associated with older adults as disabilities. Older adults who have been unemployed because of disability will have substantially improved opportunities to reenter the workforce. Under the law, individuals must be considered for employment if they can perform the essential functions of the position with reasonable accommodations.

The federal government has also been instrumental in creating employment programs for older workers. These include the Green Thumb Program, the Senior Community Service Employment Program, the Community Service

Exhibit 8.1 **Labor Force Participation for Older Adults by Age and Gender (Percentage)**

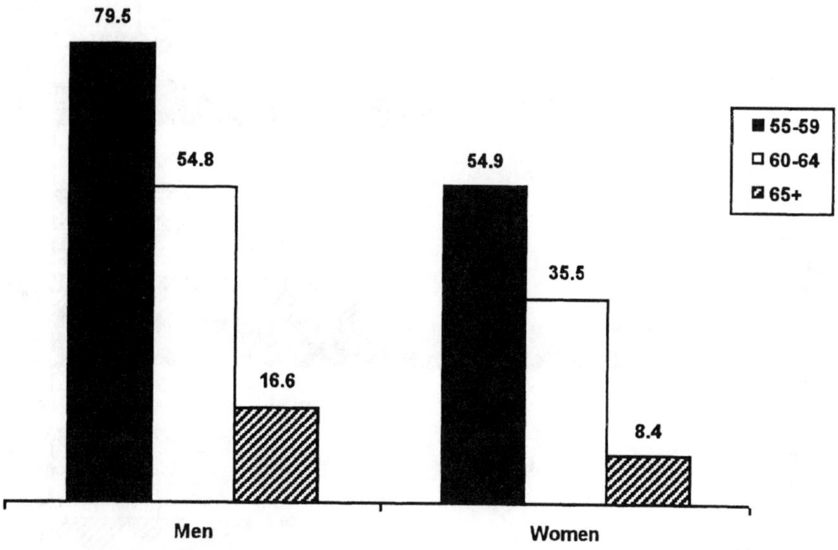

SOURCE: U.S. Department of Labor (1990a).

Employment for Older Americans under Title V of the Older Americans Act, and the Senior Employment Program. Each of these will be explained in greater detail later in this chapter.

Users and Programs

Characteristics of Older Workers

According to the U.S. Department of Labor (1990a), 79.5% of men between the ages of 55 and 59 and 54.8% of men aged 60 to 64 are in the labor force (see Exhibit 8.1). By the time men reach age 65 and older, only 16.6% are in the labor force. Labor force participation rates of older women also show a similar decline with age. Slightly more than half of all women aged 55 to 59 are working, yet only 8.4% of women over age 65 are employed. At all age groups 55 years and older, men are more likely than women to be employed.

Rates of labor force participation also vary between members of various ethnic groups. As shown in Exhibit 8.2, Hispanic men have higher rates of participation than do older white and black men. For men aged 60 to 64, 59% of Hispanic men, 56% of white men, and 47% of black men are employed. The same pattern emerges at age 70 to 74, with more Hispanic men

136

Exhibit 8.2 **Labor Force Participation for Older Adults by Age, Sex, and Race (Percentage)**

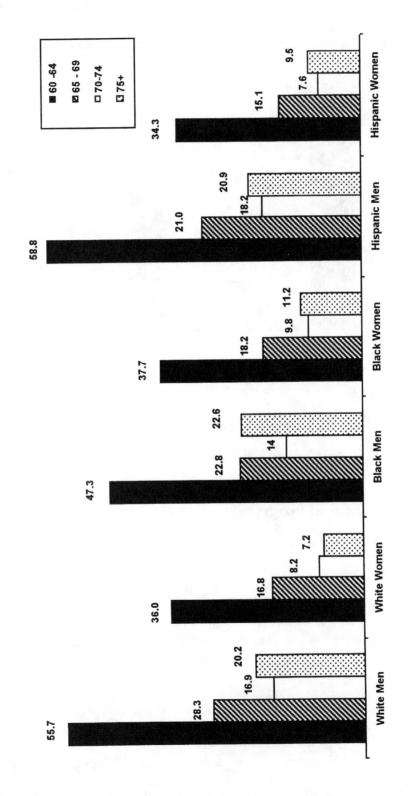

SOURCE: U.S. Bureau of the Census (1996a).

employed than either blacks or whites (18%, 14%, and 17%, respectively). A lower percentage of women at every age and in each ethnic group is employed compared with older men. Among older women, a higher percentage of black women than of white or Hispanic women is employed. At age 60 to 64, 38% of black women, 36% of white women and 34% of Hispanic women are employed.

There are two exceptions to the decline of older workers gainfully employed with advancing years (Achenbaum & Morrison, 1993). There is a shift among married couples from two-worker to single-worker units, with the wife assuming a greater share of work responsibility outside the home as her husband leaves the labor force. The second exception is the slight increase at age 73 in the numbers of male pensioners employed in full-time jobs year-round. This is most likely a result of the elimination of the Social Security earnings test at age 72.

According to the U.S. House Select Committee on Aging (1992c), older males (age 65+) represent a larger percentage of workers than other male workers in sales occupations, service occupations, farming, forestry, and fishing. Service occupations account for the largest share of older women workers; administrative support jobs (principally clerical jobs) had the second largest share of older women workers. A relatively large share of older blacks, Hispanics, and Asians also work in service occupations. These minority groups are underrepresented compared with their white counterparts in the relatively well-paid executive, administrative, and managerial occupations and the professional specialty occupations.

Of the 2.9 million older adults working in 1990, less than half were on full-time schedules (U.S. Bureau of the Census, 1992). Approximately 46% of men and 59% of women age 65 years of age and older work part-time (less than 35 hours per week). They work in jobs with lower wages than what they received at their longest job before the receipt of Social Security benefits (U.S. House Select Committee on Aging, 1992c). Compared with younger workers, more older workers are self-employed. Of nonagricultural workers, 24% of men and 14% of women are over the age of 65 (Quinn, Burkhauser, & Myers, 1990).

The availability of unearned income, particularly the availability of pension income, is a key factor in determining whether older individuals continue working after receipt of Social Security benefits. Older adults without pensions are two to three times more likely to continue working than those with pensions (Iams, 1987). Of the 36,000 readers of *Modern Maturity* who completed a survey published in the magazine in 1988, 18% reported having a second career (Bird, 1992). Of these individuals, 52% were male, 62% were married or living with a partner, and 85% were between the ages of 55 and 74. Of all respondents, 41% worked full-time, 47% were employed part-time, and 11% worked part of the year. The types of jobs the respondents held varied, with business services (e.g., office workers, environmental maintenance, and repair; 13%) and the "money business" (e.g., financial managers, bookkeepers, stockbrokers, and business consultants; 12%) the most commonly reported job fields. Most of the respondents (71%) earned less than $20,000 per year at their second career. The most common reasons these individuals reported for continuing to work were money (38%), enjoyment of work (18%), and desire to keep busy (17%).

Compared with the unemployment rate for all other age groups of workers, older workers have the lowest unemployment rate. For workers aged 55 to 64, the unemployment rate is about 3.3%; for workers 65 and older it is 3.0%. Once older workers become unemployed, however, they experience a longer spell of unemployment than do other workers. In 1990, individuals 55 to 64 years old were unemployed an average of 18.5 weeks, and those 65 and older were unemployed an average of 17.6 weeks, compared with 12.1 weeks for all workers 16 and older (U.S. House Select Committee on Aging, 1992c). Approximately 2% of older persons not in the labor force indicate that they would like to be working. The most common reasons for not working were illness or disability, the belief that they could not get jobs, and home responsibilities.

Employers of Older Workers

Federal Employment and Training Programs

Government programs provide the majority of employment and training programs for older persons. Green Thumb is the United States' oldest and largest operator of employment and training programs for older Americans. It was founded in 1965 as part of President Johnson's War on Poverty by the National Farmers Union. Originally designed to put older, rural Americans to work to beautify the nation's parks and highways, the Green Thumb program began with 280 participants in four states. By 1994, it provided employment, training, and service opportunities to more than 26,000 older Americans in 44 states and Puerto Rico (Green Thumb, Inc., 1995).

Participants in the Green Thumb program must (a) be 55 years of age or older; (b) have annual family income of not more than 125% of the established federal poverty income guidelines; (c) establish residency in the state in which they enroll in the Green Thumb program; and (d) be eligible to work in the United States. Through Green Thumb, participants receive training, experience at an approved government or private nonprofit agency (i.e., the host agency), educational opportunities, counseling, and information that help them find and keep a job. Participants average 20 hours per week

For Your Files   **AgeWorks!**

The National Council on the Aging has developed a World Wide Web site—AgeWorks!—that is devoted to employment and training issues for middle-aged and older adults. The Web site provides links to the National Council on the Aging's workforce resources, such as *America's Job Bank* (sponsored by the U.S. Department of Labor) and the Senior Community Service Employment Program (SCSEP). The site provides success stories of older adults who have entered or returned to the workforce. One success story is about a 68-year-old widow who had never worked outside the home and was frightened at the thought of finding employment. The SCSEP found her a job working 20 hours a week as an elementary school aide. Two years later, she had her driver's license and was attending a data processing class. Visitors can access AgeWorks! at

http://www.ageworks.org

of community service work at their host agencies and may not work more than 1,300 hours per year. They receive either the federal or state minimum wage, whichever is higher in the state in which they live. Employers of Green Thumb workers include schools, hospitals, housing facilities, public works and transportation, social services, and nutrition programs.

In 1969, Congress funded a demonstration project to promote useful part-time opportunities in community service activities for unemployed low-income older adults. The success of this project resulted in statutory financing in 1973 for the Senior Community Service Employment Program (SCSEP). In 1978, this program became Title V of the Older Americans Act. Although the Department of Labor manages the SCSEP, it allocates the majority of funds to 10 national organizations: AARP; Asociación Nacional Pro Personas Mayores; Green Thumb, Inc.; National Caucus and Center on Black Aged; National Council of Senior Citizens; National Council on the Aging; National Indian Council on Aging; National Asian Pacific Center on Aging; National Urban League; and U.S. Department of Agriculture, Forest Service. The governors of each state receive the remaining funds to operate the SCSEP. The governors decide which state agency in government has the authority for program management and oversight. In most states, the state unit on aging has this responsibility (Alegria, 1992).

SCSEP programs provide subsidized minimum wage jobs in community service positions in public and nonprofit organizational settings for persons aged 55 and older whose incomes are no more than 125% of the poverty level. Senior participants work 20 hours a week for the minimum wage and minimal benefits. The goal is to ultimately place these individuals in unsubsidized employment. Nationally, the placement rate is about 22%; this figure, however, varies widely by sponsor, with AARP projects achieving the highest placement levels (Freedman, 1994).

Although regulations allow contractors to provide training to participants, they devote few financial resources to this activity. Most of the efforts go into creating community jobs for participants and matching participants with existing jobs (Schultz, 1992). SCSEP workers provide whatever services are needed locally. Programs deliver two thirds of their services to the general community; the remaining services assist the older population in the community. The largest service categories are social services and education. Most participants are women (71%) and white (61%). Approximately 17% of the participants are between the ages of 55 and 59, 20% are 60 to 64, 26% are 65 to 69, 19% are 70 to 74, and 13% are 75 years of age and older. Almost one half have at least a high school degree, and 19% have some college (Freedman, 1994).

A smaller workforce program authorized under Title V is the Section 502(e) experimental projects. The purpose of these projects is to ensure second-career training and the placement of eligible Title V participants into jobs in the private business sector. In contrast to the SCSEP program, 502(e) programs can pay participants more than federal minimum wage, can subsidize a greater number of hours per week, and offer greater flexibility in the income eligibility requirements for program participants. Enrollees may have incomes of up to 150% to 165% of the poverty level, compared with 125% for SCSEP. Unfortunately, there is no separate appropriation for 502(e) programs. Sponsors must divert part of their Title V funding to run these training-oriented programs. The only in-depth examination of the 502(e) project estimates that the number of experimental project participants was about 3% of the total SCSEP enrollment (Centaur Associates, 1986). Women constituted about 70% of program enrollees. Most of these 502(e) placements were in the health, clerical, and services occupations.

The Job Training Partnership Act (JTPA) of 1982 is a comprehensive workforce development program with several programs that provide employment and training activities to persons 55 years of age and older. In general, JTPA provides basic educational and occupational skills training to persons who are economically disadvantaged and other persons with multiple barriers to employment (e.g., age discrimination) to prepare them for employment and economic self-sufficiency (Hale, 1990). Title II-A, the 3% Set-Aside program, provides funding specifically for older adults (age 55+) with low income (i.e., no more than 100% of the poverty guidelines or 70% of the lower living standard income level). These programs provide training for placement of older individuals in employment opportunities with private business concerns. Program data from the U.S. Department of Labor indicate that during program year 1989-1990, JTPA served approximately 32,092 older individuals. Approximately 66% of the states administer Title II-A 3% Set-Aside program through the state JTPA office. In 20% of the states, the state unit on aging administers the program. Most states have enacted a variety of cooperative ventures (e.g., job fairs, training sessions, special recognition events, and media events) between JTPA programs, Title V SCSEP programs, and other organizations such as vocational rehabilitation services and area agencies on aging (Alegria, 1992).

Older adults also may receive training through Title III of JTPA, which provides monies for training, placement, and other assistance to dislocated workers. The law extends eligibility to individuals who meet other criteria, including long-term unemployed persons who have limited opportunities for employment or reemployment in the area in which such individuals reside. This category includes older individuals who may have substantial barriers to employment because of age (Alegria, 1992).

Another federally funded program, involving more than 1,000 seniors nationally, is the Senior Employment Program (Ropes, 1991). Workers, age 55 and older, receive between $7 and $12 per hour in full- and part-time positions to do a wide range of environmental tasks, such as surveying schools for asbestos or working as ombudsmen for small businesses affected by Environmental Protection Agency (EPA) regulations. There are no income eligibility limitations for participation. Participants' backgrounds vary, from blue-collar trades to executives. Senior Employment Program workers can be found in practically every EPA branch in Washington, D.C., and in regional offices and laboratories throughout the United States.

Private Sector Employers

The findings from a national study of private sector firms in the United States suggests that as a group, older workers are part of alternative labor pools of clerical, semiskilled, or unskilled workers (Hirshorn & Hoyer, 1994). Approximately 47% of firms participating in the study with 20 or more employees had retiree employees in the company workforce. This proportion increased monotonically according to firm size; 45.5% of all firms with 20 to 249 employees had retiree workers, 64.2% of firms with 250 workers had retiree workers, and 73.5% of companies with at least 1,000 workers employed retiree workers. Companies hired some of these individuals mainly because they held certain needed job- and task-related qualifications that conform to the bottom-line needs of the organization. Unfortunately, many positions filled by older workers are low-wage and temporary.

A random sample of human resource decision makers representing 400 firms revealed generally positive attitudes toward older workers (AARP, 1989). Respondents rated older workers high in attendance and punctuality, commitment to quality, loyalty and dedication to the company, practical knowledge, and emotional stability. They rated older workers lower, however, in feeling comfortable with new technologies and their willingness to be flexible about doing different tasks. These stereotypes held by organizations have a direct and often adverse image on managerial behavior toward and willingness to advance older employees (Hale, 1990).

Some employers provide training and retraining opportunities for their older workers to avoid the expense and time of recruiting additional skilled personnel, to prevent skill obsolescence, to prevent workers from becoming outmoded, and to train new entrants into their workplace (Hale, 1990). Several companies have made special efforts to hire and train older workers. For example, Days Inn of America began hiring adults 50 years of age and older as reservation agents in 1986. They trained these workers to operate demanding computer software. Compared with their younger counterparts, the older workers acquired these new skills within the same time, stayed on the job longer, and generated more revenues for the company by booking more reservations (McNaught & Barth, 1992).

Job banks for retirees are also gaining in popularity. They consist of temporary pools, consultants on an on-call or project-specific basis, and in-house pools of retirees. Executives from 28 corporations reported that with few exceptions, their job banks were small programs informally managed within the human resources departments (Axel, 1989). Job banks are most prevalent in labor- and paper-intensive firms (e.g., banks and insurance companies) and in some manufacturing settings in which employers want their skills for technical and production jobs.

Challenges for Older Worker and Employment Programs

Society is redefining the meaning of work and retirement. It is not uncommon for workers of today to pursue multiple careers throughout their lifetimes. Frequently, older workers who pursued one lifelong career retire from it only to continue working in another field or in their primary field while receiving some retirement income (U.S. Department of Labor, 1994). In addition, given the changing demographics of society, there will be more older workers, as well as a greater need for them. We end this chapter by examining several challenges facing older worker and employment programs as they address the changing needs and values of an aging workforce.

For Your Files   ***Working Age***

The American Association of Retired Persons publishes a bimonthly newsletter about the changing workforce called *Working Age*. This newsletter is sent at no cost to businesses and organizations interested in employment issues that affect middle-aged and older persons. Each edition offers readers information about older workers, hiring issues, preretirement planning, and laws affecting older workers, such as the Americans With Disabilities Act (1990).

To receive *Working Age*, send a request on your organization's letterhead to *Working Age*, Worker Equity Department, 601 E Street NW, Washington, DC 20049, 202-434-2277.

Best Practice   **Senior Employment Program**

In October 1987, the De Kalb County Foundation for Aging started its own small business, named Seniors Sock-It-To-You. Older workers pair socks according to size, color, and quality—packaging approximately 50,000 pairs per week. The idea for this project began when the De Kalb County Foundation for Aging began to search for an independent long-term funding source because the local county commission, as a result of major financial problems, would be cutting the funds that historically supported the foundation's program. This creative project evolved when the foundation turned to its most obvious resource—socks! De Kalb County, home of Fort Wayne, Indiana, produces more socks than any other part of the world. Many older workers have spent a lifetime working in the hosiery mills but must leave when they can no longer keep up with the intense pace of production demands. The sock program has given productive employment to many seniors, increased their sense of well-being, and heightened self-esteem. Besides providing gainful employment to many seniors, this program has generated long-term supplemental funding for the foundation's aging programs. The nutrition program in De Kalb County is largely supported by revenue from the sock program. The foundation built a $500,000 senior center that also houses the sock-pairing operation.

For more information about this model employment program, contact De Kalb County Foundation for Aging, 600 Tyler Ave. SE, Fort Wayne, IN 46808, 205-845-8590.

Preparing for Retirement

Teaching men and women about finances and other retirement issues should begin early in their work careers. This introduction to retirement issues serves two purposes: consciousness-raising and information dissemination (Richardson, 1993). Personnel offices, training offices, and employee counseling services within organizations should provide workers with adequate information concerning financial options for retirement because many individuals are unaware of or do not fully understand their retirement benefits. This may be a particular concern for women and low-income individuals, who, because of financial concerns, may not even consider retirement as an option or have exacerbated fears about retirement (Rayman, Allshouse, & Allen, 1993; Stentzel & Steenland, 1987).

Several private organizations are testing models of flexible retirement options. These programs help upcoming retirees make an easier transition from work to retirement; companies view such programs as a cost-effective means to solving their labor shortages. For example, Polaroid allows workers to take a leave to test out retirement plans. They receive up to 6 months of unpaid leave to decide whether they want to retire; if not, they may return to work without penalty (U.S. Department of Labor, 1994). Other companies offer cafeteria-like options for older workers on a preretirement basis, such as part-time work, flextime, and vacation-work combinations. Another approach used by some companies is internal job redesign that allows for work schedule adjustments based on demographic and lifestyle changes as employees age (Mitchell, 1993). Both preretirement planning and flexible retirement plans stand to benefit both the employer and the employee by providing adequate time to prepare for the transition from work to retirement.

Addressing the Impact of Early Retirement

The trend toward early retirement continues in the United States. Many employers have encouraged early retirements through pension incentives and early retirement incentive programs. These programs can either penalize workers for remaining on the job or offer them financial incentives to encourage early retirement. For example, many workers find that remaining employed after a certain number of years on the job can cause a reduction in pension benefits (Kotlikoff & Wise, 1989). Using a different strategy to encourage early retirement, many large corporations offer workers (usually around age 50), a lump-sum cash payment equal to 6 months to 1 year's salary or additional pension credits if workers opt for early retirement (Kart, 1997).

In contrast, federal policy makes early retirement less attractive and later retirement more attractive to retain more older workers in the labor force longer. For example, the Social Security amendments of 1983 phase in a later normal retirement age from age 65 to age 67 beginning in 2000 and concluding in 2022. The 1986 amendments to the Age Discrimination in Employment Act of 1967 prohibit most employers from setting a mandatory retirement age. Beginning in 1990, the delayed retirement credit for persons working past normal retirement age began gradually increasing from 3% per year to 8% per year in 2008. Also, Congress also changed the Old Age and Survivor Insurance earnings test so that effective in 1990, persons between the ages of 65 and 69 receiving income in excess of exempt amounts now have their Social Security benefits reduced $1 for every $3 earned, rather than the previous $1 for every $2 earned. Thus, because the private sector encourages early retirement and Social Security encourages continued employment, older workers can be negatively affected by contradictory retirement policies.

Increasing Enrollments in Job Training Programs

Eligibility requirements limit the number of midlife and older persons who take part in SCSEP and JTPA programs. The inclusion of Social Security benefits and/or Title V income in calculating income eligibility for JTPA enrollment leads to the ineligibility of many older worker applicants. Beginning in 1995, states may request a waiver that allows for excluding 25% of Social Security when making eligibility calculations. Less than 1% of eligible older adults participate in the SCSEP and JTPA, however (Miranda, 1988). Program administrators at the state and local levels need to start a more aggressive awareness campaign to increase the number of older adults enrolled in this program.

Providing Opportunities for Older Workers

In both the public and private sectors, training is a key element in the successful integration of older workers in the labor force. The rapid introduction of new technologies and productive innovations requires a reorientation by employers and workers of all ages toward the concept of lifelong learning and skills upgrading. In addition, business must look beyond the "McJobs" opportunities for older workers (Hushbeck, 1990) and support the use of older workers to their full potential.

In rural areas, the agricultural economic base, low population density, and relative isolation from larger urban areas often limit the employment opportunities for older workers. The aging network needs to become more involved in offering and facilitating training programs that prepare older workers for the more limited employment opportunities in rural areas as well as helping them prepare for their retirement years.

Entry or reentry into the labor force may be difficult for some older women without recent job experience. These women may benefit from special programs designed to better integrate them into the labor force. One such program is the National Displaced Homemakers Network formed in 1981 to empower all displaced homemakers and help them in achieving economic self-sufficiency (Coles, 1991). Of displaced homemakers, 58% are age 65 or older. The network, composed of more than 1,100 local programs, agencies, and educational institutions, provides job readiness, counseling, outreach, training, job placement, and other vital services to these women.

Educating Employers

Stereotypes of aging still hold fast in the workplace. Older workers confront more restricted job opportunities than do otherwise identical younger workers. With the changes in demographics, greater awareness and understanding of older workers as resources are needed. Furthermore, employers need accurate information about the myths and realities of older workers. Many would probably be surprised to know that older workers have lower rates of absenteeism, experience less stress on the job, and remain productive workers.

Promoting Older Worker Programs in the Future

The 1995 White House Conference on Aging gave specific support for employment programs by passing a resolution supporting the expansion of training and employment opportunities for older workers. For example, the resolution supported policies that (a) provide financial incentives to industry and tax credits to individuals that reward the upgrading of worker skills and abilities, (b) ensure that older individuals are served by local, state, and federal employment and training programs at least in proportion to their numbers in the population, (c) create and maintain a national or statewide job hotline to refer older workers to the local job-finding agency in their area to assist them in their job search, and (d) develop incentives for employers to hire more older Americans—considering that 5 million Americans 55 years of age and older are capable and willing to work but are unable to find suitable jobs. In addition, delegates passed a resolution protecting the rights of older citizens and legal residents against discrimination. This included supporting policies that (a) require employers and labor unions to inform employees of their rights under ADEA and establish penalties for failure to do so; and (b) mandate, with adequate resources, the Equal Employment

Opportunity Commission's active prosecution of cases of alleged discrimination, and (c) interpret ADEA regulations to protect its intended beneficiaries sufficiently.

 ## CASE STUDY

BEGINNING THE JOURNEY TO FINANCIAL INDEPENDENCE AT MIDLIFE

Sally, a 58-year-old widow, has had no income for the last 6 months. She is unable to pay her rent and has had to move in with her sister. Before medical problems forced her to quit her job, Sally had been employed for 3 years at the local university clerking in the student bookstore. Her supervisor was complimentary about her organizational skills and how well she worked with the students and faculty. It was a pleasant job, although far from her original career goals. As a young woman, she had aspirations of becoming a chaplain or working in some aspect of the ministry, or at least in some type of helping profession. Marriage and family interrupted this dream. She left school one semester and a thesis shy of a Master of Divinity degree. During the past 30 years, a series of unfortunate events has left Sally with few resources. Other than her 3 uninterrupted years working in the student bookstore, her work history is spotty. Mostly, Sally fulfilled a traditional role as homemaker until her husband died 4 years ago. To keep in touch with her love of helping people, she volunteers at least 5 hours per week in the social ministries of her large church.

Sally and her husband had no children, and her sister is her only living relative. Although she appreciates her sister's kindness, she desperately wants to be independent. When she finally rebounded from her recent medical problems, Sally began looking for work. Sally has been searching for a job for 4 months with no promise of employment—at least employment that can support her. Sally is angry and frustrated. She is sure she is being discriminated against. She suspects that her age and being overweight are contributing to her lack of success. Overall, Sally's self-esteem at this point in her life is low, and she is running desperately short on financial resources.

CASE STUDY QUESTIONS

1. What protection does Sally have against discrimination? How realistic is it that these protections will alleviate her present situation?

2. On the basis of statistics of older workers, in what fields is Sally most likely to find employment? How do these jobs relate to her employment goals?

3. Sally could continue her job search on her own. Eventually, she might be successful. What other employment assistance might she explore? Do you believe she would qualify for these employment programs? Why?

4. Although Sally is classified as an older worker, how does her situation differ from an older worker 65 or 70 years of age? What impact does being female have on her situation, if any?

5. Which of the special employment programs for older workers described in the chapter would be most appropriate for Sally? Why? If you were the older worker employment specialist working with Sally, what would be your goals for her?

LEARNING ACTIVITIES

1. At what age would you like to retire? From what job do you see yourself retiring? How far up the career ladder will you have climbed? What will be your ending salary? What steps do you need to take throughout your adult life to achieve these goals?

2. Interview an employee counselor who deals with retirement planning. What information and training does the counselor provide? What types of employees (e.g., women, men, age, position) seek or attend retirement planning? When does the counselor recommend that employees start to plan for retirement? How much savings/pension should the average employee try to secure for retirement?

3. Plan your retirement. Will you take on a second career, travel, take classes—or do all? If planning a second career, describe what it would be and look in your local newspaper, employment agency, and senior job line to check on availability, pay, and requirements (experience and skills).

4. Interview someone who has retired from one career and has now embarked on another. How did the individual decide on the second career? How did the person find the position, learn skills, and so on? What is different about the second career compared with the previous one?

5. Interview an advocate, attorney, or someone who deals with age discrimination in employment. What type of cases has the person handled? How successful are people in fighting age discrimination? What type of positions or older adults seem more prone to age discrimination?

FOR MORE INFORMATION

National Resources

1. Green Thumb, Inc., 2000 North 14th Street, Suite 800, Arlington, VA 22201, 703-522-7272.

   Green Thumb empowers low-income older Americans who are 55 and older to remain productive and independent by providing them with employment and training opportunities.

2. U.S. Department of Labor, Office of Public Affairs, 200 Constitution Avenue NW, Room S1032, Washington, DC 20210, 202-219-8211.

   The Department of Labor is responsible for the Senior Community Service Employment Program for low-income older adults over age 55.

3. American Association of Retired Persons, 601 E Street NW, Washington, DC 20049, 202-434-2277.

   AARP is a nonprofit organization helping older adults maintain independence, dignity, and purpose. AARP has a number of publications about older workers and preretirement planning.

4. Equal Employment Opportunity Commission, 1801 L Street NW, Washington, DC 20507, 202-663-4900.

   The Equal Employment Opportunity Commission enforces the Age Discrimination in Employment Act and investigates age discrimination complaints.

Web Resources

1. America's Job Bank, U.S. Department of Labor
   http://www.ajb.dni.us

   This online listing links visitors to computerized network of 1,800 state employment offices and their active job listings. There are approximately 250,000 listed in America's Job Bank files. There is no cost to employers for posting their vacancies nor to job seekers.

2. National Council on the Aging's AgeWorks!
   http://www.ageworks.org

   AgeWorks! is devoted to employment and training issues affecting middle-aged and older workers. Web site visitors can link to the National Council on the Aging's workforce resources, other workforce-related sites, and the Senior Community Service Employment Program sites.

3. Urban Institute
http://www.urban.org/index.htm

The Urban Institute, a nonprofit policy research organization located in Washington, D.C., investigates the social and economic problems confronting the nation, including those facing older adults.

For updates on employment programs
and other employment resources, check out
Community Resource for Older Adults Web site at
http://www.hhs.unco.edu/geron.htm

9

Income Programs

Scott and Stacey are somewhat anxious as they wait for their appointment with a retirement planner. Like many couples in their mid-40s, they have not given serious thought to retirement. Most of their financial planning has centered on preparation for sending their two children to college. After hearing so much in the media lately about whether Social Security will be there for them when they retire, they are wondering if they are making the best plans for their own future. Unanswered questions for them at this time include these: Will Social Security be a retirement resource for them? Are they saving enough money and in the right way to supplement their Social Security? How do their work pensions fit into all this? What level of income will they need in retirement for quality of life? What sources of help could they turn to if something terrible and unforeseen happened to their income security?

The economic circumstances of older Americans have improved substantially during the past three decades, with average incomes and assets for persons over 65 rising dramatically. Median incomes for older adults have risen, whereas the share of older adults in poverty has dropped. As shown in Exhibit 9.1, the percentage of older adults living in poverty declined from 28.5% in 1966 to 11.4% in 1989. The decline in the percentage of older adults living in poverty coincides with the passage of public programs for income security (Moon & Ruggles, 1994).

Although the percentage of older adults who live in poverty has declined, the median income of older adults varies by age, gender, and ethnic group

Exhibit 9.1 **Poverty Rates for Older Adults: 1966 to 1989**

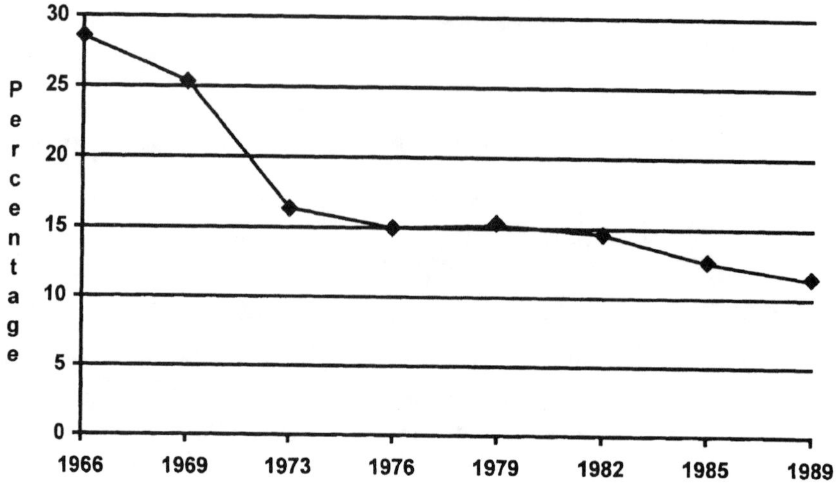

SOURCE: U.S. Bureau of the Census (1990b).

membership. People age 85 and older have significantly lower median incomes than their aged counterparts. In 1989, the median income of persons aged 65 to 74 was $10,821, $8,684 for persons aged 75 to 84, and $7,947 for persons 85 and older. In addition, there are significant income differences by gender and ethnic group membership. White older men have median incomes that are more than double those of black older men and are significantly higher than those of other older men of color as well as those of women of all subgroups (see Exhibit 9.2). Moreover, older men in all subgroups have higher median incomes than do their female counterparts. As a result of these income differences between older men and older women, older women and men of color are more likely to live at or near poverty level. The percentage of older women living in poverty in 1989 was 13.4% for white women, 36.1% for black women, and 26.6% for Hispanic women. Twenty-four percent of black older men and 19.6% of Hispanic older men had incomes below poverty level. In contrast, 6.6% of white older men had incomes below poverty level (U.S. Bureau of the Census, 1990b).

Thus, the differential income distributions among older women and older men result in greater reliance on income support programs. In this chapter, we provide the policy background for three primary income programs: Social Security, pensions, and Supplemental Security Income. We then describe the users of these programs and conclude with challenges facing income programs as the next century approaches.

Exhibit 9.2   **Median Income of Persons 65 Years and Older by Race and Sex (1989)**

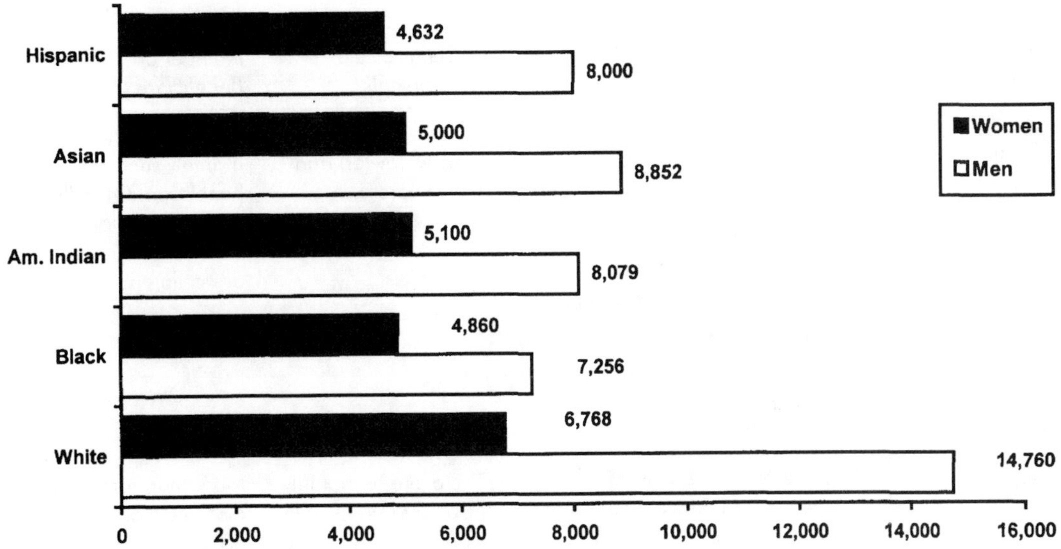

SOURCE: U.S. Bureau of the Census (1996a).

Policy Background

Social Security

The Social Security Act of 1935 established the basic old age benefits program and a federal-state system of unemployment insurance. In 1939, Congress added survivors' and dependents' benefits and, in 1956, expanded Social Security to include disability insurance to protect workers with severe disabilities. Although numerous adjustments have been made to the Social Security system since its inception, there have been few major programmatic changes (see Chapter 2 for details).

Exhibit 9.3 summarizes the various programs available under Social Security. To be eligible for retirement benefits under the Old Age, Survivor, and Disability Insurance (OASDI) program, a worker must have worked in covered employment for the required number of calendar quarters. Coverage is nearly universal for work done in the United States; it covers about 95% of all jobs. In 1996, about 142 million persons worked in employment or self-employment covered under the OASDI program (Social Security Administration, 1997b).

The three basic categories of benefits under Social Security are (a) retirement benefits, (b) disability benefits, and (c) dependents' and survivors'

Exhibit 9.3   **Benefits Provided Under Social Security**

Type of Benefit	Who Qualifies	Average Amount of Benefits Paid to Recipients	Number of Beneficiaries
Survivors Benefits	Children under 18 A child who is under 19 but still in high school A child who is 18 or older but who becomes disabled before age 22 A widow(er) who is caring for children under age 16 or disabled A widow(er) age 60 or older, or a widow(er) age 50 or older, who is disabled	$1,400 per month for a widow(er) and two children	Social Security pays monthly survivors' benefits to 7.4 million Americans, almost 2 million of whom are children.
Disability	Workers are considered disabled if they have a severe physical or mental condition that prevents them from working. The condition must be expected to last for at least 12 months or to result in death. Once benefits begin, they continue for as long as the worker is disabled and cannot work. The disabled worker and eligible family members receive checks each month.	The average monthly payment to a disabled worker is $680; for a disabled worker with a spouse and two or more children, the average payment is about $1,100. A worker who receives disability payments for two years becomes eligible for Medicare.	More than 4 million disabled workers under 65 and 1.7 million dependents (including more than a million children) receive Social Security.
Retirement	Full retirement benefits are now payable at age 65, with reduced benefits available as early as age 62. The age for full benefits will gradually rise in the next century, until it reaches age 67 in 2027 for people born in 1960 or later. Reduced benefits are still available at age 62.	Low: Wage earner $537; wage earner and spouse $805 Average: Wage earner $886; wage earner and spouse $1,329 High: Wage earner $1,248; wage earner and spouse $1,872	Social Security pays monthly retirement benefits to more than 30 million retired workers and their families. More than 9 of 10 Americans who are age 65 or older get Social Security benefits.

SOURCE: Social Security Administration (1997b).

NOTE: Of every dollar that goes to Social Security, 69 cents goes to a trust fund that pays retirement and survivors' benefits, 19 cents goes to a trust fund that pays Medicare benefits, and 12 cents goes to a trust fund that pays disability.

benefits. Once a worker qualifies for retirement benefits, he or she (and the survivors) first becomes eligible to claim early retirement benefits at age 62. To receive disability benefits, a worker must have a physical or mental impairment that prevents any substantial gainful work, and the disability is expected to last, or has lasted, 12 months or is expected to result in death (Matthews, 1992). To be eligible for dependents' and survivors' benefits, the worker has to have had enough credits to qualify for his or her own retirement or disability benefits.

Pension Benefits

The Civil Service Retirement Act was enacted in 1920, providing pension coverage for the first time to federal civilian employees (Schultz, 1995). A year later, the implementation of private, employer-sponsored pension plans was encouraged by the passage of the Revenue Act of 1921. This legislation exempted both the income of pension and profit-sharing trusts and the employer contributions to these plans from income taxation.

Through the years, serious problems (e.g., inadequate funds and misuse of funds) have undermined the worker protection provided under employer-sponsored programs. In response to the abuse and mismanagement in the private pension system, Congress enacted the Employee Retirement Income Security Act (ERISA) of 1974. It was the first comprehensive effort to regulate private pensions. The major objectives of this act are to (a) ensure that workers and beneficiaries receive adequate information about their employee benefit plans, (b) set standards of conduct for those managing employment benefit plans and plan funds, (c) determine that adequate funds are being set aside to pay promised pension benefits, (d) ensure that workers receive pension benefits after they have satisfied certain minimum requirements, and (e) safeguard pension benefits for workers whose employers end their pension plans (Coleman, 1989).

In 1990, more than 712,000 pension plans of all types in the United States covered 42 million workers (Employee Benefit Research Institute, 1994a; U.S. Department of Labor, 1994). Two primary types of pension plans are defined benefit and defined contribution plans (Barocas, 1994). *Defined benefit pension plans,* which cover the greatest number of workers, promise to pay a yearly pension benefit to workers who qualify on the basis of age and service. These plans provide retirees a steady income stream that commences with retirement and continues until that person's, or in some cases, the spouse's, death. In almost every defined benefit plan, the employer assumes the risk of making sure that adequate money is available to pay the promised benefit. *Defined contribution plans* specify employer and employee contributions but do not guarantee future benefits. Funds accumulate in an account, and the returns to the accumulated funds determine the retirement benefits. The employee is responsible for investing the contributions. The most common and frequently employed defined contribution arrangements are 401(k) plans.

Supplemental Security Income

Administered by the Social Security Administration, the SSI program provides income support to persons aged 65 and older and to children and adults who are blind or have a disability. Established in 1972, SSI replaced the federally aided state programs that had prevailed for several decades. Distribution of the first SSI payments occurred in January 1974. The program has not experienced any significant changes since its original legislation.

SSI acts as an important safety net for older adults receiving little or no Social Security benefits. Under this program, each eligible person living in his or her own household, having limited or no other income, and few assets, receives a monthly cash payment. Eligibility and federal payment standards are nationally uniform and strict. To receive SSI, a person must be aged or blind or have a disability and have assets (excluding a home, car, and personal belongings) of no more than $2,000 for an individual and $3,000 for a couple (Social Security Administration, 1996b). In addition, the recipient's monthly income (e.g., Social Security, pensions, bank account interest, and stock dividends) must not exceed the guidelines established by each state. Many recipients receive only partial SSI benefits because benefit levels are reduced by one dollar for each dollar of countable income. The maximum federal SSI benefit amounts to approximately 78% of the official poverty line for single older adults and 89% for older couples (Steuerle & Bakija, 1994).

Users and Programs

Social Security is an important source of income for many families and is the primary source of money income for older adults. As shown in Exhibit 9.4, retired workers (61%), widows and widowers (13%), disabled workers (10%), children (9%), and wives and husbands (7%) receive Social Security benefits under one of its programs. Nine of every 10 older adults receive income from Social Security. Moreover, for 13% of older adults, Social Security is their only source of income; almost one third of older adults depend on Social Security for 80% or more of their income. For unmarried older adults, 44% of their incomes comes from Social Security, compared with 34% for married older adults (Grad, 1990).

The monthly Social Security benefit amount a retired worker will receive depends on the worker's age and earning record. Nearly one half of all new

Exhibit 9.4 **Percentage and Number of Social Security Beneficiaries by Type of Benefit (September 1996)**

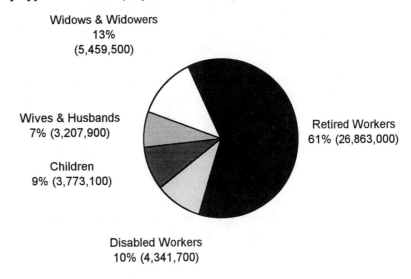

Widows & Widowers
13%
(5,459,500)

Wives & Husbands
7% (3,207,900)

Children
9% (3,773,100)

Retired Workers
61% (26,863,000)

Disabled Workers
10% (4,341,700)

SOURCE: Social Security Administration (1996a).

retired worker benefits are awarded at age 62, and more than two thirds are awarded before age 65. According to the Social Security Administration (1996a), the average monthly benefit for retired workers in 1996 was $723.00. Older male retirees received an average monthly benefit of $709.30, compared with $541.60 received by older female retirees.

Approximately 44% of couples and individuals aged 65 and older receive pension income, including both private and government employee pensions (Steuerle & Bakija, 1994). The proportion of retirees receiving pension income is greater in the middle- and higher-income brackets than the proportion in the low- to moderate-income brackets.

Approximately 9 million retirees receiving benefits from private pension plans and the majority of workers (62%) are covered by defined benefit plans. The mean income from private pensions in 1990 was $7,825 (U.S. Bureau of the Census, 1992); 66% of women and 41% of men, however, receive pension benefits under $3,000 per year (U.S. Department of Labor, 1989). Two thirds of pension recipients were men. A greater percentage of white older adults, compared with black or Hispanic older adults, received pensions. The overall mean pension incomes of white, black, and Hispanic retirees, however, are not significantly different from one another.

Approximately 2.2. million beneficiaries receive federal pension, survivor, and disability benefits, and 3.1 million former state and local workers receive pension benefits from plans sponsored by their government employ-ers (Schultz, 1992). The median benefit paid to retirees under state and local pension plans in 1990 was $7,200 (Phillips, 1992). In addition, approximately 1.6 million retirees and survivors receive military retirement benefits (U.S. Senate Special Committee on Aging, 1991b). The military retirement pro-gram, touted as the best pension in the United States, provides full benefits that begin immediately on retirement, requires no financial contribution from military personnel, pays at least 50% of basic pay to those with 20 years of service and 75% after 30 years of service, and does not subject benefits to an earnings test (Schultz, 1995).

Approximately 1.3 million older adults received SSI benefits (Social Se-curity Administration, 1996a). In 1996, the average monthly amount for an older beneficiary was $260; the maximum monthly SSI check was $470 for one person and $705 for a couple. Older women are more likely than are older men to receive SSI benefits. Black and Hispanic older adults are more likely to receive SSI than are their white counterparts.

Challenges for Income Programs

There is growing consensus among business, government, and academic experts that most Americans do not realize how much it costs to retire (Baro-cas, 1994). Younger workers think they have plenty of time to prepare for their retirement years and often do not take advantage of company-spon-sored retirement plans or savings initiatives. Midlife employees recognize the need to plan proactively for retirement but often view themselves as unable to save more. As a group, they appear conservative and do not understand much about such topics as budgeting, types of investments, risk, and the time value of money. Older employees tend to fall into one of two groups: those who have planned well and those who have not. Environmental, personal, and social circumstances prevent many older adults from having a financially secure retirement. We end this chapter by discussing some challenges facing income programs as the number and proportion of persons entering the retirement years grow.

Maintaining a Person's Standard of Living

Despite increased benefit levels, there is still a large gap for most workers between their Social Security benefits and the income needed to maintain living standards in retirement (Schultz, 1992). Experts often promote a "three-legged stool" model for financial preparation for retirement. Personal sav-ings, Social Security, and pension income represent the three components or "legs" of the retirement income stool (Barocas, 1994). As previously mentioned, Social Security benefits are a significant source of retirement income for many older adults; for millions of older adults, Social Security represents the only leg on their retirement stool. The challenge is to encourage broader pension coverage for low-wage workers and encourage financial planning for retirement.

Financial planning for retirement is a difficult and complex task. Both individuals and companies must invest more in preretirement planning as a means of helping employees take greater responsibility for their retirement income. The challenge for both the public and private sector is to (a) increase the availability of preretirement education for all individuals; (b) improve the quality of available programs by ensuring that programs assist employees in evaluating their current financial state, defining their personal goals, and identifying a financial game plan to make certain that the resources are available to achieve their personal goals; and (c) encourage people to begin preparing for retirement at an early age (Barocas, 1994; Schultz, 1992).

Enhancing the Income of Older Women

Studies have shown that women make substantially less than men in the labor market. This discriminatory pattern influences women's pensions, Social Security benefits, annuities, and bank savings. In addition, women who divorce or separate from their husbands may lose any resources developed during a marriage (e.g., rights to an ex-husband's pension and other financial assets). These women also may have discontinuous work careers that decrease their ability to achieve pension vesting rights and lower the wages on which retirement income is calculated (Richardson, 1990). To improve the income adequacy for women, policymakers must address the inequities of Social Security, particularly for working women, as well as inequities in private pension systems.

Increasing Participation in Income Programs

The federal government estimates that about 40% of older adults eligible for SSI do not participate in the program. Two key reasons appear to be lack of knowledge about it and the stigma associated with being involved with a means-tested program (Schultz, 1995). In recent years, the Social Security Administration has undertaken activities to increase awareness and participation in the program (e.g., public service announcements) but with little success. The National Commission on Social Security recommended eliminating the asset test to assist those living at or near the poverty line. Kochhar (1992) found that 16,000 aged applicants who were denied benefits because

For Your Files   **Retirement Income Planning on the Internet**

The Internet has emerged as one source of information about retirement income planning. For example, the American Express Company has developed a website that educates viewers on different retirement income options. Their webpage includes links to a brief history of retirement, information about 401K plans, and a glossary of terms. Included in the site are interactive pages that allow visitors to estimate their income needs upon retirement, what their rate of savings should be based on those income needs, and how much they will have to save to make up for earlier years when they did not save for retirement. There are no doubt other retirement income planning sites besides American Express on the Internet, so see what you can find. The American Express site is located at:

http://www.americanexpress.com/401k/other/sitemap.shtml

they were over the asset limit had assets with a mean value of $10,500. Unless there are major adjustments to the program, which has not changed significantly since its inception in 1972, participation rates of low-income older adults will remain modest.

The Long-Term Financing of Social Security

The Advisory Council on Social Security report to the Secretary of Health and Human Services in 1996 indicated no short-term financing problems with the OASDI program, but it did suggest that there were serious problems for the long-term funding of the program. In the past, efforts to deal with Social Security's financial difficulties have generally featured cutting benefits and raising tax rates on a pay-as-you-go basis. All council members agreed that this approach needs to change, but they were unable to agree on a single plan for dealing with the predicted financial difficulties. Three approaches were put forth. One group of members endorsed a *maintenance of benefits plan* that involves an increase in income taxes on Social Security benefits, a redirection of OASDI funds, coverage of newly hired state and local government workers not currently covered by Social Security, and a payroll tax increase in 2045. Other members support an *individual accounts plan* that creates individual accounts alongside the Social Security system that would involve an increase in taxation of benefits, state and local coverage, and an acceleration of the automatic increase in the age of eligibility for full benefits. The third plan, labeled the *personal security accounts plan,* creates even larger, fully funded individual accounts that would replace a portion of Social

Security. With each of these plans comes a different vision of the evolution of the U.S. retirement system. For more in-depth information about each plan, visit the Social Security Administration Web site (http://www.ssa.gov/ policy/adcouncil/findings.htm).

Maintaining and Enhancing Income Programs in the Future

The delegates to the 1995 White House Conference on Aging passed three resolutions specifically related to retirement income. The number one resolution from the delegates was keeping Social Security sound, now and for the future. For example, they supported policies that (a) maintain, strengthen, and preserve the program's current structure and purposes without means testing, with universal coverage, and with continued full protection against inflation; (b) preserve and ensure the continuing financial stability of the Social Security system for today's old and young generations; and (c) ensure that Congress or other elected officials do not use Social Security to reduce the budget deficit or balance the budget. In addition, conference delegates passed a resolution providing oversight and ensuring greater public and private pension coverage, solvency, portability, enforcement, and vestment. They pledged support of policies such as (a) preserving and strengthening traditional pension plans and devising new incentives for employers to provide them, while also creating portable retirement plans for all workers; (b) ensuring that all workers, including small business, seasonal, temporary, and other nontraditional employees, receive pensions that are adequate under defined benefit programs; and (c) improving and enforcing laws that prohibit discrimination based on gender, race, language, age, and disability, with regard to salaries, promotions, and pension benefits. Delegates also passed a resolution targeting Social Security and SSI benefits to frail older women. Under this resolution, delegates support policies that (a) amend the Social Security Act so that an individual's cash benefit level will not drop below the poverty level on reaching age 80; (b) direct the Social Security Administration to undertake an aggressive education and outreach effort to inform women of their rights and responsibilities regarding Social Security; and (c) raise the SSI benefit level to 120% of poverty.

In closing, obtaining financial security in later life will require that employment opportunities exist for older workers who wish to remain or reenter the workforce, that public and private pensions expand the number of workers covered, and that Social Security benefits continue to act as the third leg of the financial retirement stool. Perhaps the increase in the number of older adults who will be faced with retirement decisions in the next 5 years will facilitate a change in policy about work, retirement, and income security in retirement.

CASE STUDY

WHEN THE SYSTEM FAILS

Sonny, who is 66 years old, and his wife, Magdalena, who just had her 63rd birthday, never expected to find themselves so financially precarious and so frustrated with their own government at this point in their lives. When they were married 45 years ago, they had made so many plans. They were proud that their hard work had realized a modest retirement savings and that their three children were responsible, hardworking young adults. Sonny was especially proud of his service to his country during World War II.

Sonny retired at age 65 with a Social Security benefit of $1,000 per month and a union retirement benefit of $400 per month. Magdalena never worked outside the home. She had no credits toward Social Security and at age 63 is not eligible to draw an early Social Security retirement benefit on Sonny's credits of work or apply for Medicare. Nevertheless, their income had been adequate because their home and vehicles were paid for and they had no other outstanding debts.

Their retirement dreams began to fade as Magdalena's health deteriorated. Side effects from diabetes, diagnosed when Magdalena was 15 years old, have caused kidney failure. Magdalena is now receiving dialysis twice a month and spends part of her time in a wheelchair. She is also considered legally blind. The predicament for Sonny and Magdalena now is that the health plan that covered Magdalena's medical expenses expired because it had limited time coverage from Sonny's former employer, that Magdalena is not eligible for SSI because their income of $1,400 per month is too much to qualify, and that she cannot qualify for private insurance because of her preexisting condition. Although a Social Security regulation permits persons with dialysis to qualify for benefits including Medicare before age 65, Magdalena has twice been denied this benefit on the grounds that she is not disabled. Their savings have been completely depleted to pay for Magdalena's dialysis and other medical expenses. To their anger, shame, and frustration, Magdalena is receiving a 6-month limited health benefit from their state's medically indigent uninsurable program. At the end of the 6 months, they will still have another year of uncovered medical expenses before Magdalena can qualify for Social Security unless they can find some help to turn this situation around.

One day at the dialysis center, Magdalena was talking with the receptionist about not understanding why Social Security would refuse her application for early disability under the special dialysis rule. Why would Social Security not consider Magdalena disabled?

CASE STUDY QUESTIONS

1. Were Sonny and Magdalena justified in their frustration? Do they have the right to expect a source of income maintenance and health insurance coverage, given their situation?

2. Name as many help source agencies or programs that you can think of that Sonny and Magdalena might have contacted regarding this situation.

3. It is obvious that money is tight for this couple at this time. One human services professional might see the best course of help as putting Sonny and Magdalena in touch with a variety of charity programs that could help them with food, clothing, utilities, and free medical service. Another professional might see the best course to appeal their case to Social Security. Which professional would you be and why?

4. In what type of community human service environment does a dialysis center receptionist care and know where to refer a patient for help in a matter such as Magdalena's?

5. Often, in working with older adults, professionals speak of clients who "fall through the cracks." What do you think this expression means? Do you think Sonny and Magdalena fit this description? Why or why not?

6. What could have been a worst-case scenario for this couple? How typical do you think their situation is? What does it show about the importance of income maintenance programs for many older adults?

LEARNING ACTIVITIES

1. Put together a monthly budget that includes expenses such as rent or mortgage, food, utilities, medical expenses, entertainment, insurance, and other items that you believe necessary for a comfortable and satisfying lifestyle. What would you need currently to support yourself? Project your income needs to maintain that lifestyle at age 70. What changes may occur in your income needs? What is your plan to ensure that your income is sufficient?

2. Interview someone from your local Social Security office. With what issues does the office primarily deal in relation to income and benefits? Whom do the office staff see more—women or men? What are the clients' typical level of income? Do many of the recipients have alternative income sources? Does the office offer information on income planning for retirement? What counseling and information services does the office provide, and for what are beneficiaries most likely to ask?

3. Investigate retirement income plans. How accessible is the information (both in obtaining and understanding)? What places carry the information, and to whom is it targeted? Are there specific brochures for women, men, minorities, and income levels, and in languages other than English?

4. Talk to two older family members to find out what plans they have made for their income needs in their old age. Do they feel that their income is adequate? If you could, what suggestions would you make to them as to how they can plan for their income for retirement?

FOR MORE INFORMATION

National Resources

1. Social Security Administration, 6401 Security Blvd., Baltimore, MD 21235, 410-965-7700.

   The Social Security Administration is responsible for the administration of the Social Security and the SSI programs. Free publications are available.

2. Pension Rights Center, 918 16th Street, Suite 704, Washington, DC 20006, 202-296-3776.

   The Pension Rights Center works to protect the pension rights of workers, retirees, and their families. The center publishes handbooks and packets on pension law and retirement systems.

Web Resources

1. Social Security Online
   http://www.ssa.gov

   The Social Security Web site is one of the most comprehensive sites in the aging network. Visitors can request a copy of their earning record, browse information about the history and legislation on Social Security, access publications online, and review statistical information about benefits and beneficiaries.

2. Canada Pension Plan
   http://www.mb.hrdc-drhc.gc.ca/isp/retire.htm

   Check out Canada's retirement pension program and compare it with the U.S. Social Security program.

3. Benefits Link
   http://www.benefitslink.com/

   Benefits Link is a free nationwide link to information and services for employers sponsoring employee benefit plans, companies providing products and services for plans, and participating employees. There are links to new benefits information, public discussions of benefits design, Internet resources, and on-line benefits newsletters.

4. Center for Pension and Retirement Research at Miami University of Ohio

   The center sponsors an Internet discussion group on pensions and retirement. To subscribe to the list, send this e-mail message:
   To: lists@cs.muoshio.edu
   Subject: [leave blank]
   Message: subscribe pension.retire [first & last name]

5. U.S. Department of Labor
   http://www.dol.gov

   The U.S. Department of Labor's site has a number of resources, including a link that provides pension information.

> For updates on employment programs
> and other employment resources, check out the
> *Community Resources for Older Adults* Web site at
> http://www.hhs.unco.edu/geron.htm

10

Nutrition and Meal Programs

Ella wondered how often she had seen Vince make his way to the elevator at exactly 11:10 a.m. on Mondays, Wednesdays, and Fridays. Ella and Vince have lived next door to each other on the 12th floor of their senior high-rise for 10 years. She has watched Vince struggle to be independent despite his blindness. Vince probably would not admit it, but Ella knows that the noontime meals are more than just a social outing for Vince. This day as they were riding down on the elevator, they spoke of their new neighbor, Theo, who had just moved in across the hall. Theo's spouse had died 8 months ago, and they knew from their experiences that he must be lonely. They agreed to call on him after lunch and invite him to accompany them to the meal site on Friday.

The consumption of food is not only a biological necessity for health and vitality but also a social activity that is rich with symbolism. It is often an integral part of holiday gatherings and celebrations of all types. Although most of us are aware of the social nature of food consumption, we are only vaguely aware of the necessity of good nutritional habits. Good nutritional habits are important in all stages of life, but in later life, as individuals grow older, age-related changes in various body systems as well as in social relationships can place older adults at risk of inadequate nutritional intake. In this chapter, we review the extent of malnutrition and hunger among older adults, the physical and psychosocial factors that influence nutritional status in later life, the policies that support nutrition programs of older adults, the types of nutrition programs available, and the characteristics of those who use such programs.

Hunger and Malnutrition Among Older Adults

Evidence supports the notion that many older adults are at risk of poor nutritional intake, malnourishment, or hunger. A study conducted by Tufts University Center on Hunger, Poverty, and Nutrition Policy in 1990 found that approximately 3.27 million (10.5%) of adults 65 and older experienced hunger (cited in Benett, 1992). More recently, the Urban Institute (1993) conducted a national study that examined food deprivation among older adults. Researchers asked respondents whether (a) they got enough food and enough of what they wanted to eat, (b) whether food was always available and whether they had the resources to purchase food, (c) whether they skipped meals because they had no food, (d) whether they resorted to alternative action such as borrowing money to buy food, and (e) whether they had to choose between purchasing food and other necessities. The latter four questions were used to measure food insecurity. Researchers found that overall, almost 400,000 older adults reported that they sometimes or often did not have enough food to eat in the last month prior to the survey. Older adults with low incomes were twice as likely as those with high incomes to indicate that they did not get what they wanted to eat. With regard to food insecurity, 1.5 million older adults reported that they had experienced at least one of four indicators of food deprivation in the 6 months prior to the survey. Slightly less than half a million skipped meals in the past month because of lack of food or food resources. In addition, more than 600,000 had days in the 6 months prior to the survey on which they had no food or resources to purchase food. Older adults who reported that they had days with no food or food resources were asked what strategies they used to stretch their food supplies. Most reported that they bought or served less expensive meals (44%), served smaller meals (37%), borrowed money (30%), took money from savings (30%), or got food from a food bank or food pantry (20%). Many respondents had to make a decision between eating and paying for other necessities. Almost 800,000 had to make the choice between buying medicine and buying food in the 6 months prior to the survey.

Older adults who do not have adequate nutritional intake are at risk of negative physical outcomes. Researchers have found a link between inadequate nutritional intake and functional impairments such as reduced muscle mass and a compromised immune system (Arora & Rochester, 1982; Chandra, 1992). Furthermore, inappropriate diets may induce diseases such as coronary heart disease and a reduction in general well-being (Hamburg, Elliot, & Parron, 1982; Kannel, 1986).

Exhibit 10.1 **Factors Affecting Nutritional Status in Older Adults**

Physical

Cognitive status

Chronic and acute illness

Oral/dental health status

Chronic medication use

Dependence and disability

Psychosocial

Social support and isolation

Economic status

Ethnic status

Accessibility and availability of food programs

Advanced age

SOURCE: Adapted from Goodwin (1989); White, Ham, & Lipschitz (1991).

Physical and Psychosocial Factors That Influence Nutritional Status

A number of physical and psychosocial factors are thought to influence nutritional status (see Exhibit 10.1). For example, changes that older adults experience in taste, smell, and vision may inhibit their ability to enjoy food (Saxton & Etten, 1994). In addition, changes in the digestive system and the ability to chew may impair the digestion of food and make eating less enjoyable. Chronic conditions such as arthritis, orthopedic impairments, cataracts, and hypertension have been found to be negatively associated with poor nutritional intake (Dwyer, 1991). For example, those impairments that affect mobility, such as arthritis, can make shopping, preparing, and eating difficult. Individuals with cognitive impairments are at obvious risk of poor nutrition. Loss of memory, disorientation, and impaired judgment can reduce food intake (White, Ham, & Lipschitz, 1991). Because the use of medications, either over-the-counter or prescribed, is high among older adults, they are at risk of experiencing adverse drug-nutrient interactions. White et al. suggest that many drugs have adverse effects on appetite and cause the depletion of certain minerals.

Not only do physical changes make the task of eating more difficult, but changes in the social environment can have a detrimental affect on dietary patterns. Throughout people's lives, eating is an activity that we rarely do in isolation. It is a social activity associated with various rituals in our culture. Think about the food rituals in your family. Do you have a special place you like to go to eat when celebrating a birthday? Do you look forward to eating or cooking certain meals during the holidays? Are there special restaurants you enjoy? Chances are that these rituals are enjoyed with friends and family. And on those occasions when you are alone, you are probably less likely to cook and more likely to eat something of questionable nutritional value at a fast-food restaurant. Because eating is such a social activity, social isolation can result in negative changes in eating patterns. Indeed, researchers have found that living alone is associated with the lack of interest in preparing and consuming food and a less favorable dietary pattern (Davis, Randall, Forthofer, Lee, & Margen, 1985; Ryan & Bower, 1989). For example, in a national study of 4,402 adults aged 55 or older, Davis, Murphy, Neuhaus, and Lein (1990) found significant variations in living arrangement and dietary quality. Men living alone had poor-quality diets compared with men who were living with a spouse, and the percentage of men living alone with poor-quality diets increased with age. Among women aged 55 to 64, 22% of those living alone had poor-quality diets, compared with 14% of those living with a spouse. There was no significant difference in dietary quality and living arrangement for women aged 65 to 74 and 75 or more years. Overall, a higher percentage of women, regardless of their living arrangement or age, had poor-quality diets compared with men.

Included among those living alone are widowed older adults. Older adults who are widowed may be at risk of poor nutritional habits because of changes in income and social interaction patterns. Moreover, being responsible for new roles associated with meal preparation (e.g., shopping or cooking) for which they were not previously responsible can have negative dietary consequences. Although some evidence supports the relationship between living arrangement and dietary intake, other studies have found no relationship between living arrangement and nutrient intake (Green et al., 1993; Schafer & Keith, 1982). Such variations may suggest that simply measuring whether one lives alone does not adequately capture other factors that may be influencing nutritional intake, such as loneliness and number of social contacts. For example, Walker and Beauchene (1991) found a moderate relationship between loneliness and poor nutrient intake. Moreover, it may be appropriate to consider the length of time respondents have lived alone, which may reflect the degree of adjustment to altered eating patterns.

Income has an obvious effect on the quality and amount of nutritional intake. Posner (1979) points out that older adults with low income have less money to spend on food, thus reducing chances for an adequate diet. In addition, those living in poverty may not have accessibility to health care services needed to diagnose and treat diseases linked to poor nutritional status.

Rural older adults are also at risk of inadequate nutritional intake. This may be in part because rural older adults are more likely than their urban counterparts to have incomes below the poverty level, more health problems, and fewer social and health services (Rogers, 1991; Schwenk, 1992). Rural elders who were older, male, and black and had low incomes were more likely to have inadequate nutritional intake (Fischer, Crockett, Heller, & Skauge, 1991; Ralston & Cohen, 1994).

Older adults of color are also at risk of experiencing nutritional problems (Bartholomew, Young, Martin, & Hazuda, 1990). Although tremendous variations exist among and between ethnic groups in their history and cultural characteristics, they share some common sociodemographic characteristics that make them susceptible to poor nutritional intake. In general, black, Hispanic, and Native American older adults are more likely than their white counterparts to have incomes below the poverty line, lower levels of education, and poorer health status. According to U.S. Bureau of the Census (1996a), higher percentages of older blacks and Hispanics (25.2% and 25.3%) need assistance with everyday activities than do older whites (17.1%). These increased levels of functional impairment, low income, and education put older adults of color at an increased risk of malnutrition and unbalanced diets (Saxton & Etten, 1994). Moreover, language difficulties that exist among some older adults such as first-generation Asian Americans and Hispanics can act to isolate them from nutrition education and programs. Finally, Dwyer (1994) notes that nutrition education and programs that are insensitive to the cultural variations in diet may act as an obstacle to participation by older adults of color.

In response to the nutritional needs of older adults, a network of nutrition services and programs has been created. We describe these efforts in the following section.

Policy Background

Congress initiated nutrition programs for older adults with the passage of research and demonstration projects in 1968 under Title IV of the Older Americans Act. Four years later, Congress authorized the Nutrition Program for Older Americans as Title VII; the program, however, was not implemented until 1973 (U.S. Senate Special Committee on Aging, 1993). Congress reorganized the nutrition program in 1978 by placing it under Title III in the OAA.

The purpose of the nutrition program for older adults under the OAA is to provide nutritionally balanced meals and nutrition education, opportunities for social interaction, and other support services (U.S. Senate Special Committee on Aging, 1993). Specific federal goals for the program were

1. To provide persons aged 60 years and older and their spouses, regardless of age, particularly those with low income and minority individuals, with low-cost, nutritionally sound meals in strategically located centers . . . where they can obtain other social and rehabilitative services

2. To promote better health among the older segment of the population through improved nutrition

3. To reduce the social isolation of old age

4. To offer older Americans an opportunity to live out their remaining years in dignity (Posner, 1979, p. 58)

Under current OAA legislation, congregate meal programs are required to provide at least one hot meal 5 or more days a week in a congregate setting (except in rural areas and where it is deemed unfeasible); such programs may include nutrition education services. The act also authorizes home-delivered meal programs that deliver at least one hot, cold, frozen, dried, or supplement meal at least 5 days a week (except in rural areas and where it is not feasible). Each meal must provide a minimum of one third of the recommended daily allowances and be prepared with the advice of dietitians. Amendments in 1992 provided for a school-based nutrition program. Programs can use federal funds for meals and supportive services for older adults who volunteer in multigenerational school programs.

According to Senate reports (U.S. Senate Special Committee on Aging, 1993), 65% of Title III funds are for congregate and home-delivered meals. Appropriations for the nutrition program were $469,874,000 in fiscal year 1996. The program is also supplemented by participant donations, which represent 20% of program revenues (Ponza et al., 1996). The OAA also requires the U.S. Department of Agriculture to provide nutrition programs with high-protein foods, meat, and meat alternative commodities purchased by the department. Programs can opt to receive a cash payment in place of donated food (U.S. Senate Special Committee on Aging, 1993).

Food Stamp Program

The first U.S. food assistance programs were developed in the 1930s during the Depression when the government purchased surplus agricultural commodities and distributed them to the poor (Kuhn et al., 1996). In 1964, Congress established the Food Stamp program using coupons and, in 1971, enacted national eligibility standards, although the states still had a choice of food assistance programs. By 1974, however, the Food Stamp program became a nationwide mandatory program (Lipsky & Thibodeau, 1990). The goal of the Food Stamp program is to alleviate malnutrition among low-income families and individuals of all ages by providing food coupons that participants can use to buy a nutritionally adequate diet (Kuhn et al., 1996). To be eligible for food stamps, participants must meet income and asset guidelines. Older adults who receive SSI automatically meet the eligibility requirements for food stamps. According to the U.S. Senate Special Committee on

Aging (1993), older adults constitute 9% of food stamp recipients. Of these older food stamp recipients, 70% lived alone, and 80% of these individuals were single older women; almost 90% had liquid assets of $500 or less. In 1993, the average monthly food stamp amount for older recipients was $50, and approximately one fourth received the minimum benefit of $10. According to the Urban Institute (1993), two thirds of needy older people are not reached by federal food assistance programs, including food stamps.

Nutrition Screening Initiative

In response to the Surgeon General's report, *Healthy People 2000* (U.S. Department of Health and Human Services, 1990), which called for increased nutrition screening of older adults, the Nutrition Screening Initiative was conceived (Wellman, 1994). The goal of the Nutrition Screening Initiative is to promote routine nutritional screening and better nutrition care, especially among older adults. Groups such as the American Academy of Family Physicians, the American Dietetic Association, and the National Council on the Aging provide assistance with nutritional research and professional education.

The cornerstone of the Nutrition Screening Initiative project was the creation of a nutrition screening tool to be used by various professionals working with older adults. The screening tool called DETERMINE is designed to identify older adults who are at risk of poor nutritional health (see Exhibit 10.2). The screening tool asks simple questions about eating habits, illness and medication use, financial hardship, health status, and social contact. The checklist is the initial step in preventing, identifying, and correcting poor nutritional status of older adults. More than a million checklists have been distributed to laypersons and health care professionals nationwide in hopes that more older adults will be screened for nutritional deficiencies (Wellman, 1994).

In this next section, we discuss the various nutrition programs that have emerged from both the public and private sectors and provide a profile of nutrition program participants. We end this chapter with a discussion of the challenges facing nutrition programs.

Users and Programs

Nutrition programs for older adults, much like the continuum of care model discussed in Chapter 1, exist on a continuum based on functional status and socioeconomic need. Balsam and Osteraas (1987) developed the Continuum of Community Nutrition Services. As shown in Exhibit 10.3, older adult nutrition programs exist within a continuum of community nutrition programs and serve both independent and frail older adults. We explain the different nutrition programs that serve older adults in more detail below.

Exhibit 10.2

The Warning Signs of poor nutritional health are often overlooked. Use this checklist to find out if you or someone you know is at nutritional risk.

DETERMINE YOUR NUTRITIONAL HEALTH

Read the statements below. Circle the number in the yes column for those that apply to you or someone you know. For each yes answer, score the number in the box. Total your nutritional score.

	YES
I have an illness or condition that made me change the kind and/or amount of food I eat.	2
I eat fewer than 2 meals per day.	3
I eat few fruits or vegetables, or milk products.	2
I have 3 or more drinks of beer, liquor or wine almost every day.	2
I have tooth or mouth problems that make it hard for me to eat.	2
I don't always have enough money to buy the food I need.	4
I eat alone most of the time.	1
I take 3 or more different prescribed or over-the-counter drugs a day.	1
Without wanting to, I have lost or gained 10 pounds in the last 6 months.	2
I am not always physically able to shop, cook and/or feed myself.	2
TOTAL	

Total Your Nutritional Score. If it's —

0-2   **Good!** Recheck your nutritional score in 6 months.

3-5   **You are at moderate nutritional risk.** See what can be done to improve your eating habits and lifestyle. Your office on aging, senior nutrition program, senior citizens center or health department can help. Recheck your nutritional score in 3 months.

6 or more   **You are at high nutritional risk.** Bring this checklist the next time you see your doctor, dietitian or other qualified health or social service professional. Talk with them about any problems you may have. Ask for help to improve your nutritional health.

These materials developed and distributed by the Nutrition Screening Initiative, a project of:

AMERICAN ACADEMY OF FAMILY PHYSICIANS

THE AMERICAN DIETETIC ASSOCIATION

NATIONAL COUNCIL ON THE AGING, INC.

Remember that warning signs suggest risk, but do not represent diagnosis of any condition. Turn the page to learn more about the Warning Signs of poor nutritional health.

Reprinted with permission by the Nutrition Screening Initiative, a project of the American Academy of Family Physicians, the American Dietetic Association, and the National Council on the Aging, Inc., and funded in part by a grant from Ross Products Division, Abbott Laboratories.

Congregate Meal Sites

As previously mentioned, the OAA nutrition program under Title III-C provides funds to support congregate meal programs. The goals of congregate

Exhibit 10.3 **Continuum of Community Nutrition Services**

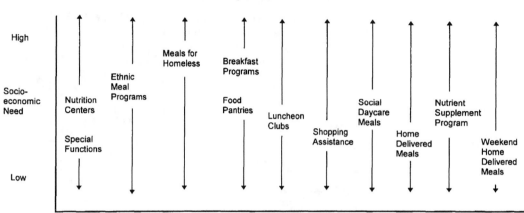

SOURCE: Adapted from "Instituting a Continuum of Community Nutrition Services: Massachusetts Elderly Nutrition Programs," by A. Balsam & G. Osteraas, 1987, *Journal of Nutrition for the Elderly,* 6(4), p. 58. Copyright © The Haworth Press. Used with Permission.

meal programs are to (a) provide low-cost meals to older adults, (b) encourage well-being through social interaction and maintenance of good health, and (c) provide nutrition information (Mullins, Cook, Mushel, Machin, & Georgas, 1993). Nutrition programs funded under the OAA are to target their services to isolated, low-income, and minority older persons. Individuals 60 years of age and older and their spouses can eat a nutritionally balanced hot meal for a suggested donation. Suggested donations range from $1 to $2; 94% of congregate meal participants and 73% of home-delivered meal participants make a contribution for their meal. Congregate meal sites are located in a variety of places, including senior centers, schools, churches, and restaurants. Meals might be prepared on site or prepared at a central kitchen and delivered to sites. All congregate meal programs serve lunch. Approximately 4% serve breakfast during the week, and 4% serve weekend meals. Almost half the programs offer modified meals to accommodate special diets. The older adults nutrition program funded by OAA dollars reaches millions of older adults. In 1994, congregate meal sites funded under the OAA provided 127 million meals to 2.3 million older persons; another 1.3 million meals were provided at 41,000 congregate sites, and 1.5 million meals were provided to 47,500 homebound older Native Americans through tribal organizations (Ponza et al., 1996).

Congregate meal programs also offer nutrition education programs, screening, and information about other community programs. Providing participants with information and referral services makes congregate meal

Best Practice **Meals on Wheels America**

Meals on Wheels America (MOWA) is a successful example of a public-private partnership that has raised nearly $12 million from private sources to deliver 3.5 million meals to thousands of homebound older adults since 1988. Its primary mandate was to show how the fund-raising ideas developed by New York City's Meals on Wheels program could be adapted for use by any meal delivery program. With funding from Joseph E. Seagram & Sons, Inc., and Bristol-Myers Products, MOWA began as a pilot project working with 20 home delivery meals programs nationwide. Each program received a matching grant and training in fund-raising techniques geared to generate private funding in its local area. Private funds that were raised would feed seniors on those days when home-delivered meals might not be available through public funding. Now there are 45 MOWA affiliate communities across the country. The technical assistance that MOWA provides has enabled all of them to meet the $5,000 first-year matching grant. The affiliates continue to be enterprising examples of public-private partnerships that make a positive difference in the lives of homebound seniors.

Just one of many creative local fund-raising examples promoted by a MOWA affiliate occurred in Los Angeles, California. In keeping with the Olympic Centennial, Meals on Wheels L.A. held a "Salute to Senior Olympians." Honoring 50 former Olympic medalists who were 60 years or older from the Los Angeles area, the luncheon attracted 350 guests and raised $20,000 for home-delivered meals. Other fund-raising successes include Atlanta's annual November "A Meal to Remember," which raises an astounding $200,000 plus annually.

One of the most visible and successful initiatives of MOWA began in 1988 when the first 20 MOWA communities launched the Thanksgiving Day Roll-Out that delivered 25,000 holiday dinners. The Thanksgiving Day Roll-Out continues to grow. In 1995, the 45 MOWA affiliates delivered more than 73,000 privately funded holiday meals. Local businesses become involved by donating tray favors such as flowers or "goodie bags." Elected officials and their families also deliver Thanksgiving meals.

The backing of corporate sponsors has been key to MOWA's achievements. The principal corporate founder and continuing national sponsor, Joseph E. Seagram & Sons, Inc., has donated funding and products. The company also has organized its employees into a volunteer army that works with MOWA affiliates by preparing and delivering meals, sitting on boards, and assisting with special events. Bristol-Myers Products, another MOWA founding funder, helped publicize the program and the needs of older Americans through two-cents-off coupon campaigns and by showcasing the program through media placements.

continued

MOWA has been so successful that the project now offers conferences for its national affiliates, a newsletter designed to share fund-raising information and ideas nationwide, a technical assistance guide given free of charge to each of the 670 area agencies on aging, and technical assistance memos featuring fund-raising "recipes."

For more information, contact Meals on Wheels America, 2 Lafayette Street, 7th Floor, New York, NY 10007, 212-964-5700, e-mail: Mowamerica@aol.com

SOURCE: "Meals on Wheels America" (1996).

programs an important link in coordinating and delivering nonnutrition programs to older adults.

Other congregate meal programs sponsored by nonprofit organizations such as the Salvation Army provide meals to low-income individuals and families of all ages. Unfortunately, the number of older adults who receive meals through these community congregate meal sites has not been documented.

Home-Delivered Meals

Home-delivered meals in most communities are provided by private nonprofit agencies and/or programs funded under the OAA. More than one home-delivered meal program may exist in any community and serve different target populations; Meals on Wheels is perhaps the most recognized home delivery meals program in the country. Eligibility to receive home-delivered meals varies by program. In general, however, individuals must have difficulty attending a congregate meal site or preparing meals. Programs receiving Title III dollars must serve individuals 60 years of age or older. Most programs have a suggested donation amount or a sliding fee scale based on income. Programs deliver one or more hot, chilled, or frozen meals directly to the recipient's home each day during the week. Many programs offer frozen meals for recipients to use during the weekend.

More recently, nutrition programs have begun offering medical nutrition therapy for older adults who are nutritionally at risk or malnourished. According to the National Policy and Resource Center on Nutrition and Aging (1996), the medical nutrition therapy process is designed to help older adults who are at risk of malnutrition obtain appropriate nutrition. On the basis of an assessment of the nutritional status of an at-risk older adult by a dietitian, a nutritional care plan is developed. The plan might recommend a change in daily diet or the incorporation of high-nutrient food into the diet. In addition, the food itself may need to be altered—chopped or pureed to help those who have difficulty chewing or swallowing. Nutritional supplements or liquid meals might also be needed to meet an individual's nutritional needs. Because of the increased cost of providing medical nutrition therapy, the funding for such programs comes from client fees, contributions, and private payers.

In addition to the nutritional value that home-delivered meal programs offer its participants, volunteers play an important role in meeting clients' social needs. Volunteers who deliver the meals are often the only source of social contact for meal recipients and, in some cases, help clients with grocery shopping or other errands. Because of the increase in the number of frail older persons, many home-delivered meals have waiting lists. Forty-one percent of home-delivered meal programs have waiting lists of persons needing home-delivered meals (Ponza, Ohls, & Millen, 1996).

According to the U.S. Senate Special Committee on Aging (1993), Title III funds provided 113 million home-delivered meals to 877,000 homebound older persons. One program, the San Francisco Meals on Wheels Program, delivers more than 1,500 meals to the homebound each day and has a waiting list of 275 individuals because of a shortage of volunteer drivers.

Food Banks

Many communities have created food banks that serve families and individuals with low incomes. Food banks distribute to qualified individuals government commodities or food that has been donated by private citizens, farmers, food manufacturers, grocery stores, and restaurants. The Emergency Food Assistance Program, administered by the U.S. Department of Agriculture, distributes to low-income individuals food such as butter, flour, cornmeal, green beans, tomatoes, beef, and pork. In 1991, the program donated 412 million pounds of food (U.S. House Select Committee on Aging, 1992b).

Another way communities have gathered surplus food to distribute to low-income individuals is to harvest unusable produce left after a commercial harvest. These "gleaning projects" have played an important role in preventing hunger in their communities. For example, the Gleaning Project sponsored by the Washington State University Cooperative Extension Program trains volunteers from low-income families to harvest unusable produce left in farmers' fields. Families are able to keep what they need, and the rest is distributed to food banks and hot meal sites. In 1995, the Gleaning Project harvested 300,000 pounds of produce, with 80% of the produce given to food banks and meal sites and the remainder going to low-income gleaners' families.

For Your Files   **Second Harvest Food Bank**

The Second Harvest Food Bank is the main provider of donated food to persons who are hungry in northern California. Its service area stretches from Gilroy to South San Francisco and from the Bay to the Pacific. It supplies 390 charities and distribution sites with 16 million pounds of donated food. An average of 105,090 persons receive food from the food bank each month.

Second Harvest has a program called Second Helpings, which collects prepared and perishable food from caterers, hotels, hospitals, and corporate cafeterias. Its Partners in Need program gives low-income volunteers the opportunity to receive groceries while helping others. Second Harvest also provides nutrition and health education and operates a food assistance hotline that helps 110 families a day. More than 11,000 low-income older adults receive a bag of groceries each week through Operation Brown Bag.

For more information, contact Second Harvest Food Bank at 415-266-8866, or check out the Web site (www.secondharvestsjca.org).

Brown Bag Programs

Brown bag programs are also supplemental food programs for low-income seniors. Typically, low-income older adults can receive a grocery bag containing fresh or frozen produce, breads, and canned foods. Food for these programs comes from local grocery stores and private donations from food drives. Distribution sites, frequency of distribution, and eligibility guidelines vary by community and by program. Operation Brown Bag, sponsored by Second Harvest Food Bank, is the nation's largest private supplemental food program for low-income older adults. According to Second Harvest program data, each week more than 10,000 low-income older persons are given bags of groceries at 61 distribution centers. Another 1,000 homebound seniors have their bags delivered to them by volunteers.

Shopping Assistance Programs

As noted above, many older adults have difficulty grocery shopping. Chronic conditions make traveling to grocery stores and selecting and carrying groceries home problematic. Lack of private transportation makes shopping burdensome as well. No doubt many of the participants who receive home-delivered meals are in need of assistance in grocery shopping. Communities have responded by offering shopping assistance services that escort older adults to food markets or deliver groceries to their home. Volunteers, in conjunction with public transportation, often help with shopping assistance. Volunteers travel to the homes of older adults, escort them to the grocery store, assist them in shopping, and return home. Grocery delivery programs allow older adults to call in their grocery order to be filled and delivered by volunteers. A study that surveyed a random sample of nutrition programs across the country found that approximately 43% of meal programs for older adults provide escort shopping services and that 15% offer grocery delivery services (Balsam & Rogers, 1988).

Users of Meal Programs

Who attends meal programs? Do these programs serve the most needy among the older population? To answer these questions, researchers have conducted studies to identify participant characteristics and benefits of attending meal programs on both the local and national level. In the last 20 years, two national studies have investigated congregate meal program participants and outcomes. One of those studies was the longitudinal study of the OAA nutrition program outcomes initiated in 1978 (U.S. Department of Health, Education, and Welfare, 1979). The purpose of the evaluation was to assess program impacts on participants and identify program characteristics and other factors that influence participant outcomes. Researchers collected information from a random sample of 91 meal sites and conducted interviews with program staff and representatives from related organizations. In addition, a sample of nutrition program participants was compared with a sample of nonparticipants. The evaluation gathered specific information about dietary and health status, isolation, life satisfaction, longevity, and independent living. Results revealed that the majority of participants had incomes below the poverty level and that one quarter of the participants were minority older adults. Participants had higher rates of social activity compared with the sample of nonparticipants. The majority attended once a week or more, and the more frequent attendees were long-term participants who were poor, more than 75 years of age, in poor health, living alone, and ethnic minorities. In the final report, Kirschner Associates (1983) concluded that the attendance did increase the nutrient intake of participants; participants also ranked the benefits of social interaction greater than the benefits of the meals.

Almost 15 years later, another comprehensive 2-year evaluation of the older adult nutrition program was undertaken. The purposes of the study were to evaluate the program's effect on participants' nutrition and socialization compared with similar nonparticipants; to evaluate who uses the program and how effectively the program serves targeted groups in most need of its services; to assess how efficiently and effectively the program is administered and delivers services; and to clarify funding sources and allocation of funds among program components (Ponza et al., 1996). Data were collected from 55 SUAs, 350 AAAs, 100 Indian tribal organizations, a representative sample of 200 nutrition projects, a nationally representative sample of 1,200 congregate meal participants and 800 home-delivered meal participants, and personal interviews of a nationally representative sample of 600 nonparticipants eligible for the congregate meal program and 400 nonparticipants eligible for the home-delivered meal program.

Ponza et al. (1996) found that participants were more disadvantaged regarding income, living arrangement, and physical health than was the older adult population in general. For example, between 80% and 90% of participants had incomes that were 200% below poverty level—a rate that is two times higher than that of the overall U.S. older adult population. Moreover, more participants were living alone (60%) compared with the overall older population (25%). With regard to physical health, participants typically had two chronic health conditions, and almost a quarter reported difficulty doing one or more everyday tasks. Racial and ethnic minorities accounted for 27% of congregate meal participants. Researchers also evaluated specific outcomes of improved nutritional status and increased social contacts. Researchers found that the nutrition program significantly influenced participants' overall nutritional intake. On a daily basis, participants had higher percentages of recommended daily allowances than did nonparticipants, and overall dietary intakes were better than those of nonparticipants as well. Results indicated that when compared with nonparticipants, participants had, on average, more social contacts per month. Overall, the results indicate that nutrition programs are accomplishing the mission of improving the dietary and social well-being of an at-risk population.

Researchers conducting studies of local older adult nutrition programs report similar outcomes, with some variation of the ethnic makeup of participants. In a study of the Boston area congregate meal program participants (n = 174), Posner (1979) found that the majority of participants were white (93%), female (69%), and widowed (44%). The average age of participants was 73 years, and most were living alone. One fifth had incomes below the poverty level; 44% had incomes that were at or below 125% of the poverty level. Respondents were asked to identify what they thought was the program's value. The opportunity for a nutritious meal and socialization were the two top reasons given by respondents for attending the meal program. Participants indicated that they realized financial as well as food-purchasing benefits (31% and 50%, respectively). That is, their participation in the nutrition program helped reduce the amount of food they bought. Significantly more older adults who lived alone realized these benefits. More than half the respondents indicated that attending the program had a positive impact on the social aspects of their lives. This included meeting more people and socializing more with peers (26%), reduced loneliness and improved morale (22%), and increased social activities outside their homes (22%). Finally, 47% of participants indicated that they engaged in social activities outside the meal program with peers they met at the site for the first time.

Similarly, in their study of 888 congregate meal participants, Mullins et al. (1993) found that the majority of participants were female (70%), white (65%), widowed (47%), and living alone (51%). A surprising number had relatively few associations with children, grandchildren, and siblings and had fewer close relationships than did respondents who received home-delivered meals. Moreover, more than one quarter (26%) reported levels of loneliness greater than the median. Half the congregate meal participants rated their health as either fair or poor, and 66% indicated that they had a health problem that affected their daily activities. Many of the participants also indicated that their economic condition was problematic; more than half (54%) reported that not having enough money to live on was a somewhat or very serious problem. Respondents were also asked if they felt healthier because of their participation in the nutrition program. More than three quarters of congregate meal participants indicated that attending the program was related to feeling healthier and making more friends.

Another study investigated the social and nutritional outcomes of a random sample of participants ($n = 140$) at 13 rural areas and 8 urban congregate meal sites in Colorado (Wacker, 1992). The majority of respondents were female (83%), and 43% were widowed. Slightly more than half the respondents reported their health status was good (52%), and 31% indicated their health was fair. Most had a high school education (47%), whereas 29% reported having less than a high school education. Reflecting data from national studies showing that meal programs primarily serve those with low incomes, many of the study participants reported a similar financial picture. When asked about their financial well-being, 32% said they had just enough income to make ends meet; 47% indicated that they had enough to make ends meet, with a little extra left over sometimes. A significant majority of respondents had been attending the program for 3 or more years and attended at least once per week. When participants were asked why they attended the program, the most popular reasons given were socializing with others (84%), getting an affordable meal (75%), and liking the food being served (72%). In addition, 75% indicated that the meal program was an important part of their diet. Of those who indicated that they had changed their health habits (e.g., reduced amount of fat and sodium in their diets), 17% said that the nutrition education presented at the meal program influenced them to change.

Examinations of users of home-delivered meal programs have shown that recipients have more physical limitations, are more socially isolated, and have lower incomes than those who attend congregate meal programs (AoA, 1983; Mullins et al. 1993). Ponza et al. (1996) found that about one half of home-delivered meal participants had incomes at or below poverty levels and that 63% rated their health as poor or only fair; 77% indicated that they had difficulty doing one or more everyday tasks. In addition, the majority of homebound older adults have poor diets compared with persons who attend congregate meal programs (Steele & Bryan, 1986; Stevens, Grivetti, & McDonald, 1992) and are at moderate to high nutritional risk (Ponza et al., 1996).

Challenges for Nutrition Programs

On the basis of empirical research during the last two decades evaluating the outcomes of nutrition programs, one can conclude that these programs are indeed successful. Programs funded under the OAA are serving older adults who are at risk of poor nutritional intake with meals that are critical to their daily food consumption. These programs also provide older individuals with social contacts that are beneficial for their psychological well-being. Despite these successes, meal programs for older adults face a number of critical issues.

Enhancing Awareness and Use of Nutrition Programs

Older adults who participate in nutrition programs derive nutritional and psychological benefits, yet many other older adults who also could benefit from attending do not participate. Peterson and Maiden (1991) explored the variables associated with awareness and use of congregate meal programs in a sample of 358 community-dwelling older adults. Those who were aware of the programs had more personal and social resources and less nutritional need. Those using nutrition programs, however, had fewer personal and social resources and greater nutritional need. Such research illustrates the need for more studies about the factors associated with awareness and use of programs to assist with outreach efforts.

On the basis of their 2-year evaluation of the senior nutrition program, Ponza et al. (1996) made the following recommendations for future directions of nutrition programs:

■ As the percentage of persons in the oldest-old category increases, the need for home-delivered meals may increase.

■ Programs must endeavor to better meet the specialized nutrition needs of its participants.

■ Changes in the delivery of health care will also have an impact on nutrition programs. As individuals continue to be discharged more quickly from hospitals and nursing homes, nutrition programs will be serving an even more frail and functionally impaired population than in the past.

■ There continue to be waiting lists at some nutrition sites for home-delivered and congregate meals, and high percentages of home and congregate meal participants continue to be nutritionally at risk. Programs will be challenged to serve the underserved population in an era of shrinking public and private dollars.

Serving a Diverse Older Population

Meal programs for older adults must be ever mindful of meeting the nutritional needs of an ethnically diverse population. Programs must ensure that the social atmosphere, as well as the meals, is welcoming to individuals of color by having culturally sensitive staff, preparing ethnic meals, offering culturally appropriate nutrition education materials, and obtaining input from minority participants (Briggs, 1992). Others have commented on the need to reach out to the most needy older persons. For example, Balsam and Rogers (1991) argue that outreach for nutrition programs must include older adults who are "socially impaired"—those who are socially isolated, are homeless, live in single room occupancy dwellings, suffer from substance abuse, or are deinstitutionalized. Because such persons might not be readily welcomed at congregate meal sites, programs targeted to older adults at the margins of society might be created (Doolin, 1985).

Funding Nutrition Programs

As always, the reliance on public money to fund nutrition programs runs the risk of cutbacks and perhaps elimination when fiscal budgets become tight. Alternative funding from businesses, civic organizations, and foundations will be sources of financial support that programs must tap to maintain and expand services (Balsam & Rogers, 1991).

Meal Programs for a New Generation of Older Adults

Finally, nutrition programs will have to change as the population ages and as cohorts with different needs and preferences replace the current participants. Because evidence indicates that nutrition and eating habits vary across age groups (Wurtman, Lieberman, Tsay, Nader, & Chew, 1988), the menus and meals offered through nutrition programs will no doubt need to accommodate those differences as well. Cappuccino, anyone?

CASE STUDY

GOOD NUTRITION: MAKING INDEPENDENCE POSSIBLE

Manuel, 75, is a shy bachelor who has lived with his mother all his adult life except 2 years when he was stationed overseas with the army. After his discharge, he returned home and worked as a cook for the local National Guard for 12 years. Everyone in town talked about the good old-fashioned food that Manuel prepared. When the local National Guard facility closed, Manuel became a self-employed janitor. He continued to work without giving retirement a second thought. His work, his flower garden, and taking care of his mother were his main activities in life. Manuel's income, barely $617 per month, supported his modest lifestyle.

One day, when Manuel was driving to the hardware store to buy garden supplies, a semitrailer broadsided him. The accident was serious and was Manuel's fault. He was rushed to the hospital with internal injuries and a broken leg and collarbone. During the hospitalization, medical tests revealed that Manuel was diabetic. His diabetes had gone untreated because he had simply ignored symptoms that had plagued him for many years. The untreated diabetes, it now seemed, was the cause of his eyesight deteriorating so rapidly in the year before the accident.

After 4 weeks, the hospital discharged him to a nursing home, where he spent 3 months in a skilled care unit. This was a difficult time for Manuel. He was making progress overcoming his injuries but not the chronic pain in his neck. In addition, his mother died, and he felt terrible that he was unable to be with her before her death. His only remaining family was his estranged sister.

Manuel's greatest desire was to return home. He reminded the nursing home staff and his doctor of that at every opportunity. He desperately missed his garden and the few neighbors with whom he used to chat over the fence. Finally, after weeks of listening to Manuel complain about neck pain and not being able to go home, his doctor ordered more X rays, which showed that Manuel's neck was broken. He was fitted for a halo cast and told by his doctor that he could return home only if he followed a strict diabetic diet and did not drive.

CASE STUDY QUESTIONS

1. Why is nutrition such a central factor in Manuel's plan of care?

2. What community-based food programs would you recommend for Manuel? Which program would you choose as the best option for Manuel? Why?

3. Is Manuel a good candidate for living at home alone if he follows the doctor's instructions? Why or why not?

4. What reasons would you give to defend Manuel's chances for successfully returning home?

5. What reasons would you give to defend Manuel's chances for having to move back to the nursing home?

LEARNING ACTIVITIES

1. Have an older adult relative keep a nutrition diary for 1 week to track what was eaten and when. Keep track of your own nutritional intake for that same week. Examine both diaries. How are they different? Similar? Are there any deficiencies in either diet? What improvements could be made in both diets?

2. Visit or volunteer at the local food bank. How many of the clients are older adults? How often is food distributed? What is the eligibility criteria for participation? How does the food bank obtain food to distribute?

3. Sign up for a congregate meal at a nearby site. How many people attend? How many times during the week are meals served? What is the suggested donation? What was the ethnic makeup of participants? Would the type of meals served attract older adults of different ethnic backgrounds?

FOR MORE INFORMATION

National Resources

1. National Urban League, 500 East 62nd Street, New York, NY 10021, 212-310-9000.

   The National Urban League is a nonprofit community service organization dedicated to assisting African Americans to achieve social and economic equality. Local league affiliates offer many programs in their area, including nutrition programs.

2. National Policy and Resource Center on Nutrition and Aging, Department of Dietetics and Nutrition, Florida International University, University Park, OE200, Miami, FL 33199, 305-348-1518.
   e-mail: nutrelder@solix.fiu.edu
   http://www.fiu.edu/nutrelder

   The National Policy and Resource Center on Nutrition and Aging works with the AoA to improve the nutritional status of older adults by disseminating nutrition information, providing technical assistance and training, and examining nutrition policies.

3. American Dietetic Association, 216 West Jackson Blvd., Chicago, IL 60606, 800-745-0775 (publications), 800-366-1655 (Consumer Nutrition Hotline).

   The American Dietetic Association is the professional society for dietitians. In addition to other services for its members and a consumer nutrition hotline, the association has numerous publications helpful to consumers, such as *Staying Healthy: A Guide for Elder Americans* and *Recommendations of Food Choices for Women.*

4. Food and Nutrition Information Center, Room 304, National Agriculture Library Building, U.S. Department of Agriculture, Beltsville, MD 20705-2351, 301-504-5719.

   The center provides information to professionals and the general public on nutrition and acquires and lends printed and audiovisual materials dealing with nutrition.

5. National Association of Meal Programs, Suite 202, 101 North Alfred Street, Alexandria, VA 22314, 703-548-8024.

   The National Association of Meal Programs provides education and training to those who plan and conduct congregate and home-delivered meals programs.

Web Resources

1. Senior Site
   http://seniors-site.com/nutritio/index.html

   Senior Site has a Web page—Nutrition and Senior Citizens—that offers a variety of information designed to inform older adults about nutrition guidelines, fats, vitamins, salt, fiber, and food eating habits.

2. Five Star Living, Inc.
   http://www.fortnet.org/fivstar/

   Five Star Living, Inc., has a home page that offers nutrition news for older adults and tips on staying healthy.

11

Health Care and Wellness

Marge had intended for years to get serious about losing weight. She could not believe it when her physician told her she was diabetic. She had just celebrated her 65th birthday, and she felt great and was as active as she had ever been. Marge discussed her options for treatment with her doctor and decided to try diet and exercise because her sugar levels were only a little above normal. She knew her personality and lifestyle well enough to know that she could not do this on her own. Her doctor suggested that she contact the Lifetime Wellness Center through the local hospital. The center encouraged her to enroll in a "Slim for Life" class sponsored by the American Heart Association and a class on "Managing Diabetes" sponsored by the hospital. After 8 weeks of classes, Marge believes she is on her way to getting control of her weight problem. She also knows the consequences of her actions and that if she needs more help, the Wellness Center is there to support her.

Although changes in physical health are inevitable as individuals age, it is possible to live a healthy life well into the ninth decade. Early detection of conditions such as Marge's diabetes and the assistance of wellness programs make it possible for her to manage her illness for many years. Indeed, older adults are living longer partly because of the advances in preventive and traditional medical care and improved access to health care services through Medicare. In this chapter, we provide a summary of the health status of older adults, the Medicare and Medicaid programs, and health maintenance organizations (HMOs). We conclude this chapter by describing health promotion and wellness programs available to older adults and the future challenges to health care policy and health promotion programs.

Health Status of Older Adults

Overall, the majority of older adults consider their health good, very good, or excellent compared with others their same age (National Center for Health Statistics, 1993). Although self-assessment is certainly one way to measure health status, the presence or absence of chronic or acute disease and the degree of inability in level of functioning are other measures of health status (Kane & Kane, 1981). Population studies of the prevalence of acute conditions reveal that older adults are less likely than younger adults to suffer from acute (i.e., temporary) conditions such as common colds (National Center for Health Statistics, 1990). The consequences of acute illness, however, are more severe for older adults than for younger adults. For example, an equal number of older adults and younger adults get respiratory infections, but death rates are 30% higher for older adults who get these infections (Hooyman & Kiyak, 1996). In contrast, older adults are more likely than younger adults to have chronic illnesses—those that are long term, often permanent, and that result in a disability that requires management rather than a cure. Marge's diabetes is a good example of a chronic condition that will require health management for the remainder of her life. According to the National Center for Health Statistics (1990), more than 80% of older adults over 65 have at least one chronic condition. Exhibit 11.1 shows the top 10 chronic conditions experienced by older persons, the most frequent of which are arthritis, hypertension, hearing impairment, and heart disease.

The presence of chronic conditions varies across subpopulations of older adults. For example, older women are more likely than older men to suffer from chronic conditions, such as arthritis, osteoporosis, hypertension, diabetes, stroke, incontinence, most types of orthopedic problems, and visual impairments (Hooyman & Kiyak, 1996). Similarly, older adults of color suffer from chronic conditions at rates that are often two times that of white older adults.

Older blacks experience hypertension, stroke, diabetes, and kidney failure more frequently than do whites. Of older Hispanic adults, 85% suffer from at least one chronic condition; by the age of 45, many Hispanics experience chronic health impairments, such as arthritis, heart disease, and diabetes, similar to a typical white 65-year-old (Cuellar, 1990). Older Native Americans have even greater rates of chronic conditions. Older Native Americans are more likely than older whites to have diabetes, hypertension, heart disease, hearing and visual impairments, and arthritis (Barresi & Stull, 1993).

Older adults are also living with and dying from AIDS. According to the National Center for Health Statistics (1993), more people over age 60 died of AIDS than did children. The number of persons aged 60 and older who died from AIDS nearly doubled from 1987 to 1992, whereas the number of children who died from AIDS remained stable.

Exhibit 11.1 **Top 10 Chronic Conditions of Persons Aged 65+ by Race: 1989 (Number per 1,000 Persons)**

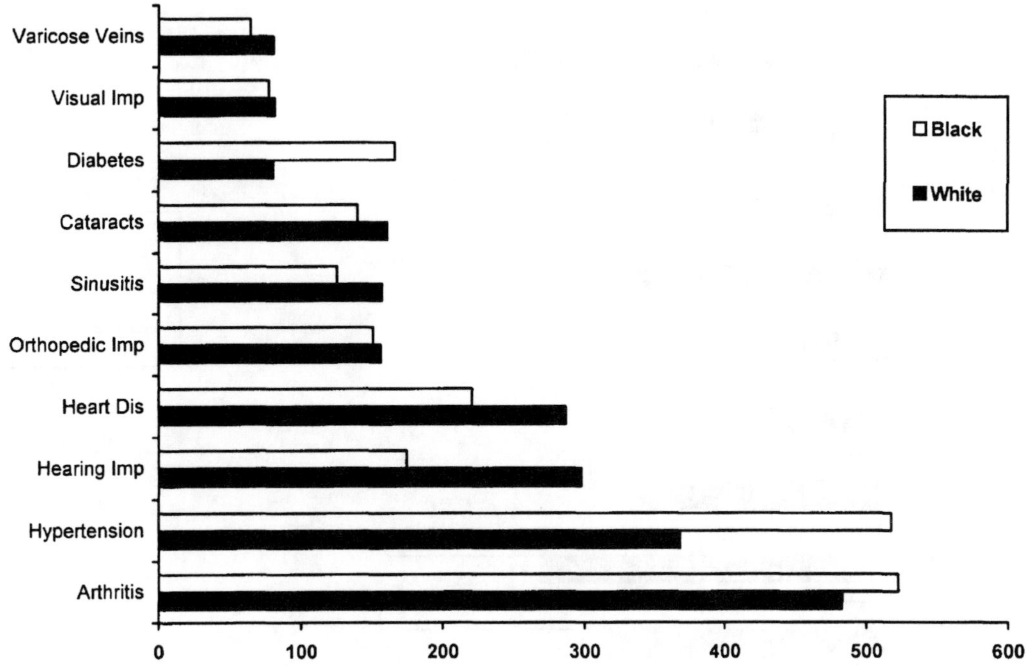

SOURCE: Compiled from National Center for Health Statistics (1990).

Persons living with chronic conditions, including HIV-AIDS, experience functional limitations for which they need assistance. Functional limitation, a measure of an individual's health status, is the inability to perform personal care tasks and home management activities. Personal care tasks, commonly referred to as *activities of daily living* (ADLs), include tasks such as bathing and grooming, toileting, dressing, and eating. Home management activities, or *instrumental activities of daily living* (IADLs), include tasks such as shopping and preparing meals, doing housework, and handling personal finances. National surveys reveal that some 6.7 million older adults have functional limitations in one or more ADL or IADL and that 5% to 8% of community-dwelling older adults need assistance with one or more ADLs (Hing & Bloom, 1990; Wiener, Hanley, Clark, & Van Norstrand, 1990). As shown in Exhibit 11.2, 9% or more of older adults aged 65 and older have trouble doing light housework, transferring (e.g., from bed to wheelchair), and bathing. Just as older women and older adults of color suffer from multiple chronic impairments, they are also likely to have multiple limitations in their everyday activities. In a sample of community-dwelling older adults,

Exhibit 11.2 **Functional Limitations of Men and Women Aged 65 to 74: 1991 (Number in Thousands)**

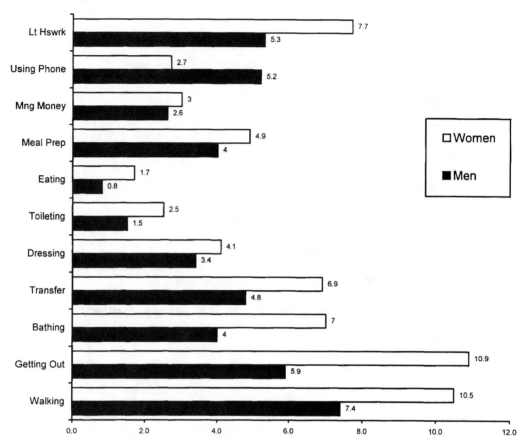

SOURCE: Compiled from U.S. Bureau of the Census (1996a).

34% of women and 22% of men had functional limitations (U.S. Bureau of the Census, 1996a). A similar disparity exists between older blacks and whites in functional abilities. Of blacks over 65, 59% have one or more functional limitations, compared with 49% of whites over 65 years of age. Furthermore, 40% of older blacks had functional limitations that were considered to be severe, compared with 27% of older whites with similar limitations.

A related indicator of functional limitation is the need for assistance in carrying out ADLs and IADLs. Not surprisingly, the need for assistance with daily activities increases with age. As shown in Exhibit 11.3, 9% of older adults aged 65 to 69 need assistance with ADLs. The need for assistance increases to nearly 50% for those over age 85.

Exhibit 11.3 **Percentage of Persons Needing Assistance With Everyday Activities by Age: 1991**

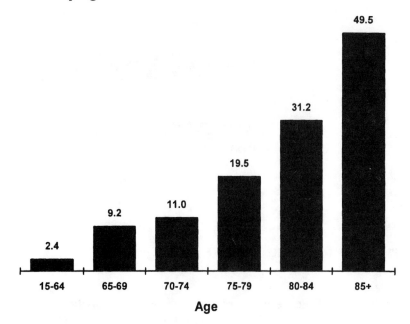

SOURCE: Compiled from U.S. Bureau of the Census (1996a).

Older women are more likely than older men to need assistance with everyday activities. Although the percentages of women and men aged 15 to 64 who need assistance with everyday activities are similar (3% and 2%, respectively), by age 75 and older, 23% of men and 33% of women need assistance with everyday activities (see Exhibit 11.4).

Partly because older adults of color experience a higher number of chronic conditions than do older whites, they are more likely to need assistance with everyday activities. As shown in Exhibit 11.5, 25% of Hispanics and blacks aged 65 and older and 17% of older whites need assistance with everyday activities (U.S. Bureau of the Census, 1996a).

In summary, most older adults do enjoy relatively good health well into their seventh decade. As people grow older and move into later life, however, they acquire more chronic conditions and experience fewer acute conditions, although the latter can result in life-threatening illnesses for some. Furthermore, health status varies between older women and men, between whites and older adults of color, and between persons of different ages. In general, women and older adults of color have more chronic illnesses and more functional limitations and are more likely to need assistance with everyday activities.

Exhibit 11.4 **Percentage of Persons Needing Assistance With Everyday Activities by Age and Sex: 1991**

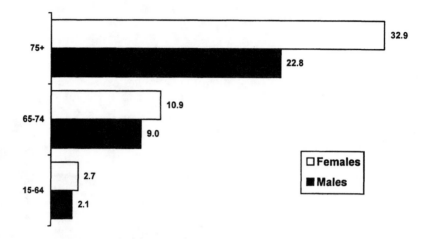

SOURCE: U.S. Bureau of the Census (1996a).

Exhibit 11.5 **Percentage of Persons 65 Years and Older Needing Assistance With Everyday Activities by Race: 1991**

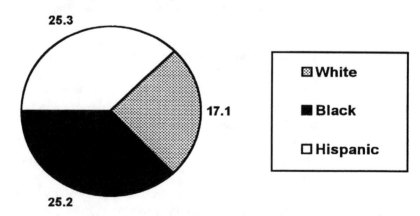

SOURCE: U.S. Bureau of the Census (1996a).

These health characteristics have significant implications for the delivery of health care and health promotion programs. For example, in later life, adults need health care programs and services that addresses chronic, rather than acute, conditions. They also need access to and coverage of rehabilitation services, including assistance with assistive technology devices that are designed to maintain functional independence. Furthermore, health promotion

---

For Your Files   **ABLEDATA**

Assistive technology devices help people maintain independent living by helping them perform ADLs. Assistive technology devices have been used by persons with disabilities for years; with the growing number of older adults with chronic conditions, however, such devices can effectively assist more older adults with their functional limitations. ABLEDATA, sponsored by the National Institute on Disability and Rehabilitation Research, is a national database of information on assistive technology and rehabilitation equipment from domestic and international sources. ABLEDATA contains information on more than 22,000 assistive technology products that consumers can search on their Web site or by phone. ABLEDATA also offers fact sheets about devices and topics related to assistive technology, consumer guides to assist with product selection, and other publications for consumers of assistive technology devices. ABLEDATA can refer callers to resources that can help them make their companies accessible. Visit ABLEDATA's fully accessible facilities at 8455 Colesville Road, Suite 935, Silver Spring, MD 20910, phone ABLEDATA for more information at 800-227-0216, or access the Web site (http://www.abledata.com).

---

programs can assist in preventing illness as well as in maintaining functioning. Later in this chapter, we will discuss the health promotion and wellness programs designed to improve the health status of older adults. In this next section, we provide an overview of the federal health insurance programs—Medicare and Medicaid.

Federal Health Care Policy

Medicare

Medicare is a national health insurance program authorized in 1965 under Title XVII of the Social Security Act as a complement to those receiving Social Security benefits. Originally, Medicare covered older adults over 65, but since its passage, coverage has been extended to persons who are entitled to Social Security disability for 24 months or more, persons with end-stage kidney disease requiring dialysis or transplant, and noncovered persons who elect to buy into Medicare (Health Care Finance Administration [HFCA], 1996d). The HCFA administers the program under the direction of the U.S. Department of Health and Human Services. The Social Security Administration is responsible for processing applications and maintaining Medicare records.

There are two parts to Medicare: *Part A, Hospital Insurance,* which covers costs associated with inpatient hospitalization and some posthospitalization care; and *Part B, Supplemental Medical Insurance,* which covers physician, outpatient care, and other medical services. Part A is funded by taxes on earnings; employers and employees each pay 1.45% of payroll, and self-employed persons pay 2.9%. Older households pay about 6% of Part A payroll taxes, and Social Security beneficiaries with incomes above a certain amount pay federal income tax to which a portion of these taxes (4 billion in 1995) is designated for Part A funds. Part B is funded primarily through premiums paid by beneficiaries and general federal revenues. Premiums cover approximately 36% of program costs, and general federal revenues cover the remainder (HCFA, 1996d). Reviewing and paying claims are done by intermediaries, such as utilization review committees (for Part A) and carriers (for Part B), such as Blue Cross and Blue Shield.

Who Is Eligible for Medicare?

All persons who are eligible for Social Security or Railroad Retirement benefits are also eligible for Medicare benefits. Therefore, individuals qualify for Medicare if they or their spouses worked 10 years (or 40 quarters) in employment that paid into Social Security. Those who lack a sufficient number of quarters can purchase Part A benefits if they also buy Part B coverage. In 1997, individuals who wished to buy Part A coverage could do so for $311 per month if they had less than 30 quarters; $187 if they had 30 to 39 quarters. For individuals who have earned enough quarters, there is no premium cost associated with Part A; older adults choosing to participate in Part B, however, pay a monthly premium ($43.80 in 1997) and $100 per year deductible for physician services.

Coverage

Exhibits 11.6 and 11.7 present a detailed explanation of the coverage provided by Part A and Part B, respectively. Medicare Part A provides coverage of inpatient hospital services up to 90 days per benefit period[1] plus 60 days of lifetime reserve days; skilled nursing facilities for 100 days following a 3-day hospital stay; intermittent home health services if skilled care is needed; and hospice care (HCFA, 1996d). Medicare Part B helps pay for the cost of physician services, outpatient hospital services, medical equipment and supplies, and other health services and supplies. Payments made by Medicare under Part A for inpatient hospital costs are based on the patient's diagnosis (referred to as diagnostic related group, or DRG). The patient's DRG dictates the payment the hospital will receive as well as the length of stay on which the payment is based. Under the DRG system, payments to

Exhibit 11.6 **Medicare Coverage: Part A**

Services	Benefit[a]	Medicare Pays	Beneficiary Pays
Hospitalization			
Semiprivate room, meals, regular nursing services, intensive care, operating and recovering room, drugs, laboratory tests, X rays, and all other medically necessary supplies	First 60 days	All approved charges but $736	$736 deductible
	Days 61-90	All but $184 per day coinsurance	$184 per day
	Days 91-150	All but $368 per day coinsurance	$368 per day
	150+ days	Nothing	All
Skilled Nursing Facility			
Semiprivate room and board, skilled nursing and rehabilitative services and other services and supplies.	Days 1-20	100% of covered services	Nothing
	Days 21-100	All but $92 per day	$92 per day
	100+	Nothing	All costs
Home Health			
Part-time or intermittent skilled care, home health aide services, durable medical equipment and supplies, and other services	Unlimited as long as Medicare conditions are met	100% of the cost of covered home health care; 80% of approved amount for durable medical equipment	Nothing for services; 20% for durable medical equipment
Hospice			
Pain relief, symptom management, and support services for the terminally ill	For as long as doctor certifies	100% of charges	May have to pay up to $5 for each prescription drug; or may charge $5 per day for inpatient care in nursing facility
Blood			
When furnished by a hospital or skilled nursing facility during a covered stay	Unlimited if medically necessary	All but first 3 pints per calendar year	For first 3 pints

SOURCE: Health Care Finance Administration (1997b).

a. A benefit period begins on the first day a beneficiary receives inpatient hospital benefits and ends after being discharged from the hospital or skilled facility for 60 consecutive days.

the hospital for a given Medicare patient may be more or less than the hospital's cost—thus the hospital either absorbs the loss or enjoys a profit. Payments for other services under Part A, (home health, skilled nursing facility, and hospice) are paid on a "reasonable cost" billed by the provider.

Exhibit 11.7 **Medicare Coverage: Part B**

Services	Benefit[a]	Medicare Pays	Beneficiary Pays
Medical Expenses			
Doctors' services, inpatient and outpatient medical and surgical services and supplies, physical and speech therapy, diagnostic tests, durable medical equipment and other services	Unlimited if medically necessary	80% of approved amount after $100 deductible Reduced to 50% for most outpatient mental health services	$100 deductible, plus 20% of approved amount and limited charges above the approved amount
Clinical Laboratory Services			
Blood tests, urinalyses, and more	Unlimited if medically necessary	Generally 100% of approved amount	Nothing for services
Home Health Care			
Part-time or intermittent skilled care, home health aide services, durable medical equipment and supplies, and other services	Unlimited as long as Medicare conditions are met	100% of the cost of covered home health care; 80% of approved amount for durable medical equipment	Nothing for services; 20% for durable medical equipment
Outpatient Hospital Treatment			
Services for the diagnosis or treatment of illness or injury	Unlimited if medically necessary	Medicare payment to hospital based on hospital cost	20% of whatever the hospital charges (after $100 deductible)
Blood			
When furnished by a hospital or skilled nursing facility during a covered stay	Unlimited if medically necessary	80% of approved amount after $100 deductible and starting with the 4th pint	For first 3 pints plus 20% of approved amount for additional pints (after $100 deductible)
Ambulatory Surgical Services			
	Unlimited if medically necessary	80% of predetermined amount (after $100 deductible)	$100 deductible, plus 20% of predetermined amount

SOURCE: Health Care Finance Administration (1997b).

a. A benefit period begins on the first day a beneficiary receives inpatient hospital benefits and ends after being discharged from the hospital or skilled facility for 60 consecutive days.

Under Part B, Medicare pays physicians on the basis of a "reasonable charge," which is the lowest of either the submitted charges or a fee schedule based on a relative value scale (HCFA, 1996d). If a provider agrees to accept

---

Best Practice   **Parish Nurse Programs**

Parish nurse programs have emerged to reduce health care costs and deliver health promotion education outside the formal health care delivery system. The Parish Nurse Program of Sinai Samaritan Medical Center in Milwaukee, Wisconsin, in cooperation with Marquette University College of Nursing, trains registered nurses and places them to work 10 to 16 hours in churches of all denominations. The role of the parish nurse is to (a) educate members about the relationship between lifestyle, attitudes, faith, and well-being; (b) counsel members about health issues, self-care to prevent disease, and coping with chronic illness; (c) refer members to the most cost-effective, appropriate community health services; and (d) facilitate programs within the church to promote healing. Specific health promotion activities include counseling on issues such as cancer, AIDS, and high blood pressure; visiting members in their homes; and offering health screenings and health seminars. Parish nurse programs are being developed across the country.

For more information about Sinai Samaritan's Parish Nurse Program, contact Parish Nurse Preparation Institute, Marquette University College of Nursing, P.O. Box 1881, Milwaukee, WI 53201-1881, 414-288-3802, Web site (http://www.mu.edu/dept/nursing/parish.html).

---

the approved rate as full payment for services, they "accept assignment." If the provider does not accept assignment for the services provided, the beneficiary is responsible for the remaining balance of the cost of the service and what Medicare will pay. Other services covered under Part B, such as durable medical equipment and clinical laboratory services, are also paid on a fee schedule. Outpatient and home health coverage under Part B is paid on a reasonable cost basis.

According to HCFA (1996d), Part A provided benefits to 33 million aged adults and 4 million disabled enrollees. Part B provided coverage to almost 36 million enrollees. Combined benefit payments for Part A and Part B averaged $4,978 per enrollee.

Medigap Policies

Many older adults purchase Medicare supplemental insurance policies, commonly referred to as Medigap policies. Medigap policies are designed to assist with the costs of health care services not covered by Medicare. Medigap policies usually pay deductibles, co-payments, and the remaining 20% of the approved charges for physician and hospital services. Limited coverage is sometimes provided for prescription drugs, home care, and preventive care.

Medicaid

In the same year in which Congress enacted Medicare (1965), Medicaid became law as Title XIX of the Social Security Act. Medicaid provides medical assistance for low-income families and individuals. Unlike Medicare, Medicaid is funded through the joint effort of federal and state governments to help states pay for health care of those who are needy. The federal government provides broad national Medicaid program guidelines and funding to the states. Every state that participates (all do but Arizona) develops its own eligibility standards; determines the type, amount, and scope of benefits and the rate of payment for services; and administers its own program (HCFA, 1996a). Therefore, Medicaid programs vary by state, and not all low-income individuals are eligible for Medicaid.

Who Is Eligible for Medicaid?

States have some flexibility in setting Medicaid eligibility guidelines. They determine who will be covered and the income guidelines necessary to be eligible. Eligibility falls in two categories—the *categorically needy* and *medically needy*. Those who are categorically needy must meet certain income and asset guidelines established by the state. Some groups of categorically needy persons, however, are required by federal law to receive Medicaid coverage. For example, persons who receive federal income maintenance assistance, such as SSI and Aid to Families With Dependent Children (AFDC)[2] must receive benefits (HCFA, 1996c). In addition, certain groups are required to receive Medicaid coverage. These groups include (a) Medicare beneficiaries and certain aged, blind, or disabled adults who have income above those requiring mandatory coverage but below the federal poverty level; (b) institutionalized individuals with income and resources below specified limits; (c) persons who would be eligible if institutionalized but are receiving care through home and community-based services; and (d) recipients of state supplementary payments, such as Old Age Pensions (HCFA, 1996a).

Some states opt to include individuals considered medically needy but who have too much income to qualify as categorically needy. Under this option, states allow members of selected groups (e.g., aged, blind, and/or disabled persons) to spend down to Medicaid income eligibility guidelines by using their medical expenses to offset their excess income, thus reducing their income level to meet the Medicaid guidelines (HCFA, 1996a).

Coverage

States participating in Medicaid must provide basic medical services to its beneficiaries. The following are medical services provided to those who qualify[3]:

- Inpatient hospital services
- Outpatient hospital services
- Physician services
- Nursing facility services
- Rural health clinic services
- Home health care for persons eligible for skilled nursing services
- Laboratory and X-ray services

States also may receive federal assistance if they choose to provide other optional approved medical services. Some optional medical services covered by Medicaid include

- Clinic services
- Optometrist services and eyeglasses
- Prescribed drugs
- Prosthetic devices
- Dental services

Payment for services is made directly to the provider, and the provider must accept the Medicaid payment as payment in full. States may also require beneficiaries to pay co-payments or a deductible for certain services (HCFA, 1996b).

After obtaining permission from HCFA, states can require beneficiaries to enroll in managed care plans and offer home and community-based services to those individuals with chronic impairments who are eligible for Medicaid. As of 1997, 14 states have established managed care enrollment plans for Medicaid beneficiaries (managed care will be discussed below; American Public Welfare Association, 1997). The states that have been given approval to establish an all-managed-care Medicaid program are Delaware, Florida, Hawaii, Illinois, Kentucky, Maryland, Massachusetts, Ohio, Oklahoma, Oregon, Rhode Island, Tennessee, and Vermont. States also can request a waiver that allows states to offer a package of services to persons who, without community support services, might otherwise be institutionalized. Such services include case management, adult day program services, respite care, and homemaker/home health care.

Medicaid also provides benefits to persons who qualify for Medicare. For persons who are eligible for both Medicare and Medicaid, called *dual eligibles,* Medicaid pays for all the premiums, deductibles, and coinsurance costs associated with Part A and Part B. Medicaid may also pay for services beyond what is covered under Medicare (e.g., hearing aids and skilled nursing after

100 days; HCFA, 1996d). The Medicare program must pay for services before any payments are made by Medicaid.

Other Medicare beneficiaries who can receive assistance from Medicaid are those who have incomes at or below 100% of the poverty line and whose resources are at or below 200% of the SSI guidelines (HCFA, 1996d). Known as *qualified Medicare beneficiaries* (QMBs), these individuals receive assistance from Medicaid in paying the cost-sharing provisions of Medicare. *Specified low-income Medicare beneficiaries* also receive assistance from Medicaid in paying expenses associated with Medicare. Medicaid will pay Medicare Part B premiums for persons who are eligible for Medicare whose incomes are above the QMB levels but below 120% of the poverty level.

Persons who are aged, blind, and disabled represent about 30% of Medicaid recipients and account for 68% of Medicaid spending (Ford, 1996). HCFA (1997a) data indicate that much of the Medicaid spending for this group is for long-term care—an amount totaling 48 billion, or 34% of total Medicaid spending. Federal Medicaid spending in 1995 was $120.1 billion, with spending on nursing home care totaling $29.1 billion and spending on home health care totaling $9.4 billion. As a result of the growth in the cost of health care for low-income and older adults under Medicaid and Medicare, managed care has emerged as a way to control health care costs.

Managed Care

As health care costs continue to escalate, the idea of managed care has moved into the forefront as a way to deliver health care more effectively and efficiently. Managed care is defined as the "efforts to coordinate, rationalize, and channel the use of services to achieve desired access, service, and outcomes while controlling costs" (Kane et al., 1996, p. 9). HMOs deliver managed care that provides comprehensive health services for a fixed payment. HMOs combine insurance and the delivery of medical care in one entity and offer enrollees comprehensive health care services in exchange for a premium while at the same time try to control the quality and access to health care services (Cain, 1996; Kane et al., 1996).

Types of Managed Care Organizations

The delivery of physician services varies by managed care organizations (Kane et al., 1996). The *staff model HMO* hires physicians as salaried employees representing most of the common specialties. The *group model HMO* contracts with a multispecialty physician group to provide all physician services to its members. The *network model HMO* contracts with more than one group practice to deliver physician services to its members. Finally, the *direct contract model HMO* contracts directly with individual physicians and compensates them for delivering services to HMO members.

The two most common types of plans under which Medicare beneficiaries may be covered are risk contract and cost contract (Kane et al., 1996). Providers under *risk contract* plans receive 95% of the projected average expenses for a fee-for-service per beneficiary regardless of the amount of services used. Risk contract HMOs assume full financial risk for all care provided to Medicare beneficiaries. In addition, they also must provide all Medicare-covered services, and many offer additional services as well (HCFA, 1996d). Members of risk plan HMOs must receive all their care through providers associated with the HMO, although emergency services provided outside the plan can be covered.

Medicare enrollees who participate in *cost contract* plans and use the HMO providers will have their Medicare deductibles, coinsurance, and any excess beyond Medicare's allowable charges paid for by the plan. Enrollees are responsible for the plan's co-payment cost. If enrollees seek care from a provider outside the HMO network, they assume costs associated with using Medicare, including deductibles, coinsurance, and excess charges. Seven percent of Medicare beneficiaries—2.8 million—are enrolled in risk plans, and 2% were enrolled in cost plans (GAO, 1996b).

Cain (1996) has identified a number of advantages that Medicare beneficiaries enjoy when they join HMOs. They usually do not have to pay deductibles or coinsurance payments required under Part A or Part B, and HMOs agree not to charge more than Medicare's approved amount. Therefore, for many older adults, HMOs are an alternative to buying supplemental Medigap policies. In addition, HMOs often provide a wider range of services, including preventive health care, outpatient mental health services, prescription drugs, and eyeglasses. HMOs usually charge a small per-visit fee or a co-payment for selected services. Disadvantages include restrictions on choice of doctor and hospitals who are not associated with the HMO; there is also a fear that older adults will not get the health services they need (Kane et al., 1996). Other problems include misunderstandings among enrollees about the terms associated with HMO enrollment, restrictions, and denial of services (Wilson, cited in National Association of Area Agencies on Aging, 1996).

Health Promotion and Wellness

The focus on health promotion and wellness has been driven, in part, by the desire to enjoy a high level of functioning in later life. Growing evidence shows that individuals who engage in healthy lifestyle behaviors have positive health outcomes. For example, 7 of the 10 leading causes of death (e.g., heart disease and stroke) can be reduced by changes in lifestyle, including proper nutrition, exercise, reduced alcohol consumption, and not smoking (Belloc & Breslow, 1972). For older adults in particular, health promotion activities can prevent illness in those who are healthy, prevent those who are ill from becoming disabled, and help older adults who are disabled to preserve function and prevent further disability (Institute of Medicine, 1991). Therefore, numerous health promotion programs targeting older adults have emerged. The OAA has supported the funding of health promotion programs, and the AoA has been instrumental in supporting initiatives designed to enhance the well-being of older adults. These efforts will be discussed below.

Policy Background

The 1992 amendment to the OAA authorized the creation of Part F, Disease Prevention and Health Promotion Services, under Title III. Health promotion programs under Part F included the funding of the following health promotion programs:

- Health risk assessments
- Routine health screenings
- Nutrition counseling and education
- Health promotion programs relating to chronic conditions
- Alcohol and substance abuse, smoking cessation, weight loss, stress management, and physical fitness programs
- Home injury control services
- Mental health
- Education about the availability of preventive services covered under Medicare
- Medication management
- Information about age-related diseases
- Gerontological counseling
- Counseling regarding social services and follow-up health services

Funding for preventive health services under Part F for fiscal years 1995 and 1996 was $16,982,000 and $15,623,000, respectively. Although the House proposed eliminating funding for Part F programs in 1997, both the president's and Senate's proposed budgets included funding for preventive health programs. For fiscal year 1997, Congress has funded preventive health programs at $15,623,000 (AoA, 1997a).

The AoA has been instrumental in sponsoring a number of nationwide initiatives designed to promote health and wellness of older adults. The National Health Promotion Initiative sponsored by the AoA and the U.S. Public Health Service in 1986 was designed to facilitate collaboration between state and local health departments, state and local AAAs, and volunteer organizations in developing and implementing health promotion programs (Fall-Creek, Allen, & Halls, 1986). The initiative targeted four areas of health promotion—injury control, proper drug use, better nutrition, and improved physical fitness. The initiative was responsible for the development of resource materials, including the *Health Promotion and Aging: A National Directory of Selected Programs* (FallCreek et al., 1986), *A Healthy Old Age: A Sourcebook for Health Promotion With Older Adults* (FallCreek & Mettler, 1982), and *Health Promotion and Aging: Strategies for Action* (FallCreek & Franks, 1984).

In 1989, the AoA launched the Historically Black Colleges and Universities Initiatives to address the health promotion needs of older adults of color. Ten schools were awarded grants under this initiative to develop strategies and demonstration projects to promote better self-care habits among minority older persons. Health promotion strategies included church-based health promotion programs, programs for low-income older blacks living in inner cities and rural areas in Georgia using peer counselors, and the creation of videotapes and instructional guides targeted to older African American audiences through public access television (DHHS, 1993).

Another major initiative sponsored by the AoA was the Action for Health: Older Women's Project in 1990. The goal of the project was to demonstrate the feasibility of developing and implementing an innovative community-based, peer educator-facilitated health and wellness promotion program for older minority and low-income women (Herman & Wadsworth, 1992). In 1994, the AoA became a participant in the National Coalition on Disability and Aging to focus attention on the common concerns of aged persons and persons with disabilities. The delivery of care under managed care is just one of the topics coalition members examine.

Health Promotion Programs and Users

For many years, older adults were not targets of health promotion programs (McGinnis, 1988). As Walker (1989) pointed out, health promotion programs excluded older adults because it was thought that they could not benefit from activities in which the benefits would emerge in the future. In addition, many believed that health promotion programs would not be successful in changing the lifelong behaviors of older adults. Fortunately, health promotion programs that target older adults have become more frequent in recent years.

Best Practice **HELP Program**

Older adults often need health care more than any other group but are the least able to afford or access the health care they need. Through the HELP Program, sponsored by the Los Angeles Department of Aging and the Charles R. Drew University of Medicine and Science, free services are delivered to older adults at each of the city's 15 multipurpose senior service centers. Organizers of this program have described it as almost equivalent to the good old days when doctors made house calls.

The HELP Program is anchored by the state-of-the-art Rosa Parks Mobile Health Vehicle. This 33-foot traveling health clinic provides the medical equipment necessary for senior health care at centers that do not have the facilities in-house. In 1995, experienced physicians specializing in gerontology provided free services to more than 1,000 seniors 60 years and older in the city of Los Angeles. Typical health care procedures included testing of blood sugar, blood pressure, hearing, prostate, cholesterol, and eyes. The physician leader is usually a Drew University staff member. The geriatric medical staff members at the Drew/King Medical Center are strong advocates for early detection and prevention. Through the HELP Program, they hope to reach seniors who are afraid to go to the doctor because they don't want the doctor to find anything. This unique public-private partnership is committed to making health care convenient for Los Angeles older adults so that hospitalization among them will be reduced. For more information, contact City of Los Angeles, Department of Aging, 2404 Wilshire Boulevard, Suite 400, Los Angeles, CA 90057, 213-368-4000.

Health promotion programs for older adults have shifted from focusing on the management of specific disease conditions to including prevention of illness and injury and the enhancement of health (Walker, 1989). Thus, health promotion programs can address a multitude of concerns and be defined in a variety of ways. For example, Teague (1987) defined health promotion as

> Any combination of health education and related organizational, political, and economic interventions, designed to facilitate behavioral, and environmental changes which prevent, delay the occurrence, or minimize the impact of disease or disability while promoting the independence and well-being of older adults. (p. 23)

Health promotion programs can be illness specific, such as programs designed to reduce high blood pressure, or can be broad based and include physical fitness, stress management, nutrition, and environmental awareness. In addition, there are different levels of health program intervention strate-

---

For Your Files   **SMILE Program**

The SMILE program (*So Much Improvement with a Little Exercise*) was developed by researchers and practitioners to help older persons maintain their independence and mobility. SMILE is a low-intensity exercise program for individuals who are physically inactive and chronically impaired. Classes are held in senior centers and adult day programs and are led by peer leaders and professionals. The program has a 41-minute exercise video demonstrating warm-up, simple stretching, range of motion, deep breathing, and cool-down exercises. An instructor's manual teaches the peer leaders to perform the exercises and adapt the exercises to fit the clientele. A participant manual that can be used alone or in conjunction with the videotape is also available. An evaluation of the effectiveness of the program is under way. For more information about the program or obtaining the videotape or manuals, contact SMILE Program, University of Michigan Mail Services, 1032 Greene Street, Ann Arbor, MI 48109-1445.

SOURCE: American Association of Retired Persons (1994a).

---

gies (O'Donnell & Ainsworth, cited in Teague, 1987). *Educational health promotion* programs provide participants with information designed to increase awareness, education, and behavior change. Health education can be delivered through lectures, flyers and posters, health fairs, and resource libraries. *Evaluation screening* programs test past, current, and potential health problems. Fitness assessments are perhaps the most popular evaluation screening programs. *Prescription* programs are used in conjunction with evaluation screening and give participants the information they need to correct or prevent a current health problem. Finally, *behavior change support* programs provide participants with evaluation screening, a prescription for change, and the support system needed for participants to be successful in changing health habits.

Health promotion programs may be sponsored by hospitals, universities, churches, departments of public health, local AAAs or aging network members, insurance companies, and community organizations such as the Red Cross. Programs may be delivered in a variety of settings including shopping malls, senior centers, hospitals, senior housing, and local schools.

Although information about health promotion activities is widely available, little empirical published research documents who participates in formal health promotion programs. Admittedly, the generalizability of such research is limited because of the wide variation in program content, format, and participant characteristics. A handful of studies, however, can provide a tentative understanding of participation rates and benefits.

Some evidence suggests that participants of health promotion programs have higher incomes and education, have higher levels of community involvement, and are more often women (Lefebvre, Harden, Rawkowski, Lasater, & Careton, 1987; Pirie et al., 1986). For example, Buchner and Pearson (1989) examined the characteristics of participants in an HMO senior health promotion program. Demographic factors associated with participation included being older and female, having higher levels of income and education, and being a nonsmoker. Ratings of general health status were not related to participation, and participants were more likely to have lower mental and social health ratings than nonparticipants. Wagner, Grothaus, Hecht, and LaCroix (1991) evaluated a senior health program involving a sample of people who were 65 years and older and who were enrolled in an HMO. The health promotion program consisted of a nurse educator visit to assess health risks, follow-up classes, written materials, and a review of prescription medications. Researchers interviewed the enrollees who chose not to participate. Nonparticipants had lower levels of education and family income, were less likely to be members of community organizations, were more likely to smoke, and had more negative self-evaluations of chronic conditions and health status compared with participants. Other studies comparing participants and nonparticipants in health promotion programs generally conclude that participants are individuals who already have preventive attitudes toward health care and engage in a variety of preventive health behaviors (Carter, Elward, Malmgren, Martin, & Larson, 1991).

Finally, there is some concern that health promotion programs do not have lasting results (Hickey & Stilwell, 1991; Warshaw, 1988). Lalonde, Hooyman, and Blumhagen (1988) investigated the long-term effectiveness of the Wallingford Wellness Project. This project was a 3-year community-based health promotion demonstration project that offered 21 weeks of education and behavior change training to persons 55 and older in physical fitness, stress management, nutrition, and environmental awareness and action. An experimental group (n = 90) was recruited from the community, and a comparison group (n = 44) was recruited through social groups. Follow-up studies revealed that the project was most effective in the short term—up to 6 months following graduation from the program. Participants reported sustaining behavior changes initiated in physical fitness, stress management, and nutrition; these behavioral changes declined, however, when measured 6 months later. With regard to retaining health information, participants sustained their increase in health information over pretest levels, except for nutrition information. The project was ineffective in reducing health service use among participants. Clearly, more rigorous studies are needed to evaluate and compare the different types of health promotion and wellness programs offered to older adults.

Best Practice **Healthwise for Life**

Healthwise for Life is a self-care education program designed to help older adults do a better job of caring for their health. This 90-minute workshop includes a self-care workbook, presenter's guide, and a stop-action videotape presenting scenes aimed at triggering discussion. The program was pilot tested in urban settings and then distributed in rural areas. The four key program sponsors for the rural initiative were the Brookdale Foundation, who provided funding; the National Rural Health Network; the National Rural Electric Women's Association; and Healthwise, Inc., of Boise, Idaho, which developed the course materials and training program.

Workshop participants receive a copy of the *Healthwise for Life: Medical Self-Care for Healthy Aging Handbook*, which covers 120 of the most common health concerns of older adults, including chronic and acute ailments, staying healthy, independent medical consumerism, and caregiving. Volunteer or agency facilitators, such as local extension agents, lead the participants through a step-by-step approach on how to recognize health problems, provide home treatment, and decide when to call a doctor.

In 1993, an independent postworkshop evaluation indicated that most older adults receiving the handbook and taking part in the workshop used the book and workshop information. Participants also asked more questions of their doctors and felt they had saved money by being more involved in their health care (Mettler & Kemper, 1995).

Twenty-three counties and more than 3,300 older adults have participated in the program. Colorado is a good example of a state in which the Healthwise for Life program has been broadly implemented. In many counties, the Colorado State University Cooperative Extension Program and the Area Agencies on Aging have coordinated the program. AAAs underwrite the cost of the handbooks and recruit the participants, whereas the extension program facilitates the workshops. A postevaluation study conducted in one rural Colorado county showed that 92% of the participants had made improvements in their nutrition and diet habits because of the program, 67% used their book more than three times to address health problems, 68% shared their book with others, and 42% felt the program had resulted in making fewer doctor visits (Liess, 1996).

For more information or to order books, contact Healthwise, Inc., P.O. Box 1989, Boise, ID 83701, phone 208-345-1161, fax 208-345-1897.

Challenges for Health Care and Health Promotion Programs

Serving Diverse Groups of Older Adults

Extending health promotion and prevention programs to all individuals, especially older adults and vulnerable populations, was one of the many resolutions made at the 1995 White House Conference on Aging. Delegates recommended supporting policies that encourage a total wellness approach by emphasizing fitness programs, stress management, and available and affordable preventive health measures and screenings. Although education about preventive health behaviors is an important factor in changing personal behavior, scholars have criticized health promotion programs for focusing too much on individual behaviors while ignoring other factors related to poor health, including poverty, racism, sexism, ageism, and environmental hazards (Hickey & Stilwell, 1991; Minkler & Pasick, 1985). Health promotion programs will be meaningless if issues such as access and affordability to health care services continue to be problematic for many older adults.

Health promotion programs must be sensitive to the cultural characteristics of their participants. Ralston (1993) identified programmatic strategies for health promotion programs targeting older blacks, including using an educational framework with scheduled classes to deliver information, using black churches to sponsor programs, and using peer leaders to act as liaisons between older adults and the health care delivery system. In addition, health promotion programs must be sensitive to participants' sociodemographic characteristics. Something as simple as instructing older inner-city participants to take daily walks may be unsuccessful because they fear walking in their neighborhood (Minkler & Pasick, 1985).

Increasing Research and Program Evaluation

Further empirical research is needed to examine the factors associated with participation in health promotion programs. Researchers also must use theoretical models that can assist in investigating the motivational forces that are associated with participation in a wide variety of formal health promotion programs (Pascucci, 1992).

Supporting Health Programs and Policies in the Future

Traditional health care, with its focus on acute care, does not adequately address the health care needs of older adults who must live with and manage chronic conditions. Moreover, older adults need regular primary care to help them prevent illness and maintain their health. Preventive services for the control of high blood pressure, cancer screenings, immunizations, and therapies to help manage chronic conditions are key to extending a healthy life in later life (DHHS, 1990). Delegates to the White House Conference on Aging (1995) recommended that preventive health care, such as immunizations, annual Pap smears, mammograms, and nutrition screening be covered under Medicare and Medicaid. Indeed, the challenge facing U.S. society in the next century is creating a health care system that provides all its members, of every age, accessibility to health care, including regular primary care and health promotion.

 ## CASE STUDY

HEALTH CONCERNS AFTER RETIREMENT

David, 60, retired a year ago from a high-level executive position with a major auto company. His retirement meant the end to 25 years of long hours in fast-paced, high-stress management work. It also meant the end to grueling overseas travel and weeks of separation from his family. During this past year, David has been helping his wife, Evelyn, move into a smaller, but new, home. He has had a lot of time to think about what he would like to do next. David has decided to use his experience by developing a part-time international consulting business that would allow him to work in his home office part of the time.

Lately, David has been feeling tired and sleeping poorly. He decided that he should have a complete checkup before launching into his new endeavor. He was both anxious and excited about meeting his new doctor, recommended by another retired executive. He told David not to expect to leave this doctor's office with a prescription in hand after a 30-minute visit. The friend was right. The checkup ended up taking 2 weeks and consisted of a thorough recounting of David's medical history, family medical history, and lifestyle choices. It also included an examination and a series of laboratory tests.

When David returned for the results of his evaluation, he was presented with some startling facts. His doctor told him frankly that he was headed into a lifetime of chronic health problems unless he drastically changed his lifestyle. Specifically, his blood pressure and blood sugar levels were too high, and his insomnia problems were probably due to too much alcohol consumption on a daily basis. The doctor complimented David for quitting smoking 10 years ago. Because of these other factors and because David's father died of heart disease, however, David was still at risk of heart disease and other complications. The doctor strongly recommended some major lifestyle interventions.

CASE STUDY QUESTIONS

1. Would you say that David's doctor is being responsible by strongly recommending lifestyle changes for David? What research supports your answer? Why might David not have encountered such medical recommendations 10 or 15 years ago?

2. In what ways does David fit or not fit the profile of someone who would participate in a health promotion program? Would you say that David has a preventive attitude about his situation?

3. The chapter describes four possible models of health promotion programs. Describe each model and how each model might apply to David's situation.

4. Without knowing the specific community in which David and his doctor live, where generally might David look for health promotion support for his lifestyle change work?

5. First and foremost, David's doctor is concerned with David's health and well-being. In light of current health care trends, how is this case an economic concern for the doctor and for society?

■ LEARNING ACTIVITIES

1. Interview an older adult about his or her physical health. What chronic conditions does the individual have? How do these interfere with activities of daily living? What has the person done to adjust to any impairments? Does the person use any assistive technology devices (low- or high-tech) to help with activities?

2. Ask an older family member or friend to share with you a recent hospital or doctor bill and the Medicare invoice that corresponds to that health care episode. After gaining the person's permission, report to the class the type of health care episode, the amount the health care provider charged, the amount Medicare paid, the amount paid by a Medigap policy (if there is one), and the amount paid by the patient. How easy or difficult was it to gather this information from the invoices sent by each provider?

3. Investigate whether HMOs are in your area. If so, phone each HMO and ask them to send you information about plans for Medicare patients. Find out what model of HMO they adhere to (they will no doubt be impressed with your knowledge!). Compare the plans with Medicare and a standard Medigap policy. What are the differences in coverage?

4. What health promotion programs are available in your community for older adults? Who sponsors these programs? What services and information are offered in these programs?

FOR MORE INFORMATION

National Resources

1. American Diabetes Association, 1660 Duke Street, Alexandria, VA 22314, 703-549-1500 or 800-342-2383.

   The American Diabetes Association works to prevent and cure diabetes and to improve the quality of life of persons affected with diabetes. It provides information about the diagnosis and treatment of diabetes and resources available to assist people with this disease. Local chapters of the association provide support and educational materials. The association publishes *Diabetes Forecast,* a monthly publication about living with diabetes, and numerous pamphlets including *Older Adults: Diabetes and You.*

2. American Health Foundation, 1 Dana Road, Valhalla, NY 10595, 914-592-6317.

   The American Health Foundation conducts research in preventive health care and has developed a public education program to promote health promotion behaviors. It publishes the *Health Passport,* designed to inform readers about heart disease and cancer, and *Live Well,* which shows readers how to eat a low-fat diet.

3. American Heart Association, 7272 Greenville Avenue, Dallas, TX 75231, 214-373-6300 (http://www.9mhrt.org).

   The American Heart Association funds research and conducts public education programs on the prevention and control of heart and cardiovascular disease. It distributes a number of pamphlets for older adults including *Walking for a Healthy Heart* and *An Older Person's Guide to Cardiovascular Health.*

4. American Red Cross, 430 17th Street NW, Washington, DC 20006, 202-737-8300.

   The American Red Cross, most noted for its disaster relief program, also provides health education programs and health services. Local chapters offer health screening programs and wellness and family health programs.

5. Arthritis Foundation, 1314 Spring Street NW, Atlanta, GA 30309, 404-872-7100 or 800-283-7800.

   The Arthritis Foundation offers health education programs, brochures, and a bimonthly magazine about resources and programs to help persons with arthritis. Local chapters sponsor exercise programs, support groups, and resource materials.

6. Centers for Disease Control National AIDS Clearinghouse, P.O. Box 6003, Rockville, MD 20849, 800-458-5231.

   The National AIDS Clearinghouse, a referral source for identifying health care resources for persons with AIDS, can help callers locate educational materials. Inquirers can obtain a number of publications, including *Coping With AIDS* and *Caring for the AIDS Patient at Home*.

7. Health Care Finance Administration, P.O. Box 340, Columbia, MD 21045, 410-786-3000 or 800-638-6833 (http://www.hcfa.gov).

   HCFA coordinates the Medicare program and has publications for consumers including *The Medicare Handbook* and *Guide to Health Insurance for People on Medicare*.

Web Resources

1. Healthtouch Online
   http://www.healthtouch.com

   Healthtouch's home page offers health resources and health information. Its Web site provides a searchable database of prescription and over-the-counter drugs and a health resource directory that provides information about how to contact health organizations for more information about specific health topics. The site also has information about many topics related to health, wellness, diseases, and illnesses.

2. Monash Health Promotion Unit, Monash University, Australia
   http://www.monash.edu.au/health

   Monash University's Department of Medicine has constructed a Web site designed to encourage health education and promotion. The site has numerous links to information about a wide variety of health issues such as Alzheimer's disease, arthritis, eye problems, ethnic and minority health, physical activity, and much more. It's worth the trip to Australia!

3. Colorado HealthNet Home Page
   http://www.bcn.boulder.co.us/health/chn

   Colorado HealthNet home page offers information about health concerns including arthritis, asthma, cancer, chronic pain, diabetes, elder care issues, and an opportunity to submit or read about patients' stories.

4. Homebound Program
   http://www.crm.mb.ca:80/scip/health/homebond.html

   This site describes the Homebound Program in Winnipeg, Manitoba, Canada. The Homebound Program is a health promotion outreach service for retired shut-ins over age 50 and their caregivers in Winnipeg. The Homebound Program offers, among other services, an audiovisual lending library of more than 80 health promotion and wellness topics. The Homebound Program has received many awards, so stop by and learn more about what they are doing in Manitoba!

5. National Center for Chronic Disease Prevention and Health Promotion
   http://www.cdc.gov/nccdphp/needhome.htm

   The center has a site with links to information about chronic disease, disease prevention and control, and community health promotion.

6. Family Health, College of Osteopathic Medicine at Ohio University
   http://www.tcom.ohiou.edu:80/family-health.html

   The College of Osteopathic Medicine at Ohio University has developed a series of 2½-minute audio programs designed to reach a general audience with practical, easy-to-understand answers to some frequently asked questions about health and health care. Topics currently available include arthritis, frailty and older adults, urinary incontinence, and exercise. Check out this new way of delivering health education over the Net!

NOTES

1. A benefit period begins on the first day a beneficiary receives inpatient hospital benefits and ends after being discharged from the hospital or skilled nursing facility for 60 consecutive days.

2. Under the recent welfare reform act (Personal Responsibility and Work Opportunity Reconciliation Act of 1996), AFDC is replaced by Temporary Assistance to Needy Families (TANF). Under this legislation, states have been given more leeway to determine Medicaid eligibility for families with children.

3. Services to mothers and children under the categorically needy of Medicaid are not listed.

12

Mental Health Services

Phil, a 78-year-old widower, lived independently until about 6 months ago. At that time, he realized that he no longer could get around without the help of a walker. Just as he was accepting this restriction, his eye doctor told him that nothing more could be done to treat his macular degeneration. Now, Phil is legally blind. Because of his independent nature, the eye specialist referred him to a rehabilitation counselor for persons with visual impairments. Despite progress on learning new skills, the counselor became increasingly concerned about Phil's extreme mood swings from anger to despondency. The rehabilitation counselor referred him to the mental health center's peer counseling program. After a few weeks of talking one-on-one with the peer counselor, Phil agreed to participate twice per week in a group of other older adults with similar experiences. Phil likes the idea of talking through his problems with someone his own age. He says, "I am getting the help I need without people thinking I am crazy."

Approximately 532,000 community-dwelling older adults have a serious or chronic mental illness (e.g., any psychiatric disorder present during the past year that seriously interferes with one or more aspects of daily life) that they have coped with throughout their adult lives (Barker et al., 1992). For other older adults, like Phil, factors such as a decline in physical health, loss of independence, lower socioeconomic status, multiple stressful life events, and limited social support seriously influence their mental health status for the first time in their lives.

This chapter focuses on mental health services for older adults and their families. We begin by examining federal support for mental health programs and services. Next, we profile older adults with mental health problems and describe the various types of programs designed specifically to address their needs. We conclude this part of the chapter with a discussion of the current and future issues in delivering mental health programs. The second part of the chapter examines mental health services targeted to caregivers of elders with physical and/or cognitive impairments.

Policy Background

The Community Mental Health Act of 1963 created a major change in the provision of mental health services in the United States. It changed the focus of care from long-term, custodial, institutional care in state hospitals to active, outpatient, community-based care. A major goal of outpatient care for all individuals, including older adults, is to encourage maximum independence. This translates into the need for mental health programs and services aimed at keeping older persons within their own homes and communities.

Mental health services for older adults constitute only about 2.5% of Medicare expenditures. Medicare coverage for mental health services was expanded in 1990 (via the Omnibus Budget Reconciliation Act [OBRA] of 1989), but coverage of specialized services is still limited. For example, although there is no limit on the total number of hospitalization or inpatient days for psychiatric care in general hospitals, coverage for inpatient care in freestanding psychiatric hospitals is limited to 190 days during an individual's lifetime. For outpatient services, there is no limit on allowable charges, although there is a 50% coinsurance. OBRA (1989) also expanded the coverage for services provided by nonphysician providers. Psychologists and clinical social workers rendering mental health services now are eligible for direct reimbursement; previously, reimbursement was made only when the services provided by these professionals were under the direct supervision of a physician.

In response to the changes put forth by OBRA, the National Association of Insurance Commissioners revised the model Medicare Supplemental (Medigap) insurance regulations. All Medigap policies are now required to cover the 50% coinsurance for outpatient mental health care under Medicare Part B (Finkel, 1993). Unfortunately, this change is prospective, therefore it does not apply to older adults holding Medigap policies in effect prior to their state's adoption of the new model regulation.

Medicaid services for mental health care for older adults vary substantially among states. Coverage is divided into mandatory and optional services (Taube, Goldman, & Salkever, 1990). General hospital inpatient care, physician services, outpatient services in general hospitals, emergency room services, and nursing home care are mandatory. These services focus on the needs of patients with acute illness episodes and persons who need to be in a nursing home. The optional services help persons with chronic mental impairments living in community settings. These services include care by nonphysicians, freestanding outpatient clinics, case management, rehabilitation, and home health care. Many states have not adopted Medicaid's optional elements. In those states that have, providers are often reluctant to participate because of the low rates of reimbursement.

In 1987, the Omnibus Budget Reconciliation Act was passed by Congress as part of Medicaid reform. This legislation requires that all prospective nursing home applicants who have a primary or secondary diagnosis of a major mental disorder undergo a preadmission screening to determine if they are appropriate for nursing home admission and if they need active treatment for mental illness. The mental disorders covered by OBRA include schizophrenia, paranoid disorders, major affective disorders, schizo-affective disorders, and atypical psychoses. Nursing homes who admit older adults with designated psychiatric conditions without conducting the prescreening are denied Medicaid payments.

The Social Security Administration administers several programs that provide cash payments or other benefits to persons with mental disabilities. Persons with adequate work histories usually receive monthly cash payments as Social Security benefits, and persons with minimal resources and insufficient work history usually receive a monthly payment under the Supplemental Security Income (SSI) program. Approximately 46,000 persons 65 years of age and older receive government disability payments because of their mental disorders (Barker et al., 1992).

Older American Act funds also may be used to support mental health services for older adults under Title III-B and III-F. Title III-B, which allocates spending for a wide range of supportive services, includes funding for mental health programs as well. Local AAA funds can be used to support mental health programs and services designed to enable older adults to attain and maintain mental well-being. Funding also may be authorized under Title III-F, which funds disease prevention and health promotion services. Health promotion services can include screening for the prevention of depression, coordination of community mental health services, provision of educational activities, and referral to psychiatric and psychological services. Thus, local AAAs have the opportunity to fund a wide variety of mental health programs and services under the OAA.

Users and Programs

Characteristics of Mental Health Clients

Between 15% and 25% of people 65 and older are purported to suffer from mental illness or emotional distress that affects their quality of life (Buckwalter,

Smith, & Caston, 1994). Approximately 60% of the mental health problems experienced by older adults are due to nonorganic psychiatric disorders (e.g., affective and anxiety disorders), with the remaining due to organic mental disorders (i.e., dementia; George, Blazer, Winfield-Laird, Leaf, & Fischbach, 1988).

Depression is the most common reason for referring older persons for mental health services (Kent, 1990; Mosher-Ashley, 1993). As many as 15% of community-dwelling older adults and 50% of elders living in long-term care facilities suffer from depression (Blazer, 1989). In the majority of cases, their depression is viewed as a reactive depression (i.e., the person is reacting to a major life loss or transition) rather than as stemming from other etiologies. Other reasons older adults are referred for mental health services include (a) Alzheimer's disease and other organic mental disorders, affecting approximately 10% of individuals 65 years of age and older living in the community; (b) suicide behaviors—17% of all suicides are committed by adults 65 years of age and older; and (c) alcoholism, which affects about 10% to 15% of older adults, the same rate as found in the general population (Ostrander, 1992). Greater percentages of older adults of color (i.e., African Americans, Hispanics, American Indians, and Asian-Pacific Islanders) report having mental health problems than do their white counterparts. Within these minority groups, women tend to have higher rates of affective and anxiety disorders, whereas men tend to have higher rates of substance abuse-dependence disorders (Stanford & Bois, 1992).

Several demographic variables are associated with the use of mental health services among older adults (Freiman, Cunningham, & Cornelius, 1993). For example, increasing age is associated with a lower probability of mental health, as is being a person of color. Women and individuals recently widowed have a significantly higher probability of health care use for mental problems than do men and married persons. Also, the more acute and chronic health problems reported by older adults, the more likely they are to be using mental health services.

Only about 5% of rural community mental health centers' patients and less than 2% of rural private patients with psychiatric problems are older adults (Buckwalter et al., 1994). Buckwalter et al. suggest several factors that adversely influence the appropriate use of mental health services by rural elders, including sociodemographic, economic, and cultural issues; the lack of mental health professionals to work with aged individuals; and the stigma surrounding mental illness and its treatment.

Older adults with serious or chronic mental illness represent the most severely disabled persons with psychiatric disorders, yet there is almost no research concerning the use of community services by these individuals (George, 1992). One study of 111 deinstitutionalized older adults with chronic mental illnesses revealed that those individuals receiving care and support from family members were most likely to be living in the community (Meeks et al., 1990). Among these individuals, 59% were on psychotropic medications, but only 17% were seeing a mental health professional on a regular basis.

Residents of long-term care facilities also benefit from mental health services. The three major nursing home resident groups needing such services are persons who are physically ill but cognitively capable; persons who are mentally ill but cognitively capable; and those with dementia. Although different therapeutic issues arise and different interventions are needed for each group, all long-term care residents face similar situations in which they may require emotional support, including (a) making the transition into the facility, (b) establishing relationships with staff, (c) adapting to the institution's schedule, (d) adjusting to new roles with family caregivers or to a lack of family caregivers, and (e) accommodating to a new activities schedule (Lichtenberg, 1994). Unfortunately, results of a national survey revealed that less than 5% of older nursing home residents have contact with a mental health professional or receive some type of mental health care from a general physician (Burns et al., 1993). Those receiving mental health services were more likely to have a specific mental health diagnosis, were exhibiting mood disturbances, and had been transferred from a psychiatric hospital. This suggests that services are more likely to be directed toward individuals with more serve impairments. In addition, age was a factor. Individuals between the ages of 64 and 74 were more likely than older patients to receive care.

Mental Health Programs

For most older adults, mental health intervention does not mean going into a counselor's office or receiving help from a specialized mental health care center. Fewer than 2% of persons seen in private psychiatric offices and only 4% to 6% of patients who receive community mental health services are 65 years of age and older (Wykle, Segall, & Nagley, 1992). This can be attributed to several factors: (a) Most centers are not widely accessible and tend to be isolated from the mainstream of community health and social services for older adults; (b) mental health service programs have not aggressively engaged in outreach and case finding; rather, they tend to rely on referrals and self-identification of potential clients; and (c) reimbursement for treatment of mental disorders under Medicare is substantially less complete than for physical disorders (Lebowitz & Niederehe, 1992).

The aging service network provides a wide range of mental health services for older adults. The results of a national mail survey of AAAs (Bane, Rathbone-McCuan, & Galliher, 1994) indicate that the most common services available in rural planning and service areas (PSAs) were telephone reassurance, mental health screening, individual counseling, and Alzheimer's support groups. In mixed PSAs (i.e., areas with rural, urban, and suburban counties) the most common mental health services were Alzheimer's support groups, counseling, and mental health referral and materials. Great variability in the community resources that facilitate these services to older adults was found in both the rural and mixed PSAs. For example, more than 80% of respondents in both areas reported the availability of adult protective service intervention for older persons with mental health problems, whereas only 12% of the rural PSAs and 31% of the mixed PSAs reported having a mobile mental health team that traveled to the person's home.

Mental health services and counseling may take place in a health care setting (i.e., physician office or clinic), the client's residence (i.e., own home or nursing home), a senior center, or an adult day center. For example, more than 350 persons 55 years of age and older have participated in a counseling program located at *Mature Minglers* multipurpose senior center in Michigan (Grady, 1990). The *Geriatric Service Program* located in Baltimore County provides psychotherapy sessions at the suburban homes of older adults unable or unwilling to come to a senior center, where services are also provided, or to the community mental health center in which the program is housed (DeRenzo et al., 1991). The *Senior Adult Growth and Enrichment Program* in North Carolina is a mental health outreach program that provides home-based services to rural older adults living in their own homes or in long-term care facilities (Atkinson & Stuck, 1991).

Relatively little is known about the community-based services available to older adults with serious or chronic mental illness who are at risk for or who have a history of psychiatric hospitalization. A nationwide survey of 73 mental health agencies providing outpatient psychiatric services to this group of older adults provides some descriptive information about the services provided and the problems facing agencies serving older adults with chronic mental illness (Mosher-Ashley & Allard, 1993). The majority of agencies surveyed were community mental health centers (87%). The primary services provided to older adults with chronic mental illness were counseling, crisis intervention, case management, group therapy, case consultation, in-service training, and day treatment. The most common problems agencies faced in providing services to older clients with chronic mental illness were insufficient funds, lack of residential services, lack of transportation, and insufficient staffing.

Although community-based treatment of older adults with mental health problems is preferred by both older adults and mental health professionals, a small proportion of older individuals need more intensive care provided by institutions. Persons older than age 65 represent less than 7% of all individuals

---

Best Practice **Gatekeeper Program**

This program, originally developed in 1978 in Spokane County, Washington, is designed to seek out and offer assistance to at-risk older adults living in isolation. This is accomplished through "gatekeepers," nontraditional referral sources such as postal workers, meter readers, phone operators, and others who come into contact with older adults on a regular basis. Gatekeepers are trained to identify and refer at-risk older adults to appropriate support agencies that can intervene and solve a problem before it becomes a major crisis.

For more information about the Gatekeeper Program, contact Elderly Services Program, Spokane Community Mental Health Center, 107 South Division, Spokane, WA 99202, 509-458-7450.

SOURCE: American Association of Retired Persons (1996).

---

receiving inpatient psychiatric services. Symptoms of depression, anxiety, dementia, paranoia, delusional ideation, and alcohol and drug abuse are the most likely reasons for admission of older persons to psychiatric hospitals. The need for hospitalization is dependent on the severity of symptoms and the older person's ability to carry out activities of daily living. In addition, patients frequently have concomitant physical illnesses that also must be addressed. The major goal of residential treatment programs is to alleviate symptoms and provide care and training in skills of daily living (Wykle et al., 1992).

The number of specifically trained individuals to provide mental health services targeted for geriatric patients is small but growing. Four major clusters of professionals treat older adults: psychiatric nurses, clinical social workers, psychologists, and psychiatrists (Gottlieb, 1990). They work in settings such as community mental health centers, inpatient settings, HMOs, public and private agencies, hospitals, nursing homes, and private practice. Mental health services for older adults may also be provided by physicians certified in geriatric medicine, counselors and therapists, and pastoral counselors.

The last 15 years have seen a growth in the use of paraprofessionals providing psychological and psychosocial interventions with older adults (Lichtenberg, 1994). In some cases, they offer formal mental health services, whereas in others, they provide informal support. Paraprofessionals work alone or in conjunction with or under the supervision of trained professionals. One type of paraprofessional program that has grown rapidly during the last two decades is peer counseling programs for older adults. These programs train and supervise older adults to provide counseling and support to other older individuals. Peer counselors typically address a broad range of issues including depression; loneliness; problems that result from physical impairments; and other concerns related to aging, gender, and ethnicity. They receive supervision from a professional counselor employed by the agency sponsoring the program. Programs often begin because they are a cost-effective means of providing mental health services for older adults. The benefits of peer counseling programs for older adults include these: (a) Many older people talk more readily to older people than to professional therapists; (b) peer counselors serve as positive models for their clients; (c) peer counseling enriches the lives of both the client and the counselor; and (d) peer counselors may be more effective than professionals because they are often more aware of the problems indicative of the older individual (Bratter & Freeman, 1990).

Challenges for Mental Health Programs

The graying of America and the deinstitutionalization of persons with mental illness have resulted in increased attention to the mental health needs of older adults. Although great improvements in the delivery of mental health services have been made since the passage of the Community Mental Health Act in 1963 and the funding of mental health programs under the OAA, many challenges remain to improve the delivery of mental health services to older adults.

Connecting the Delivery Systems

The two primary systems involved in providing community services to older adults with mental health concerns are the public mental health system (primarily community mental health centers) and the aging service network. A formal relationship between community mental health centers and the aging network, however, often is the exception, rather than the rule. This is unfortunate for older adults because those centers with formal relationships with local AAAs tend to provide a larger range of services to older adults, provide services to older adults in more settings, and provide mental services to higher proportions of older adults than do those without formal affiliations (Lebowitz, Light, & Bailey, 1987). Thus, joining forces appears to be the most effective and efficient means of reaching and servicing older adults with mental health concerns.

Reaching Diverse Groups

Older adults of color use mental health services to a lesser extent than their white counterparts, yet they appear to have the same, if not greater, need for such services. Use is affected by language barriers, limited access to information regarding available services, transportation, cultural dissimilarity, and reduced social and economic resources (Stanford & Bois, 1992). Because individuals from ethnic minority groups represent a rapidly increasing segment of the total older adult population, mental health services must recognize the importance of cultural sensitivity and cross-cultural training of mental health professionals as one means of eliminating the barriers to use of mental health services by ethnic minority elders.

The rural older adult population also is vastly underserved by the mental health system (Bane et al., 1994; Buckwalter, Smith, Zevenbergen, & Russell, 1991). As with most other service sectors, rural providers are faced with the issues of availability, accessibility, and acceptability of mental health services. In addition, the closure of rural physician practices and hospitals has forced rural citizens either to use local emergency services, regardless of whether they are capable of responding to mental health problems, or to seek health care in distant urban areas (U.S. Congress, Office of Technology Assessment, 1990).

Training Providers

Needed are more providers trained specifically to address the mental health concerns of older adults. By the year 2020, as many as 500 additional academic geriatric psychiatrists will be needed to offer leadership in education, training and research in this area (Committee on Personnel for Health Needs of the Elderly, 1988). Similar needs are projected for the other specialities constituting the core disciplines of geriatric mental health—psychology, social work, and psychiatric nursing. Continuing education programs also are needed for current mental health practitioners, many of whom lack the knowledge and skills necessary to effectively work with older adults needing mental health services.

Providing Mental Health Programs in the Future

The 1995 White House Conference on Aging gave specific support for programs that meet the mental health needs of older adults. Delegates passed 14 resolutions that supported policies related to mental health, including those to (a) amend Medicaid to include provisions that ensured the availability of home and community-based mental health services; (b) amend all statutes that regulate public and private health and long-term care insurance plans to achieve parity in coverage and reimbursement for mental and physical health disorders; and (c) expand educational and training programs in mental health and aging for professionals as well as for older persons, their families, and other gatekeepers in the community.

Because the vast majority of older adults exist in and interact with a family network, the mental health needs of those within the family network must be addressed. We now turn our attention to the mental health needs of family caregivers.

Mental Health Services for Family Caregivers

One potential consequence of providing care for older adults with physical and cognitive impairments is an increased risk of mental health problems among family caregivers. Caregivers are highly vulnerable to stress-related physical and emotional complaints. They frequently report experiencing bouts of depression and a high use of psychotropic drugs (George, 1992). Community services for caregivers include educational programs, support groups, respite care, and assistance with handling their emotional reactions to the changes in their loved ones. These services may be partially funded or supported by various state, local, and nonprofit voluntary agencies. In this section, we describe the characteristics of caregivers who use mental health services and the types of services available to them. We end with a discussion of the challenges facing programs trying to reach and serve these caregivers.

Users and Programs

Characteristics of Caregivers Using Mental Health Programs

Family caregivers who seek support from mental health professionals present a wide array of problems and concerns. A study of 51 family caregivers who participated in weekly individual counseling sessions revealed nine pressing issues and problems: improving coping skills (time management, dealing with stress, and other coping mechanisms); family issues regarding spouse, siblings, and children; responding to the older person's emotional and behavior needs; physical well-being and safety; legal and financial affairs; quality of relationship with the care receiver; eliciting formal and informal support; feelings of guilt and inadequacy; and long-term planning (Smith, Smith, & Toseland, 1991). These problems and issues are consistent with findings of other researchers and suggest areas in which practitioners need to be prepared to help caregivers with a broad range of problems and concerns.

Group interventions also provide caregivers with skills and support to cope with the stressors of caregiving. An extensive review of the caregiver support group literature (Toseland & Rossiter, 1989) revealed that the typical support group is composed of predominantly middle-class women, mostly the wives and daughters of those receiving care. Although participants range in age from 16 to 80, most are between the ages of 40 and 65. The majority provide care for a parent or relative with some form of mental impairment.

Mental Health Programs for Family Caregivers

Programs designed to meet the mental health needs of family caregivers include individual counseling, support groups, and educational programs. A review of these intervention strategies suggests positive outcomes for the caregivers who participate (Gallagher-Thompson, 1994). With respect to individual counseling, spouses of persons with Alzheimer's disease report less depression after their participation in brief psychodynamic psychotherapy. This approach offered caregivers the opportunity to understand how past conflicts were influencing their reactions and responses to their current situation (Rose & DelMaestro, 1990). After completion of brief cognitive-behavioral therapy whereby participants were taught to identify and modify the negative thoughts that contributed to the development and maintenance of depression, caregivers reported a significant reduction in symptoms associated with depression (Gallagher-Thompson, 1994). Behavioral therapy approaches also are effective in teaching management skills to family caregivers of persons with dementia, thereby reducing the stressfulness of the situation for the caregivers (Fisher & Carstensen, 1990). A study of individual counseling for daughters and daughters-in-law who were primary caregivers for physically frail elders also revealed positive outcomes for those who received treatment, compared with a no-treatment group (Toseland & Smith, 1990). Caregivers participating in counseling demonstrated more effective coping skills, improved psychological well-being, and improved relationships with the care receivers than did caregivers who did not receive counseling.

Support groups, a popular form of caregiver intervention, are widely available and generally well attended (Gallagher-Thompson, 1994). Most groups are limited to six to eight sessions. Almost all include both education and support, focusing on seven major themes: information about the care receiver's situation, the group and its members as a mutual support system, the emotional impact of caregiving, self-care, problematic interpersonal relationships, the development and use of support systems outside the group, and home care skills. The majority of leaders report positive outcomes for regular attendees, and the participants report high satisfaction with the group. These outcomes, however, tend not to be substantiated by data obtained either through the use of standardized measures in case study evaluations or by more rigorously designed research studies (Toseland & Rossiter, 1989).

For Your Files   ***Caregiver Support Groups in America***

Caregiver Support Groups in America, a new directory published by the National Council on the Aging, lists 750 support groups for caregivers. The caregiver groups are listed state by state and include specific types of support groups such as for children of aging parents or for persons taking care of individuals with Alzheimer's disease. The guide also includes a listing of manuals on how to start a support group. For more information, contact National Council on the Aging Publications, Department 5087, Washington, DC 20061-5087, 202-479-1200.

Numerous educational programs have been developed to meet the needs of individuals faced with the challenges of providing care for frail, aging relatives. Most of these programs are for spouses and adult children who have assumed the primary responsibility for a family member experiencing physical or cognitive decline. The majority of these programs cover a variety of topics including community resources, sensory changes, communication skills, normal aging, behavioral changes, living arrangements, coping with stress, and chronic illness (Roberto, 1990). Among the few program descriptions or evaluations found in family or gerontological journals, several commonalities existed. First, the presentation formats are similar. A two-hour session offered during several weeks is the most popular model. Second, almost all programs use a multiple topic approach. Third, although the majority provided similar content, most programs are designed for a specific target population (Brubaker & Roberto, 1993).

Many cooperative extension programs provide support in meeting the mental health needs of caregivers of frail elders. Through the facilitation of formal educational programs (Epstein & Koenig, 1990) and support groups (Marsden, 1990), family members learn how to more effectively carry out their roles and responsibilities as primary caregivers while reducing feelings of stress and burnout. For example, the *Volunteer Information Provider Program* initially designed to help rural Missouri families deal with the stress of caregiving has been replicated in at least 24 states and the District of Columbia (Halpert & Sharp, 1989). The goal of this program is to train peer volunteer information providers to deliver information to family caregivers on topics such as the normal aging process, communication skills, and stress management.

Since the pioneering efforts of the Travelers Companies in the mid-1980s, workplace support for caregivers has increased (Neal, Chapman, Ingersoll-Dayton, & Emlen, 1993). Employers provide support for their employees with elder care needs through their policies (e.g., job-sharing options; flex-time; and medical, personal, or family leave time), benefits (e.g., insurance, tax credits, dependent care reimbursement plans, and subsidized care), and services (education, information and referral, counseling, and case management).

Challenges for Family Caregiver Mental Health Programs

As the number of frail older persons increases and more family members occupy the role of caregiver, the emotional support provided by mental health services will be in greater demand. A number of challenges need to be addressed to meet the mental health needs of family caregivers.

Increasing Participation in Programs

A limited number of caregivers attend mental health-related programs or use services that may enhance their ability to provide care. This may be because many do not identify themselves as caregivers or because they may lack a caregiving alternative that would allow them to attend therapy or other types of programs. When caregivers do access these services, it usually is because they have reached a crisis stage. Health care and other service providers need to inform caregivers of the availability of supportive services and encourage their use before caregivers experience distress. Caregivers need to be continually reminded to "take care of themselves." They also need reassurance that using services does not mean that they are failing to meet their caregiving responsibilities, but rather that through the use of such services, they are maintaining and enhancing their coping abilities. Employers also need to recognize the benefits of mental health programs for their employers who are family caregivers and make those services available through employee assistance programs.

Reaching Diverse Groups

Despite research that demonstrates that minority caregivers experience burden and depression, they are less likely to participate in caregiver support programs. The lack of seeking mental health support may be due in part to the caregiver's reliance on others in the informal network for caregiving assistance and the internalization of the caregiver role, which makes seeking formal services contradict strong cultural norms of family responsibility (Cox & Monk, 1993). Because cultural norms may make it difficult for caregivers to turn to the formal network for support, services must be sensitive to the differing personal and cultural expectations held by caregivers of various ethnic and racial groups. Cox and Monk suggest that support groups need to be created within ethnic communities in which caregivers would feel more comfortable discussing their problems with those who have similar cultural experiences and expectations.

Mental Health Programs in the Future

The delegates of the 1995 White House Conference on Aging endorsed mental health programs that support caregivers of older adults. Specifically, delegates passed resolutions promoting policies that (a) provide culturally, ethnically, and linguistically sensitive education and support for intergenerational family caregivers through the efforts of volunteers and revenue-neutral support groups and (b) expand the Family and Medical Leave Act of 1993 for individuals who render care for aging relatives.

 ## CASE STUDY

SCHIZOPHRENIA COMPLICATES CARE NEEDS

Katherine is a 77-year-old divorced woman who has a diagnosis of schizophrenia. Although Katherine has most likely been a schizophrenic since her early 20s, she was not formally diagnosed until her mid-50s. Since her diagnosis and subsequent treatment, Katherine has enjoyed long periods when she has felt good. Like many mental health patients, however, when Katherine is feeling good, she stops taking her medicine. Gradually, mood changes occur that escalate to hostile and paranoid behavior. On many occasions, she has had to be hospitalized in the psychiatric care unit of the local hospital. The length of time under such care varies, depending on how long it takes to regulate her medication.

Despite her illness, Katherine raised four sons. Two of her sons are dead, one lives out of state and takes no interest in his mother, and the fourth and youngest son, Tom, lives nearby. Tom tries to help his mother, but it isn't easy. She keeps to herself and does not let people, even her son, get close to her. In her community, she is known as a character who doesn't mince words. Although she is fiercely independent, she is dedicated to her church. One of her favorite rituals is communion, which she always takes twice a year.

Now, age has compounded her problems. Katherine is overweight, is unsteady on her feet, and has arthritis and poor vision. It is increasingly difficult for her to get around. At this stage, her isolated, simple life is also becoming problematic. She requires more services such as transportation, shopping assistance, and daily monitoring to make sure she is taking her medication. Although her disease has leveled out some, she continues to have relapses when she is noncompliant with her medicine. These events are more frequent than necessary. Both her son Tom and her mental health worker of 3 years are concerned about her future.

CASE STUDY QUESTIONS

1. What mental health research data discussed in this chapter best describe Katherine?

2. Do you think Katherine's mental health diagnosis, coupled with her physical problems, makes her more at risk of institutionalization? Why or why not?

3. Katherine probably would not qualify for nursing home care as a Medicaid recipient solely because of her physical health. Under what circumstances described in the chapter could Katherine receive nursing home care paid for by Medicaid?

4. Fortunately, Katherine has the services of a professional mental health worker. From which of the mental health programs described in the chapter has Katherine most likely been receiving services?

5. What types of support may be available for Tom to help him understand and care for his mother?

LEARNING ACTIVITIES

1. Interview a mental health professional who works with older adults. What are some of the primary issues with which many older adults seek or need assistance? What are some of the difficulties in getting older adults to participate in mental health services? Why has this professional decided or been chosen to work with older adults? How might the skills needed be similar to or different from those needed to work with other populations?

2. Ask a mental health service provider to share with you copies of the assessment tools that are used for younger and older adults. Are they similar or different? Would you have difficulty in answering some of the questions?

3. Sit in on a peer counseling or other type of mental health training. What was the topic? How did it relate to older adults, family caregivers, or those providing services to them? What did you learn?

4. What do you believe are the benefits and issues related to mental health services for older adults and their family caregivers? What did you learn were some of the barriers, and what might the agency and the community do to break down the barriers? What might keep you from accessing mental health services currently and in the future?

FOR MORE INFORMATION

National Resources

1. National Institute of Mental Health, Information Resources and Inquiries Branch, Room 7C-02, 5600 Fishers Lane, Rockville, MD 20857, 301-443-4513.

   The National Institute of Mental Health conducts and supports research to learn more about causes and treatment of mental and emotional disorders. Available are free publications including *Plain Talk About Aging, If You Are Over 65 and Feeling Depressed,* and *Plain Talk About Handling Stress.*

2. National Mental Health Association, 1021 Prince Street, Alexandria, VA 22314-2971, 703-684-5968; National Mental Health Information Center, 800-969-6642.

   The National Mental Health Information Center, established by the National Mental Health Association, provides inquirers with information about mental health topics and has a wide variety of written information about mental health topics.

3. Alzheimer's Association, 919 North Michigan Avenue, Suite 1000, Chicago, IL 60611, 800-272-3900 (http://www.alz.org).

   The Alzheimer's Association sponsors education programs and support services to patients and families who are coping with Alzheimer's disease. The association offers a 24-hour hotline with information about Alzheimer's disease and local chapters and resources. Educational materials are also available.

4. National Self-Help Clearinghouse, 25 West 43rd Street, Room 620, New York, NY 10036, 212-642-2944.

   The National Self-Help Clearinghouse collects and distributes information about self-care and self-help groups across the United States and offers such groups technical assistance. Publications and guides to organizing self-help groups are available.

Web Resources

1. Mental HealthNet
   http://www.cmhc.com/

   This is quite a site! This site offers more than 4,200 individual resources on mental health issues. Links to a reading room, professional resources, self-help resources, and other mental health Web resources are listed. Definitely worth the visit when you have some time to spend between classes!

2. Psych Central, Dr. John Grohol's Mental Health Page
   http://www.coil.com/grohol/web.htm

   This psych Web pointer helps visitors locate information on the Web and is organized by topic or alphabetically. There is an incredibly lengthy list of general support resource links to other sites on the Web with a brief description. It's the most comprehensive mental health listing we found.

3. Emotional Support Guide
   http://asa.ugl.lib.umich.edu/chdocs/support/emotion.html

   This site, created by the University of Michigan Library, has links to emotional support resources, such as Griefnet and Caregiver Information, chronic illness resources, and bereavement resources.

13

Legal Services

Fernando telephones the local area agency on aging requesting emergency food. The agency staff member arranges for food to be delivered and then asks Fernando why he has none. It seems that he has not received his Social Security check for 2 months. He did get a couple of letters from Social Security a few months ago, but he does not read well, so he set them aside and forgot about them. He did not pay his rent this month or last and ran out of medicine 2 days ago. The agency staff member arranges for Fernando to receive daily meals and medication. She also calls the local senior legal assistance program and makes an appointment for Fernando. With the assistance of a senior legal aid attorney, his Social Security checks were reinstated, and his landlord has agreed not to evict him.

Fernando's situation illustrates how one problem, a lack of food, can in turn reveal a cascade of other additional problems, many of which are or become legal issues. Older adults may experience legal problems brought about by changes in work, family, and physical health. These problems can have devastating consequences on their quality of life. For example, a retired person may be unable to collect an expected pension. After the divorce of a child, the ex-son- or daughter-in-law might refuse to let grandparents visit grandchildren—or because of other circumstances, grandparents may find themselves as parents once again, caring for grandchildren. Upon the death or divorce of a spouse, tangible property must be divided, and when physical or mental capacity wanes, substitute decision makers might need to be appointed to make decisions on behalf of an older adult. Legal problems may also occur because older adults do not have access to legal advice before signing legal documents (Moore, 1992).

231

In this chapter, we review the federal policies that facilitated the development of legal programs serving older adults. We then briefly discuss the legal problems that older adults often encounter and consequently need assistance with and the different types of legal programs designed to serve older adults. We conclude this chapter by discussing the challenges that legal programs face in meeting the legal needs of older adults.

Policy Background

In 1974, Congress passed legislation that created the Legal Services Corporation (LSC). Its purpose is to provide low-income individuals with minimum access to legal assistance. The LSC is a private, nonprofit organization directed by an 11-member board appointed by Congress and the president. Currently, the LSC funds 323 local legal services programs in all 50 states, as well as 23 national and state support centers that provide technical legal assistance and expertise on a variety of poverty law issues. The National Senior Citizen Law Centers in Los Angeles and Washington, D.C., the Legal Counsel for the Elderly, and Legal Services for New York City are examples of LSC-funded centers that specialize in elder law. In addition, the LSC provides funding to numerous law school clinics, some of which specialize in serving older clients (U.S. Senate Special Committee on Aging, 1993).

Individuals can receive legal assistance through a local legal services office, provided that their income does not exceed 125% of the poverty line and their legal problem is civil, rather than criminal. The majority of cases handled by legal services staff on behalf of older adults include housing issues, such as landlord-tenant disputes and subsidized housing complaints; family issues, such as divorce; and public benefits issues, such as Social Security and SSI. Of the 1.4 million cases closed by legal services advocates in 1993, 12% of those cases involved legal assistance to clients older than age 60 (U.S. Senate Special Committee on Aging, 1993).

Since its inception, the LSC has not been without its critics. Every year during the Reagan and Bush administrations (1980 to 1992), the budget submitted by the White House proposed to eliminate the LSC and its programs. Severe cuts in LSC funding through the years have resulted in fewer attorneys and paralegals available to handle cases. Staff reduction has caused many offices to limit the type of cases accepted and the number of people served. For example, the LSC Act of 1974 defined minimum access to legal assistance as having two legal services attorneys for every 10,000 poor persons. Funding levels to meet minimum access standards were obtained in 1980 and 1981 ($300 million and $320 million, respectively); presently, however, there is only one attorney for every 10,000 poor persons. This compares with approximately 28 attorneys for every 10,000 persons with incomes above the poverty line (U.S. Senate Special Committee on Aging, 1993). For fiscal year 1995, Congress appropriated $415 million to fund the LSC programs. Appropriation for fiscal year 1996 was $278 million and was $283 million in 1997. (Legal Services Corporation, 1997; U.S. Library of Congress, 1995a, 1995b).

Older Americans Act Support of Legal Assistance

Legal programs became eligible for funding under the Older Americans Act in 1973. Amendments to the OAA in 1981 required that AAAs spend an "adequate proportion" of Title III-B dollars on legal services. A subsequent amendment in 1987 required state units on aging to set minimum percentages that area agencies must spend on providing legal assistance. AAAs must contract with legal providers who have experience in delivering legal assistance and must involve the private bar in efforts to improve older adults' access to legal assistance. In fiscal year 1994, $20.4 million Title III-B dollars were spent on legal services that served 286,805 older adults and provided 1,151,561 units of service (AoA, 1994b).

In addition to Title III-B dollars allocated to fund legal assistance programs, the Vulnerable Elder Rights Protection Activities program (Title VII), authorized in 1992 amendments to the OAA, also directs funding for legal assistance services. Title VII monies are available to states that establish focal point programs at the state level for elder rights policy review and advocacy. These state programs, usually called Legal Services Developers (listed in Appendix 2), must create statewide standards for legal service delivery, provide technical assistance to AAAs and legal service providers, promote training to representative payees and guardians, and promote pro bono programs in cooperation with the private bar. Title VII monies are also used for programs that are designed to prevent elder abuse, neglect, and exploitation. Funding is made available for programs that

- Conduct public education about elder abuse and outreach to help identify possible cases of abuse and exploitation
- Promote the development of information and data systems for elder abuse reporting systems and conduct analyses of state information concerning elder abuse
- Conduct training on the identification, prevention, and treatment of elder abuse and exploitation as well as conduct training that assists the victims of elder abuse
- Promote the development of an elder abuse, neglect, and exploitation system to identify, investigate, and resolve cases

Users: Legal Problems of Older Adults

Obtaining a profile of who uses legal assistance programs is a difficult task because many programs do not compile detailed information about client characteristics (i.e., marital status, age, income, and education) or are hesitant to publicly reveal client characteristics to protect client confidentiality, or such data are only provided to local AAAs or SUAs and not published in academic journals. Thus, statistical information on Title III-B legal assistance clients is inadequate. Some inferences about client characteristics can be made, however, by examining the type of legal problems for which they seek assistance. In addition, the type of cases that legal programs accept will also affect the type of clients served by those programs. Moreover, legal assistance programs funded under the OAA target socially and financially needy older adults. An older adult with a sizable estate will no doubt be served by the family attorney or be referred to an estate lawyer rather than to a Title III legal aid program. In the next sections, we will review the civil and criminal legal problems of older adults and, when available, the extent to which older adults report having those problems.

Legal problems emerge in various ways. Older adults who lack an understanding about what constitutes a legal problem or how laws originate may not be able to identify that a legal remedy exists when problems occur. Persons who work with older adults also must be aware of potential legal problems, so that referrals can be made to appropriate legal services.

Legal problems can be categorized as either civil or criminal. Civil legal problems are disputes between individuals or organizations, whereas criminal legal problems are those acts that threaten the well-being of the state and include crimes against the person such as assault, homicide, rape, and robbery. Civil legal problems commonly experienced by older adults are presented next, followed by criminal problems.

Family Issues

Divorce

Only 5% of individuals older than 65 are divorced (U.S. Bureau of the Census, 1996a). Although divorce is uncommon in later life and less frequent than in other age groups, its consequences can be financially devastating to older women who divorce. Many women in the current cohort of older adults have been lifelong homemakers and often have no financial support apart from those benefits associated with being a spouse. When husbands file for divorce, lifelong homemakers may discover that the house, utilities, bank accounts, credit cards, and automobiles do not have both names on titles and accounts. Divorce might even exclude the wife's access to her husband's pension. Such arrangements leave them financially vulnerable and in need of legal assistance to protect their rights to marital property.

Grandparent Visitation

Of older adults, 80% have children, and of those, 94% are grandparents (Hooyman & Kiyak, 1996). Researchers have documented that grandparents occupy important roles within the family network. For example, grandparents provide emotional and instrumental support, offer stability in times of crisis, assume parental responsibilities of grandchildren when parents are unavailable, and serve as the keepers of family history (Matthews & Sprey, 1984; Minkler & Roe, 1996). Strong emotional bonds are not uncommon between grandparents and grandchildren (Hodgson, 1995; Roberto & Stroes, 1992).

Various disruptions in the nuclear family can fracture the relationship between grandparents and grandchildren. For example, divorce, death of a parent, adoption of a grandchild by a friend or relative, or termination of parental rights may sever intergenerational bonds. Until recently, grandparents had no legal recourse to aid them in reestablishing contact with their grandchildren. Now, however, all 50 states have enacted laws that allow grandparents to petition the court for visitation rights. State statutes vary with regard to who can petition, the circumstances that must be present in the nuclear family before visitation rights are considered, and how the court determines whether grandparent visitation would be in the best interests of the grandchildren.

Other grandparents have a different set of problems concerning their grandchildren. Growing numbers of grandparents have found themselves parenting their grandchildren (Minkler & Roe, 1996). Grandparents take on the parental role when, for a variety of reasons, parents are unable to care for their children. Grandparents who become parents might need assistance in filing for additional benefits or in securing the legal documents needed to authorize their parental authority.

Estate Planning

A will provides a means to specifically identify and distribute tangible property after death. Dying without a will (*intestate*) results in the distribution of property among family members in accordance with state law. Thus, the distribution of the assets of a person who died intestate can be complicated, time-consuming, and subject to conflicts among family members regarding the value and ownership of the property. Therefore, many older adults, even those with small estates, can benefit from drafting a will. In a statewide survey of older adults in Wisconsin designed to determine the extent of

unmet legal needs, problems with wills and estates were the second most frequently mentioned legal problem experienced by respondents (Spangenberg
Group, 1991).

Income

Many older adults live on fixed incomes and rely wholly or in part on public
income programs such as Social Security, SSI, Railroad Retirement, or Veterans benefits. Some 13% of older adults rely on Social Security for their sole
source of income; 2.1 million receive SSI benefits (GAO, 1995; U.S. Senate
Special Committee on Aging, 1993). When one considers the complex and
complicated regulations that govern the administration of these programs, it
is not surprising that many legal problems can arise.

Legal problems occur when program intake workers refuse to process
applications because older adults do not have the documents needed to
prove their age, work history, marital status, or financial status. In addition,
eligibility criteria are often excessively complicated, confusing, or easily mis-
interpreted. State and federal programs such as old age assistance programs
and SSI base eligibility on financial need, and applicants must prove that their
income and asset levels are below eligibility amounts. Definitions of income
and assets can create confusion because in-kind assistance, such as gifts of
food, can count as income. An otherwise qualified individual may be denied
access to critical financial assistance. Finally, legal problems can surface even
after individuals are receiving benefits. For example, because eligibility for
Social Security is based on work history, an error in an earnings record can
result in a smaller benefit amount. Mistakes occur in an estimated 2% to 3%
of earnings records (Matthews & Berman, 1990).

A second type of legal problem related to income assistance programs
occurs when participants receive a notice of overpayment or notice of termination of benefits. Overpayments occur when income amounts exceed
eligibility criteria or when the benefit amount paid to the recipient is miscal-
culated. For example, the father of one of the authors of this book sought
legal assistance after he received a $13,000 overpayment notice from Social
Security (the notice suggested that he send Social Security a check for the
entire amount within 30 days!). Further investigation revealed that an error
made by a Social Security technician in recording his working income into
his monthly Social Security benefit amount for a 3-year period had caused
the overpayment. A legal services paralegal was able to negotiate with Social
Security a repayment plan that took a small amount of money from his
monthly check until the overpayment was paid.

Overpayments also can result when older adults receive income benefits
from more than one program. Consider the case of Mary Espinosa, who

received a small Social Security check, based on her husband's earnings, and an SSI check, for a total monthly income of $425. On Mr. Espinosa's death, Mary went to the Social Security office to report his death, so her technician could adjust her benefit amount. Mary continued to receive both checks until one day, she received a notice of overpayment demanding that she repay $3,000 of SSI benefits. Mary did not realize that although her SSI intake worker sat next to her Social Security intake worker in the same office, she needed to notify both workers of her change in circumstances. A legal advocate can determine if the overpayment actually occurred and, if warranted, appeal the overpayment decision or, if needed, negotiate a repayment schedule.

Although older adults can appeal these adverse decisions, they may not understand why they have been denied benefits or have had their benefits reduced and assume that nothing can be done. A reduction or termination of benefits could place the older adult in a position of being unable to pay for rent, food, or necessary medical assistance. Therefore, it is critical that older adults consult legal advocates when there are changes in benefit eligibility or amount. In the Wisconsin study mentioned earlier (Spangenberg Group, 1991), problems with public benefits were the third most frequently reported legal problem experienced by respondents. Older black adults in the study experienced problems with public benefits at twice the rate of their white counterparts.

Employment

Age Discrimination

Persons aged 55 and older represent 13% of the nation's workforce. Some 56% of workers over 64 are employed part-time as well (Employee Benefit Research Institute, 1994b; U.S. Bureau of the Census, 1996a). Older adults who wish to remain working or obtain work may encounter age-based discriminatory employment practices. Although the number of older adults who have experienced workplace discrimination is unknown, researchers report that many managers have negative stereotypes about older workers. These include the perception that older workers will not perform as well as younger workers, that older workers are not cost-effective, and that older workers are not suitable for training (Rix, 1994; Sterns & McDaniel, 1994). Such attitudes and beliefs, although not supported by empirical research (see Commonwealth Fund, 1993), can lead to discrimination against older workers.

To counter age discrimination against older workers, Congress enacted the Age Discrimination in Employment Act (ADEA) in 1967. Although some exceptions exist, the ADEA prohibits employment discrimination against persons aged 40 or older. Under the act, employers must not refuse to hire individuals on the basis of their age; discriminate with respect to compensation, terms, conditions, or privileges; limit, segregate, or classify employees in such a way that adversely affects their employment status or opportunities because of age; or retaliate against employees who exercise their rights under ADEA (Strauss, Wolf, & Schilling, 1990). The ADEA also prohibits employment agencies from engaging in discriminatory employment practices. Older workers who feel they have been discriminated against can file a claim with the Equal Employment Opportunity Commission and may also have claims under state law. In 1993, the commission received 19,884 age discrimination complaints (U.S. Senate Special Committee on Aging, 1993). The number of age discrimination complaints will likely increase with the aging of the baby boom cohort.

Pensions

For some older adults, private pension plans provide additional income in retirement. According to the Employee Benefit Research Institute, the number of private pensions doubled during the years 1975 to 1987 from 340,000 to 870,000 (cited in Strauss et al., 1990). As of 1993, 45% of private sector workers, 83% of state and local public sector workers, and almost all federal workers were covered by a pension plan (Employee Benefit Research Institute, 1994c; U.S. Department of Labor, 1993). Unlike Social Security, whose regulations apply uniformly to all older adults, pension plans vary from employer to employer. We review the types of pension plans in more detail in Chapter 9.

The Employee Retirement Income Security Act (ERISA) of 1974 regulates the administration of pensions. Retirees can file a federal suit if pension benefits have been unfairly denied, if future benefits are affected by changes in the pension plan, if the plan or funds have been improperly managed, if other rights outlined in the plan are breached, or if the plan does not disclose information required by ERISA (Matthews & Berman, 1990). Although retirees have various legal safeguards to their pension funds, it is probable that the majority of retirees are unaware of their rights under ERISA.

Health Care

Medical Insurance

As with income assistance programs, older adults can encounter legal problems with Medicare and Medicaid (We discussed these in greater detail in Chapter 11.) Most legal difficulties with Medicare Part A can occur when coverage is denied for services rendered. A denial most often occurs when the Medicare insurance carrier determines that services were not medically necessary, that services could have been provided on an outpatient basis, or that services were custodial rather than medical (Matthews & Berman, 1996). Disputes of payments under Part B usually concern the scope of coverage or the amount approved for payment by Part B carriers. Appeals of adverse decisions are made to the Social Security Administration.

Because Medicare does not cover all medical expenses and older adults must pay for deductibles and uncovered services out-of-pocket, many purchase supplemental insurance (Medigap) policies to help pay medical expenses. Unfortunately, older adults are often victims of Medigap insurance fraud—pressured to switch companies or to purchase duplicate policies, denied coverage because of preexisting clauses, or refused for renewal of a policy for reasons other than nonpayment. In recent years, the selling of Medigap policies has come under scrutiny and regulation. Federal law requires each state to adopt standardized Medigap benefit policies. When violations in these regulations occur, advocates can pursue legal remedies with the state insurance commissioner or through civil court.

Medicaid eligibility is based on income and asset levels and on being age 65 or older, blind, or disabled or having dependent children. Because Medicaid is a state and federal program, income and asset levels for eligibility vary among states. Under the Medicaid program, adverse decisions with regard to eligibility and coverage can be appealed.

Medically related legal problems because of difficulty managing medical paperwork were the type of legal problem Wisconsin elders reported most frequently (Spangenberg Group, 1991). Experiencing a problem with private health insurance also was mentioned by a large percentage of older black and white individuals.

Advance Directives for Health Care

Readers may remember hearing about the case of Nancy Cruzan. Nancy was in a fatal car accident and never regained consciousness. After she was in a vegetative state for 5 years, her family petitioned the court for the authority to remove her from artificial life support systems (*Cruzan v. Harmon*, 1988). Initially, the court did not grant the family permission to withdraw life supports because the family had no way of knowing what Nancy would have wanted in this situation. In part because of the Cruzan case and the increase in the number of persons who wish to remain in control of health care decisions after they are unable to articulate their desires, states have enacted laws that allow for the creation of *advance directives*. Advance directives are legal documents that convey the wishes of an individual regarding personal health care decisions and that must be executed while the individual is still competent. Two types of advance directives are the durable power of attorney for health care and the living will.

Older adults who want to articulate their health care wishes can do so in many states by executing a durable power of attorney for health care decisions. A durable power of attorney appoints an agent to make health care decisions outlined in the document. A living will also provides a legal mechanism that enables individuals to express their wishes regarding life-sustaining treatment. Living wills are more narrow in scope because they authorize the withdrawal of certain life-sustaining procedures only in situations in which the individual has a terminal illness or is comatose (Alexander, 1991). Only a small percentage of older adults, however, report that they have executed a living will (High, 1988). Providing preventive legal assistance to older adults by drafting these documents before they are needed can reduce the occurrence of problems in the future.

Consumer Fraud

Older persons constitute approximately 60% of all health-related consumer fraud and 30% of all white-collar crime victims (U.S. House Seclect Committee on Aging, 1984). For a variety of reasons, older adults may be more likely than others to be victims of consumer fraud. First, physical frailty or mental impairments may leave older adults at a disadvantage in understanding and negotiating with persistent salespersons. Second, older homebound persons may welcome opportunities to shop at home and may enjoy the company of friendly visiting salespersons. Third, older adults with low incomes may be especially susceptible to apparent opportunities to increase their incomes, take advantage of promised low prices, or send away for prize money. Consumer fraud against older persons is particularly widespread in home repair and mail schemes (U.S. House Select Committee on Aging, 1984). Federal and state consumer protection laws provide legal remedies for consumer fraud cases. Older victims of consumer fraud need to consult legal advocates to help them recover the costs of their fraudulent purchases.

Nursing Homes and Long-Term Care

Of older adults, 5%, or approximately 1.5 million persons, reside in long-term care facilities at any one time; of adults aged 65 and older, however, 43% can expect to stay in a long-term care facility (Murtaugh, Kemper, & Spillman, 1990). A variety of legal concerns may unfold during a resident's stay in a long-term care facility. One source of legal problems can be with the admission agreement. Studies evaluating the legality of nursing home admission agreements found that many contained illegal or questionable provisions

(Amborgi & Leonard, 1988; Wacker, 1985). Unfortunately, when problems do occur with the provisions set forth in the admissions agreement, older adults or their family members might not realize that they have a valid legal challenge to those contracts.

A second concern is the enforcement of residents' rights. Federal and state governments have enacted numerous laws to protect the rights of nursing home residents and to promote a high standard of care. Nursing homes must provide care and services to residents in a way that promotes and maintains the residents' physical, social, and mental well-being (Eldeman, 1990). Federal law protects residents' rights, including the right to privacy, the right to speak freely, the right to refuse treatment, and the right to freedom of association (see Chapter 19). Although nursing home residents and their family members can call on an ombudsman to advocate on behalf of the resident, there may be instances when a breach of residents' rights calls for a legal remedy.

Substitute Decision Making

Imagine for a moment that you have failed to open your mail for a couple of months. What would be the consequences of such a seemingly innocent mistake? No doubt your utilities would be on the verge of being turned off. Your car payment and insurance bills would be overdue, and letters threatening repossession would be in the stack of unopened letters. Checks would go undeposited. Bank accounts would be left unattended and important notices left unanswered. Such a scenario is not hard to imagine happening to older adults who are cognitively impaired and unable to manage their personal affairs.

Older adults who need assistance managing their personal affairs have legal ways to appoint a substitute decision maker. Legal documents such as a power of attorney or durable power of attorney are used to appoint someone to manage financial affairs. Individuals must be mentally competent before they can execute these documents. A durable power of attorney, unlike the power of attorney, continues to remain in effect upon the incapacity of the executor.

Another type of substitute decision maker is a guardian or conservator. Courts can appoint guardians or conservators who have the authority to make personal or financial decisions on behalf of an incompetent adult. Before a guardian or conservator can be appointed, the individual must file a petition with the court and prove that the older adult, called a ward, is mentally incompetent. Once appointed, guardians have the power to make decisions about every aspect of the ward's life, including living arrangements, financial affairs, health care, and social relationships. Because of the

Exhibit 13.1 **Victimization by Type of Crime and Age (Rate per 1,000 Persons)**

Age	Sexual Assault	Robbery	Assault	Personal Theft
< 19	8.2	23.8	205.5	6.8
20-34	7.9	18.8	133.5	5.8
35-49	1.6	5.2	32.8	1.9
50-64	0.2	2.3	12.6	1.7
65+	0.1	1.4	3.6	2.1

SOURCE: U.S. Bureau of the Census (1996b).

extensive nature of the guardian powers, guardianships should be sought only when other less restrictive options are unavailable (Keith & Wacker, 1994).

Criminal Legal Problems

Criminal legal problems include assault, robbery, rape, burglary, larceny, and motor vehicle theft. Many researchers report that older adults are more fearful of crime than are younger adults, and a higher percentage of older blacks express a fear of crime than do older whites (62% vs 28%, respectively; Lee, 1983; Lindquist & Duke, 1982; Michigan Offices of Services to the Aging, cited in Kart, 1997). Nevertheless, older adults are far less likely to be victims of crimes (U.S. Bureau of the Census, 1996b). As shown in Exhibit 13.1, the crime rate for selected crimes against older adults is markedly less than the rate for adults under age 65. Although older adults are less likely to be victims of crime, the outcome is often more physically, emotionally, and financially devastating than for younger victims of crime (Covey & Menard, 1988; Crandall, 1991). One of the more significant crimes affecting older adults is elder abuse.

Elder Abuse

Elder abuse most often occurs within the family context, and perpetrators are usually the elders' primary caregivers (Pillemer & Finkelhor, 1989). Elder abuse includes physical, psychological, and financial abuse as well as neglect. Victims of physical and psychological abuse are often in poor emotional health; the victims of neglect are usually older women, with multiple frailties, who are cognitively impaired and socially isolated (Wolf, 1996). The prevalence of elder abuse and neglect ranges from 3% to 10% of the persons 65 and older (Pillemer & Finkelhor, 1989; Wolf, 1996). All 50 states have legislation that allows for intervention and protection of vulnerable, disabled, or incapacitated adults. The responsibility for investigating such cases rests with either the state social services department or the SUA (Wolf, 1996).

Best Practice **New Hampshire Coalition to Prevent Elder Abuse**

One effective approach to increasing awareness and action related to elder abuse is through coalition building. The New Hampshire Coalition to Prevent Elder Abuse has an impressive list of accomplishments. The New Hampshire Coalition consists of 31 professionals from service agencies across the state. Professional fields represented include the University of New Hampshire and other colleges, law enforcement, the state legislature, elder housing providers, the clergy, legal service providers, public and private nursing homes, medical care providers, and AARP.

Each agency designates "the person in your organization whom you would go to for help." One striking accomplishment of this working coalition has been the distribution of 15,000 awareness brochures as of March 1996, mainly through the New Hampshire Council of Churches. Other activities include distribution of posters to the offices of medical professionals, an active speakers' bureau, sponsorship of state level conferences on elder abuse, and displays at health fairs and conferences. The coalition has been particularly successful at getting their message across in brief but effective contacts.

For more information, contact the National Committee for the Prevention of Elder Abuse, University of California at San Francisco/Mount Zion Institute on Aging, 3330 Geary Blvd., 3rd Floor, San Francisco, CA 94118, 415-750-4188.

Because a family member is most often the abuser, and the older adult is often frail and dependent on the caregiver for assistance, intervention can be difficult. For competent older adults, legal assistance can help evict or restrain the abuser; for incompetent victims, protective services can be implemented. The designated state agency, usually the department of social services, offers protective services to help the victim resolve the abuse, or as a last resort, may seek a guardianship to protect the victim from exploitation. Protective services are also called to intervene in cases of self-neglect.

Legal Assistance Programs

Despite the creation of legal programs through the Older Americans Act and the Legal Services Corporation, many older adults—particularly low-income and minority elders—do not receive legal assistance with civil problems. This is particularly true for those older adults with incomes just above the LSC guidelines yet who cannot afford the costs of a private attorney. Furthermore, the limited numbers of attorneys and paralegals staffing legal assistance programs are serving fewer clients and accepting fewer numbers and types of cases. To address the lack of available legal assistance for older adults, SUAs and local AAAs have developed unique methods of delivering legal assistance and have formed partnerships with state and local private bar associations to broaden their involvement in the delivery of legal services for older adults. These different methods of delivering legal assistance are discussed below.

Legal Hotlines

According to Moore (1992), access to legal assistance must begin by improving the entry point to legal assistance and increasing the provision of preventive legal assistance. Legal hotlines have emerged as one way to address both problems. The Legal Council for the Elderly sponsors nine statewide legal hotlines through funding from the AoA. Residents of the state aged 60 and older can call a toll-free number and speak directly to an attorney. Attorneys offer legal information or advice, refer those who need representation and can afford to pay for it to attorneys who charge a fixed rate per hour, or refer those who cannot afford legal assistance to a local legal services program. Users of hotline services, who frequently have low income, report high levels of satisfaction, and the majority would recommend the services to a friend. Advantages of a telephone hotline service include being accessible to persons who are homebound or without transportation, being able to give prompt information and thereby reduce the anxiety level of older adults, and being able to resolve simple problems quickly.

Moore (1992) describes a hotline program tested by the Legal Counsel for the Elderly that targets older adults of color. Minority volunteers are trained to act as mediators between the older adult and the hotline attorney. A volunteer conducts the preliminary interview of the older adult and gathers an understanding of the problem. The volunteer then contacts the hotline attorney, obtains information about the proper course of action, and has the responsibility of helping the client follow the advice given.

Bar Association Services

Edelstein (1996) outlined bar association services that may be useful to older adults. These include lawyer referral services, referral and information services, reduced fee panels, and volunteer lawyer panels.

Lawyer Referral Services

A lawyer referral service is typically composed of a panel of attorneys who will give advice or represent individuals with legal problems. Callers are

---

For Your Files **Institute on Law and Rights of Older Adults**

The Institute on Law and Rights of Older Adults at the Brookdale Center on Aging at Hunter College acts as a legal support program for social workers, paralegals, attorneys, and other professionals engaged in advocacy assistance to older persons who are poor. An interdisciplinary staff of attorneys and social workers has expertise in Medicare, Medicaid, SSI, Social Security disability, home care, health care decision making, adult protective services, Medigap, and long-term care insurance. The staff is available to provide technical assistance on public benefit laws and regulations to elected public officials and staff of other not-for-profit agencies.

More than 2,500 professionals are trained annually, and telephone case consultations average 350 calls per month. The institute publishes many publications including *The Senior Rights Reporter* and *Help for Seniors*, as well as entitlement bulletins, a benefits checklist, and training manuals.

For more information, contact the Institute on Law and Rights of Older Adults, Hunter College, Brookdale Center on Aging, 425 East 25th Street, New York, NY 10010-2590, 212-481-4433 (Web page: http://www.hunter.cuny.edu/health/htmls/iol_hp.html).

---

referred to an attorney who has some expertise with the type of legal problem encountered and who is located nearby. The initial consultation is provided free of charge or for a small fee with no obligation to continue with that particular attorney. No prescreening is done on the legal merits of the case.

Lawyer Referral and Information Services

A lawyer and information service is similar to the lawyer referral service except that calls are screened more carefully for legal merit, and simple problems are often resolved before the referral is made. The service is provided at no cost or for a nominal fee, and there is no further obligation by the client to continue with the attorney.

Reduced Fee Panels

Reduced fee panels are coordinated by local or state bar associations and are composed of attorneys who will provide legal assistance in specialized areas of law. For example, the Maryland State Bar Association sponsors a *Sixty-Plus Legal Panel* through which participating attorneys offer low-cost assistance with wills, living wills, powers of attorney, and small estate administration.

Volunteer Lawyer Panels

Some communities have created pro bono legal programs staffed with volunteer attorneys who provide free legal assistance to older adults. These pro bono programs usually require clients to meet some financial guidelines and often limit the type of legal problems they accept. One pro bono program enlists volunteer paralegals who deliver free legal services at "Saturday clinics" at a different site each month in minority communities (Moore, 1992).

State and local bar associations also are involved in educating older adults about potential legal problems. Bar associations may sponsor continuing education sessions about legal problems germane to older adults, produce legal handbooks for senior citizens, and sponsor "law days" for older adults (Coleman, Wood, Sabatino, Nelson, & Baker, 1986).

Dispute Resolution Programs

Mediation services offer individuals an alternative to the costs associated with traditional court litigation. Mediation is done through a neutral third party who guides the parties to a mutual resolution. Mediation is usually less expensive, less time-consuming, and less stressful than traditional legal methods, and mediation settlements tend to be more lasting than settlements imposed by the courts (Edelstein, 1996).

Dispute resolution programs are emerging across the country as a viable alternative to going to court. Many dispute resolutions programs are sponsored by local or state bar associations and university law school programs. For many older adults who have legal problems, a dispute resolution program may be a better option than the traditional court system, although the extent to which older adults use dispute resolution services is unknown.

Money Management Programs

For some older adults, paying bills and managing their finances becomes an overwhelming task because of health limitations or inexperience. Although family members frequently assist with money management tasks (Stone, Cafferata, & Sangl, 1987), many older adults who do not have an informal support network to turn to are not able to easily secure this type of assistance. Money management programs have been created to assist older adults with their financial activities. These programs help clients with bill paying and check depositing, sorting through medical bills and filing claims to insurance companies, budgeting, and preparing durable powers of attorney or burial trusts (Tokarek, 1996).

Best Practice   **Dispute Resolution Center**

The Dispute Resolution Center in Saint Paul, Minnesota, is a private non-profit organization founded to provide mediation, facilitation, training, and referral services in the Twin Cities. As a community resource, the center assists individuals, families, community groups, government agencies, and businesses in resolving conflicts. A majority of the individuals served by the center are people in lower-income ranges. Through the use of constructive means such as mediation and facilitation, the center has helped in thousands of matters to prevent the need for costly litigation.

The Dispute Resolution Center is a Certified Community Dispute Resolution Program under the guidelines administered by the Supreme Court. The center works with social service and government agencies and handles between 400 and 500 cases on average each year. Community problems handled include matters of public safety concerning traffic and parking; rental arrangements; consumer-merchant disputes; neighborhood conflicts about noise, pets, and property lines; and small claims concerning money, property damage, or breach of contract.

To accomplish its goals of fostering open communication and encouraging positive responses to conflict, the Dispute Resolution Center recruits and trains a diverse group of volunteer mediators. The center benefits from more than 50 volunteers who represent a broad cross section of the community. In 1995, the volunteers contributed approximately 2,000 volunteer hours as mediators, office workers, and board members.

The Dispute Resolution Center also provides workshops and presentations on conflict resolution and communication for community groups and organizations such as schools, colleges, landlord or tenant unions, community councils, block clubs, youth centers, and other audiences. For more information, contact Dispute Resolution Center, 265 Oneida Street, Saint Paul, MN 55102, 612-292-7791, or visit the Web site (http://www.spacestar.net/users/tkhedeen/drc.htm).

SOURCE: Dispute Resolution Center (1997).

Challenges for Legal Programs and Services

Removing Barriers to Legal Services

One important challenge for legal assistance programs is to identify and remove the barriers that impede older adults in obtaining legal relief. Although no empirical research has documented the reasons why older adults might hesitate to seek legal assistance, anecdotal information from individuals

---

Best Practice **Jewish Family and Children's Services**

The Jewish Family and Children's Services offers a personal affairs management program for frail older adults who live in San Francisco and San
Mateo counties. The fee-for-service program provides different levels of
assistance to its clients. In "no authority" cases, staff members assist clients
in paying bills, budgeting, and processing medical claims. When a client's
physical health makes it difficult to write checks or sign documents, a
durable power of attorney is executed by a staff member. This enables the
staff member to sign documents on behalf of the client. If the client becomes or is unable to make decisions on his or her own behalf, a staff
member can seek a conservatorship. A court-ordered conservatorship
awards a staff member legal authority to manage a client's assets. The
program has approximately 95 clients and is staffed by two full-time
employees.

One case involved an older man who had been isolated in his apartment
because of his difficulties with emphysema. When program staff members
met with him, they discovered $60,000 worth of undeposited Social Se-
curity, pension, and disability checks, as well as a year's worth of unpro-
cessed medical claims. In addition to taking care of the client's financial
needs, staff arranged to have meals delivered to his home.

For more information about the Personal Affairs Management program,
contact the Jewish Family and Children's Services, 1600 Scott Street, San
Francisco, CA 94115, 415-561-1229.

SOURCE: Tokarek (1996).

---

providing legal assistance suggests that numerous barriers act to keep older
adults from seeking legal services. Among them are personal factors, such as
a lack of knowledge about legal rights, fear of the legal system, and embarrassment, and structural factors, such as geographic distance, that act to limit
access to services.

As mentioned earlier, if older adults are not aware that a problem they
are experiencing has legal remedies, they will not be inclined to seek out
legal advice or assistance. Even when it is apparent that the problem encountered needs a legal professional, for many older adults, the legal system
seems complicated, foreign, and intimidating. It is often difficult to find an
appropriate attorney, and frail older adults might not have the physical or
mental stamina to fight what they imagine will be lengthy litigation with its
complications and confusing legalese. Furthermore, having a legal problem
can elicit feelings of embarrassment, especially when the legal problem has
occurred because of poor judgment or lack of foresight.

Making Legal Programs More Accessible

Another challenge is to make legal programs easily accessible. Programs that do provide legal assistance are often not readily accessible to those without transportation or living in rural areas. Although legal services may be available in a given community, if they are located away from low-income neighborhoods or neighborhoods of color, such programs will be less available to these at-risk populations. Language barriers and a lack of cultural sensitivity can keep many older adults from various ethnic backgrounds from seeking legal assistance. This is especially significant because elders of color have greater unmet legal needs than do their white counterparts (AARP, cited in Moore, 1989).

Supporting Legal Programs in the Future

Finally, in recent years, legal assistance programs have been underfunded and understaffed. If the legal needs of low-income and middle-class older adults are to be addressed, funds for legal programs that serve older adults should be increased. The 1995 White House Conference on Aging delegates passed resolutions that supported policies that ensured authorization and adequate funding of legal assistance programs under the OAA and through the LSC. Specifically, delegates recommended policies to

- Promote state and national training and support services for providers of legal assistance
- Promote coordination of legal assistance among private bar and publicly funded practitioners
- Promote legal assistance outreach to ethnic and minority populations, persons with disabilities, isolated older persons, and those with low incomes

As the number of older adults increases in the coming decade, there will no doubt be a greater demand for legal assistance programs and services. This increase in demand for services will likely occur without an increase in funding levels, and legal service providers and AAAs will be challenged to develop creative methods of legal education and service delivery.

 ## CASE STUDY

A WIDOW IN LEGAL TROUBLE

Jean is a 66-year-old woman who was widowed at age 65. She and her husband, Fred, had been married for 42 years when he died suddenly of a heart attack. For most of their working years, they managed apartments. Jean assumed the office duties, and her husband maintained the physical building and grounds. This employment gave them an apartment, utilities, and an income of approximately $20,000 per year. It was a dependable existence, and they were well liked and respected by their renters.

Like many husbands of that generation, Fred paid the bills and balanced the checkbook. Jean always depended on Fred to handle the couple's finances. After Fred's death, Jean, of necessity, had to take over the finances. Within 2 months, Jean realized that she was in deep trouble. Unbeknownst to her, Fred had been taking cash advances from eight credit cards to support a gambling habit. The credit card receipts were arriving, it seemed to Jean, almost daily. To her horror and distress, the cash advances totaled $40,000. Now, unemployed and frail from her advancing emphysema, Jean was barely getting by on $812 Social Security per month. Quickly, Jean realized that after rent, utilities, groceries, prescription drugs, and other necessities, she could not pay off this incredible debt.

Jean's daughter, Susan, was sympathetic and supportive but unable to provide financial assistance. A few years earlier, Jean and Fred had invested the little savings they had in a grocery business for their daughter. This was an unsuccessful venture that eventually went bankrupt. The first credit collection calls have begun, and Jean is completely distraught. When she finally mustered up the courage to tell her best friend what happened, it took her another 2 weeks to pick up the telephone and call the senior paralegal program at the local area agency on aging.

CASE STUDY QUESTIONS

1. Jean, like Fernando in the introduction to this chapter, has multiple problems. List all possible problems that could be brought on by Jean's husband's actions.

2. Which of Jean's problems are legal issues? Which fall into other service categories?

3. Of all Jean's problems and worries, what is the single thing that could be addressed that would bring her the most peace of mind? Defend your choice.

4. Considering the chapter's discussion of why older adults might hesitate to seek legal assistance, what factors in Jean's case substantiate her reluctance to call an attorney?

5. Jean's health situation suggests that possible end-of-life legal issues could be addressed. Referencing the chapter, suggest one or two other legal areas that could be approached with Jean.

LEARNING ACTIVITIES

1. Make an inventory of the legal aid programs that serve older adults in your community. What type of cases do they accept? Where are people referred when they cannot take their cases? What is the breakdown of the cases they accept in a given year?

2. Contact your local district attorney's office and arrange an interview to find out about elder abuse and fraud cases involving older adults the office prosecutes each year. Does the office sponsor any public education for older adults about consumer fraud or elder abuse?

3. Make a list of the legal problems discussed in this chapter. Obtain permission from 10 older adults to ascertain whether they have had any of these legal problems in the last year. If so, ask them if they sought legal advice for the problem and the outcome of the situation. Be sure to keep your interviewees' names confidential when reporting your findings.

FOR MORE INFORMATION

National Resources

1. American Bar Association, Commission on Legal Problems of the Elderly, 740 15th Street NW, Washington, DC 20005, 202-622-8690.

   The commission focuses on the legal concerns of older adults and provides technical assistance, models of legal assistance projects, telephone and written assistance, publications, and speakers.

2. American Association of Retired Persons Legal Counsel for the Elderly, 601 E Street NW, Washington, DC 20049, 202-434-2120.

   The AARP Legal Counsel for the Elderly offers training in law and advocacy skills, assistance in establishing legal hotlines, and delivery systems models as well as numerous pamphlets on legal topics of concern to older adults and their families.

3. National Senior Citizens Law Center, 1815 H Street NW, Suite 700, Washington, DC 20006, 202-887-5280.

   The center offers advice, litigation assistance, and training and program development assistance to legal services providers and state and local area agencies on aging.

Web Resources

1. Administration on Aging's Elder Law Page and Elder Abuse and Safety Page
   http://wwwaoa.dhhs.gov/aoa/webres/

This is a great place to start when looking for legal resources for older adults. The AoA has compiled links to legal resources and resources about elder abuse. Updates to the page are made regularly.

2. Senior Law Home Page
   http://www.seniorlaw.com

   A home page sponsored by a New York law firm that has specialists in elder law, the site provides information about Medicare and Medicaid, elder law, legal resources, and elder law attorneys.

3. National Senior Citizens Law Center
   http://www.nsclc.org

   The center has information about its services, manuals, and publications, as well as information about Social Security and SSI, Medicare, Medicaid, nursing home residents' rights, home care, pension rights, age discrimination and mandatory retirement, and Older Americans Act services.

4. AARP Legal Questions and Answers Page
   http://www.aarp.org/programs/legal/home.html

   AARP's home page provides basic information about legal issues relevant to older adults.

5. Elder Law Center: Court TV
   http://www.courttv.com/legalhelp/elder/

   Court TV? But its Web page has links to information about national and state organizations, legal sources for older adults, Medicare and Medigap policies, pensions and retirement plans, Social Security, and wills and trusts.

6. Manitoba Senior Citizens Handbook: Legal and Consumer Rights and Services
   http://www.crm.mb.ca/scip/other/genmb/msch/msch17.html

   This might be a long address to type in, but it is well worth it to visit this site. This Web page is a good example of the vast amount of legal information that can be made available to older adults via the Web. There are links to information about lawyer referral programs, legal clinics, consumer rights, victim assistance programs, mediation services, and others.

7. National Center on Elder Abuse
   http://www.interinc.com/NCEA/indexnf.html

   The objectives of the center are to perform clearinghouse functions, develop and disseminate information, provide technical assistance and training, and conduct research about elder abuse. The home page offers information and statistics about elder abuse, links to other resources, and a list of publications. Visitors can also access the quarterly newsletter, *NCEA Exchange*.

8. East Bay (California) Elder Abuse Prevention
   http://www.aimnet.com/oaktree/elder

   East Bay Elder Abuse Prevention's home page offers information about what elder abuse is, how to recognize abuse, who must report elder abuse, and where to report suspected abuse. The site even has a link to Benedict monks in Canada who raise cats to be placed with older adults who have been abused or neglected.

9. New York Elder Abuse Coalition
   http://www.drica.com/ian/eac/comsvc.htm

   The coalition has created a home page with links to community-based and protective services available to elder abuse victims in New York.

 **14**

Transportation

An older man in a wheelchair was picked up by a paratransit system in El Paso, Texas to go from the nursing home where he resided to K-Mart. The trip did not take more than 15 minutes. During the trip the man expressed how pleased he was to be getting out. He said that he had been a resident of the nursing home for seven years and that this was his first outing during that time that was not medically related. (Peterson, 1995, p. 12)

It is difficult to understand how most of us would feel if we could not do something as common as take a trip to K-Mart. We jump in our cars at the drop of a hat to run this or that errand. For most Americans, taking several trips per day to a variety of locations is a common occurrence. This gentleman, however, was grateful that accessible transportation was available and thrilled to be enjoying a nonmedical outing. The actual purpose of his trip may have been less important to him than the opportunity for an outing.

Mobility attained through the private automobile is the American way. We all remember the anticipation of getting our first driver's license. Most teenagers are excited to obtain a driver's license, and having a car is a rite of passage. Aside from deriving enjoyment from car travel, without transportation, we could not meet our basic needs. Going to work, buying groceries, seeing the doctor, going to the park, visiting with friends—all become difficult and often impossible without transportation. Thus, we enter later life being accustomed to having the ability to come and go as we please.

Transportation plays a critical role in the physical, social, and psychological well-being of older persons. Physical health depends on access to medical facilities and other social services. The ability to maintain an active social life in old age depends on accessibility to family and friends as well as recreational and cultural activities. Key ingredients of psychological health that are enhanced by mobility are freedom from isolation and the ability to choose one's range of activities (Wachs, 1979).

In this chapter, we review the legislative history of transportation services, the transportation patterns of older adults, and the different models of transportation services. We conclude by identifying some of the challenges in meeting the transportation needs of an aging society.

Policy Background

Twentieth-century growth patterns, coupled with America's emphasis on travel by personal automobile, have contributed greatly to decline in travel options. Private transportation has come to dominate travel in this country to such an extent that the United States is less connected via public transportation in the 1990s than it was in the late 1920s. Previously, through a series of easy transfers, passengers could travel from Burlington, Iowa, in the southeast corner of the state, along the Mississippi River, to Waverly in central Iowa—a distance of more than 150 miles—and back in the same day. The same journey today would be impossible ("Community Service Is Key," 1994). In an attempt to reverse this trend, federal and state transportation legislation has been enacted during the last 25 years to increase transportation options for persons who are transit dependent.

Responsiveness to mobility needs began in the 1970s when the United States made significant gains in providing transportation options for elders and persons with disabilities. Beginning in 1970, an amendment to the Urban Mass Transportation Act of 1964 advanced the cause of transportation for older adults and persons with disabilities by mandating that these individuals have the same right as other persons to use mass transportation facilities and services. Spurred on by demands made by older adults, persons with disabilities, and their advocates, approximately 4,000 or more special purpose transportation systems were in operation by the end of the decade (Ashford, Bell, & Rich, 1982). These programs varied from a single vehicle to a fleet of buses serving urban and rural areas, resulting in a mosaic of transportation programs across the country. During this same period, transportation was the "sleeper" issue at the 1971 White House Conference on Aging, ranking third in importance, preceded by income and health.

Another important statute of the 1970s, the Rehabilitation Act of 1973 (Section 504), directed federally assisted transit providers to offer half-fare service to older persons in off-peak periods. These regulations also required that local transit planning processes make special efforts to plan public mass transportation facilities and services that could effectively be used by older and disabled persons. Transportation planners and operators responded to

Section 504 mandates by implementing special transportation systems for the older adults and persons with disabilities. These systems used smaller buses and vans and could provide door-to-door service. Such systems became known as *paratransit* operations.

During the 1980s, the United States entered a second generation of specialized transportation developments. Although the 1970s were a decade of growth and development of specialized transportation systems, the 1980s were a decade of retrenchment in response to a general tightening of the availability of financial resources at all levels of government (Ashford et al., 1982). The 1980s were also a time when transportation systems emphasized cost-effectiveness and efficiency in providing public transportation. Federal legislation required that programs applying for federal transit funds develop a transit development plan. These plans identified present and future needs and how transportation would be coordinated with other providers. Only with an approved plan could local or regional transit groups compete for federal transit funding. Today, transit development plans are still a requirement to receive federal transit funding.

In the 1990s, two laws were passed that greatly influenced public transit. The first was the Americans With Disabilities Act (ADA), signed into law in July 1990. This far-reaching law prohibits discrimination against people with disabilities in almost all aspects of American life and extends comprehensive civil rights to people with disabilities similar to those conferred on racial minorities by the Civil Rights Act of 1964. ADA requirements cover transportation services, facilities, and equipment of all entities, public and private. A key requirement of the ADA is that all new transit vehicles must be accessible to persons with wheelchairs. Fixed route systems must offer a paratransit or specialized service for persons with disabilities who cannot access the fixed route system. Furthermore, this paratransit service must be comparable to the fixed route service in fares, hours and days of operation, response times, and geographic areas covered. The ADA also provides specific eligibility criteria for the comparable paratransit service for what constitutes disability.

Prior to the ADA, many paratransit systems transported elders because of age or disability. Ironically, because age alone is not a factor in determining ADA eligibility, the passage of the ADA may have proved to be a barrier for older adults who rely on public transportation services. Could older passengers who do not meet the stricter disability guidelines lose their mobility so that the program has the resources to meet the ADA obligations? The act, it was feared, would motivate transit operators to reduce service because they would lack the resources to respond effectively to all mobility needs (Rosenbloom, 1993b). A 1992 study commissioned by the AARP looked at 300 ADA implementation plans and interviewed 18 communities for an in-depth analysis of how they would approach ADA implementation. The study found

For Your Files   **National Eldercare Institute
on Transportation**

The National Eldercare Institute on Transportation is a joint project of the National Association of Area Agencies on Aging, National Caucus and Center on Black Aged, the National Council on the Aging, and the Administration on Aging. The goal of the institute is to increase public awareness of the transportation needs of at-risk older people, forge effective cooperation between the aging and transportation networks, and provide practical training and technical assistance on aging and transportation issues. The institute offers a toll-free transit hotline and issue briefs on best practice models of community transit systems, elder transportation programs, and cost sharing in transportation. The institute offers training workshops on management issues in elder transportation and coordination efforts between transportation and aging networks.

For more information, contact the National Eldercare Institute on Transportation, 725 15th Street NW, Suite 900, Washington, DC 20005, 800-527-8279.

that most of the 18 case study cities admitted that many older persons would be found ineligible by new screening and certification procedures (Rosenbloom, 1993c). How many older Americans meet the stricter ADA requirements, how many will actually be displaced by the ADA from paratransit service, and how local communities will ultimately respond to this situation all remain unanswered questions at this time. After the final 1997 implementation deadline, we may have a better idea of how the ADA has affected older Americans.

The Intermodal Surface Transportation Efficiency Act (ISTEA) of 1991 made several significant changes to the federal transit program. One obvious change was renaming the federal agency that oversees the transit industry. The agency that had been called the Urban Mass Transportation Administration since its birth in 1964 was renamed the Federal Transit Administration (FTA). This name change reflected an awareness by Congress and the federal government that public transportation is vital to all citizens, urban and rural (Rucker, 1995a). ISTEA specifically addresses the mobility needs of older persons, persons with disabilities, and those who are economically disadvantaged. The legislation also places great emphasis on local, regional, and state planning and coordination; it makes funding of capital and operating costs dependent on assurances that local transit systems are coordinated with regional and state transit plans. ISTEA holds promise for older Americans and those with disabilities by setting the stage for a postinterstate highway era by requiring that highways and transit be planned together. Local communities committed to transit find reason for hope in ISTEA's limited amount of flexibility to transfer highway funds to public transit projects (Zeilinger, 1994). This complex legislation offers many opportunities for transportation planning and funding that could improve the mobility possibilities for older Americans.

Users and Programs

Factors Associated With Transportation Patterns of Older Adults

Older Americans largely rely on private vehicles for their transportation needs. In 1991, more than 14 million Americans aged 70 years and older had driver's licenses—90% of all men and 80% of all women (Rosenbloom, 1993a). Up to age 75, the majority of older adults have good driving records and appear to perform as well as middle-aged drivers; after age 75, however, older adults are two times as likely to be in a crash per mile driven (U.S. Senate Special Committee on Aging, 1993). Exhibit 14.1 shows the percentage of older urban and rural adults who rely on various forms of mobility. The majority of older adults, regardless of location, rely on private vehicles for transportation needs.

Gender

Overall, both urban and rural older women are less likely to rely on a private vehicle, and more likely to use public transportation, than are older men. Higher percentages of older men and women, regardless of residence, rely on walking more than they do on public transit systems. Public transit use by older adults is low in both urban and rural locations (see Exhibit 14.1).

Health

Many factors influence the mobility of older persons and, consequently, the use or nonuse of public transportation. The most obvious is health. Of the more than 30 million Americans aged 65 or older, 16% (almost 5 million) report some sort of mobility limitation because of a health condition that has lasted for 6 or more months and has resulted in difficulty going outside the home alone. The incidence of health-related mobility problems is substantially higher for women and is higher among rural residents (21%) than among urban residents (12%; National Eldercare Institute on Transportation, 1994). Thus, older adults with mobility limitations will be among those who are transit dependent.

Exhibit 14.1 **Travel Modes by Gender and Residence for Persons Aged 65 Years and Older**

| | Urban | | Rural | |
Mode	Men	Women	Men	Women
Private vehicle	89.9%	86.8%	95.0%	93.1%
Public transit	2.4%	2.6%	0.2%	0.7%
Taxi	0.2%	0.5%	0.3%	0.5%
Walking	6.8%	9.2%	2.6%	5.6%

SOURCE: Murakami, 1994, p. 1.

Geographic Location

Geographic location also affects mobility options. Rural residents who are aged, disabled, or poor are particularly transit dependent. Nationally, 76 million people are considered transit dependent, and rural areas account for 29 million, or 38%, of the total. Specifically, 32% of all rural residents are classified as transit dependent (U.S. Bureau of the Census, 1996b). By contrast, only 30% of urban residents are so classified. Another factor resulting in rural transportation deficiency is the loss of long-haul bus service to 15% of rural communities. More than 50% of the nation's rural residents live in areas with no federally assisted public transit service (National Eldercare Institute on Transportation, 1994).

One way to analyze transit ridership by older adults is to break ridership patterns into urban, small urban, and rural components. This is useful because there are differences among each of these areas. A study prepared for the Administration on Aging showed that in the 33 largest cities (those with more than 1 million in population), transit resources are substantial, yet many of the mobility needs of older adults are still unmet (National Eldercare Institute on Transportation, 1994). In those areas, only 6% of the total ridership, and 13% of the noncommuter ridership, was composed of older persons. In small urban areas (areas of 50,000 to 200,000 persons), the total served is substantially less than in the large urban areas. Furthermore, the total amount of service per senior is substantially less, at 12.5 trips annually in small urban areas, 20 trips annually for areas between 200,000 and 1 million, and 37 trips annually for the largest urban areas. Transit ridership by older adults in rural areas is even more bleak. Of the 7.9 million persons aged 65 and older living in nonmetropolitan areas, 36% (2.8 million) live in places without public transportation. Another 48% (3.8 million) live in areas in which use of public transit services is less than 2 rides per year.

Income

Economic problems also magnify transportation problems. Almost 12%, or 3.7 million, of older adults in the United States live in poverty. Elders living in rural areas are poorer than their urban counterparts (16% of older adults living in rural areas are poor, compared with 11% living in urban areas). Older adults of color are more at risk of being poor than are their white peers. For example, nearly a third of all African Americans aged 65 or older are poor (44% in rural areas). For Native Americans, the poverty rate is 29% overall and 35% in rural areas. For Hispanics, the figures are 23% overall and 30% in rural areas (National Eldercare Institute on Transportation, 1994). Approximately 10.9% of white older adults live below the poverty line. Thus, the expense of maintaining a private vehicle is beyond the means of many low-income older persons and low-income minority elders. Some older adults find that even transit fares are beyond their means. The cost of purchasing, maintaining, and operating an automobile is increasing faster than many other goods and services. This will make car ownership for low-income older adults even more prohibitive.

Barriers to Public Transit Use

Why is the rate of public transit use by older adults so low in areas in which public transportation is available? A variety of barriers exist to keep older adults from using public transportation. If you have some free time one afternoon, try getting from your house or apartment to the senior center, grocery store, or medical clinic *via public transportation,* and try to envision yourself as an older adult. While on your trip, think about the following:

> How difficult was it to figure out the route you needed to take to get to your destination? What times did the bus service not run?
>
> How long did it take you to get to the bus stop? What would it be like waiting there in bad weather?
>
> How high was the first step into the bus? Were the seats comfortable? Could you get in and out of them easily?
>
> How many transfers did you have to make during your trip?
>
> How close did the bus drop you to your final destination?
>
> How long did it take you to complete your trip?

If you are a veteran of using public transportation, you probably do not think twice about making your way across town and complete your journey without much trouble, but how would an older adult fare? Those of you who use

---

Best Practice   **Tri-Met of Portland, Oregon**

Tri-Met of Portland, Oregon, has proved that accessibility is more than lifts on buses and paratransit plans. The transit staff and bus drivers were increasingly concerned with the needs of persons with hearing impairments and how to effectively communicate with them. Because of the pressing priority needs of persons in wheelchairs, the accessibility needs of persons with hearing impairments had fallen through the cracks. When the accessibility manager for Tri-Met spotted an advertisement for pictograms of restaurant food to help international travelers, an idea was born. Why couldn't pictograms be used to communicate with people with hearing impairments? Her idea was to produce a set of pictograms that illustrate situations that typically arise during fixed route travel, particularly with persons with hearing impairments.

Tri-Met wrote a proposal and was funded to develop a standardized picture language for expressing various situations that can occur during fixed route travel. The Oregon Deaf Resources Center supported the proposal and helped the project by soliciting suggestions for the pictograms from deaf communities across the country.

Another aspect of this project was the production of a transit personnel training video, created and produced by people who are deaf, to educate transit drivers about deaf culture. They expect the benefits to go beyond improving communication with persons with hearing impairments. Enhanced communication capability will also improve communication with other passengers with disabilities, such as older persons and others who have cognitive impairments.

For more information, contact Tri-Met, 4012 Southeast 17th Street, Portland, OR 97202, 503-238-4904.

SOURCE: Community Transportation Association of America (1995).

---

your car to get around probably experienced some uncertainty—we hope that you did not get lost! But from an older adult's perspective, using public transportation can be challenging.

Structural Barriers

Older adults report that they have to walk long distances to the nearest bus stop and that bus stops have inadequate shelters, no benches, and poor lighting. The buses themselves pose problems because steps into the bus are often high and narrow, the seats are difficult to get in and out of, bus windows are so dirty that they are difficult to see out of, and buses are often overcrowded (Patterson, 1985; U.S. Department of Transportation, 1980).

Fear of Crime

Fear of crime is also a concern for many older adults (Lowy, 1980; Patterson, 1985). In his study of older transit riders, Patterson found that older adults' fear of crime was significant in all aspects of the trip. For example, 77.3% reported fear while waiting at the bus stop, 69.5% were afraid while walking to and from the bus stop, and 64.8% were afraid while riding the bus.

Bus Schedules

Another barrier to riding transit systems relates to bus schedules. Most transit systems are designed for commuters going to work, rather than to hospitals, clinics, and senior centers (Huttman, 1985). In Patterson's (1985) study, many older transit riders reported a lack of frequency of bus service during the daytime (66.9%) and evenings (78.0%).

The National Eldercare Institute on Transportation (1992) conducted focus groups of older adults around the country to ascertain anecdotal information about transportation barriers. Older adults reported that the ideal transportation system would have drivers who are courteous and patient, travel shorter distances, have smaller buses that were for seniors and persons with disabilities only, not require transferring, have bilingual staff, and have more flexible bus schedules to meet the needs of community people, not just workers.

Social Barriers

Elders of color may face additional barriers that result from cultural perceptions and a lack of sensitivity by the transportation service system. For example, many minority elders shy away from all services including transportation because they have experienced hurtful discriminatory practices in the past. Other barriers include language and literacy barriers, discomfort if the rider is the only minority using the transportation system, fixed route services that do not adequately service minority neighborhoods, and service providers who assume that minority elders rely on their families for transportation (Heath, 1993).

Transportation Programs

Community transportation programs vary greatly in funding and design. Transit resources available to older persons have been described as a mosaic,

Best Practice **Chickasaw Nation, Oklahoma**

In 1991, the Chickasaw Nation received a demonstration grant from the Federal Transit Administration to develop a transportation system for all 11 counties within the Chickasaw service area. A needs assessment was conducted, and a transportation plan was written that was evaluated and approved by the tribal council and the FTA. The backbone of the new system was coordination. The Chickasaw Nation Transportation System became the lead agency for all coordination efforts including vehicle acquisition, facility storage and maintenance, dispatching and scheduling, operations, and administration.

With this model, the system operates a demand responsive and fixed route service to a large number of tribal members in isolated areas and still meets the needs of heavily populated areas. Some of the agencies and services this coordination includes are tribal Head Start programs, tribal boarding school, the Carl Albert Indian Hospital, two medical centers, the alcohol and drug treatment center, senior citizen nutrition programs, and youth programs. This is a good example of how coordination eliminates duplication of service, offers the community efficient transportation, and uses transportation resources wisely.

For more information, contact the National Transit Resource Center, 800-527-8279.

SOURCE: Shawn (1994).

rather than as an integrated network. This mosaic is made up of public systems supplemented by transportation programs provided by nonprofit organizations, human service agencies, caregivers, and communities of faith (National Eldercare Institute on Transportation, 1994). A transportation program could be as basic as a group of volunteers working on their own or under the auspices of an umbrella human service agency to transport older adults to medical appointments and other important destination points in their community. At the other end of the spectrum, the transportation program could be a sophisticated, multifaceted system including fixed route service with complementary paratransit service that is scheduled through a fully computerized central dispatch component. In each community, it is the challenge of the human service professional to find out what programs exist and who is eligible for service and under what circumstances.

To best understand any discussion about transportation programs, it is necessary to have a basic knowledge of a few transportation terms that describe general types of transportation delivery systems (see Exhibit 14.2).

Public transportation and specialized transit have been referenced several times in this chapter. *Public transportation* is defined as service that is available for any trip purpose to any person of any age and is operated by public agencies or supported by public funds to some extent. *Specialized transit,* on the other hand, is service that is provided for a variety of trip purposes and open to older, disabled, and/or low-income persons but usually not to the general public. Specialized operators range from urbanized operators with large fleets of more than 30 vehicles to rural systems with only one van and volunteer drivers. Another term, *incidental transit* or *human service agency transportation,* describes those programs in which transit is "incidental" to the agency's main program purpose. For example, mental health centers, senior centers, hospitals, and nursing homes often provide some transportation for their clients. The transportation, however, most likely is an optional service that the organization is providing to enhance its main program. *Commercial service* is defined as service provided by for-profit entities on a for-hire basis. Taxi service, shuttles, limousines, and charter services fall under this category.

Within these general categories of transportation programs are several types of service that describe how the service is organized. A *fixed route* service is a regularly scheduled service operated on a set route. A *deviated fixed route* service is a fixed route service that will deviate from its regular route to pick up special riders such as persons who are older or disabled, depending on its passengers' requests. Let's suppose a county transportation program runs several routes a week at scheduled days and times to the county's rural senior centers to transport groups of seniors to a major shopping center. Depending on the needs of the seniors, the driver will pick up or drop off seniors in neighboring towns that are off the route. The driver is also able to change the destinations according to the needs of the group being transported. This system has the capability to modify the usual route to meet the needs of the riders. Opposite of fixed route and deviated, or modified, fixed route services is the *demand responsive* system, a personalized service provided usually for older and disabled persons. It is provided on an immediate demand basis or on an advanced reservation basis. This term is often used interchangeably with *paratransit, dial-a-ride,* or *specialized service.* This service can be curb-to-curb (the passenger must come out to the vehicle), door-to-door (driver goes to the door of the passenger's residence and provides assistance if needed), and/or door-through-door (driver goes into the home and/or final destination to provide more assistance, especially to frail or disoriented individuals). An important feature of demand responsive service is that transportation services are tailored to the needs of individual riders. Most demand responsive systems operate minivans, vans, or minibuses to provide this service. Passengers call, usually a

Exhibit 14.2 **Selected Transportation Terms**

ADA: The Americans With Disabilities Act, a federal law requiring that facilities and services be made accessible to persons with disabilities

APTA: The American Public Transit Association, representing the interests of public transit agencies, particularly those in large urbanized areas

Complementary paratransit: Service that must be offered by fixed route public transportation operators to persons with disabilities who cannot access or use regular fixed route service

CTAA: The Community Transportation Association of America, representing the interests of specialized transit operators and those who operate in rural and small urbanized areas

Curb-to-curb service: A demand responsive service system in which the passenger must come out to the vehicle

Deadhead: The time and/or distance that a transit vehicle does not spend in revenue service or moving passengers (e.g., the travel from a garage to the beginning of a route)

Demand responsive: Personalized, direct transit service provided usually for persons who are older or disabled, either on an immediate demand basis or an advanced reservation basis; often used interchangeably with *paratransit, dial-a-ride,* or *specialized service*

Deviated fixed route: A fixed route service that will deviate from its regular route to pick up special riders such as older or disabled persons and then return to its regular route without significantly detracting from its schedule

Door-through-door service: A demand responsive system in which the driver goes into the home and/or final destination to provide more assistance, especially for frail or disoriented individuals

Door-to-door service: A demand responsive service system in which the driver goes to the door of the passenger's residence and provides assistance if needed

E&D: Elderly and disabled; in the past, the more common term was E&H ("elderly and handicapped")

Fixed route service: A regularly scheduled transit service operated over a set route

FTA: Federal Transit Administration, a federal agency in the U.S. Department of Transportation that provides funding for various transit services; formerly known as the Urban Mass Transportation Administration

Human services transportation: Transportation provided to persons served by human service programs such as Medicaid and Title III of the Older Americans Act; most transportation is provided to older, disabled, or low-income persons on a demand responsive basis

Incidental provider: An organization that provides transit only to its own clients and primarily as a service incidental to its primary service

ISTEA: Intermodal Surface Transportation Efficiency Act of 1991, usually referred to as "ice tea"; the federal authorizing legislation for transit and highway programs, best known for its creation of flexible funding mechanisms—provisions that allow funds to be transferred between highway and transit programs

Match: State or local resources that must be provided to support a project to qualify for federal financial assistance

Paratransit: Transportation that is more flexible and personalized than conventional fixed route, fixed schedule mass transportation service, but not including exclusionary services such as charter or sightseeing trips (see also demand responsive)

SOURCE: Mauser (1994).

minimum of 24 hours in advance, to schedule a van for an appointment. The transit scheduler will match the request with the appropriate vehicle and routes. Whether a transportation system is fixed route, modified fixed route, demand responsive, or a combination of service modes depends on the needs of the community and the resources available to meet those needs (Mauser, 1994).

Federal Transit Administration

Of the types of transportation described above, most visible are the programs funded with federal funds, which provide 55% of all public money for transportation for older persons. Most of that money comes from two sources: the FTA and the U.S. Department of Health and Human Services (Lee, 1993). This network provides an estimated 95 million trips per year in rural areas and 7.7 billion trips per year in urban areas (Rucker, 1995b).

Three principal funding sources through the FTA are critical to meeting the mobility needs of older and disabled persons (see Exhibit 14.3). One FTA program, called Section 5311 (formerly Section 18), apportions funds to states for public transportation in nonurbanized areas of less than 50,000 residents. Service cannot be client specific or limited to older and disabled persons and must be promoted to the general public. In most Section 5311 programs, however, the majority of riders are older persons or persons with disabilities. Section 5311 programs are made up of a network of approximately 1,200 public, private for-profit, and private nonprofit agencies that cover a service area of 1.5 million square miles and 53 million people (Rucker, 1995b). Most Section 5311 vehicles are vans carrying 8 to 15 passengers (53%). Nearly half of all Section 5311 vehicles are wheelchair accessible. Demand responsive service is the most common mode of service among Section 5311 providers (86%). The remaining service is fixed route or modified fixed route. The average operating budget for a Section 5311 provider is $316,150. State and local funds account for 40% of this total and Section 5311 funds for 24% (Rucker, 1994).

A second FTA program, Section 5310 (formerly Section 16), offers funds to assist with the purchase of capital equipment to agencies serving older persons and persons with disabilities in either urbanized or nonurbanized areas. Historically, the funds were offered only to private nonprofit organizations. The ISTEA legislation now allows these funds to be awarded to public organizations as well. These grants provide funds for the rehabilitation of used vans and lift equipment, the purchase of new vans, purchase of radios, and other equipment needs. Nearly 3,700 transportation providers in the United States operate vehicles obtained through the Section 5311 program (Rucker, 1994).

Third, Section 5307 (formerly Section 9) makes federal monies available for public transportation in urbanized areas. Formula grants are available to communities of 50,000 or larger for the purposes of transportation planning, equipment costs, and operation costs. Recipients of these funds may not serve nonurbanized areas and are not required to serve the entire urbanized area they represent. For example, unincorporated areas surrounding a large city may not be served by the city's Section 5307 program (Mauser, 1994).

Exhibit 14.3 **Federal Transit Administration Programs Vital to Community Transportation**

Funding Source	Eligible Recipients	Program Description
Section 5311 (formerly Section 18) of the Federal Transit Act	Awarded to state transportation agencies; eligible subrecipients include local public bodies, private for-profits and nonprofits, and Indian tribal organizations serving areas less than 50,000	Provides both operating and capital and administrative assistance to non-urban areas
Section 5310 (formerly Section 16) of the Federal Transit Act	Awarded to state transportation agencies; eligible subrecipients are private nonprofits or public bodies providing coordinated transportation services for elders and persons with disabilities	May be used to purchase capital equipment such as vans, radios, and wheelchair lifts
Section 5307 (formerly Section 9) of the Federal Transit Act	Monies flow directly to local providers, not to a state department of transportation; public or private providers of transportation services in urban areas of 50,000 or greater population; private transportation companies may be eligible through contractual arrangements	May be used for both capital equipment purchases and continuing operational expenses

SOURCE: Adapted from "Federal Funding Resources," 1995, *Community Transportation Reporter, 13*, pp. 24-25.

Department of Health and Human Services

Under DHHS, transportation programs are funded primarily through the Older Americans Act, the Community Services Block Grant, and Title XIX of the Social Security Act (Exhibit 14.4). Title III, Part B of the Older Americans Act authorizes transportation services to facilitate access to supportive services, nutrition services, or both. How these monies flow to the states and local AAAs is explained in Chapter 2.

The network of Title III-funded older adult transportation providers includes more than 2,400 agencies using an estimated 15,800 vehicles. Some 30% of these Title III agencies also receive FTA Section 5310 funding, and another 10% to 12% receive other FTA funding including Section 5307 described above. Expenditures of Title III funds on transportation services totaled nearly $74 million in fiscal year 1992. Program data for fiscal year 1993 show that Title III programs provided 40,258,849 one-way trips to 820,583 older adults and that 356,450 of those trips served rural elders. Of these participants, 19% were minorities and 39% were persons with low income. Expenditures under Title III of the OAA in 1993 for transportation for older adults totaled $64,672,074. Because the AoA discourages the use of Title III funds for the purchase of vans, the major portions of these monies were allocated for operational rather than capital expenses (National Eldercare Institute on Transportation, 1994). Often, Title III funds are part of a public-

Exhibit 14.4 **Important Sources of Transportation Support Through the U.S. Department of Health and Human Services**

Funding Source	Eligible Recipients	Program Description
Title III	State agencies on aging and local area agencies on aging who subcontract with local providers	Funds are available through Title III, Part B of the Older Americans Act to provide community-based systems of transportation, legal, and in-home services for elders, as well as for multipurpose senior centers.
Title VI	Tribal organizations and public or private nonprofit organizations that serve Native American elders	Funds are available through Title VI of the Older Americans Act to provide nutrition, information and referral, transportation, and other services to Indian elders.
Community Services Block Grant	Local agencies, often county based, to serve low-income persons	Funds may be used for employment, education, housing, nutrition, energy, emergency assistance, and related needs such as transportation for older, low-income, and disabled persons.
Title XX Social Services Block Grant	State and local social service agencies	Enables states to address goals of reduced dependency on social programs; services can include transportation.
Medicaid	State and local medical assistance agencies	Funds available through Title XIX of the Social Security Act to enable states to provide health care services to medically needy low-income persons. States are to ensure transportation to medical services for Medicaid beneficiaries.
Developmental Disabilities Basic Support Grants	State and local developmental disabilities agencies often called Community Center Boards	Funds provide medical services, support services— programs that enable persons with developmental disabilities to become independent and productive; transportation is key service for independence.

SOURCE: Adapted from "Federal Funding Resources," 1995, *Community Transportation Reporter,* 13, pp. 25-28.

private partnership. A private or corporate entity will work with a government entity—in this case, the local AAA—to deliver a service to needy older adults. This is a growing trend to maximize resources.

An example of such a public-private venture is in Springdale, Arkansas, where the AAA issues coupons to offset a portion of the cost of a taxi trip with the local taxi company. The city gains a valuable service for its older adults and residents with disabilities. Meanwhile, the taxi company increases its ridership (Lee, 1993).

Two other important sources of support for public transportation are the Community Service Block Grant and Title XIX Medicaid, both DHHS programs. Under the block grant program, states and Indian tribes receive fund-

For Your Files   **Rural Transit Assistance Program**

The Rural Transit Assistance Program, a program of the Federal Transit Administration of the U.S. Department of Transportation, is a national resource center to help rural transit operators with questions and problems faced every day on the job. This full-service information and assistance clearinghouse on rural and specialized transportation maintains more than 10,000 computerized entries on topics including human resources, transit funding, legislation, and regulations. High-quality training materials, technical assistance, bulletins, and special reports are offered. Public domain materials are available for the cost of reproduction and shipping. No user fee is charged.

For more information, contact Federal Transit Administration, RTAP National Resource Center, c/o Community Transportation Association of America, 1440 New York Ave. NW, Suite 440, Washington, DC 20005, phone 800-527-8279 or fax 202-737-9197.

ing to provide a broad range of social services for low-income persons. These funds are awarded on a formula basis to states, which pass the majority of these funds on to local nonprofit community action programs. Transportation services commonly are provided by many of these local programs.

Title XIX of the Social Security Act, the Medicaid Program, establishes and supports essential health care for low-income people—primarily older persons, persons with disabilities, and single-parent households with dependent children. Nonemergency transportation has been part of the Medicaid program since 1969, when federal regulations mandated that states ensure the service for all Medicaid recipients who have no other means of transportation available to them. A Community Transportation Association of America study in 1991 (cited in Bogren & Hyman, 1994) discovered that about 1% of Medicaid expenditures are spent on transportation services. Although tiny by comparison with the entire Medicaid budget, by 1992 Medicaid transportation funding was four times that of the FTA's Section 18 (now Section 5311) program. Rural transit agencies are particularly reliant on Medicaid nonemergency transportation funding, which provides from 8% to 70% of their transportation budgets.

Successful transportation programs can tap many other sources of funding to meet the needs of mobility dependent persons. Examples include other federal sources, foundations, advertising, rider fees, and special fundraising events (see Exhibit 14.5).

Exhibit 14.5 **Additional Federal and Other Sources of Transportation Funding**

Funding Source	Eligible Recipients	Program Description
Congregate Housing Services Program	Public bodies and private non-profit corporations managing housing for elders and persons with disabilities	Funds are available to provide meals and nonmedical support services, including transportation services, to allow frail elders or disabled persons to maintain maximum independence in a home environment.
Foster Grandparent Program	State and local government agencies, private nonprofit organizations	Funds may be used to provide stipends, transportation, and other support services for low-income elders working as volunteers in programs serving infants, children, or youth with special needs.
Retired Senior Volunteer Program	State and local government agencies, private nonprofit corporations	Funds may be used to provide transportation and other support services for elders to work as volunteers in community service activities.
Senior Companion Programs	State and local government agencies, private nonprofit corporations	Funds may be used to provide transportation and other support services for low-income elders to work in community service activities serving elders with physical, mental, or emotional impairments.
Other	Examples of other sources of funding include United Ways, fares, local tax initiatives, service clubs, foundations, contracts with programs to provide services to a specific group of recipients, and in-kind donations.	

SOURCE: Adapted from "Federal Funding Resources," 1995, *Community Transportation Reporter, 13*, pp. 28-30.

Challenges for Transportation Programs

Meeting Transit Needs

Despite an annual count of 95 million rural transit trips and 7.7 billion urban transit trips, public transit systems in many communities are inadequate. Much of rural America remains without service. Of the nation's rural residents, 38% live in areas without any public transit service, and another 28% live in areas in which the level of transit service is negligible. The per capita rural transit service levels lag substantially behind service levels available to urban residents (Rucker, 1995b). In urban areas with more than 1 million in population, public transit resources are substantial compared with rural areas; the mobility needs of many urban older adults, however, are still unmet.

Barriers to service use discussed earlier in the chapter must be addressed to increase ridership of young and old alike. Furthermore, several factors are likely to increase the demand on public transit systems in the future. One point of view concludes that because older drivers are more vulnerable to injury and their visual and cognitive performance on driving-related tasks diminishes with age, unprecedented numbers of drivers, along with other older adults who depend on them, will lose their mobility for transportation. As a society, then, we must be projecting and planning for increased need for public transit and paratransit to meet this demand. Because transit budget cuts have been on Congress's agenda, it will be increasingly difficult to depend on federal transit funds to meet these increased needs.

Despite all this, a great deal has been achieved in the last 20 years to meet the transportation needs of older adults. A recognized network of transportation professionals is growing and becoming more efficient, effective, and creative in specialized transit delivery. Federal legislation has promoted a return to increased transit availability while at the same time emphasizing local coordination in meeting the transit needs of older adults. Much remains to be done, however.

Improving Coordination of Resources

One of the biggest problems that plague the public transit system is the lack of coordination. The U.S. General Accounting Office (1991a) conducted a study of special transportation services for older adults to assist the Senate in considering the reauthorization of the Older Americans Act and the Federal Transit Act (1988). Of the 19 special transportation programs studied, 18 showed that fragmentation of special transportation is a pervasive, long-standing problem and that in many communities, agencies operate in isolation from one another. This fragmentation occurs despite federal legislative mandates in both acts to encourage coordination. Multiple funding sources for special transportation services result in differing program guidelines for operational practices. For example, the Federal Transit Act encourages the charging of fares, whereas the Older Americans Act explicitly prohibits charging for services but allows voluntary donations. Another problem affecting coordination and efficiency is that many community agencies such as adult day programs, nursing homes, and senior centers purchase a van or vans to respond to the needs of their clients. Other groups of seniors and people with disabilities may see such a vehicle operating in their community and wonder why their own mobility needs are not being met (National Eldercare Institute on Transportation, 1994). After a time, the program and the community learn that an expensive piece of equipment is not being used to its potential. There can be much misunderstanding in a community about the use of such vehicles, and often, these programs lack the expertise, understanding, and will to coordinate their transportation resources with the overall needs of the community.

Not only does lack of coordination result in a community not being adequately served within its own boundaries, but there is an incredible imbalance in service levels from community to community and in traveling from one community to another when public transportation is required. One community could be adequately served by a transit program while a neighboring community has no transit service at all. Even large metropolitan areas, which overall have better coverage from public transportation, have unserved population pockets. Less likely to be found is public transit service between communities, particularly small to midsized communities.

Currently, the federal government, through the Federal Transit Act of 1988 and the ISTEA of 1991, places a heavy emphasis on local transportation coordination and a balanced, flexible funding approach to transportation. Many advocates, however, feel that the emphasis is not strong enough and that specialized transit will continue to be underserved. Because most of these flexible funds were formerly earmarked for highways, transit and human service advocates will need to form coalitions and become integrally involved in the new and complex ISTEA planning processes to ensure that the transportation needs of older adults are adequately addressed. This includes advocating for their fair share of funding. Whether the new coordination planning and flexible funding rules under ISTEA will favorably affect transportation delivery in the United States remains to be seen.

Another future issue with strong relational ties to transportation is the delivery of home and community-based services. Since the 1980s, states and local communities have developed a network of community-based services to support older adults who want to remain in their own homes for as long as possible. These home and community-based services are designed to prevent premature institutionalization through the provision of housing, home health care, nutrition, chore services, respite care, and day services. These programs are discussed in greater detail in other chapters. A report on the Mini-White House Conference on Aging and Transportation (Schauer & Weaver, 1994) noted that policy issues currently being discussed on a national level will affect the quality of life for older adults in the 21st century. Elder mobility as an issue is unique from any other. Without adequate mobility, most social delivery programs lose much of their impact, and any reforms made in health care will be moot without health care access.

Another future funding challenge is the uncertainty of Medicaid, as the federal and state governments debate how to make this program more cost-effective. The future of Medicaid transportation funds is uncertain, at best. In addition, speculation abounds that many other federal programs will be block granted to the states in the future, leaving the states with considerably more flexibility than they currently have to determine how federal monies are expended. Will transportation for older and disabled persons be a priority against a myriad of other pressing human needs that states are facing?

Enhancing Mobility Options

We should not assume that the only answer to the mobility needs of future older Americans lies exclusively with increased funding and better coordination of public transit. Vitally significant to mobility as it relates to the well-being of elders is America's roadway system. Many planners and policymakers are asking questions about how to maximize the ability of older adults to meet their mobility needs in a safe manner. As alluded to earlier in this chapter, federal and state funding for transit dependent persons is minuscule compared with the billions expended on highway infrastructure each year. Realistically, travel by car will continue to be central to U.S. society, including older adults. Older persons of 2020 will have grown up during a period when use of the automobile became an integral part of everyday life. These older persons will probably have high expectations about driving. Therefore, as a society, it may be a question not only of how to expand and make public transit more accessible and attractive to older adults but also of how to improve the safety of older adult drivers, many of whom believe that the automobile will continue to be their principle means of meeting their mobility needs (Committee for the Study on Improving Mobility and Safety for Older Persons, 1988).

The committee's study also concluded that age is a poor predictor of performance and should not be the sole determination of when persons relinquish their driver's licenses. The study suggested that many steps could be taken to improve the mobility and safety of older drivers and pedestrians: improving roadway markings; making highway signs more legible; improving vehicle safety; and establishing, among other things, better standards for left-hand turn lanes (older drivers in particular have difficulty with left-hand turns). A specific example is the current standard highway signage. The standard assumes that an inch-high letter is legible at 50 feet. This standard corresponds to a visual acuity of 20/25, which exceeds the visual ability of about 40% of drivers who are 65 to 74. This is just one example of how a better-designed roadway system that takes the needs of older adults into consideration would go a long way in maintaining the mobility of future older adults.

Jette and Branch (1992) concluded that future generations of older drivers are likely to be even older and drive more miles than the older drivers of today by virtue of their increasing numbers and their continued reliance on the car in old age. Because America has supported a national policy during the past 50 years that places high priority on private automobile transportation, some argue that roadway design, automobile engineering, and licensing and retraining of drivers are all critical considerations in enabling older adults to use their automobiles as long and as safely as possible.

Today and in the future, there will be significant challenges to make roadway systems safer for older drivers. Although today, older people drive fewer miles than the rest of the population, their future mileage is likely to increase for several reasons. More older people, especially older women, have driver's licenses than previous cohorts of older women. Furthermore, as today's young people age, they will be more likely to retain their driver's licenses compared with the current cohort of older adults (Eberhard, cited in Committee for the Study on Improving Mobility and Safety for Older Persons, 1988). Also, more older people now reside in suburbs where reliance on the automobile is greater. Finally, as people age, they are less likely to change residential location, leading researchers to expect that the graying of the suburbs will continue (U.S. Senate Special Committee on Aging, 1991b). Ideally, future planning for the mobility needs of all populations will not center on transit versus cars but will focus on how to build communities that give older adults a range of mobility options that they could self-select on the basis of their particular capabilities and situation.

 CASE STUDY

A NEED FOR TRANSPORTATION PLANNING AND COORDINATION

Daylight, Inc., is a small, social-model adult day program. Daylight's mission is to help older adults remain independent in the community and to give caregivers time apart from the daily stresses of caregiving. At first, the Daylight staff and board of directors thought that they would have to close for lack of interest. Fifteen years later, with consistent marketing, great personal effort by the executive director, and excellent support from an active board of directors, Daylight has increased its average attendance from 6 to 17 persons per day. Family calls and agency referrals to the program are coming in weekly. Two years ago, Daylight opened a satellite program 35 miles away to serve seven rural communities in the southern half of the county. Now, there is a need for a modern facility and to expand services to include weekend and overnight respite. Daylight has embarked on a major capital development project in partnership with a home health care agency. The proposed facility will house both agencies and permit program expansion and flexibility not currently possible.

At a recent annual planning retreat, the staff receptionist commented about the many callers who ask about the program but who ultimately do not enroll their family members in Daylight. After much discussion, the board directed the executive director to conduct a follow-up survey with those callers to learn why they chose not to use Daylight. A telephone survey was prepared and volunteers called 37 families.

The survey results showed that 42% of the families contacted did not choose Daylight as a respite option because of the lack of transportation. Nearly 55% of those surveyed in the southern part of the county listed transportation as the principal barrier to enrollment. Transportation barriers were due to age, disability, and conflicting work schedules. When the executive director brought this information to the next board meeting, the board decided to form a task force to develop a plan of action for board consideration that would address the transportation problem.

CASE STUDY QUESTIONS

1. Assume you are a member of the task force. What additional information would you want to know before you proceed with the development of a plan of action to address these transportation barriers?

2. Daylight is planning to build a new facility. What relationship does this transportation issue have with the success or failure of the new facility, if any?

3. On the basis of what you have learned from reading the chapter, what types of transportation programs might you need to contact? What questions would you need to explore with these entities to write your report and proposal for the Daylight Board of Directors?

4. What transportation options should the task force explore? Describe at least three transportation options for Daylight and list the advantages and disadvantages of each option.

5. How is this situation relevant to the chapter's discussion of the relationship between mobility needs of frail elders and home and community-based services?

6. List the transportation terminology that best describes the Daylight passenger and the type of service most suited for this passenger.

⑤ LEARNING ACTIVITIES

1. Contact your state transportation association. To find the name and phone number of the transit association in your state, go to the *Community Resources for Older Adults* Web site (http://www.hhs.unco.edu/geron.htm). Find out the association's stance on transit issues, gaps in service for older adult riders, and future public transit plans.

2. Select a destination to which an older adult might travel, such as the bank, Social Security office, senior center, grocery store, or doctor's office. Use the local public transportation system to get there. Try to select a location that is

not close to your home. If you are familiar with riding public transportation, select a location you have not been to before. Record your observations and make note of the following:

a. How long did it take for you to get to the bus stop?

b. How long did you have to wait?

c. How long did it take to get to your final destination?

d. How many older adult riders were there?

e. How many barriers to riding public transportation could you identify that you think would make it difficult for older adults to ride the bus? Look for things such as these:

    1. Bus stop location and condition

    2. Height of steps into the bus

    3. Seating

    4. Ability to see upcoming stops

Make note of your general feelings. Did you feel any apprehension? How hard was it to figure out your route and bus stop location? On the basis of your observations, what suggestions do you have for making public transportation older adult friendly?

3. Interview an older adult who is currently driving and one who uses public transportation. Ask the current driver how the person's driving has changed through the years, whom the driver would rely on if he or she were no longer able to drive, and if the driver would consider using public transportation, and if not, why? Ask the public transportation user what the user likes and dislikes about public transportation and what suggestions the user has for improving transportation services.

FOR MORE INFORMATION

National Resources

1. National Caucus and Center on Black Aged, Inc., 1424 K Street NW, Suite 500, Washington, DC 20005, 202-637-8400.

   The National Caucus and Center on Black Aged sponsors a number of transportation initiatives and programs.

2. National Eldercare Institute on Transportation, 725 15th Street NW, Suite 900, Washington, DC 20005, 800-527-8279.

   The National Eldercare Institute on Transportation offers a toll-free transit hotline and issue briefs on best practice models of community transit systems, elder transportation programs, and cost sharing in transportation. The institute offers training workshops on management issues in elder transportation and coordination efforts between transportation and aging networks.

Web Resources

1. Community Transportation Association of America, 715 15th Street NW, Suite 900, Washington, DC 20005, 202-628-1480
   http://www.ctaa.org

   The association's Web page has links to state and local transportation systems, federal transportation news and budget information, and transportation funding that describe more than 90 transportation grants available, along with links to other related transportation sites.

2. The Transit-Center
   http://www.transit-center.com

   The Transit-Center's home page is geared more for transportation professionals but does have a good resources page that offers links to ADA paratransit coalitions, news groups, and transit-related sites.

3. Wandsworth Community Transport
   http://web.ukonline.co.uk/wct

   Take a trip to the United Kingdom and check out the transportation services offered by the Wandsworth Community Transport System.

4. Federal Transit Administration
   http://www.fta.dot.gov

   The FTA's home page is a great place to start to access a tremendous amount of information about transportation. Visitors can search the National Transit Library by using key words; read reports about transit accessibility, the history of transit, public participation, and outreach; and access directories and references.

 **15**

Housing

It has been a year since Lois sold her home and moved into a federally subsidized senior housing complex. The move was a difficult decision, and the 2 years she waited for an opening were difficult and frustrating. Once settled into her new apartment, she had no regrets. Her modest income of $623 per month had been totally inadequate to meet the expenses of keeping up her home and paying for her heart medication, groceries, and utilities. She rarely had as much as a dime left over at the end of the month. She couldn't even begin to consider a major roof repair that was sorely needed. She misses her old neighborhood, but she doesn't miss the worries of taking care of a house and yard. Now that her money goes a little further, she can enjoy some outings with her new friends.

The majority of older individuals perceive their homes as one of their most prized possessions. A home is much more than physical shelter. It gives those who dwell within its confines a sense of security, privacy, comfort, and independence. It also plays a major role in facilitating social interaction with family and friends (Blank, 1988). A home holds for its residents a multitude of memories and a sense of continuity in life. Findings from a recent study suggest that the vast majority of persons aged 55 and older want to stay in their homes and never leave (AARP, 1992). The quality and type of dwellings in which older adults live depend on many things, such as their income, age, marital status, gender, and race, as well as their health and functional status.

We begin this chapter by describing the theoretical concept of *person-environment fit* as a framework for understanding the relationship between older individuals' place of residence and their physical, psychological, and social needs. We then discuss the various independent and supportive housing arrangements in which older adults reside and policies that support these arrangements. The chapter concludes with a discussion of several emerging issues that are likely to influence the housing options and needs of older adults in the future.

The Person-Environment Fit Model

For older individuals to be satisfied with their environment, an appropriate "fit" needs to exist between their level of competence and the demands of their environment (Lawton, 1980; Lawton & Nahemow, 1973). Competence refers to the upper limits of an individual's abilities and extends across several areas of functioning including (a) health, (b) sensory-cognitive abilities, (c) capacity for self-care, (d) ability to perform instrumental activities, (e) mastery, and (f) social skills (Lawton, 1982). If the environment is too demanding for an older adult's competence or if the environment puts too few demands on the older adult's competence, there is a poor fit.

Elders enjoy a range of comfort and display adaptive behavior when their physical and social living environments are compatible with their personal abilities and resources. A moderately challenging environment is beneficial because it encourages growth and therefore stretches the person's abilities. Too wide a discrepancy between personal competence and the demands of the environment results in maladaptive behavior and personal stress and might impede the person's abilities to carry out activities of daily living (ADLs). For example, we know that living in their own homes is the preferred housing choice of most older adults. If, however, the home becomes too costly to manage or the older person is physically unable to maintain it, the demands of the environment may be too stressful. Relocation decisions often occur when older adults, or others in their support network, decide that they are no longer competent to remain living in their current housing environment.

When selecting a new housing option, older persons should avoid moving to a residence that requires too little from them or lacks the stimulation necessary to challenge their existence. When older adults find that their skills and abilities are limited by their environment, they often become bored and give up doing many things for themselves. Just as overstimulation by the environment can cause distress, understimulation can be just as stressful for the individual and result in greater dependence and feelings of helplessness (Lawton, 1982).

In summary, when considering outcomes related to the person-environment fit model, the preferences of the individual and the nature of the environment must be considered. The older adult's decision to move often is prompted by a need for greater physical, psychological, and/or social security (Parmelee & Lawton, 1990). An older person's security needs, however, may be in direct conflict with his or her need for autonomy and independence. To successfully adapt to a new, more structured living environment, older adults need to actively pursue a level of autonomy appropriate to their personal resources and competencies. We now turn to a discussion of the different types of housing environments that older adults occupy.

Users and Programs: Independent Living Environments

Independent living environments are designed for older adults who are able to manage daily activities, such as housekeeping, cooking, and personal care, with little assistance from others. Widely varying living environments exist that allow older adults to live independently. Each of these will be discussed below along with the programs and services that help older adults remain in their independent living environment.

Single-Family Dwellings

The majority of noninstitutionalized, community-dwelling older adults own or rent their dwellings. The majority live in detached, single-family dwellings (76%), whereas the remainder live in multiunit buildings (13%), semi-detached houses (5%), and mobile homes (6%; see Exhibit 15.1; AARP, 1992). More than half (59%) of older adults own their homes, 23% are making mortgage payments, and 17% are renters.

Personal variables such as age, race, gender, marital status, and income influence home ownership in later life (Naifeh, 1993; U.S. House Select Committee on Aging, 1992a). Individuals aged 65 to 74 are more likely to be homeowners than any other age group of seniors. Ownership levels are higher for older men than for older women and higher for those individuals who are married than for those who are not married in later life. Older persons with incomes greater than $25,000 and white elders are more likely to be homeowners than their less financially well-off and minority counterparts (see Exhibit 15.2).

Compared with younger individuals, older adults who live in single-family dwellings (a) have lived in their homes longer, (b) have homes more likely in need of repairs, and (c) spend more money on their homes. According to Naifeh (1993), 35% of persons 65 or older moved into their current place of residence before 1960. Women, whites and blacks, and persons with lower incomes are most likely to remain in the same home for the longest period.

Exhibit 15.1 **Type of Dwelling Unit of Older Adults**

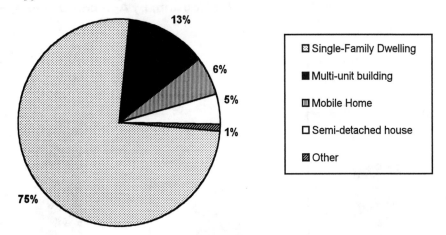

SOURCE: American Association of Retired Persons (1992).

Exhibit 15.2 **Percentage of Householders 65 Years of Age or Older Who Are Homeowners, by Race and Income**

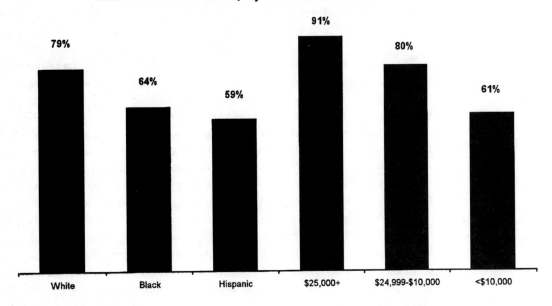

SOURCE: Naifeh, 1993, p. 5.

Although many older homeowners do not have a mortgage and consequently spend less on housing than do younger adults, aged homeowners

Exhibit 15.3 **Percentage of Householders Spending 30% or More of Their Household Income for Housing, by Age and Ownership**

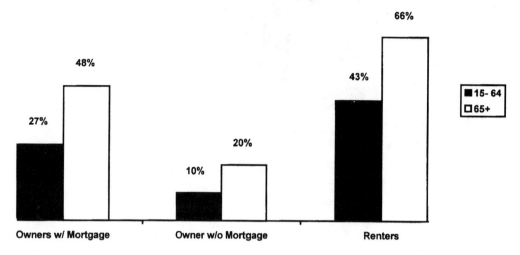

SOURCE: Naifeh, 1993, p. 25.

spend a greater percentage of their yearly income on housing (see Exhibit 15.3). Furthermore, as elders grow older, they are likely to spend more of their income on housing than they did when they were younger. Almost one half of all older homeowners spend 30% or more of their income on housing; younger homeowners spend approximately 27% of their income on housing (Naifeh, 1993). This pattern holds true for old-old and young-old homeowners, with and without mortgages, as well as for renters.

Especially hard hit when it comes to housing costs as a percentage of income are older adult homeowners with low incomes. Of older adults with incomes below $10,000, 93% spend 30% or more on housing, compared with 24% of older adults with incomes greater than $25,000 (see Exhibit 15.4). A full 62% of older adults spend 50% or more of their incomes on housing costs. For example, an older household with an income of $9,999 is likely to spend $417 or more per month on housing costs, leaving them with $416 or less for living expenses. These older adults clearly represent the predicament of being "house rich" but "cash poor." Low-income older adults who rent also spend a higher percentage of their income on housing than do older adult renters with higher incomes (Naifeh, 1993).

Housing Programs

As we mentioned at the beginning of the chapter, the majority of older adults, such as Lois, desire to remain living in their own homes as long as possible.

Exhibit 15.4 **Percentage of Older Adults Spending 30% or More of Their Income on Housing, by Income and Ownership**

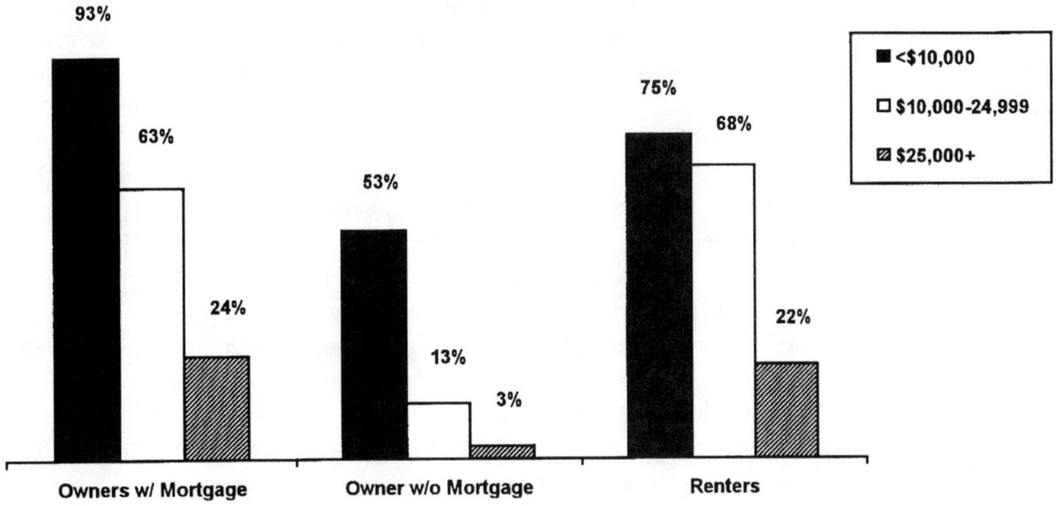

Legend:
■ <$10,000
□ $10,000-24,999
▨ $25,000+

Owners w/ Mortgage: 93%, 63%, 24%
Owner w/o Mortgage: 53%, 13%, 3%
Renters: 75%, 68%, 22%

SOURCE: Naifeh, 1993, p. 28.

This may be more difficult for older adults with low and middle incomes and those with houses that are in need of repair. Most communities offer programs that can provide economic and tangible assistance to make housing costs and repairs more affordable.

Home Equity Conversion Programs

Older adults who own their homes can convert part of their home equity into cash while still living in their home through home equity conversion programs. There are no restrictions on how the income generated through an equity conversion program can be used. Older adults may choose to use the income for home repairs, health care costs, living expenses, or as a source of discretionary income. Scholen (1990) has identified four types of equity conversion programs. One type of home equity conversion is the *deferred payment loan* program. Under this program, the homeowner can borrow a lump sum from a lending institution with no repayment of the principal or interest until the end of a specified term or until the homeowner dies or sells the home. Under the *reverse mortgage program,* the lender provides the borrower with monthly advances or a line of credit that can be tapped into as needed. Payment on the reverse mortgage is not due until the end of the loan term, which may be related to the length of time the borrower occupies the home. *A sale-leaseback program* allows the homeowner to sell the home to a buyer, who then leases it back to the seller for life. The new owner is usually responsible for taxes, repairs, and insurance and pays the seller a down payment and a monthly payment. The seller pays a monthly rent and has the right to live in the house until he or she dies or moves. The final type of equity conversion program is the *life estate option*. Under this program, the older homeowner sells the home but retains a life estate—or total ownership—until death.

Although not a home equity program, *property tax relief* programs allow older homeowners to defer property tax payments until they sell their homes or die. State or local governments offer tax deferral programs to low-income older adults who are unable to keep up with rising property taxes as a way to remain living in their own homes. Property tax relief programs can differ slightly in how the program is administered. State or local governments might make loans to homeowners so they can pay property taxes, reduce the assessed value of the home, or authorize a deferred payment of property taxes until the homeowner sells the property or dies (Scholen, 1990; U.S. Senate Special Committee on Aging, 1993).

Home Repair Programs

Home repair and maintenance are a considerable expense for many older adults because the majority have lived in their homes for more than three decades. Although most older homeowners are forced to cut back on cosmetic aspects of home upkeep, findings from the 1987 American Housing Survey (Golant & LaGreca, 1994) indicate that they "do not allow vital housing components to deteriorate" (Reschovsky & Newman, 1991, p. S296). Of older households, however, 6% report problems with poorly functioning plumbing, leaky roofs, and inadequate electrical wiring (Mikelsons & Turner, 1991). Inadequate housing conditions are more likely to be present for elders of color and elders with low income. Greater percentages of older blacks and Hispanics report moderate to severe housing problems compared with older whites. In addition, elders with incomes below $5,000 are more likely to report inadequate housing conditions than are elders with incomes between $10,000 and $15,000 (Norry & Williams, 1994).

Besides needing specific repairs, many homes do not support frail older adults in conducting daily activities within the home. Older adults who are aging in place may need to modify their homes' structure to accommodate their physical limitations. Modifications in lighting, accessibility, mobility, and bathing facilities can improve functioning and enhance safety (Pynoos, 1992).

In response to the increasing demand for assistance with housing upkeep and repair, a number of home repair programs have emerged across the

Best Practice **SWAT Home Repair Program**

Students Working Against Threats to the Aged and Disabled (SWAT) began in 1994 to help elders and adults with disabilities in rural east Texas. Adult Protective Services caseworkers and students at Stephen F. Austin State University in Nacogdoches are working together to clean up the homes of older adults who have financial, mental, or physical problems that make it hard for them to take care of themselves. Caseworkers for the Adult Protective Services Unit in the Texas Department of Protective and Regulatory Services team up with student groups to clean and repair substandard dwellings. First, caseworkers orient SWAT team members about the person for whom they will be working. This helps the volunteers connect with the person they are helping. Teams are encouraged to interact with the client as much as possible. SWAT team members literally converge on a client's home armed with paintbrushes and buckets labeled "elbow grease." The process is much like an old-fashioned spring cleaning with the entire contents of the home carried out onto the lawn. Depending on the condition of the dwelling, SWAT teams provide many services from disinfecting, to painting, to minor repairs. Once the work is done, the interior of the home is spruced up with donated curtains, rugs, and bed linens.

In 2 years, hundreds of volunteers have refurbished 25 homes. The program is successful on many levels. Volunteers receive immediate gratification because the final results are so obvious and the recipients are openly grateful. The caseworkers are inspired and invigorated from working with the volunteers, and there are no administrative costs because the program is run exclusively by volunteers.

For more information on SWAT, contact Stephen F. Austin University, Sociology Department, P.O. Box 13047, Nacogdoches, TX 75962, 409-468-4405.

country. Home repair programs provide assistance with home maintenance or minor repairs. The funding for many of these programs comes from community development block grants or Title III monies from the Older Americans Act. Programs vary with regard to the type of repairs they subsidize but typically include emergency repairs for plumbing, electricity, heat, and leaking roofs; minor repairs; exterior painting; and the removal of debris.

Two programs that help low-income adults with the costs of heating and cooling their homes are the Department of Energy's Weatherization Assistance Program and the Low Income Home Energy Assistance Program (LIHEAP). Under the weatherization program, the federal government provides funds to the states, which allocate money to local nonprofit agencies that purchase and install insulation and make energy-related repairs. From 1991 to 1993, more than 2 million homes were weatherized, half of which were older adult households (U.S. Senate Special Committee on Aging, 1993). A Department of Energy report cited by the Senate Special Committee on Aging found that the weatherization program reduced utility costs of the homeowner, that the cost of weatherization was less than the average energy savings per household, and that U.S. carbon emissions were reduced. Funding for the weatherization program in fiscal year 1996 was $109.7 million and was increased to $120.8 million in fiscal year 1997 (Northeast Midwest Institute, 1997).

The LIHEAP provides financial assistance to low-income households regardless of age, either directly, through vendors, or to landlords for home heating and cooling costs, energy crisis intervention, or low-cost weatherization. According to the U.S. Senate Special Committee on Aging (1993), 7,366,379 individuals received assistance through the LIHEAP; more than 70% of LIHEAP recipients had annual incomes of less than $8,000, most of whom were older or single-parent households. Funding for LIHEAP in fiscal year 1997 was $973 million (DHHS, 1997).

Home Sharing

When home expense becomes burdensome, home sharing can be a viable solution to managing those expenses. Shared housing is a living arrangement in which two or more unrelated people share a home or apartment to their mutual advantage (Mantell & Gildea, 1989). "Tenants" often pay modest rent or provide services to the householder in exchange for room and board. For older adults with extra living space in their homes, this housing option can provide financial assistance, companionship in a familiar and comfortable setting, and help with household chores.

Although generally thought of as an urban phenomenon, home sharing is not limited to any particular community (Robins & Howe, 1989). Elders most interested in shared housing often have low incomes, large uninsured medical expenses, poor health, and limited physical mobility (e.g., difficulty climbing stairs; Varady, 1990). Older home sharers who are economically secure and active but live alone typically are interested in having someone in their homes at night or someone who will do periodic home maintenance chores (e.g., shoveling snow) but do not expect routine daily assistance or companionship from their "boarder" (Jaffe & Howe, 1988).

Federal Housing Programs

Federal legislation has created a number of housing programs that assist older adults who have limited incomes through Section 8, Section 202, and public housing. In addition, programs under the auspices of the Rural Housing and Community Development Service (formerly the Farmers' Home Administration) offer housing assistance for older, low-income individuals living in rural areas.

Section 8

Project-Based Assistance. Under Section 8, rental subsidies are given to landlords who agree to rent to low-income individuals and families. The subsidy covers the difference between the tenants' contribution, an amount that totals 30% of their adjusted income, and fair market rents (U.S. Senate Special Committee on Aging, 1993).

Tenant-Based Assistance. In contrast to the Section 8 project assistance component, the tenant-based assistance component offers rental assistance directly to the tenant in the form of rental certificates or vouchers. Tenants must obtain a dwelling with rent that is not higher than the fair market value determined by the U.S. Department of Housing and Urban Development (HUD). Tenants are responsible for paying 30% of their income for rent. If the rent is higher than the fair market value, the renters are responsible for the difference (U.S. Senate Special Committee on Aging, 1993; Zedlewski, Barnes, Burt, McBride, & Meyer, 1990).

Section 202

Section 202 is the primary construction program that makes low-cost federal loans to nonprofit sponsors for new construction or rehabilitation of existing structures to provide subsidized rental housing for low- and moderate-income elders. Tenants aged 62 and older living in these units pay rent that is about 30% of their adjusted income (U.S. Senate Special Committee on Aging, 1993). These housing complexes usually offer supportive services, such as transportation and meals.

Public Housing

Public housing is the oldest federal housing program assisting individuals and families with low incomes, including older renters. Older adult renters occupy an estimated 45% of public housing units. Local public housing authorities usually operate these housing units, and renters pay rent equal to 30% of their adjusted income. Of older public housing tenants, 70% have annual incomes between $3,000 and $6,000, and 15% of these households have at least one member with a physical disability (U.S. Senate Special Committee on Aging, 1991b).

For Your Files   **B'nai B'rith**

B'nai B'rith is the largest Jewish sponsor of nonsectarian, federally subsidized housing for older adults in the United States. B'nai B'rith, through its Senior Citizens Housing Committee, has been involved in a cooperative partnership with the Housing and Urban Development to make available rental apartments for low-income older adults. They have a network of 29 apartment buildings in 21 communities across the United States, which encompass more than 3,700 apartment units serving more than 4,500 persons. Each project has a volunteer board of directors that makes sure each apartment building is responsive to its residents. Professional staff offer support and assistance to individual apartment building board of directors. For more information, contact B'nai B'rith at 1640 Rhode Island Avenue NW, Washington, DC 20036-3278, 202-857-6581 (http://www.bnaibrith.org/sch/over.html).

SOURCE: B'nai B'rith (1997).

Rural Programs

Two housing programs are available to rural elders under the Rural Housing and Community Development Service program. Section 515 offers low-interest construction loans for rental and congregate housing for low-income individuals. Approximately half of Section 515 housing projects are occupied by older adults (U.S. Senate Special Committee on Aging, 1993). Section 504 provides loans and grants to low-income rural residents 62 years of age and older to repair new or existing single-family housing.

Congregate Housing Services Program

The Congregate Housing Services Program provides grants to public housing agencies and owners of Section 202, Section 8, and Section 515 units for meals and supportive services for frail older adults (and other persons with disabilities). Ninety-eight sites received such funds in 1994; the program was not funded, however, in 1996 or 1997. It is likely that these funds will be folded in with other block grant funds given to states or housing authorities (J. Sheehan, personal communication, April 22, 1997).

Planned and Naturally Occurring Retirement Communities

Although the majority of older adults live in age-integrated communities, almost one third of all older adults live in a naturally occurring retirement

---

Best Practice   **Sunflower Supportive Services Program**

In recognition of the large number of older adults aging in place, the Kansas Department of Commerce and Housing, Division of Housing, requested and received a $67,000 grant in 1994 from the Robert Wood Johnson Foundation for a demonstration supportive services program in four senior housing sites in Kansas. The goal of the program is to demonstrate that the state of Kansas, working with senior housing developments and local service providers, can provide and finance supportive services in response to the needs and preferences of older residents.

A key element of the Supportive Services Program is its reliance on consumer choice in determining supportive services to be offered. Key features of the program are these:

■ The program is targeted to the entire housing development, not to frail older individuals. This approach has the advantage of reducing stigma because older persons do not need to declare themselves frail or disabled; all residents are eligible for services.

■ There is significant consumer involvement in establishing the program through resident input, which includes market surveys, focus groups, and regular discussions with residents.

■ The program is organized around a service coordinator skilled in organizing people and accessing community resources. Individuals are referred for professional services as needed.

This program has the potential to serve approximately 351 senior residents. All four sites have a resident services coordinator. The state supportive services coordinator provides training, consultation, technical assistance, and support to the senior housing providers in the program.

For further information, contact Kansas Department of Commerce and Housing, Division of Housing, 700 SW Harrison, Suite 1300, Topeka, Kansas 66603-3712, 913-296-5865.

SOURCE: Kansas Department of Commerce and Housing (1997).

---

community, in which at least half of the residents are 60 years of age or older. Naturally occurring retirement communities emerge through long periods as people living in the same location age in place. Residents typically have annual incomes under $20,000, are members of minority groups, and live in small towns (AARP, 1992).

An estimated 1% to 2% of older adults live in planned retirement communities such as Leisure World in California and Sun City in Arizona. Such communities, which tend to be located in the suburbs or in rural areas, often have an extensive offering of activities. For example, the 21,000 residents of Leisure World in Laguna Hills, California, enjoy six clubhouses for classes and crafts. They have access to table tennis, billiards, lawn bowling, a swimming pool, hot tubs, a Jacuzzi, golf courses, tennis courts, equestrian facilities, an extensive library, and private garden plots, as well as some on-site municipal services (Barrow, 1996). Often-cited advantages to living in age-segregated planned communities include living with peers who have similar interests, in a quiet environment, and among helpful, friendly people (AARP, 1992).

Most residents in these planned communities live in single-family dwellings or in town houses. The vast majority of residents are white, married, and between the ages of 65 and 74 and have higher incomes than most other groups of seniors (Blank, 1988). Both personal and demographic variables influence an older person's interest in moving to a planned retirement community. Specifically, older persons who perceive themselves as extroverts, security minded, physically active, and fairly self-reliant express a higher degree of interest in moving to a planned retirement community than those individuals who are highly family oriented, introverted, and less self-reliant (Loomis, Sorce, & Tyler, 1989).

Single Room Occupancy Hotels

Single room occupancy hotels (SROs) are "cheap hotels and rooming houses located in areas adjacent to the downtown business districts" (Erickson & Eckert, 1977, p. 440). They can be remodeled hotels, tenements, school buildings, hotels that have always served as SROs, or newer buildings built specifically as SROs. Typically, SROs provide inner-city residents with a private room and a shared kitchen, bath, and common area. More recently, some SROs have been built as micro efficiency units that include a small kitchenette and a bathroom with a shower (Regnier & Culver, 1994). Services provided to tenants range from nothing to highly managed care. Sometimes, SROs will offer limited security, light housekeeping, or an errand service (Rollinson, 1991a). Although perceived to be at the bottom rung of the housing ladder, SROs provide emergency, transitional, and permanent housing for single low-income persons of all ages (Regnier & Culver, 1994).

Researchers estimate that some 400,000 older adults live in SROs across the country (Eckert & Murrey, 1987). In studies of SROs located in Chicago and New York, the percentage of tenants who are older adults ranges from 15% to 33%. Most of these individuals indicated not only that they were lifelong residents of the city but also that many had lived in the same neighborhood during their childhood (Crystal & Beck, 1992; Rollinson, 1991b).

In contrast to the image of the SRO tenant as primarily male and alcoholic, older adults who live in SROs represent a diverse group with regard to gender, age, health status, marital status, race, and education (Crystal & Beck, 1992; Rollinson, 1990). Approximately 40% of older tenants are women. The age and health profile of tenants creates a picture of an older adult, usually in his or her 70s, coping with chronic conditions such as arthritis and other musculoskeletal problems, diabetes, heart conditions, and sensory losses. Few older SRO residents report a past or current drinking problem. Almost one half of the older SRO tenants reported never being married; most others were either widowed, divorced, or separated. Approximately one third of the tenants have less than a ninth-grade education, whereas almost one fourth report that they have attended or graduated from college. Researchers also report a diverse picture with regard to race of the tenants. Although in the majority of studies, most of the residents were white, the percentage of white residents ranged from 54% to 97% (Bild & Havingurst, 1976; Community Emergency Shelter Organizations, 1985, cited in Rollinson, 1991b; Crystal & Beck, 1992). Residents live on small incomes from SSI and Social Security. The majority of older tenants report average incomes falling below current poverty levels, with their housing costs (i.e., rent and utilities) taking up as much as half of their monthly income.

Researchers and service providers characterize residents of SROs as fiercely independent individuals who are protective of their autonomy and who receive little assistance from relatives, friends, or neighbors (Rollinson, 1990). Rollinson quoted one resident, confined to a wheelchair, as saying, "Some people say, 'can I help you do this and help you do that,' and being bullheaded as hell I tell them no, except to go to the [grocery] store" (p. 201).

Challenges for Independent Living Programs

As we discussed at the outset of the chapter, the majority of older adults reside in independent living settings and desire to do so as long as possible. Many issues need to be addressed, however, to promote independent living in the community.

Removing Barriers to Shared Housing

Several barriers can impede the use of shared housing in later life (Mantell & Gildea, 1989). The most frequently cited barrier is a lack of financial support for programs that help match older individuals with prospective housemates. Limited federal, state, or local support is available for these programs, and the clients served are often unable to pay the actual cost of providing the service. Second, restrictive zoning regulations and building and fire codes prohibit shared housing in many residential neighborhoods. A third barrier is older adults' fear that their income from SSI, food stamps, or fuel subsidies will be reduced if regulatory agencies base decisions on the income of the household. In addition, older adults may be hesitant to share their homes with a stranger. Such attitudes, no doubt, are tied to deep-rooted values of privacy and independence.

Serving Older Adults Living in Public Housing

Several problems have emerged for older adults living in public housing. Many units are in need of extensive repair and remodeling—three fifths of the nation's public housing units are more than 20 years old (U.S. Senate Special Committee on Aging, 1992). New housing stock has not been built because funding for HUD-assisted housing programs declined by 80% from 1981 to 1990 (U.S. Senate Special Committee on Aging, 1990). Furthermore, there are lengthy waiting lists to get into public housing. In some cities, 28 older persons apply for every vacancy that occurs in newer units. The lengthy waiting lists are due in part to the lack of available units and a low turnover rate of 13.4% annually. Finally, public housing does not provide services for tenants who, as they age, may require assistance with ADLs. As the low turnover rate suggests, many older tenants who move into public housing stay there until they are no longer able to live independently, creating a tremendous need for supportive services to help them age in place.

Promoting Communities for Older Adults

The future of planned retirement communities is uncertain because many of the original residents are aging in place. In addition, some older individuals who move to a planned community find that they miss interacting with children and younger adults, who typically live within traditional community neighborhoods.

Because naturally occurring retirement communities typically emerge within traditional residential environments, health and other supportive services are not usually available within or close to the immediate neighborhood. Residents, therefore, must be able to seek out and obtain these services on their own.

Enhancing SROs

Although SROs offer the most vulnerable persons in society a place to live, they provide little in the way of comfort, security, or support. Many buildings

Best Practice **Coming Home Program**

The Coming Home Program is a 6-year demonstration program created to meet the health, social, and housing needs of older adults, particularly those who are frail. It is a joint project of the Robert Wood Johnson Foundation and the National Cooperative Bank Development Corporation. Although the Coming Home Program endeavors to work with all economic groups, the majority of its effort goes toward creating "affordable" models for low- to moderate-income seniors, particularly in rural areas. The Coming Home Program combines grants, technical assistance, and debt financing to design and build systems of care that coordinate and integrate health, social, and personal care services with housing for older adults.

Grants are made available for feasibility assessment and for a portion of technical assistance. Generally, grants are made on a matching basis and provide sufficient capital to explore the economic viability of a proposed project, including development, operational, and financing alternatives. For example, a rural community that shows an initial need for senior housing and/or assisted living may work with Coming Home Program staff to develop a nonprofit sponsor for the feasibility study. The sponsor must be community based, such as a social service provider, a health system organization, or a community development agency. The community-based sponsor must contribute a cash match of approximately 20%, or usually $3,000, toward the cost of the study. If the feasibility study shows positive need and economic potential, the development process may begin. An interesting and positive feature of the Coming Home Program is that all project planning and development are facilitated through the community-based nonprofit organization whose board of directors represents the community served. Community citizens are given an integral advisory role during the development of the project. The Coming Home Program is operating in 20 states nationwide. By 1996, the program had 23 housing/supportive housing units in seven states. Many more projects are in the development stages.

For more information, contact National Cooperative Bank Development Corporation, 44 Montgomery Street, Suite 610, San Francisco, CA 94104, 414-834-6985.

are in deteriorating condition and poorly maintained. Many SROs in New York, San Francisco, and Los Angeles were built before or at the turn of the century (Ovrebo, Minkler, & Liljestrand, 1991). The rooms are sparse and small; most cannot easily accommodate wheelchairs. Kitchenettes often consist of a nonworking stove (Rollinson, 1990). Elevators frequently break down, leaving frail residents stranded in their rooms. Lack of adequate heating in the winter and extreme heat in the summer, holes in the wall, and rodents are problems reported by residents (Crystal & Beck, 1992; Rollinson, 1991a).

The internal environment of SROs may restrict social interaction, and the external environment contributes to social isolation as well. SROs are often located in dilapidated parts of the city. Fear for their personal safety greatly restricts older residents' movement during the day, and movement at night is nonexistent (Rollinson, 1991b). Rollinson reported that during the summer months, residents typically spent just over 15 hours in their rooms and more than 18 hours during the winter months, with most spending a typical day alone in their rooms.

Although SROs are fraught with serious problems, they provide housing to a group of older persons who are at risk of being homeless. The SRO as a housing option for low-income older persons, however, is diminishing. Since the 1970s, the number of SRO units has rapidly declined. An estimated 1,111,000 SRO units were eliminated from 1970 to 1980 (Hooper & Hamberg, 1986). The major forces behind the loss of SROs include downtown revitalization, gentrification, and lack of funding to rehabilitate deteriorating buildings (Ovrebo et al., 1991). This loss of housing represents a serious problem for older SRO residents, many of whom reported that they did not know what they would do if they had to move.

Supportive Living Environments

Supportive living environments are designed to help older adults who are self-sufficient and are capable of self-care to some extent but who need some assistance with ADLs. Generally, supportive environments provide older adults varying degrees of assistance and oversight.

ECHO Housing and Accessory Apartments

Elder Cottage Housing Opportunity (ECHO) housing is a unique housing option for older adults and their families. ECHO housing units (sometimes called "granny flats" or garden suites) are small, self-contained, movable housing units located next to the home of a family member. The units also can be made to fit into the space of an attached garage or connected directly to the main house. They have their own electrical system, temperature controls, and plumbing. Meters can be attached to the unit to keep utility costs separate from the main house. Configurations of the units vary; most have a living room, kitchen, bedroom, and bath. Once the units are no longer needed, they are removed. In some cases, where space is available, mobile homes may serve as ECHO housing (Hare, 1990).

To create an accessory apartment, families remodel an existing room, basement, or garage into a living area in which a frail older adult can live. As with ECHO housing, accessory apartments provide the same benefits of privacy and support, although the construction is more permanent.

Both ECHO housing and accessory apartments allow older adults to live with or near their families. They offer families a way to provide assistance to older family members yet allow privacy and independent living. Other benefits include lower housing costs, increased intergenerational interaction, and a possible delay of institutionalization.

ECHO housing is a relatively new concept in the United States. Early efforts to publicize the idea generated a great deal of interest, but that interest did not result in the development of ECHO housing to any great extent (Hare, 1991). In a nationwide study conducted by AARP (1992), 3% of the respondents (n = 1,505) indicated that they had purchased or rented a small, removable house on their relative's property. Another 18% said they would consider this alternative living arrangement.

Congregate Housing

Although public housing often is referred to as congregate housing, many congregate facilities are privately owned. Most congregate housing facilities have separate apartments for each resident plus common, shared areas for meals and recreation, including "congregate dining, social lounges, laundry facilities, recreation spaces, and a secure barrier free environment" (Heumann, 1990, p. 46; Monk & Kaye, 1991). These facilities provide services in a residential setting for persons who can no longer independently manage tasks of everyday living. The typical on-site staff includes a building manager, janitorial services, and social/activity organizer. Medical personnel are not usually on-site in a congregate facility.

Residents in congregate housing receive at least one major meal served congregately per day and have the option of receiving assistance with additional meals, housekeeping, personal care, transportation, and other support services if needed. Residents typically have some limitation that precludes independent living but that does not require continuous medical or nursing care nor full-time personal care.

Continuing Care Retirement Communities

Continuing care retirement communities (CCRCs) provide a full range of housing options for retired adults, from independent living through nursing home care. There are more than 700 CCRCs in the United States with more than 200,000 residents (Ernst & Young, 1989). The average CCRC has been in operation for fewer than 30 years; the CCRC industry experienced its most dramatic growth during the 1970s and 1980s (Ruchlin, Morris, & Morris, 1993). Religious groups and other nonprofit organizations are frequent sponsors of CCRCs. Although there are many variations, the typical CCRC averages about 200 independent living apartments, 40 assisted living beds, and 90 skilled nursing beds (Chellis & Grayson, 1990).

CCRCs offer incoming residents a contract that remains in effect for the balance of their lifetime. There are three basic types of CCRC contracts (American Association of Homes for the Aging, 1987). An *all-inclusive contract* includes shelter, residential services, and amenities as well as long-term nursing care for little or no substantial increase in monthly payments, except for normal operating costs and inflation. A *modified contract* also includes shelter, residential services, and amenities but offers only a specified amount of long-term nursing care for little or no substantial increase in monthly payments, except for normal operating costs and inflation adjustments. After using the specified amount of nursing care, residents pay either partial or full per diem rates for the care they require. A *fee-for-service contract* includes shelter, residential services, amenities, and emergency and infirmary nursing care. Access to long-term nursing care is guaranteed but at full per diem rates. A continuing care contract typically requires a lump-sum entrance fee, paid on moving into the community, and monthly payments thereafter. In 1988, the median entrance fee for CCRCs ranged from $32,800 for a studio apartment to $85,000 for units larger than two bedrooms; median monthly fees ranged from $695 for studios to $1,000 for larger units (Ernst & Young, 1989).

As one might expect from the high contract fees, CCRCs typically attract an affluent older population. The typical CCRC resident is a white, widowed, divorced, or never married female in her early 80s (American Association of Homes for the Aging, 1987). Residents also are more likely than the population at large to be childless (Sherwood, Ruchlin, & Sherwood, 1989). A comparison of 1,552 randomly selected CCRC residents and a randomly selected group of 1,552 elders living in a traditional community found CCRC residents more likely to be older, to be female, to have higher levels of income and educational attainment, and to have more limiting health problems and greater problems with the IADLs (e.g., shopping and cooking) than their community counterparts (Ruchlin et al., 1993).

Assisted Living

Assisted living is one of the most recent and fast-growing innovations in housing options for older adults. Assisted living is "any group residential program that is not licensed as a nursing home, that provides personal care to persons with need for assistance in the activities of daily living (ADLs), and that can respond to unscheduled needs for assistance that might arise" (Kane & Wilson, 1993, p. xi). These settings may include personal care boarding homes with additional services, residential care units owned by and adjacent to nursing homes, congregate housing settings that have added services, purpose-built assisted living programs, or the middle level of CCRCs. Ownership of these facilities may be either nonprofit or for-profit.

Most developments built specifically as assisted living communities are small, with few having more than 70 units (Evans, 1994). They most often offer private occupancy units with at least full bathrooms, kitchenettes with refrigerators and cooking capacity, and lockable doors; three meals a day in a group dining room; general housekeeping and maintenance services; personal care according to individual needs; on-site delivery or coordination of nursing, health, and social services; and supervision and oversight for persons with cognitive limitations. Facilities use fewer medical staff than non-medical staff, and the majority of facilities contract services from a variety of consultants, ranging from beauticians to physicians (Kane & Wilson, 1993).

Rents for assisted living vary from approximately $1,000 to $3,000 per person per month (Evans, 1994), with most facilities having base rates for various sizes of accommodation and a minimum service package and higher rates for added services. Most of the rates, even at the high end, are substantially less than nursing home care for private paying residents. Insurance companies are increasingly allowing holders of long-term care policies to use their benefits for assisted living if the services are cost-effective. Public payment for assisted living includes supplemental payments to the facility for housing for services for SSI clients; through reimbursement in Medicaid, Medicaid waiver, or state long-term care programs; or some combination of these sources.

One of the most common comments of administrators of assisted living programs nationwide is that their facilities tend to attract residents more disabled than those initially targeted (Kane & Wilson, 1993). They described their typical assisted living resident as having one or more of the following characteristics: female; over the age of 80; in need of help with ambulating; in need of medication reminders; forgetful; and in need of help with bathing or dressing. Most facilities admit and retain residents with a variety of disabling conditions and physical health care needs, but few residents typically need moderate or heavy care. The most frequent reasons residents leave a facility is that they need more care than can be provided for them.

Personal Care Boarding Homes

Board and care homes are "non-medical community-based living arrangements that provide shelter (room), board (food), and 24-hour supervision or protective oversight and personal care services to residents" (Hawes, Wild-fire, & Lux, 1993, p. 3). The names used to identify board and care homes, and the nature of the homes, vary considerably. Small homes may provide for as few as two residents, whereas some institutions may designate all or a large percentage of their beds for board and care residents. All states license board and care homes, although licensing requirements differ.

According to census reports, there are approximately 18,000 licensed board and care homes accommodating 360,000 residents in the United States (U.S. Bureau of the Census, 1994c). In addition, officials estimate that approximately 28,000 unlicensed homes exist (U.S. Senate Special Committee on Aging, 1990). Unlicensed homes include facilities excluded from mandatory licensure because of size or service criteria established by the state in which they operate as well as homes that meet a state's criteria for obtaining an operating license but avoid securing one.

We know little about the characteristics of board and care residents except that persons seeking this type of housing alternative are likely to need some supervision and personal care. Most residents are characterized as physically or cognitively frail and at risk for further health and functional declines (Hawes et al., 1993). About half the residents of board and care homes pay for their care with private resources (U.S. Senate Special Committee on Aging, 1990). Others rely on assistance from federal and state programs to pay at least part of the cost of living in a board and care home. For example, the monthly check of a SSI recipient may go toward the payment of the home's charges. Most states also provide some form of additional payment to supplement an older person's SSI payment. In some states, payment for board and care homes comes from Medicaid waiver program funds, block grants, or county funds.

Foster Care

Adult foster care "serves people who, because of physical, mental, or emotional limitations, are unable to continue independent functioning in the community and who need and desire the support and security of family living" (U.S. Department of Health, Education & Welfare, 1964, p. 2). Foster care includes support services, supervision, and personal care provided by a private host family or individual who takes a small number of older adults and encourages them to participate in the lives of the family and in the community (Sherman & Newman, 1988). Foster care homes are considered to be a social care model in contrast to the medical model of nursing homes. The average cost per month for a person to live in foster care is approximately $1,000.

Best Practice **Mary Sandoe House**

The Mary Sandoe House assisted living project in Boulder, Colorado, is an exemplary housing alternative that has been operational since 1988. Its multiple sponsors include City of Boulder Housing Authority, Boulder County Community Action Program, the Boulder Gray Panthers Service Project, Inc., and an interfaith housing group. Funding for the project was leveraged through the Community Development Block Grant program, Colorado Housing and Finance Authority low-interest loans, and local fund-raising. Juniper Partners, Inc., provides day-to-day oversight of management and conducts board development training and technical assistance.

A small project built in an existing neighborhood, the Mary Sandoe House accommodates 12 private bedrooms adjacent to shared living and dining areas. The average age of the residents is 86. Many have mobility limitations because of a stroke or arthritis, and some suffer from mild dementia. Support services include some bathing assistance, supervision of medications, personal laundry, social activities, and arrangements for special transit. Meals are served family style.

The underlying philosophy that influenced the design of the house and continues to influence its day-to-day management can be summed up in two words: *good neighbor.* Residents of Mary Sandoe House are regarded as part of the neighborhood. Neighbors are invited to outdoor barbecues, and neighbor children are encouraged to visit the residents. Typical residential activities, such as tending a garden, picking up the mail, and socializing on the patio, are part of the daily routine of the residents.

Another attractive and unique aspect of the Mary Sandoe House is that half the residents have low to moderate incomes. Rents vary from $900 to $1,650 per month. This price range is comparable with similar but much larger projects.

Often, group living projects in single-family neighborhoods meet with strong resistance. When they do, city planning committees are compelled to deny special use permits for these projects. Mary Sandoe House planners launched a successful proactive approach to allay fears that neighbors might have about building a small assisted living project in their neighborhood of single-family homes. In teams of two, planners visited neighbors close to the proposed project. They discussed the nature of the project and showed architectural sketches of the house. One of the 20 neighbors who were contacted spoke out against the project at a public meeting. This neighbor was not against the group living project but felt that the land should be retained as open space.

continued

Persons associated with Mary Sandoe House believe it has been successful, in part, because many sectors of the community, public and private,
were committed to the concept of a small residential program that could
blend in with the day-to-day activities of an existing neighborhood.

For more information, contact Juniper Partners, 1603 Fourth Street, Boulder, CO 80302, 303-443-7752.

For the most part, individuals who can benefit from foster care need
supervision and assistance but not continuous medical attention. Elders generally go into foster care because they do not have family who can take care
of them or because their family is unable or unwilling to provide daily care.
Sherman and Newman (1988) conducted an extensive study of three populations of foster care residents: residents with mental illness, residents with
mental retardation, and frail elders. The elder residents in foster care are
likely to have one of three histories: They may have been in foster care for
many years, they may have been residents of institutions (e.g., a psychiatric
hospital) for many years and only recently been placed in foster care, or they
may have been recently placed with a foster family from the community.
Many elders in foster care will remain with their family until their death.
Others will leave the family for a more specialized care center, such as a
nursing home, psychiatric hospital, or residence for persons with mental
retardation.

Long-Term Care Facilities

At the most dependent end of the housing continuum are long-term care
facilities, known more commonly as nursing homes. At any one time, approximately 5% of individuals 65 years of age and older reside in nursing
homes. The typical nursing home resident is female, white, not married, and
over the age of 75 (U.S. Bureau of the Census, 1990a). The patient requires
skilled, 24-hour care because of severe physical or cognitive limitations.
Given their unique role in the continuum of care and the broad range of
issues to consider, we will consider nursing homes separately in Chapter 19.

Challenges for Supportive Living Environments

Supportive living environments make it possible for many frail elders to
continue living in the community. A wide range of supportive living options,
including long-term care facilities, is needed to address the physical, psycho-

Exhibit 15.5 **Spectrum of Housing Options**

Housing Option	Little or No Assistance	Moderate Assistance	Cannot Perform Without Assistance
Single-Family Dwelling	▓		
Public Housing	▓		
NORC—Naturally Occurring Retirement Community	▓		
House Sharing	▓		
Home with Chore Services Nutrition Services Home Repair Home Equity Conversion Low-Income Energy Assistance	▓	▓	
Congregate Housing	▓	▓	
ECHO Housing Accessory Apartments		▓	
Home with Delivered Meals Homemaker Home Health Aide Telephone Reassurance Visiting Programs		▓	
Home with Adult Day Services		▓	
Assisted Living/Personal Care Boarding Homes		▓	
Foster Care		▓	▓
Long-Term Care Facilities		▓	▓
Continuing Care Retirement Communities		▓	▓

SOURCE: Adapted from American Association of Retired Persons (1985).

logical, and social needs of older adults. Exhibit 15.5 displays a summary of the different housing options discussed in this chapter and the level of assistance appropriate in each option. We now turn to the concerns that will need to be addressed in the future regarding supportive living arrangements for older adults.

Removing Barriers

Although ECHO housing promises many benefits, Hare (1990) identified several barriers facing elders and their families interested in ECHO housing. In some jurisdictions, zoning laws prohibit the addition of such a unit, and neighbors may complain of its use. In addition, few vendors for ECHO housing exist, limiting the purchasing opportunities for families who are looking for solutions for immediate housing problems.

Enhancing Services

Almost all the research shows cost savings with congregate housing compared with long-term care facilities. The major reasons for the lower costs are the limited availability of expensive on-site personal and nursing care and the greater independence of the residents (Heumann, 1990). Congregate housing, however, relies on community-provided services. Heumann points out that where such services are not readily available, staff at the congregate facility must carefully monitor residents and coordinate their care to avoid "undercaring."

Protecting Residents

The long-term financial stability of CCRCs is often a concern of bankers and other investors who are asked to support the development of new CCRCs. Floyd (1993) cites a *Consumer Reports* study that found between 5% and 10% of those communities applying for accreditation "unfit," mostly because of shaky finances. Specifically, CCRCs often have too many liabilities and too few reserves to cover their health care commitments. Unfortunately, some senior CCRC residents who believed that their housing and long-term care needs would be taken care of find out that moving to the next level of care may not be an option when they need it.

Few states have developed specific policies or regulations or have specific regulatory bodies for assisted living units. Kane and Wilson (1993) report that assisted living programs may often need one or more additional licenses beyond a basic residential care or board and care license. Common state-level regulatory concerns are avoiding quality problems; deciding how much to regulate; deciding how to pay for the services for low-income elders; and conceptualizing assisted living in relationship to overall state long-term care planning.

States and licensing agencies give a wide variety of titles to board and care homes and have different requirements for licenses (Hawes et al., 1993). Some states require a license for every residential setting that houses people who need personal care or supervision; most states require licensure only if the home actually provides such services or advertises that it provides care and supervision. Licensure requirements also may depend on the size of the facility and the number of persons receiving care.

The content of the licensure standards also varies from state to state (Hawes et al., 1993), although most licensure standards have requirements for fire safety, physical structure, sanitation, basic safety and services, the characteristics of the residents who can be admitted, and resident rights. Approximately one half the states have established minimum staffing levels; they are often so low (e.g., one staff member for 30 to 60 residents), however, that they may be meaningless if a large percentage of residents need personal assistance with ADLs. In addition, the staff members caring for persons in board and care homes often receive little or no formal training.

Enhancing Opportunities for Foster Care Residents

Socialization and social network interactions beyond the immediate household are often low among residents of foster homes (Sherman & Newman, 1988). Thus, although these individuals are physically residing within a neighborhood, their participation in community activities appears marginal. In addition, communities often oppose the development of foster homes, regardless of the age or other characteristics of the residents (Mangum, 1985). Residential communities that consist primarily of single-family homes are particularly unwelcoming of foster homes.

In closing, although older adults have a myriad of options regarding their living arrangements, problems in housing availability and affordability continue to exist. As boomers age, the tension between the issues of person-environment fit will become apparent for many more older adults, and a variety of housing options and programs will continue to be in demand.

 CASE STUDY

FINDING A NEW HOME

Ellen, an active 77-year-old widow, had resided in a triplex rental for 8 years. Ellen was happy with her living arrangement and said that she planned to "live here the rest of my life." An outgoing person, she became well acquainted with her neighbors and enjoyed the convenient location of her home. She spent many hours out-of-doors tending her roses and helping with other yard duties voluntarily. Because she had established herself as an excellent renter, the owner considered Ellen's fixed income of $1,000 per month and, in 8 years, had increased her rent by only $75, bringing it to $350 per month. She could cover her living expenses and enjoy recreational activities at a local senior center.

In 1994, the owner notified Ellen that he had turned over his property to his daughter and that she would raise the rent to $700 per month. Ellen reported that "the rent increase devastated" her and that for days she "cried at the drop of a hat" because she had no idea what she was going to do. Ellen did not want to depend on her two children who lived nearby. She wanted to be independent. If she found another rental, the same thing could happen to her again. Where would she find affordable rent now that this midsized community was growing rapidly and rentals were in great demand?

Ultimately, a friend advised her to contact the manager of a small mobile home park in a nearby community of 7,500. Ellen knew nothing about mobile homes and was skeptical but open-minded. She had heard that the manager was "very strict" about whom he accepted into the park. Initially, the manager told her that nothing was available. As the conversation progressed, Ellen won him over with her pleasing personality. He offered that she could look at one unit that was available. Ellen was more than impressed with the well-kept home that was for sale by an older couple.

Her next problem was financial. Her banker advised her to use a certificate of deposit of $35,000, her entire savings, for collateral. This would more than cover the full cost of the mobile home at $28,000 and generate enough interest to pay the interest of the loan. The lot fee was $175 per month and included water and trash rates. Ellen pays on the principal each month in an amount that varies depending on her monthly finances. Ellen has settled into her two-bedroom mobile home with an attached garage and "more storage space" than she has "ever had." Her children like her new home and visit often. Ellen's grandson says, "Grandma, you do not live in a mobile home, you live in a home." Ellen tells her friends, "I love it, I have never been happier in my life, please God don't do anything to my little house."

CASE STUDY QUESTIONS

1. Citing research, explain why Ellen's emotional reaction to having to move from her apartment home of many years could be expected.

2. What factors does Ellen have working in her favor in this situation? What circumstances could be working against her?

3. Ellen has advanced arthritis in her hips and knees. What bearing does this condition have on her future housing choices?

4. On the basis of the environmental fit model, what housing options would be appropriate for Ellen? Why?

5. Where might Ellen go to find out more about housing options in her community?

LEARNING ACTIVITIES

1. Investigate the housing opportunities available for older adults in your community. What types of services, if any, are offered? Do the residents reflect what you have learned about senior housing in this chapter?

2. Interview someone from the public housing authority. What does the person see as the primary issues facing housing for older adults? What policy changes have had to be implemented during the last decade?

3. Conduct a review of recent housing legislation (federal, state, and local) that deals with housing for older adults. What is the focus of legislation or policy? What are its strengths and weaknesses?

4. Interview residents that reside in public or residential housing facilities. What do they like about the facility? What are their primary concerns? What do they like about living in an age-specific environment? What don't they like about it? What do you perceive to be the advantages and disadvantages for residents living there? Would you encourage a family member to live in age-specific housing? Would you consider it as an alternative for yourself?

FOR MORE INFORMATION

National Resources

1. National Resource and Policy Center on Housing and Long-Term Care, Andrus Gerontology Center, University of Southern California, Los Angeles, CA 90089-0191, 213-740-1364 (e-mail: natresctr@usc.edu).

   The mission of the policy center is to make housing a more integral part of long-term care. The center conducts research, policy analysis, training, and technical assistance and disseminates results to aging and housing networks, consumers, practitioners, policymakers, and researchers. The center has best practice guidelines, fact sheets, and other resources about housing, along with a Web site (http://www.scf.usc.edu/hknapp).

2. National Council on the Aging, 409 3rd Street SW, Suite 200, Washington, DC 20024, 202-479-1200.

   The National Council on the Aging has resource materials on a wide variety of topics, including senior housing and supportive services available to older adults living in their own homes.

3. National Council of Senior Citizens, 1331 F Street NW, Washington, DC 20004, 202-347-8800.

   The council is an advocacy organization of older adults whose primary purpose is to work for legislation to benefit older adults. The National Council of Senior Citizens is one of the major sponsors of housing for older adults—its Housing Management Corporation manages buildings across the country.

4. Assisted Living Facilities Association of America, 10300 Eaton Place, Suite 400, Fairfax, VA 22031, 703-691-8100.

   The Assisted Living Facilities Association of America is a nonprofit membership organization whose mission is to enhance the quality of life in assisted living residences as well as to promote the interests of the assisted living industry. It offers a number of publications including *Assisted Living Today* magazine, *Staff and Training Guide,* and other publications of interest to consumers.

5. American Association of Homes and Services for the Aging, 901 E Street NW, Suite 500, Washington, DC 20004, 202-783-2242.

   This national association of nonprofit organizations represents 5,000 nonprofit nursing homes, continuing care retirement communities, assisted living residences, senior housing facilities, and community service organizations for older adults. This group also sponsors the Continuing Care Accreditation Commission that accredits continuing care retirement communities. Free information on long-term care and housing for older adults is available on its Web page (http://www.seniorsites.com/aahsa), along with links that explore different housing options.

Web Resources

1. Be sure to check out the home pages of two organizations we've already talked about—the American Association of Homes and Services for the Aging (mentioned above) and B'nai B'rith (http://bnaibrith.org).

2. Manitoba Senior Citizens' Handbook
   http://www.crm.mb.ca/crm/other/genmb/msch05.html

   Our friends up north have put together a great page that explains all the types of living accommodations available to older adults. Take a look at the different housing options available for older adults in Manitoba.

3. U.S. Department of Housing and Urban Development
   http://www.hud.gov

   This is the place to start to look for information about housing policy or programs. Visitors can search HUD's database and gain access to housing reports, program information, and a variety of housing data. The site also has consumer information about housing.

16

Case Management

Ruby, 86, suffers from Parkinson's disease. Widowed for 5 years, Ruby lives in a small house one block from the main street of the town in which she has lived for 25 years. Ruby is becoming quite frail and must always use a walker. She has wonderful neighbors who are helpful, a 76-year-old sister-in-law who lives 5 miles away, and two nieces who are caring and attentive but live out of state. To help her remain independent and to continue to live in her own home, Ruby's case manager recommended a variety of service options including meals on wheels, home health care, and the use of the senior bus for visits to the doctor when her neighbors are not available to take her.

Case management is central to the integrative delivery of services for older adults. Without it, many older adults such as Ruby become frustrated when seeking help from an often fragmented, complex, and costly service system. Case managers serve as navigators, guiding older persons in their pursuit of services that will foster their independence. The National Advisory Committee of Long-Term Care Case Management defines case management as "coordinating services that helps frail elders and others with functional impairments and their families identify and secure cost effectively administered services appropriate to the consumers' needs" (Connecticut Continuing Care, Inc., 1994, p. 5). This dual mission of planning and individualizing services to promote client independence while controlling costs makes the role of case management a cornerstone of community-based service provision for older adults (Rife, 1992).

Known by a variety of names (e.g., care management, case coordination, and service management), case management occurs in a diverse range of long-term care programs for older adults. Although programs differ in how they implement, access, and monitor their services, they do agree on the core

Exhibit 16.1 **Case Management Process**

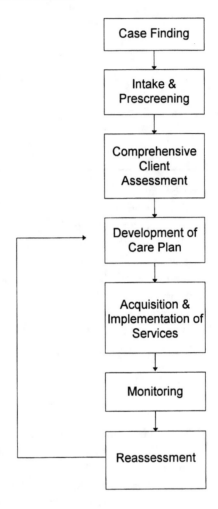

elements of case management (Austin, 1996; Quinn, 1993; Schraeder, Fraser, Bruno, & Dworak, 1990; Urv-Wong & McDowell, 1994).

The case management process begins with *case finding* (see Exhibit 16.1). The purpose of case finding is to locate individuals who might benefit from services. Case managers often rely on referrals from other professional service providers to help them in identifying viable clients. Gatekeepers, or individuals who by the nature of their day-to-day work come into routine contact with many people, can be trained to successfully identify isolated, older individuals with functional limitations and refer them to case management programs (Emlet & Hall, 1991). Once identified, case managers begin the *intake and prescreening* process by obtaining basic information about

Exhibit 16.2   **Case Management: Comprehensive Assessment**

When the case manager determines that a client is eligible for case management services, the case manager conducts a multidimensional assessment that profiles details of the client's needs and support systems. Although the specific assessment tools used vary across programs, the following questions are typical of some of the areas addressed during the assessment process:

■ What are the history and current nature of the client's illness?

■ What medications does the client take?

■ What is the client's perception of his or her health?

■ How is the client coping with his or her situation?

■ How good is the client's short- and long-term memory?

■ How well is the client able to dress, eat, bathe, walk, and toilet him- or herself?

■ Who, if anyone, helps support the client among family, friends, church, and neighbors?

■ What physical characteristics of the client's dwelling help or hinder the client's mobility?

■ What financial resources are available to the client to pay for services?

SOURCE: Quinn (1993).

the client (e.g., presenting problem, age, income, living arrangements, current level of both formal and informal service use, and type of disability). Case managers also evaluate potential clients according to program criteria (i.e., income and level of frailty) to determine eligibility for particular services.

After a client is accepted via the prescreening, the case manager continues the process by conducting a more *comprehensive client assessment*. Using a multidimensional assessment tool (see Exhibit 16.2), the case manager gathers in-depth information about the person's physical well-being and medical history, psychological and mental functioning, functional ability (i.e., ADLs and IADLs), social activities, formal and informal service use, economic and financial status, in-home safety, and family relationships (Krout, 1993a; Quinn, 1993). From the assessment, the *development of care plan* occurs. The care plan describes the type of problem the client has and the planned outcomes of the services. The case manager operationalizes the needs of the individual in conjunction with a client's values and preferences to set desired outcome goals and to design a care plan of informal and formal services to best meet the needs of the individual. The case manager then identifies, coordinates, and negotiates service provision and funding. How the case manager handles the *acquisition and implementation of services* depends on which case management model is being used (the different models will be described later in the chapter).

Monitoring is also a function of the case manager. After arranging for services, the case manager continues to periodically monitor client satisfaction with the plan, the appropriateness of the plan, and the implementation of the plan (e.g., quality, timeliness, and duration). Finally, after a specified time, the case manager conducts a *reassessment* of the client and care plan to detect changes in the client's needs and to evaluate the effectiveness of the care plan in meeting the client's goals. On the basis of this evaluation, the case manager revises or adjusts the care plan as appropriate to reflect the client's current needs, or the client may be discharged from the program.

In the remainder of this chapter, we focus our attention on the rapidly developing field of case management. We begin by examining the political influence and support for case management services. This section is followed by a profile of case management users and providers. We end the narrative portion of the chapter with a discussion of the challenges facing case management programs now and in the future.

Policy Background

Federal support has been critical to the development of case management programs serving older adults. With the passing of the Comprehensive Health Planning and Public Health Service Amendments of 1966, case management began to surface as a method for helping individuals overcome the federal bureaucracy and improve their access to federal health care programs (Spitz & Abramson, 1987). In the 1970s, when the government began to allocate significant dollars for the development of community-based services, many programs incorporated case management as a key service (Quinn, 1993). By 1979, 333 case management programs for older adults existed throughout the United States (Downing, 1985).

Federal initiatives supporting the development of community-based services continued through the 1980s but with greater focus on cost containment. With the Omnibus Budget Reconciliation Act of 1981, Congress attempted to reform the Medicaid program by allowing states to modify Medicaid regulations. States could apply for waivers that either limited the services offered from a statewide program, allowed reimbursements to provider organizations for services not ordinarily part of the state's Medicaid plan, or allowed modifications of the existing eligibility criteria for the client applying to the Medicaid program. This was a significant policy change because public programs could now include a range of both health and personal care services and case management services through one funding source (Quinn, 1993). Currently, more than 40 states have federal waiver programs

---

Best Practice **Philadelphia Corporation for Aging**

The Philadelphia Corporation for Aging is leading the way in the development of clinical protocols for community-based long-term care. This private nonprofit area agency on aging for Philadelphia, Pennsylvania, was awarded a grant from the Administration on Aging to produce and disseminate a series of 12 clinical protocols for care management in community-based long-term care. Since 1989, a team of professionals including care managers, administrators, and clinical experts has been working to develop protocols on the common conditions that can threaten a client's ability to continue living in the community. These conditions are incontinence, falls, risk of abusive behavior by a caregiver, depression and suicide, noncompliance/symptom self-care behavior, alcoholism, financial management, dementia, limited physical mobility, chronic pain management, and families with dysfunctional dynamics. The project tests each protocol before it is finalized to incorporate modifications and refinements.

Clinical protocols have been operational in the health care system for some time. The purpose of this project is to implement minimum standards in care management that will help address complex client problems. The protocols are concrete procedures that can be taken at each step of the care management process. They show how to identify the clients' problems, how to act on the problem, and how to monitor it. For example, the protocol manual for incontinence includes definitions, prevalence, treatments, providers, a decision tree, a protocol chart, and case discussions. Protocol training sessions for participants teach the best practices in the field to improve the quality of life for their clients. Data collected on the project show that the protocols have broad applicability. At least one protocol was in use for 95% of the clients of the agency.

For more information, contact the Philadelphia Corporation for Aging, 642 N. Broad Street, Philadelphia, PA 19130-3409, 215-765-9000.

---

that allow reimbursement for case management as part of their specialized home and community-based services (Raiff & Shore, 1993).

The Older Americans Act (OAA) began supporting case management demonstration and research projects with the act's 1978 revisions. The 1985 reauthorization of the OAA identified case management as a basic service. This legislation authorized area agencies on aging to "support services designed to avoid institutionalization including case management" (§ 321 [5]). The reauthorization of the OAA in 1992 once again directed funding under Title III, Part B for case management services, and case management was identified as an important component of in-home services for frail older adults under Part D.

Users and Programs

Public and private case management services have proliferated during the past decade in response to demographic changes, increased concern about the cost of services, and the complexity of the health care and service systems. In this section, we describe the general characteristics of individuals using case management and the persons and programs providing case management services. In addition, we briefly present evaluation outcomes from several long-term care demonstration programs built around the provision of case management.

Characteristics of Case Management Clients

It is difficult to profile the typical case management client because most authors describe the consumers of case management in descriptive (e.g., frail or nursing home eligible) rather than in empirical terms. Typically, publicly funded programs require a predetermined level of client frailty to qualify for case management services (Quinn, 1993). Private case management services often are available to any individual who has the resources to pay for the service. The following examples show the similarity and diversity of clients found among and within case management programs.

Like Ruby, whom we met at the beginning of the chapter, many case management clients are white, older, female, and widowed. A national study of 553 rural, primarily community-based case management providers found that most clients were women, over 75 years of age, and widowed (Krout, 1993a). Most of the clients lived alone and had yearly incomes below $15,000. Approximately one half of the individuals receiving services were Medicaid eligible. The agencies retained the older adults as case management clients for an average of 32 months. The most frequently noted reasons for termination of services were the client's recovery, death, institutionalization, relocation, and need for a higher level of care.

The 864 clients referred to hospital-based case management programs located primarily in urban areas of New Mexico and Arizona ranged in age from 60 to 106, with an average age of 78.7 years (Warrick, Netting, Christianson, & Williams, 1992). Two thirds of all clients were female; the greatest proportion of clients were white (80%), followed by Hispanics (13%). They reported having an average of 11 years of formal education and a yearly income of approximately $9,600. Overall, 41% of the clients said that they had experienced a major health deterioration within the previous 6 months of receiving case management services, and 13% had major surgery. Clients enrolled in the program immediately following hospitalization presented case management needs different from those of individuals referred from other community service programs. Many hospital-referred clients needed

---

For Your Files **National Advisory Committee on Long-Term Care Case Management**

The National Advisory Committee on Long-Term Care Case Management, consisting of a group of case management experts from academia, provider organizations, and state and federal government, developed case management practice guidelines for long-term care (Geron & Chassler, 1994, 1995). The committee formulated 104 guidelines in nine areas of case management: (a) consumer rights, preferences, and values; (b) comprehensive assessment; (c) care plan; (d) implementation; (e) monitoring; (f) reassessment; (g) discharge and termination; (h) quality of case management and provider services; and (i) efficient use of resources. The guidelines outline the normative bounds of long-term care case management practice and summarize what is known about the effectiveness of case management and what research is needed. The intent of these guidelines is to help case management agencies, programs, and practices, whether privately or publicly funded, in understanding the clinical, legal, and theoretical parameters of long-term care case management.

For more information, contact the National Case Management Partnership, Connecticut Community Care, Inc., 43 Enterprise Drive, P.O. Box 2360, Bristol, CT 06011-2360, 800-231-8524.

---

intensive, immediate assistance as they exited the hospital. They did not need long-term intensive case management services as required by community-referred clients, who, in comparison, were older, less likely to have informal caregivers, and more likely to be functionally dependent. Approximately 36% of all clients continued in case management for at least 1 year. Clients terminated from the program because of death, nursing home admission, self-sufficiency, referral to another case management agency, or relocation outside the hospital service area.

The general profile of private case management clients resembles that of individuals served by publicly funded programs. Results of a national survey of 117 private case management firms suggest that the typical client is late 70s or early 80s in age, female, widowed, and living alone (Second, 1987). Most clients had an annual income of less than $35,000. For most agencies, less than 25% of their clients were eligible for Medicaid.

Case Management Programs

Program staff composition, qualifications, and numbers vary, depending on the size and mission of the organization providing case management services.

Typically, case management programs set minimum qualifications for their case managers, usually expressed in varying combinations of academic and work experience in human services (e.g., gerontology, nursing, and social work). Besides the primary case managers, some organizations employ case manager assistants to work with clients, families, service providers, and other internal agency staff to help the case manager in the day-to-day management of the client caseload (Quinn, 1993; Schraeder et al., 1990). There also may be a case manager supervisor who maintains a supportive and consultative environment for the case managers by helping them with clinical and stress management issues (Applebaum & Wilson, 1988). The supervisor typically is responsible for managing program staff and supervising the case managers, negotiating service provider contracts, maintaining and analyzing data for program evaluation, and implementing quality assurance protocol (Schraeder et al., 1990).

Agencies and organizations use various approaches to carrying out case management, ranging from simple referral services to the actual delivery of comprehensive services. Each model varies both organizationally and operationally. The main differences between models are the level of authority directly controlling service use, the types and systems of service provision, and the method of payment. No evaluation data exist demonstrating that any one approach to case management is better than another (GAO, 1993).

In the *broker model,* case managers act as brokers for clients and service providers by linking the two through a referral system (Howe, 1994; Quinn, 1993). The purpose of broker case management is to match the target population with appropriate services based on predefined agreements and standards of practice. The broker model supplies individuals with objective information from which to make decisions, a care plan with options and recommendations to help guide them, and a neutral party to help with the process of securing services. They have no service dollars to spend on the clients' behalf; thus, they cannot guarantee their clients that services are delivered as prescribed. This model works particularly in "service-rich" communities in which the client has many service options and the case manager has no direct conflict of interest with the various providers. Case management provided under this model is usually a freestanding service provided by both public and private organizations (Milne, 1994).

Schraeder and colleagues (1990) describe four variations of the broker model. *Simple broker models* of case management inform and arrange needed services. Case managers under this model do not authorize or purchase services, nor are they directly responsible for the delivery of services. In the *combined broker model,* the organization providing case management furnishes some services for the client and coordinates the remainder with external agencies. The *complex broker model* authorizes types and levels of

---

Best Practice **Pennsylvania Care Management Institute**

Pennsylvania Care Management Institute is a private, nonprofit organization dedicated to providing knowledge and developing skills to enhance the professional growth of care management staff and other professionals in community-based long-term care. The institute was founded in 1987 from a recognized need among care management providers to increase skills through education, professional development, and consultation. The organization has recognized that it must support the role of care managers to ensure quality.

Pennsylvania Care Management Institute develops a curriculum and provides training combining up-to-date information and current theory to help participants improve their job performance and satisfaction. The curriculum covers topics ranging from the aging process, to record keeping, to ethical issues in long-term care. Also, the institute taps nationally recognized authorities in the field for consultation when agencies are interested in developing or revamping a care management program.

Care managers who want to improve their professional status may become certified through the institute's Care Management Accreditation Programs. Two levels of certification are offered—Certified Care Manager and Advanced Care Manager. The certification is verification that the care manager has completed a comprehensive series of training courses and has attained a level of competency in the practice of care management. Pennsylvania Care Management Institute's leadership in the field of care management certification is evidenced by its membership representing organizations throughout the Commonwealth of Pennsylvania. Others are beginning to enter the certification field, including Connecticut Community Care, Inc., the National Association of Professional Geriatric Care Managers, and Lynn University in Florida.

For more information, contact Pennsylvania Care Management Institute, 935 S. Trooper Road, Norristown, PA 19403, 610-650-0496.

---

services provided with certain financial controls or capped expenditures. The *consolidated broker model* consists of a single or merged provider system delivering a full range of services through directed provisions or contracts. This case management model exists within a prepaid, capitated funding structure housed under one administrative umbrella.

Under the *service management model,* used by many of the Medicaid waiver programs, case managers have funds available for services. The case management agency contracts with area providers to deliver the services authorized in each client's care plan. Most states have policies that limit the total cost of services that can be authorized by case managers. "Cost caps" usually are 60% to 80% of a state's comparable Medicaid nursing home rate (Quinn, 1993). Under this model, the case manager is fiscally accountable, and the case manager's authority to purchase services is constrained by the range of services offered and the supply of those services in the local delivery system (Austin, 1996).

Based on prospective financing, whereby programs receive a specific dollar amount for each client they serve, regardless if it costs more or less to deliver the care that is needed, the *managed care model* operates much like a health maintenance organization (GAO, 1993; Quinn, 1993). Clients pay a predetermined fee, and case managers are responsible for providing all needed services to clients. The case managers have control over a pool of funds to purchase services for clients. Providers are prepaid, placing the liability on the case managers for excess costs. Often, the managed care agency will control cost by providing services directly or by selectively contracting with outside providers to offer services to clients at a discounted price.

The *medical group model* provides a direct link between primary care physicians, nurse or social work case managers, and older patients (Shelton, Schraeder, Britt, & Kirby, 1994; White, Gundrum, Shearer, & Simmons, 1994). This model emphasizes a collaborative team approach under the leadership of the primary care physician. It stresses patient targeting, comprehensive multidisciplinary office-based and in-home assessment, individualized care planning, arrangement and coordination of needed services, continuing case management, follow-up, monitoring, and patient/caregiver education. The case manager helps facilitate the person's medical care by addressing the psychosocial and environmental influences affecting care. The use of case management in this setting complements and enhances the medical group's practice by providing a direct link between clients/caregivers in their homes and primary care physicians (Schraeder et al., 1990).

Under the auspices of the *acute care hospital-based model,* there is a linking of previously disconnected disciplines and departments within the hospital (e.g., finance, patient care delivery, and administration). This model organizes patient care from a team approach, which in turn results in better quality of care for the patient (Cohen & Cesta, 1994). Most hospitals view case management as a cost-effective means of shortening the patient's length of hospital stay while reducing the use of unnecessary tests, treatments, procedures, and other hospital resources (Cohen, 1991; DelTogno-Armanasco, Olives, & Harter, 1989; Sinnen & Schifalacqua, 1991).

Episodic care case management occurs only when called for by providers in any of the other models of case management (Howe, 1994). The key feature of this model is that it can be only reactionary. It occurs in reaction to the admission, consultation, or phone call. The objective of this approach is to provide, during periods of stress, specialized diagnostic services and intervention services that are beyond the capabilities of the client and the primary care provider. The suppliers of episodic case management services include hospitals, specialized treatment centers, and health care specialists (e.g., physical therapist).

Evaluation of Case Management Programs

Does case management prevent or delay institutionalization? Is it cost-effective? To answer these questions, during the past 25 years, the federal government and several private foundations have funded 18 community-based long-term care demonstration projects that included case management services (Austin, 1996). The fundamental hypothesis tested by these projects is whether community care can be a cost-effective substitute for institutional care. Some of the evaluations indicate that the use of home and community-based services is not cost-effective when compared with nursing home costs. The findings also suggest, however, that the use of case management is an effective and successful way to control the total cost of home and community-based care programs.

Probably the most notable demonstration project was the National Long-Term Care Channeling Project, a federally funded program started in 1980 that examined the effects of case-managed community-based long-term care services at 10 sites across the country. Specific benefits for those participating in the channeling project included increasing their use of home care, reducing their unmet health care needs, increasing their confidence in receipt of care and satisfaction with arrangements for it, and increasing their satisfaction with life while not resulting in large reductions in informal caregiving (Kemper, 1988). Contrary to its original intent, however, the project increased costs of care. The evaluators suggested that one reason for increased costs was that although the population served was extremely frail, they were not at high risk for nursing home placement. Thus, the costs of the additional home care were not offset by reductions in nursing home placements.

In 1985, the Social/Health Maintenance Organization Demonstration Project began at four sites across the country (Abrahams, Nonnenkamp, Dunn, Mehta, & Woodard, 1988) and continues to be evaluated. Each federally funded site has a case management unit responsible for allocation of long-term care services. Individuals enrolled in the organizations pay premiums to receive services. The project sites consolidate services and providers to provide a full range of medical, personal care, and social services. They pool funding resources (e.g., Medicare, Medicaid, private insurance premiums, and client out-of-pocket fees) to provide members acute health care plus expanded long-term care services. The case manager must administer service dollars judiciously because payments for services are capitated and prospective (Quinn, 1993). With the introduction of "provider risk" in the case management process, the project provider organizations can remain financially sound only if they keep their costs below the negotiated capitation rate.

Support from private organizations stimulated hospitals' interest in the use of case management services. The Robert Wood Johnson Foundation provided 4-year demonstration grants to 24 hospitals throughout the country under its 1983 program for Hospital Initiatives in Long-Term Care (MacAdam et al., 1989). The purpose of the program was to encourage hospitals to develop new programs to better meet the needs of older persons. The participating public and not-for-profit hospitals set up unique projects. Each program initiated organizational changes; administrative improvements; educational activities for clinicians, staff, and consumers; case management programs; and community-oriented long-term care services. Case management was the only service that the foundation required all grantees to implement. Although most of the hospitals viewed case management as a valuable, relatively low-cost addition to the widening range of services they provided older adults, on completion of the demonstration period, most were unable to document changes in outcomes because of the provision of case management. Twenty-two hospitals reported, however, that they planned to continue some level of case management activities, one hospital ended the service, and one hospital was unable to report the future course of the service.

The Flinn Foundation sponsored the Hospital-Based Coordinated Care demonstration project at six sites in Arizona and New Mexico from 1986 to 1989 (Christianson et al., 1991; Warrick et al., 1992). The purpose of this project was to encourage private, not-for-profit hospitals to provide case management services to older adults at risk of rehospitalization after discharge. The clients and the community network of long-term care service providers had a positive view of the case management program. It delivered quality services to older individuals who met conventional eligibility criteria related to need. In contrast, the case management programs encountered several obstacles when trying to integrate into their own hospitals. For example, top administrators often lacked a strategy for blending long-term care with acute care service delivery in their organizations. Internal conflicts with hospital social workers, discharge planners, and home health agency staff about "ownership" of the patients in the hospital emerged during the implementation period and persisted throughout the project. In addition, most physicians had limited contact with the program case managers. They were not frequent users of, nor effective advocates for, the program. After the grant funding ended, most hospital administrators chose not to continue the program primarily because of the inability of case management to pay for itself (Christianson et al., 1991).

The Program of All-Inclusive Care developed through a combination of private and public funding. The 12-site demonstration project seeks to replicate On Lok, an innovative community-based model of capitated acute and chronic care for nursing home-eligible seniors in San Francisco's Chinatown. The On Lok program emphasizes the use of day health care and a reliance on an extensive multidisciplinary team to manage and deliver services for frail, older participants (Ansak, 1990). The program sites receive support from the Health Care Finance Administration, which provides waivers that allow capitated contracts using Medicare and Medicaid funds, and private foundations and sponsoring organizations largely support the initial costs of the demonstrations (i.e., site support, staff development, and service expansion). Although the program is still in the early stages of development, its advocates have learned several critical lessons from the start-up experiences of the first eight replication sites (Kane, Illston, & Miller, 1992). First is the necessity for sites to obtain sufficient start-up funds. Without such funds, the financial viability of the program is a constant source of concern. The slower than expected growth in the number of persons participating in the program at several of the replication sites also affects the financial viability of the projects. Another issue is the importance of building and maintaining staff with the skills and abilities to work in a multidisciplinary setting. Finally, case managers must develop the right patient mix in both acuity and dementia to accommodate the needs of all clients in a capitated system.

Challenges for Case Management Programs

Case management provides the entry into the community-based long-term care system. It plays a significant role in the coordination of services and resources for many older adults. We end this chapter by addressing several current and future challenges facing case management programs.

Providing Case Management Services

Considerable debate has emerged about where in the structure of services the case management role should reside, whether agencies that provide home care services should be allowed also to be case managers, and how case managers should interact with other agencies and individuals who are authorized to bill the program for service (Kane & Frytak, 1994). To address these issues, two criteria need to be considered: the client's well-being and the interest of the organization paying for services. As Kane and Frytak point out, the care provided should meet unmet needs and result in improved or maintained physical, social, and emotional functioning of the individual. Service should be provided in a courteous and respective manner and should be perceived as satisfactory. From a payer's perspective, the program should make efficient and effective expenditures. Kane and Frytak report that proponents of case managers in the provider role say that using independently employed case managers to authorize and monitor service is inefficient and redundant and does not lead to allocation in the patient's best interest, whereas proponents of nonprovider case management argue that publicly funded long-term care programs are efficient and effective only to the extent that they are under the authority of case managers who are not providers of care. Given these opposing positions, policymakers and researchers must explore more specifically what case management means operationally to home care agencies, nonprovider case management agencies, and state programs that fund both types of programs.

Ensuring the Effectiveness of Case Management Programs

How effective programs are in delivering case management services rests with several critical elements. First, case managers must receive proper training. Interviews with 95 case managers from six states in the GAO study (1993) identified the following as key practices essential for effective case management: the ability and skills to comprehensively assess client needs, time to have adequate contact with clients, knowledge of resources available in the community, and continual training to maintain and improve skills. Second, large caseloads limit the ability of case managers to give clients sufficient attention to ensure that clients' needs are met and that services are provided adequately. Other effects of large caseload sizes include limited time available to spend with each client and increased risk of burnout for case managers. Third, some barriers to effective case management outcomes are outside the control of local case management agencies. These include a lack of financial resources, inadequate availability of services in the local area, and extensive administrative requirements imposed by state administering agencies. In rural areas, the vast geographical areas for which many rural case managers are responsible often limit their ability to see their more "low-risk" clients regularly (Urv-Wong & McDowell, 1994).

Providing Quality Case Management Services

Although most publicly funded case management programs have some requirements concerning qualification, training, and timely completion of activities (Justice, 1993), there are no uniform state or federal guidelines for the practice of case management. As case management services continue to grow and mature, Geron and Chassler (1995) call for guidelines that reflect changing practice and legislative realities; that promote flexibility in practice according to consumer values, preferences, and needs; that foster the efficient use of resources; and that ensure the equitable provision of quality services to those who are in need.

Diversifying Caseloads

Case managers can increasingly expect to manage a more diverse caseload; it is expected that persons of color will constitute 40% of the service delivery system by the year 2000. To successfully work with minority populations, it is vital for case managers to develop cultural competencies. This will require greater understanding, sensitivity, respect, and appreciation of the cultural norms (i.e., history, lifestyles, experiences, and beliefs) of older clients and their families (Raiff & Shore, 1993).

Addressing Ethical Issues Facing Case Managers

Sometimes, case managers find their personal and professional ethics in conflict (cf. Kane & Caplan, 1993). For example, many case managers have control over the services used by their clients by virtue of the funding for the services and the contracts or agreements the case management agency has with other organizations to provide services. This controversial issue questions the control by case managers of the use of particular services by their older clients. Case management firms that also provide direct services in addition to case management services may restrict client access to a greater variety or less costly selection of services.

The increasing medicalization of aging also jeopardizes the capacity of case managers to provide the social services critical to meeting the needs of older persons and their family caregivers (Binney, Estes, & Ingman, 1990). The problem stems from public policy decisions that often define long-term care as need for medical services. This either makes the need for medical services an absolute condition for access to "free" social services or makes the medical services "free" and charges for social services. Consequently, case managers sometimes provide unnecessary medical services to make individuals eligible for social services (Shapiro, 1995).

Promoting Case Management in the Future

Delegates of the 1995 White House Conference on Aging promoted case management as part of several resolutions made for policy recommendations. For example, case management was (a) identified as part of an integrated, affordable system that provides a seamless continuum of quality services; (b) included as a means of providing supportive individual and cost-effective service arrangements; and (c) viewed as a way to promote the independence of older persons in their homes.

Case management services will continue to evolve along with the health care system in this country and will undoubtedly become even more important as the number of Medicare and Medicaid recipients enrolled in managed care programs increases. Thus, it is critical to continue to evaluate the effectiveness and efficiency of both public and private case management services.

CASE STUDY

WHEN INFORMATION AND REFERRAL ARE NOT ENOUGH

Five years ago, Helen, 83, was diagnosed with a benign brain tumor that is causing partial memory loss. The tumor also may be the cause of several other physical symptoms such as excessive tearing in one eye, constant postnasal drip, imbalance, and difficulty swallowing. Because Helen no longer drives or arranges appointments and is unable to keep house or cook, Ross, her husband of 55 years, has taken over most of the household duties. Helen taught high school English for many years and was an avid reader. She continues to read with encouragement, but she loses her concentration quickly. Her math skills are completely intact, and she is an avid cribbage player. Helen's social skills are appropriate but repetitive. She offers visitors coffee and sweets often during the visit and forgets that they previously discussed subjects. She has a keen memory for some aspects of her past and has completely lost her memory of other past events. Within a year of diagnosis, she lost the memory that her parents were killed in an automobile accident when she was 19 years old.

Ross is a retired electrical engineer. An organized person, he keeps lists and has an established routine for everything he does. These habits carry over into his approach to caregiving. He reads constantly; writes letters to the editor and to his elected representatives; and keeps abreast of local, state, and national events. He is interested in the status of the educational system and the future of children. Ross has suffered from periods of depression throughout his life. He sought professional counseling several times, once within the last year after becoming depressed about Helen's memory loss and overwhelmed with the caregiving responsibilities. Meal preparation was especially worrisome to Ross. He was placed on an antidepressant. Ross had serious physical and psychological reactions to the drug. As a result, their two daughters, who live 100 miles away, encouraged and helped their parents to move into an alternative care facility. They stayed at the facility for 2 months. After Ross stabilized, he arranged to return home.

Home is a small, modest house near a midsize university. Although hardly considered wealthy, Ross and Helen receive retirement pensions from their engineering and teaching professions and Social Security totaling $2,225 per month. Ross speaks of investment savings as well. They have excellent health insurance coverage. In short, they can purchase most items that they want, but they want little.

Once, they were moderately involved in the community. Ross volunteered for a congregate meal program and was an advisory board member for several human service agencies. Because of Helen's condition, however, they have withdrawn from all their social activities. They continue to go for daily drives in the country when the weather is pleasant. They no longer go out to eat. Recently, Helen was hospitalized for a blood clot in her leg. This has added to Ross's worries, and a friend who visits the couple weekly fears that Ross is headed for another bout of depression that could destabilize the couple's situation.

CASE STUDY QUESTIONS

1. Case finding, that is, locating individuals who might benefit from case management services, is the first step of the case management process. Who might be possible referral sources for this case? What elements make this case an appropriate referral?

2. What information provided in this case study would be the most critical for a case manager to consider in the prescreening process? Do you believe that Helen and/or Ross are in danger of institutionalization? Why or why not?

3. The comprehensive assessment is a detailed step in case management. The following are only a few of the many questions to consider.

   Who is the client in this case scenario?

   What is the central problem?

   What additional information would you want to know about Helen and Ross?

   What outcomes would you as a case manager like to see achieved for Helen and Ross?

   What strengths and/or resources do they already have in place?

4. If you were to develop a plan of community services for Helen and Ross, what would you include and why?

5. Considering the outcome(s) and the community resources you have determined for Helen and Ross, what would be considerations in monitoring the progress of this case?

LEARNING ACTIVITIES

1. Interview an area agency on aging director or staff member who works closely with case management. What is perceived to be the benefits of and issues related to case management? Does the staff member want to see amendments to the Older Americans Act to address concerns? What type of direction does the agency receive from the Administration on Aging and the state office on aging?

2. Interview the director of a case management program or a case manager. What are the requirements (education and experience) to be a case manager? What are the responsibilities of a case manager? What are primary concerns with the program? What does the individual believe are the benefits of case management (to older adults, caregivers, service providers, and the community)?

3. Interview a caregiver or client receiving case management. How has this service affected the lives of the caregiver and client? How would they manage without it? What changes would they like to see in the program?

 FOR MORE INFORMATION

National Resources

1. National Long-Term Care Resource Center, University of Minnesota, Institute for Health Services Research, School of Public Health, 420 Delaware Street SE, Minneapolis, MN 55455, 612-624-5171.

   The resource center has issued reports on case management in long-term care, including *Models for Case Management in Long Term Care: Interactions of Case Managers and Home Care Providers.* Contact the center for a list of publications about case management.

2. National Association of Professional Geriatric Care Managers, 1604 North Country Club Road, Tucson, AZ 85716, 520-881-8008.

   The National Association of Professional Geriatric Care Managers is an organization of practitioners whose goal is the advancement of dignified care for older adults. Association members assist older adults and their families in coping with the challenges of aging. The association publishes a national referral directory as well as the *Geriatric Care Management Journal,* which is published four times a year.

3. Aging Network Services, 4400 East-West Highway, Suite 907, Bethesda, MD 20814, 301-657-4329.

   Aging Network Services is a nationwide, for-profit organization of private practice geriatric social workers who serve as care managers for older adults by providing a comprehensive assessment of older adults in their own homes and assist in arranging the delivery of home care services.

Web Resources

Not much has emerged via the Web on case management except for a few private case management agencies that have a home page. Take a look at how this growing field is advertising its services (we do not endorse these programs; we list them only as a source of information).

1. Florida Health Consultants, http://www.flahealth.com
2. Elder Care Solutions, http://www.caring.com/elderhome.htm
3. Aegis Care Management Network, http://www.aegiscare.com

 **17**

Home Care Services

Margaret, 72 years old, has had multiple sclerosis for 20 years. For approximately 15 of those years, she and her husband, Wilbert, have lived a relatively normal life. The disease, however, has progressed to the point that Margaret needs assistance with most of her activities of daily living. Wilbert has been a model caregiver but the last 5 years have taken their toll on him. Wilbert never thought that he could afford regular home health care for Margaret. He was relieved to learn that she qualified for home health care under Medicare because she is totally confined at home. The home health agency schedules aides early in the morning. This allows Wilbert to attend his weekly Lions Club breakfast meeting. Wilbert would never complain about his caregiving responsibilities, but he does admit that he really enjoys the weekly breakfast outing.

Home care is a continuum of comprehensive care, providing individuals services that allow for maximum health, comfort, function, and independence in a home setting (Harper, 1991). Older adults such as Wilbert and Margaret choose to use home care services for several reasons, including the hope of avoiding institutionalization, familiarity of the home environment and sense of independence associated with this familiarity, lower perceived costs, and the continuity of family life and care (Salamon & Rosenthal, 1990).

In the United States, there are three primary types of home care: skilled home health care, nonmedical home care, and hospice care. Individuals receive home health care services in their homes to promote, maintain, or restore health or reduce the effects of illness and disability (Harris, 1988). Skilled home health care represents the largest segment of public expenditure for home care. Nonmedical home care services are care services of a nontechnical nature that emphasize the daily needs of individual users. The services include home aides, homemaker services, respite care, and home-delivered meals. The intent of hospice care is to provide supportive and palliative care for persons who are terminally ill and their families but not to treat the underlying conditions.

Research on home care often combines skilled and nonskilled services without specifying which services are being analyzed. This makes it difficult to profile the users and providers of these services. Because specific chapters in this book are devoted to services that fall under the rubric of nonmedical home care (e.g., case management, nutrition services, and respite care), our primary focus in this chapter is on home health services and related nonmedical services (i.e., home health aide and homemaker services) that provide personal assistance to older persons confined to their homes. The latter part of the chapter focuses on hospice care.

Policy Background

The first home care agencies were established in the 1880s to serve individuals who otherwise would not have medical care (Arneson, 1994). From this time until the mid-1960s, the industry grew slowly. With the passage of Medicare and Medicaid in 1965, the use of formal home care services increased dramatically.

To be eligible for home health coverage under Medicare, a person must meet five qualifying criteria (Rosenzwieg, 1995). First, a physician must certify the need for services, and, second, the individual must remain under the care of a physician. Third, the person must be homebound, meaning that the individual is unable to leave the home because of illness or injury without the assistance of a person or device and without a considerable and taxing effort. Fourth, the individual must need part-time or intermittent skilled nursing care (defined as up to and including 28 hours of skilled nursing and home health aide services combined provided on a less than daily basis[1]) or physical therapy or speech therapy. If the older adult meets these conditions, he or she may also receive occupational therapy, medical social services, and home health aide services. Fifth, Medicare must certify the home health agency providing services.

If a person meets all five of the above qualifying criteria, Medicare will pay for the types and amounts of home health services covered, if the services are "medically reasonable and necessary." Services are covered in full with no deductible or co-payment from the beneficiary. The passage of the 1980 Omnibus Budget Reconciliation Act (OBRA) greatly expanded Medicare's home care benefit. Specifically, it removed the 100-visit limit, and an acute care hospitalization was no longer necessary to receive home care services. Because one must need skilled nursing or therapeutic care to obtain home care services from Medicare, typical coverage averages 2 to 3 months. Thus, services normally do not address chronic needs for home care.

The introduction of Medicare's prospective payment in 1983 also has contributed to the growth of the home care industry, particularly with respect to home health care services. The cost containment strategy has promoted earlier hospital discharges, thereby sending patients home "quicker and sicker" with initiation and maintenance of treatments formerly performed only within the hospital now provided in the home. As a result, the acuity of illness, types of therapeutic care administered, and the amount of direct care to persons in their homes have increased dramatically. The home health care benefit, however, still represents a relatively small proportion of Medicare expenditures. In 1995, Medicare spent about 8% of its budget for home health care services (National Association for Home Care, 1995).

States may also provide home care services under three provisions of the federal Medicaid statute: (a) state plan home health services, (b) state plan optional services, and (c) waiver programs (Rosenzwieg, 1995). Federal law sets forth minimum mandated benefits and allows states the option of providing other services. States must provide the following home health services for all individuals eligible for Medicaid and entitled to nursing facility placement: part-time or intermittent nursing, home health aide, and medical equipment and supplies. Although all states require the provision of these particular home health services, federal law does not set the amount of service provided. The optional home care services that states may provide to individuals include personal care services, home and community-based care for functionally disabled elders, private duty nursing, and respiratory therapy for ventilator dependent individuals. Both mandatory and optional services offered under the Medicaid state plan must meet the following federal requirements: (a) Services must be uniformly offered throughout the state; (b) the recipient must have free choice of providers; (c) comparable services must be available to all individuals; and (d) any limits placed on the amount of services must be sufficient in amount, duration, and scope to achieve the purposes of the Medicaid program.

If states want to provide services without complying with mandated and optional state plan requirements, they may obtain a waiver of one or more of them under certain federal provisions (Rosenzwieg, 1995). OBRA 1981 revised Medicaid's funding to allow states to cover home and community-based services for individuals who would otherwise require institutional care. The Section 2176 waiver program permits states to provide a comprehensive range of home and community-based services to individuals who but for the provisions of such services would be institutionalized. Services that states may cover include case management, homemaker, home health aide, personal care, adult day care, health care, habilitation, respite care, and other services approved by the state Medicaid agency and HCFA as cost-effective (Miller, 1991). Section 1396 legislation, enacted in 1987, waives the same rules but applies only to persons aged 65 and older. As of April 1996, 49 states had waiver programs serving older adults. Only Pennsylvania and the District of Columbia do not have Medicaid waiver programs for older adults (GAO, 1996a).

Three other federal programs also authorize home-based services—Title III of the Older Americans Act, the Social Services Block Grant Program under Title XX of the Social Security Act, and the Department of Veterans Affairs. Area agencies on aging have the option of funding home health care services under Title III-B. In 1987, legislators added Title III-D to the OAA, which provided additional financial support for nonmedical in-home services for frail older persons (e.g., case management, lifeline systems, and deep cleaning). The intent was that they provide new and additional services, not just increase the services that already existed. Although states have broad authority to spend their Title XX allocations on a wide array of social services, 39 states use some portion of their funds to support home services (e.g., homemaker and chore aide) for frail elders (AoA, 1994a).

The Department of Veterans Affairs provides limited home care to qualifying veterans living within a 30-mile radius of Veterans Administration medical centers with a home care unit. The services covered are similar to those provided by Medicare. There is a co-payment for services based on eligibility category, secondary insurance status, and ability to pay.

Funding of home care can also come from private sources. National studies indicate that private payment accounts for as much as 30% to 40% of unskilled custodial home care services (Kane, 1989). Private long-term care insurance policies also cover the cost of home care. Most policies cover skilled nursing and therapist services; fewer cover the costs of nonmedical home care services such as home health aides or homemakers.

Users and Programs

Characteristics of Home Health Care Clients

On the basis of estimates from three national data sets, between 21% and 31% of older individuals use home care services (Benjamin, 1992). A review of the small body of research on use of home care shows, with some consistency, several factors directly associated with home care use. First, with increasing age, the odds of home service use grow. According to the 1987 National Medical Expenditure Survey, of the nearly 6 million Americans receiving home health services, half are 65 years of age and older (Altman &

Exhibit 17.1 **Percentage of Home Health Clients Needing Assistance With ADLs**

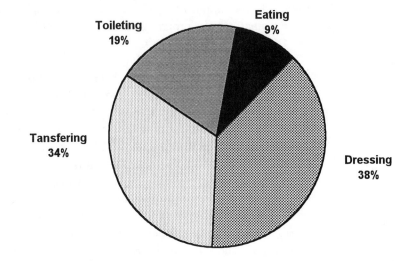

SOURCE: Hing (1994).

Walden, 1993). Among these older adults, the likelihood of using home health care services increased with age: 7.1% of persons aged 65 to 74, 14.5% of those aged 75 to 84, and 30.9% of persons 85 and older use home health care. Persons 85 years of age and older also averaged a greater number of home health visits per year (71 visits) than the younger elder groups; persons aged 75 to 84 averaged 67 visits per year, whereas individuals aged 65 to 74 averaged 56 visits per year. A second variable associated with use of home care is gender. Undoubtedly reflecting the longer life expectancy of women, more older women than older men use home care services (Grabbe et al., 1995; Hanley & Wiener, 1990).

Another consistent predictor of service use is functional disability. Persons with moderate and severe levels of dysfunction are more likely to use formal home care than those with mild functional impairments (Grabbe et al., 1995; Rowland & Lyons, 1991). A national survey of older home health patients revealed that nearly three fourths of these individuals received help with either an ADL or an IADL (Hing, 1994). Bathing, dressing, and transferring in or out of a bed or chair are ADLs with which older clients most frequently need assistance, followed by using the toilet and eating (see Exhibit 17.1).

The most frequent IADL with which older home health clients received help is light housework (Exhibit 17.2). In addition, one quarter of home health clients need assistance with taking medications, and 16% need assistance preparing meals and shopping.

Exhibit 17.2   **Percentage of Home Health Clients Needing Assistance With IADLs**

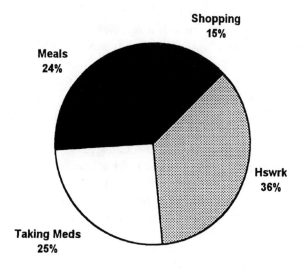

SOURCE: Hing (1994).

According to the national survey findings (Hing, 1994), 80% of older home health patients received skilled nursing services, whereas 50% received personal care services. Less frequently used services included physical therapy (16%), homemaker and/or companion services (11%), social services (10%), medications (7%), and occupational and/or vocational services (4%).

Family status also influences the use of home care services. Most older adults rely on family members, particularly their daughters and daughters-in-law, for daily support and assistance. When family members are not available or unable to provide care, reliance on formal home services increases. For example, Hanley and Wiener (1990) reported that unmarried older persons use more home services than do their married counterparts. They also found higher rates of home care users among people without any children. For individuals with children, the number of daughters negatively influences the use of home care services.

Mixed evidence exists regarding the relationship between other personal background characteristics and the use of home care by older adults. One such variable is cognitive status. Some researchers suggest that individuals with fewer cognitive limitations are more likely to be using home care services, whereas others report no relationship between cognitive abilities and home care use (Grabbe et al., 1995). Hanley and Wiener (1990) found that although cognitive functioning was not a predictor for obtaining home care, it did predict the amount of care received after implementing formal care. Individuals with lower levels of cognitive functioning were more frequently users of home care than were those with more intact cognitive abilities. Part of this confusion comes from the use of different definitions of home care in these studies.

Race rarely is a significant predictor of the use of home care, although the findings of a national survey suggest that older whites are the predominant users of home care services (Hing, 1994). Similar variables, however, appear to influence home care use among older adults of color and their white counterparts. For example, a study of home health service use by older Hispanic immigrants revealed that predisposing and illness level factors predicted the use of home health services, whereas enabling factors were not significant (Ailinger & Causey, 1993). Specifically, being female, being older, and having a higher level of education were significantly associated with use of home health services. The illness level factors significantly correlated with the use of home health care were increased ADL impairment and lower self-assessed health.

Home Health Care Programs

In 1995, there were 14,011 home health agencies (not including those providing primarily hospice services) in the United States (National Association for Home Care, 1995). Of these, 62% are Medicare-certified agencies. Approximately 41% of the agencies are proprietary, 37% are nonprofit, and 23% are government and some other type of ownership (Jones, 1994). One third of all the home health agencies are in six states: California, Florida, Illinois, New York, Pennsylvania, and Texas. Texas, with 557 home health agencies, has the highest number of agencies, whereas Alaska reports the fewest agencies, with 10.

It is relatively easy for new home care agencies to establish themselves, especially if they are not providing Medicare-certified home health care. Nonmedical home care services are not subject to federal regulation. States put forth their own definitions of and regulations for home care; both vary from state to state (Arneson, 1994). Although 39 states require state licensure for nonmedical home care services (Riley, 1989), standards are minimal and are not difficult for most agencies to meet.

Home care staff consist of both skilled professionals (e.g., doctors; nurses; physical, occupational, and speech therapists; lab technicians; and social workers) and paraprofessional members (e.g., homemakers, home health aides, and companions). Nurses are the most common providers of home health care, whereas home health aides provide the greatest mean number of home health visits (Altman & Walden, 1993; Kaye, 1992).

The majority of home health aides are middle-aged women, disproportionately minority, who provide personal care and assistance with daily living

---

For Your Files   **National Association for Home Care**

The National Association for Home Care is a trade association that represents the interests of more than 6,000 home care agencies, hospices, and home care aide organizations. Its members are primarily corporations or other organizational entities in addition to state home care associations, medical equipment suppliers, and schools. The association also offers individual memberships. Increasingly, professionals such as social workers, nurses, and physical therapists who are employed by home care agencies or are interested in home care are joining one of the forums established by the National Association for Home Care to serve the specific needs of these fields. It also has publications such as *How to Choose a Home Care Agency: A Consumer's Guide* and *Basic Statistics About Home Care 1995*. For more information, call 202-547-7424.

SOURCE: National Association for Home Care (1997).

---

to frail elders (Feldman, 1993). These workers are the least skilled and lowest paid workers in the home care industry. As a group, they do not belong to unions and have little job security, few fringe benefits, limited training, and little opportunity for advancement. On a positive note, most aides report that their positions afford them time and schedule flexibility, autonomy, independence, and an opportunity to provide concrete help. They find their work intrinsically satisfying because they are committed to their older clients and the clients' families and feel that they accomplish something worthwhile (cf. Schmid, 1993).

Challenges for Home Health Care

As the health care delivery system continues its evolution, receiving health and supportive care at home will be part of the normal pathway of care. For many older adults, receiving medical care and nonmedical services in their home is less expensive than institutional care. It is the most preferred care modality among older adults. We end our discussion of home health care by addressing several current and future challenges facing home health care agencies.

Working With New Clients

The majority of new home health care clients are recent hospital discharges who are likely to be in a state of partial recovery from the conditions that

---

Best Practice **Visiting Nurse Association of the Treasure Coast**

Health Care on Wheels, operated by the Visiting Nurse Association (VNA) of the Treasure Coast in Indian River County, Florida, is a unique program addressing the needs of residents who do not have a primary care physician or health insurance. A mobile medical unit, staffed with a nurse practitioner and basic screening and testing equipment, operates 70 hours per week in neighborhoods with high concentrations of residents lacking access to primary health care. The van also carries a computer that allows staff to quickly and easily manage demographic data associated with the program. Services include screening such as blood pressure, blood sugar, physicals, flu shots, and a few diagnostic activities. Colds, ear infections, and urinary tract infections are examples of illnesses the nurse practitioner is prepared to diagnose and treat.

Since 1992, the program has processed 4,200 visits to the mobile unit with clients divided almost equally between children and adults. Older adults represent about 10% of the caseload, with some of these patients being monitored on a regular basis. Most of the older clients are without a primary health care provider. Through collaborative agreements with a number of programs in the area, the VNA also has been able to provide vouchers to help their low-income outreach clients pay for prescription medications.

Financial support for the VNA Health Care on Wheels Program comes from a special tax district set up within Indian River County. The tax district governing board provides direction to the VNA by designating the areas in which the mobile medical unit can best meet community needs. Once an area has developed needed medical services such as access to a medical clinic and primary care providers, the mobile unit is assigned to another area.

For further information, contact Program Director for Health Services, VNA of the Treasure Coast, 1111 36th Street, Vero Beach, FL 32960, 561-567-5551.

---

first precipitated their acute care stay (Liebson, Naessons, Krishan, Campion, & Ballard, 1990). These older individuals may encounter overwhelming stress as they attempt to adapt not only to the illness and hospitalization but also to the continuing need for physical care and emotional support. In addition, cognitive limitations are prevalent in new admissions, which can seriously impair the older person's ability to absorb and retain discharge information or acclimate to the home environment (Dellasega & Stricklin,

1993). Four major types of stressors face the home care patient: (a) inadequate patient teaching and insufficient discharge planning; (b) acute illness at discharge resulting in having home care demands, high use of complex and sophisticated technology in providing care, and client dependency; (c) home setting poorly adapted for client care, resulting in an unsafe environment; and (d) inadequate or inappropriate resources, including informal caregivers and insufficient finances, and inability to access the service system (Wagnild & Grupp, 1991). Agencies need to work with older patients to reduce the impact of these stressors because older persons unable to manage them will not achieve optimal care outcomes.

Serving Older Adults in Rural Communities

Many rural communities have a greater need for in-home medical and non-medical services than they can meet. Kenney and Dubay (1992) found that although rural areas have more home health care agencies per population than urban areas, rural elders have less access to home health services. The reason for this discrepancy is not clear. It may be a result of attitudinal and behavioral characteristics of rural elders, the lack of available needed services/therapies, or other factors not yet identified (Redford & Severns, 1994).

Financing and Paying for Services

Although public funds pay for a large amount of home care, many older adults also must pay for some of their care. Studies suggest, however, that only between 10% and 20% of all older adults can afford quality policies that provide adequate home care coverage (Weiner, Illston, & Hanley, 1994). As new strategies are considered to improve the financing available for home care services, a key policy decision that legislators must address is determining an appropriate balance between public and private sector financing that meets the needs of frail older adults, does not undermine the efforts of informal caregivers, and is equitable and politically viable (Rowland & Lyons, 1991).

Recruiting and Retaining Staff

Given the growth and diversity in the health care system, there often is competition for employees among home care agencies, hospitals, and nursing homes as well as from other service sectors (e.g., discount stores). This competition, along with minimal wages and benefits, the lack of job security, and limited opportunity for career development, contributes to high turnover rates, particularly among nonmedical health care staff. These personnel issues present concerns about the quality of care to recipients. With the future increase in the demand for the frontline workers in home health care, the home health industry will need to develop and implement creative strategies for recruitment, retention, and professional development of their non-medical workers.

Ensuring Quality Care

Home health care agencies must continually address the issue of quality assurance. The traditional approach to quality evaluation in home care has been through the establishment of standards by national professional groups or state associations. Their usefulness, reliability, and validity have not been tested (O'Neill & Sorensen, 1991). There also is a lack of consistency in home care research as to the definition of client outcomes, which makes it difficult to generalize the findings beyond the specific study population. Although Medicare program's quality assurance is the most elaborately developed, Regan (1990) notes that one missing element is significant consumer involvement. He recommends taking several steps to have greater involvement of the public in improving the quality of home health care, including formal roles for consumer advocacy groups within the state regulatory agency and having an ombudsman authorized to monitor the survey agency's inspection and investigative efforts. There is precedent for involving the long-term care ombudsman; some states (e.g., Alaska, Connecticut, Idaho, Maine, Pennsylvania, Wisconsin, and Wyoming) have authorized ombudsmen to investigate complaints regarding home care (Miller, 1991).

In the wake of health care reform, enrollment in Medicare HMOs has increased (see Chapter 11). The outcomes for HMO patients compared with fee-for-service patients, however, have come into question. A national sample of 1,260 patients receiving home health care for 12 weeks revealed that although the cost for HMO patients was about two thirds as much as for the fee-for-service patients, patients in fee-for-service programs had better outcomes (Schlenker, Shaughnessy, & Crisler, 1995). Approximately 57% of fee-for-service patients improved in their ability to perform ADLs, compared with 43% of HMO patients. Schlenker et al. suggest that HMOs provide too few home health care visits to patients and attribute the difference in care, in part, to the capitation payments provided to HMOs by Medicare. With the trend toward more managed care, agencies must continually evaluate their services as related to client outcomes.

Supporting the Future of Home Health Care

The 1995 White House Conference on Aging gave support for home health care services by endorsing policies that expand and enhance payment for these services. Specific resolutions included these: (a) Refocus the emphasis of existing funding toward home and community-based care by eliminating the current institutional bias; (b) broaden the options of Medicaid long-term care benefits to include choices other than institutional care, such as personal assistance services, adult day health care, assisted living, mental health services, respite care, and home and community-based services; and (c) develop culturally sensitive long-term care insurance regulations that standardize private policies to encompass home and community-based services, as well as institutional care, that are affordable and accessible and that provide basic consumer protection. Whether the federal government and the private sector are able to meet the challenges facing home health care remains to be seen.

Hospice

Hospice is a philosophy of caring for individuals who are terminally ill and their family members. It is a comprehensive approach providing palliative medical, social, emotional, and spiritual support. As of 1995, there were approximately 2,544 operational or planned hospice programs in all 50 states and Puerto Rico (*Hospice Fact Sheet,* 1995). Although most hospice patients are older adults, persons of any age may receive hospice care.

Policy Background: Hospice

The Tax Equity and Fiscal Responsibility Act enacted in 1982 created the Medicare hospice program. Originally, reimbursement for coverage was limited to 210 days. The passing of OBRA (1990) removed this limitation. Medicare now provides for unlimited days of coverage for hospice care when provided by a Medicare-certified hospice program for as long as the doctor certifies that there is a need. To be eligible for hospice care, a person must be certified as terminally ill, with only about 6 months to live, by the patient's physician or a hospice staff physician, and the hospice care must be part of the written plan of treatment established by the attending professionals. Medicare entitles the person to the following services: physician services; nursing care; medical social services; home health aides; counseling for the patient, family, and other caregivers; short-term inpatient care; physical, speech, and occupational therapy; homemaker services; and medical supplies, appliances, and equipment. When a patient receives these services from a Medicare-certified hospice, Medicare pays providers one of four fixed prospective per diem rates, based on service level and setting, for every day of hospice benefit coverage. Medicare hospital insurance (Part A) pays almost the entire cost of care. Hospice can charge the patient $5 for each prescription drug provided on an outpatient basis by the hospice program and $5 per day for inpatient care if the patient moves to a nursing home or hospital for up to 5 days of respite care (Matthews & Berman, 1996). In 1995, Medicare spent less than 1% of its approximate $200 billion budget on hospice services (*Hospice Fact Sheet*, 1995).

Although Medicare is the most common source of funding for hospice services, other entities also cover the cost of participation in hospice. Medicaid provides hospice coverage in 36 states plus the District of Columbia. Hospices also receive reimbursement from private health insurance, HMOs, preferred provider organizations, private pay, and to a lesser extent from local (e.g., United Way), state, and federal sources (Delfosse, 1995). More than 80% of employees in medium and large businesses have coverage for hospice services, and 82% of managed care plans offer hospice services (*Hospice Fact Sheet*, 1995).

There is current nonmandatory nationwide accreditation or a "seal of approval" for hospice programs. Many programs undergo voluntary certification by Medicare and the Joint Commission on Accreditation of Healthcare Organizations. In addition, 35 states have hospice licensure laws, 6 have laws pending, and 10 states plus the District of Columbia do not have hospice licensure (*Hospice Fact Sheet*, 1995).

Users and Programs: Hospice

Characteristics of Hospice Clients

The National Hospice Organization estimated that in 1994, 340,000 patients were served by hospice in the United States (*Hospice Fact Sheet*, 1995).[2] That translates to hospice programs tending to one of every seven deaths. Although most hospice users are individuals with terminal cancer, about 22% of hospice patients have other types of illness. Of those with other illnesses, 10% had heart-related diagnoses, 4% had AIDS, 1% had renal (kidney) diagnoses, 1% had Alzheimer's disease, and 6% had some other illness.

Information derived from the 1994 National Home and Hospice Care Survey (Haupt, 1997) indicates that 45% of hospice patients were male and 55% female. Of the male patients, 61% were 65 years of age and older, whereas 75% of the female patients were age 65 or older. Approximately 81% of hospice patients were white. Nearly half (48%) of the patients were married. Men were more likely to be married than were women, whereas women were more likely to be widowed. The average time patients received care from hospice was 64 days. Most (77%) hospice patients died at home; 14% died in acute inpatient facilities; 9% died in other institutions.

Hospice Programs

In 1995, there were 3,550 hospice programs in the United States, of which 1,795 were Medicare certified (National Association for Home Care, 1995). A variety of organizations provide hospice services. Approximately 33% of hospices are independent community-based organizations; 29% are divisions of hospitals; 22% are part of home health agencies; 3% are divisions of hospice corporations; 1% are divisions of nursing homes; 12% are "other" or not identified. Approximately 74% of hospices are nonprofit, 4% are government organizations, 12% are for-profit, and 10% are "other" or unidentified. Most states provide care to fewer than 1,000 hospice clients; only 14 states provided care to 1,000 or more clients in 1991. Almost 95% of the population lives within 25 miles of a hospice program (Harper, 1995).

Hospice patients receive individualized services, depending on their personal needs. Hospices employ more than 25,000 paid professionals. These individuals include medical personnel such as physicians and nurses, home health aides, social workers, clergy, and pastoral counselors. In addition, 96,000 volunteers (75,000 women, 21,000 men) provide emotional and spiritual support to patients and their caregivers. Forty-two percent of the female volunteers and 47% of the male volunteers were over age 60. Approximately 92% of primary caregivers in home health agency-based hospices were white, as were 95% in hospital-based hospices and 97% of all hospice volunteers (Delfosse, 1995).

Hospices also offer bereavement groups and services for families and caregivers to help them with their grief. Eighty-one percent of hospices offer these programs and services to the community at large, not just those families served directly by hospices. Bereavement services include follow-up phone calls and visits, information regarding meetings or group offerings, and literature and material on grief. A survey completed by 268 hospice providers indicated that either nurses or individuals with human services backgrounds (e.g., social work, clergy, and counseling) coordinate bereavement services (Lattanzi-Licht, 1989). Some programs had no specific bereavement personnel; these programs said that all personnel were involved with the follow-up of families.

Challenges for Hospice

Hospice programs in the United States focus on home care and dehospitalization (Mor & Allen, 1995). Family members, along with the hospice staff, provide care to their terminally ill loved ones. Hospice, along with other health care providers, will be affected by the ever changing nature of health care and the graying of the population. We end this section with a discussion of the challenges facing hospice programs now and in the future.

Serving a Greater Diversity of Patients

White, middle-class patients are the predominant users of hospice programs. For hospices to respond to the needs of ethnic minority patients, workers need to be sensitive to culture-specific issues and practices. Challenges to overcome in providing hospice services across cultures include language differences, family values, lack of trust, and feelings of discrimination or inequality by the hospice patient (Noggle, 1995). To successfully expand services into minority communities, hospices must establish a pattern of education and communication appropriate to consumers, volunteers, and professionals of all races and ethnicities (Harper, 1995).

Supporting Patients Without Families

By design, the hospice home care model supports the efforts of families caring for terminally ill patients at home. An increasing number of hospice candidates, however, do not have home support available, or the support that is available is inadequate or unreliable (MacDonald, 1992). Thus, hospice programs face either not serving this group of individuals or providing care for patients whose needs far exceed available resources. To address this issue, hospices need to develop creative approaches to serving patients without primary caregivers. Without strong community support (e.g., donations and volunteers) and supportive legislative action, most hospices will continue to struggle with how to provide care to individuals who are for the most part alone.

Enhancing Bereavement Programs

Bereavement programs are often the most underdeveloped component of the hospice program. Programs cite lack of sufficient staff time, lack of personnel, and funding pressures as the most frequent barriers to the delivery of bereavement services (Lattanzi-Licht, 1989). Thus, lack of resources for bereavement services is an issue facing most hospice programs.

As we mentioned in Chapter 1, the increase in the numbers of oldest-old persons in the coming decade will put an additional strain on the demand for home care and hospice services. Issues of delivery, access, and affordability of home care services will be of critical importance to the well-being of an aging population.

⧉ **CASE STUDY**

WILL HOME HEALTH CARE WORK FOR HARRIET?

Harriet is a 79-year-old woman who has never married. She lives in a small mobile home situated on land several miles from a rural town of 2,500 persons. Until 3 years ago, she lived with her bachelor brother who had been at the center of her life. His sudden death left Harriet confused and depressed because her life had revolved around the companionship and care of her brother. Her health has deteriorated steadily since his death.

People in her community describe Harriet as a colorful character. She dropped out of school when she was 16 years old and took a job as a ranch cook's assistant. Her interest in ranching led to several years of traveling the rodeo circuit assisting well-known bronco riders. Eventually, Harriet ended up owning a small grocery store in the town where she now lives. Her independent spirit became well-known by her customers and business acquaintances. Harriet made no time for other social contacts beyond work and her brother. Harriet is not a religious woman and has little patience for "frivolous" socializing. Until recently, she devoted her spare time to raising and showing an exotic breed of house cat.

Although she accumulated considerable savings, she spent most of it supporting her brother, who had an alcohol problem. She does receive a monthly Social Security check of $524. Because she owns her mobile home and the acre of land on which it is situated, her monthly expenses average only $225. She has Medicare and a small supplemental health insurance policy. Harriet has a history of diabetes and high blood pressure, which have gone untreated. She has fallen several times, and it is becoming difficult for her to get in and out of her bathtub. This, combined with some incontinency, has made it difficult for her to maintain her personal hygiene. She recently was discharged from the hospital after gallbladder surgery. Her wound is not healing quickly.

CASE STUDY QUESTIONS

1. The chapter discusses several predictors of use for home health services. Describe these predictors. Which apply to Harriet?

2. What are the social and environmental dynamics of Harriet's situation that a home health agency would take into consideration when assigning a worker to this case?

3. What criteria would Harriet have to meet to qualify for Medicare home health services? What other payment sources might be available to Harriet?

4. Harriet is likely to resist the idea of home health care. What arguments could best make the case to Harriet that this is a good option for her?

LEARNING ACTIVITIES

1. Review current Medicare, Medicaid, or Older Americans Act legislation that pertains to home care services. What do the various legislations mandate? How do they differ, and where do they overlap? What areas do you believe legislation needs to address in preparation for future growth of the aging population?

2. Interview a home health care provider or hospice staff member. What situations does the provider encounter? What type of on-the-job training or in-service do workers receive? What are the education and experience requirements for staff positions? What are some of the obstacles as well as benefits of the service? What changes would the staff like to see?

3. Interview someone who receives or is the caregiver of someone who receives home health or home care services. What does the recipient or caregiver feel are the benefits of the program? Where are the gaps? How would the individual change, if at all, the program or services? What would the individual do without the program or services? How did the household find out about the program and select the provider?

4. Check local newspapers, television, radio, and magazines for home care service and hospice ads. Whom are they trying to reach? How would you respond to the ads?

5. Design a new home care or hospice program. What elements would be primary? Who would you serve? How would you market your program?

FOR MORE INFORMATION

National Resources

1. National Association for Home Care, 228 7th Street SE, Washington, DC 20003, 202-547-7424.

   The National Association for Home Care represents home health agencies, hospice programs, and homemaker/home health aid agencies. *Caring Magazine* and *Home Care News* are published by the association. Contact them for a list of publications.

2. National Hospice Organization, 1901 N. Moore Street, Suite 901, Arlington, VA 22209, 703-243-5900 or 800-658-8898.

The national office offers technical assistance and training to local hospice organizations. It operates a toll-free referral line to local hospice programs. Numerous free publications are available.

3. Visiting Nurse Association of America, 3801 East Florida, Suite 900, Denver, CO 80210, 303-753-0218 or 800-426-2547.

   The VNA is the parent organization of local VNAs that provide personal care; speech, physical, and occupational therapies; and nutritional counseling. A fact sheet is available.

4. Foundation for Hospice and Home Care, 513 C Street NE, Washington, DC 20002, 202-547-6568.

   The foundation promotes home care and hospice care through the establishment of standards of care, educational programs, and research. Free consumer guides about home care and hospice are available.

5. Catholic Charities, 1731 King Street, Suite 200, Alexandria, VA 22314, 703-549-1390.

   Catholic Charities is a social service agency that offers assistance to people of all ages and has extensive support services, including homemaker services, through its local offices.

Web Resources

1. GriefNet
   http://rivendell.org

   GriefNet is a Web page that can connect visitors with a variety of resources related to death, dying, bereavement, and major emotional and physical losses. It offers interactive discussion and support groups—all for bereaved persons and those working with the bereaved, both professional and laypersons. The support and discussion groups are accessed by e-mail. Groups include *grief-chat,* a general discussion list for any topic related to death, dying, bereavement, or other major loss; and *grief-widowed,* a support group for anyone who has lost a partner or a spouse at any age, at any time, of any sexual orientation. This is a great site. Be sure to stop by for a visit.

2. National Hospice Organization
   http://nho.org

   The National Hospice Organization site offers a wide range of links, including How to Find a Hospice, Basics of Hospice, Discussion Groups, NHO Store (which has a list of publications and resources), and Specific Diseases. This well-designed site furnishes much useful information.

3. HomeCare On Line

   http://www.nahc.org

   This Web page of the National Association for Home Care offers information about state associations, consumer information, news updates, and legislative information. Visitors also can search the database for information.

4. ElderCare

   http://www.eldercare-info.com

   ElderCare is a private, nonprofit referral agency that provides referrals to in-home and other community resources at no cost.

NOTES

1. Additional hours and days of services may be provided subject to review by fiscal intermediaries on a case-by-case basis, on the basis of documentation justifying the need for and reasonableness of such additional care.

2. Unless otherwise noted, the statistical information on patient and provider characteristics comes from the *Hospice Fact Sheet* (1995).

18 🎨

Respite Services

William, 78 years old, was at the end of his rope when he called the area agency on aging. He had resisted making the call for months, but a close friend urged him to get help. William had watched his wife's memory fade year by year, but he couldn't completely accept that she had Alzheimer's disease. His doctor was advising him that the stress and continuous physical exertion were aggravating his arthritis. The case manager suggested that William consider having a trained respite worker come into his home twice a week. Reluctantly, William agreed. After a month of respite help, he is beginning to appreciate the 6 hours per week when he can concentrate on other things.

Respite care refers to temporary, short-term supervisory, personal, and nursing care provided to older adults with physical and/or mental impairments (George, 1987). Programs provide respite services in the older person's home or at a specific site in the community (e.g., adult day services, nursing home, or hospital). Although older adults are the recipients of care, these dual-purpose programs also provide temporary periods of relief or rest for caregivers away from their care receivers.

As with William, the primary caregiver tends to be a spouse who assumed the role of caregiver because of the failing physical or mental health of his or her partner. The role of spousal caregiver often comes at a time in the couple's lives when they may be experiencing health problems or the reduction of functional capacities associated with aging. When a spouse is not available or is unable to provide care, adult children assume the caregiving responsibilities for their aging parents. It is usually a daughter or daughter-in-law who takes on the major responsibility. These women often face the competing demands of caring for an aging parent, managing a household, and working outside the home (Bowers, 1987; Horowitz, 1985; Neal et al., 1993; Stone et al., 1987).

Although family caregivers experience a sense of pride and emotional gratification when they perceive themselves as successfully fulfilling their caregiving responsibilities (Kaye & Applegate, 1990; Motenko, 1988, 1989), the demands of providing daily care for an older family member are not without physical, psychological, and social liabilities. Caregivers often experience poor physical health and emotional distress. Fulfilling the role of primary caregiver often restricts the use of personal time, interferes with employment responsibilities and obligations, and strains family relationships (Gallagher, Wrabetz, Lovett, Maestro, & Rose, 1988). To help alleviate the burden and stress of caregiving, respite services have become an integral part of the continuum of support services for older adults. They provide relief for caregivers from the constant responsibilities of caring for dependent older adults and allow both the caregivers and care receivers time for independent relationships and activities (Klein, 1989).

In this chapter, we present information about the types of respite programs available for older adults and their caregivers. The chapter begins with an overview of federal support for respite services, followed by a presentation of the general characteristics of older adults who participate in respite programs and a description of the primary types of respite services. We end this chapter with a discussion of the challenges facing providers of respite services now and in the future.

Policy Background

Some of the first support for respite care for older adults came from the Older Women's League. In the early 1980s, the league sponsored model legislation in several states to encourage the development of statewide respite programs for caregivers of frail older adults. As a result, several states mandated respite care as part of their state-sponsored programs for older adults and their families (e.g., Illinois's Alzheimer's Disease Program, New York State's Expanded In-Home Services for the Elderly Program, California's Alzheimer's Disease Institute; Petty, 1990).

In its 1987 report, *Losing a Million Minds*, the U.S. Congress, Office of Technology Assessment, firmly established the need for respite care, particularly for persons with dementia. Of the top 10 services rated by caregivers of persons with dementia as essential or most important, six related to respite care: (a) a paid companion who can come to the home for a few hours each week to give caregivers a rest; (b) a paid companion for overnight care; (c) personal care for the older person; (d) short-term respite outside the home in nursing homes or hospitals; (e) adult day care; and (f) nursing visits at home. In addition, the OTA report suggested that the provision of respite services postpones the need for nursing home placement.

Despite these findings and other research documenting the need for and effectiveness of respite services, the federal government provides limited financial support for respite services. Because the government defines respite care for the older individual as "personal care," it is not a reimbursable service under Medicare. Medicaid allows for such care through its waiver programs and can cover both in-home respite and adult day services.

Some respite programs receive support through OAA funds under Title III-D, which authorizes the support of in-home services including in-home respite and adult day care. In addition, the act provides funds for educational programs that teach caregivers about Alzheimer's disease, how to cope with the disease process, and how to use behavior management techniques. Funding for in-home programs under the OAA in fiscal year 1995 was $9,263,000 and was the same for fiscal year 1996 (AoA, 1997a).

Family caregivers who work and must pay for respite services for their care receivers may benefit from dependent care assistance plans (Canan & Mitchell, 1991; Neal et al., 1993). Authorized under Section 129 of the Internal Revenue Code, if employers offer this benefit option, dependent care assistance plans provide reimbursement of up to $5,000 per year for out-of-the-home dependent care expenses. Qualifying individuals include spouses or dependents who are unable to care for themselves, regardless of age, and regularly spend at least 8 hours each day in the employee's household. This time requirement makes such plans less useful for adult children and other individuals with elder care responsibilities because many of these employees do not share a household with the older person whom they are helping (Scharlach, Lowe, & Schneider, 1991). In addition to dependent care assistance plans, a federal tax credit for employment-related expenses incurred is also available to individuals who have dependent care responsibilities. The federal dependent care tax credit reduces the amount of income tax the employee owes by a percentage of the expenses the employee has incurred because of dependent care responsibilities. Individuals eligible to receive care and the types of expenditures allowed are the same as those that apply to the dependent care assistance plan. Thus, employees with children are the primary users of dependent care tax credits; only about 20% of the benefits claimed are for elder care (Biegel, Schultz, Shore, & Morycz, 1988).

Users and Programs

Respite programs typically provide care for older adults with a wide range of physical and mental disabilities. Some programs, however, provide services for specific subgroups of older adults such as persons with Alzheimer's disease (Lawton, Brody, & Saperstein, 1991; Seltzer et al., 1988) or developmental disabilities (Factor, 1993). The small number of reports that include data on client and family characteristics makes it difficult to develop an accurate profile of respite care users. Thus, we begin this section by providing a general profile of older adults who use respite services. We then focus our attention on the three most common types of respite programs: (a) in-home respite care, (b) adult day care, and (c) institutional respite care. When data are available, we will provide information about the older adults and caregivers using each type of respite care.

Characteristics of Older Adults Using Respite Services

Drawing on the limited research literature, Montgomery (1992) profiled older adults participating in respite programs. Typically, these elders are around 80 years of age. Male participants tend to be younger than their female counterparts. They also are overrepresented in the client population in comparison with the gender distribution of this age group in the general population—about 40% of the clients are male, and 60% are female. More than 85% of the older adults live with their caregivers, who are either spouses or adult children. Most older respite users have multiple impairments that limit their ability to perform daily activities of living.

Respite Programs

A variety of agencies operate respite programs including both for-profit and nonprofit organizations. Programs differ with respect to their definitions of respite, target populations, eligibility criteria, and the amount and type of respite offered. Costs for respite services vary, depending on the type and level of care provided to the participants. Most programs rely on contributions from their clients, who pay either a preset amount or on a sliding scale according to their financial resources.

In-Home Respite Care

In-home respite care takes place in the home in which the older person lives. Depending on the needs of the caregiver, in-home respite can occur on a regular or occasional basis and can take place during the day or evening hours. Some programs provide personal and instrumental care for the older person, whereas others provide only companionship or supervisory services (Klein, 1986; Lawton et al., 1991). Professionals and nonprofessionals, employed by community-based agencies that offers respite services (e.g., home health agencies, senior support programs, and church-affiliated organizations), typically provide the care. Several communities have developed programs that rely on trained volunteers to provide in-home respite care (Klein,

For Your Files   **Alzheimer's Association**

The Alzheimer's Association has more than 200 chapters and 1,600 support groups nationwide and offers a wide range of materials containing information and advice for persons afflicted with Alzheimer's disease and for their caregivers. To obtain information about Alzheimer's disease or about services available through Alzheimer's Association chapters, call the Information and Referral Service Line at 800-272-3900 or contact the Alzheimer's Association, 919 N. Michigan Avenue, Suite 1000, Chicago, IL 60611-1676, 800-272-3900. Information can also be obtained from the association's home page (http://www.alz.org).

1989). For example, the Visiting Nurse Association of America created a partnership with older adults in Senior Companion Programs in 18 cities across the country designed to expand the scope of long-term care services. The Senior Companion Program trains volunteers to assist older clients and their families by developing a relationship with dependent elders and, in the process, providing family caregivers much-needed respite (Fischer & Schaffer, 1993).

Older adults who receive in-home care typically exhibit more frequent social and behavioral problems than do participants of other types of respite programs (Lawton et al., 1991). Their caregivers report a higher degree of burden and provide more intense care compared with caregivers using other types of respite. Caregivers using in-home respite services also spend fewer hours per day away from their care receivers than those using adult day services (Berry, Zarit, & Rabatin, 1991). These caregivers, however, spend less time on caregiving activities on days in which they use in-home services compared with caregivers using adult day programs, perhaps because of the amount of time consumed preparing the older adult for the out-of-home program.

In-home respite is the type of respite most acceptable to family caregivers (Conlin, Caranasos, & Davidson, 1992; Lawton et al., 1991). It typically is more flexible than other forms of respite because it most easily accommodates to the specific day and time that the caregiver wants. Caregivers also view in-home respite as more acceptable than other types of programs because they do not have to take the older adult out of the environment in which they are most comfortable. It also has its limitations because in-home respite services can be expensive, particularly if frequently used for several hours per day. Families also may be reluctant to use in-home respite services because they do not like having strangers in their homes or taking care of their loved ones (Miller & Goldman, 1989).

Adult Day Care

The Adult Day Services Association (formerly the National Institute on Adult Day Care) defines adult day care as a

> community-based group program designed to meet the needs of adults with functional impairments through an individual care of plan. It is a structured, comprehensive program that provides a variety of health, social, and related support services in a protective setting during any part of a day but less than 24-hour care. (National Institute on Adult Day Care, 1990, p. iv)

Since 1974, the number of adult day care centers operating nationwide has grown from 18 (Weissert, 1977) to more than 3,000 (Geller, 1994).

In the past, the terms *medical* and *social* were used to distinguish between types of adult day centers. Programs following a medical model offer intensive health and therapeutic services prescribed in individual plans for each participant. Social-oriented programs focus more on the socialization needs of the participants through the provision of individual and group activities, meals, and health maintenance programs. It is difficult to identify any given center as falling into either category, however, because all centers provide varying degrees of social programs and health services. The findings from a national survey of 774 adult day centers support this perception (Conrad, Hughes, Hanrahan, & Wang, 1993). Except for special purpose centers (e.g., Alzheimer's family care and rehabilitation), the distinction among most centers is more clearly delineated on the basis of the *intensity* of services and activities provided, rather than on the philosophical orientation of the centers. Whatever a program's primary emphasis, the Adult Day Services Association recommends that all adult day care programs provide eight essential services: personal care, nursing services, social services, therapeutic activities, nutrition and therapeutic diets, transportation, emergency care for participants, and family education (National Institute on Adult Day Care, 1990).

Approximately three fourths of all adult day care centers are in urban settings (Conrad, Hanrahan, & Hughes, 1990). Although some adult day centers are freestanding agencies, other organizations such as churches, senior centers, nursing homes, community hospitals, or the Veterans Administration sponsor and operate most day programs (Webb & Heide, 1991). Most centers are private not-for-profit (70%), 20% are public, and 10% are private for-profit agencies (Conrad et al., 1990). Regardless of the hosting agency, most centers are small, averaging 20 participants per day. Typical staff members for adult day centers include an administrator (or executive director), program director, and one or more of the following: program assistants/aides, recreation or activity aides, nurse and nurse aides, therapist, social workers, custodial workers, van drivers, administrative personnel, and office staff (National Institute on Adult Day Care, 1990; Weissert et al., 1989). Volunteers, including students, also play an essential role in the staffing of many adult day care programs.

Most adult day care programs serve populations mixed in age and impairment. The typical day care participant is a woman, in her mid- to late 70s, white, unmarried, but not living alone (Conrad et al., 1990; Weissert et al., 1989). More than one half of the day care participants are functionally dependent, and almost 40% suffer cognitive limitations. Although the background characteristics of day care participants appear fairly consistent across studies, characteristics of caregivers who rely on adult day care services vary. For example, in a study of 59 day care programs in Pennsylvania, caregivers were most likely to be daughters of the care receivers, in their mid-50s, who had served as the primary caregiver for 1 to 5 years (Kirwin & Kaye, 1991). A comparative study of 118 female caregivers of persons with Alzheimer's disease found that users of adult day care were younger, had higher education and income levels, were more likely to have children living in the household, and reported more symptoms of stress and depression than those caregivers who did not use this type of respite service (Guttman, 1991). The 42 caregivers who used a dementia-specific day program in New York, however, were more likely to be older, spousal caregivers, most of whom had served as the primary caregiver for less than 2 years (Monahan, 1993).

An advantage of day care over in-home respite care for the care receiver is that it provides important peer group support and greater opportunities for social interaction. For the caregiver, adult day care offers freedom from caregiving responsibilities for potentially long, continuous blocks of time at a lesser cost than in-home services (Lawton et al., 1991). A disadvantage of using adult day care is the physical and emotional effort required to prepare care receivers to attend a day program. For example, transportation to and from the center is a major issue that caregivers and programs must resolve. Caregivers often view getting the care receiver ready to leave home more consuming and exhausting than providing the usual care (Berry et al., 1991). In addition, many caregivers and their care receivers have an adverse emotional reaction to the term *day care,* which they perceive is a program for children, not an appropriate setting for older adults (Bane, 1992).

Institutional Respite Care

Institutional settings such as nursing homes, Veterans Administration hospital-based nursing homes, and hospitals provide respite services. In most

Best Practice   **Parker Jewish Geriatric Institute**

The Parker Jewish Geriatric Institute in New Hyde Park, New York, instituted an Alzheimer's Respite Center on February 1, 1989. The center began through a grant from the Dementia Care and Respite Services Program, a national demonstration program funded by the Robert Wood Johnson Foundation with direction and technical assistance provided by the Bowman Gray School of Medicine of Wake Forest University. The National Alzheimer's Association and the Administration on Aging also cofunded this program. By 1991, Parker had shown that day centers can meet the needs of people with dementia and their caregivers and achieve financial self-sufficiency. By the third quarter of its second year of operation, Parker had an operating surplus of $15,696.

The keys to the success of Parker are flexible hours, drop-in service, and a 7-day-a-week operation. Caregivers are free to drop off their loved ones at the last minute. Initially, this policy was a "management nightmare." Training and orienting a pool of per diem workers solved the problem, however. With the center open from 7:00 a.m. to 7:00 p.m. and from noon to 7:00 p.m. on weekends, families have greater flexibility in arranging their schedules. Parker is even willing to be flexible on those hours. The center will open earlier in the morning for caregivers, such as for a police officer who needed to drop off his father at 5:00 a.m. because he worked an early shift. Special hours can be arranged with families who have special events. The center will open on a holiday if that is what a family needs.

Another customer-driven service that has been popular with caregivers is an à la carte approach to purchasing services. Instead of one daily or hourly rate, caregivers may purchase meals, shaves, transportation, and other special services separately. This type of customer choice is unique in the adult day care business. Parker is also a site for a dementia care training program of the New York chapter of the Alzheimer's Association. Home health aides from various agencies are trained in a 4-week program to be dementia specialists. Four days each week are spent on-site at Parker and one day in classes. Staff members at Parker continue to be available to the home health aides for advice on how to handle situations with Alzheimer's patients even after they have completed the program. The center also provides field work for students in gerontology and recreation therapy. A survey of Parker's caregivers showed that 85.6% rated the center as excellent and reported that the participants generally were happier since they began attending.

For more information, contact Parker Jewish Geriatric Institute, 271-11 76th Avenue, New Hyde Park, NY 11040, 718-289-2160, or Dementia Care and Respite Services Program, Partners in Caregiving, Bowman Gray School of Medicine of Wake Forest, Department of Psychiatry and Behavioral Medicine, Medical Center Boulevard, Winston-Salem, NC 27157, 910-716-4941.

situations, caregivers pay out-of-pocket for institutional respite care. This type of respite care differs from in-home and day programs in that it provides overnight and/or extended services. Beds may be available for both emergency respite care (e.g., illness of a caregiver) and planned respite stays, such as when a caregiver plans an extended vacation or a short weekend of relaxation (Lawton et al., 1991; Looney, 1987).

Nursing homes indicate that almost 80% of their respite clients have functional impairments that would make them eligible for institutional placement, with approximately 50% of these clients eligible for a skilled nursing facility (Montgomery, 1992). Caregivers of elders using institutional respite services typically are older and spend more time in the caregiver role than caregivers using other types of programs. Perhaps, because these care receivers are at a point of requiring intense care and supervision, caregivers often use this type of respite service on a trial basis before permanent nursing home placement (Miller & Goldman, 1989; Miller, Gulle, & McCue, 1986; Scharlach & Frenzel, 1986).

Institutional respite programs have their advantages and disadvantages with respect to cost, caregivers' perceptions of care and the facility's ability to provide care, and the additional burden of preparation required of the caregiver (Gonyea, 1988; Harper, McDowell, Turner, & Sharma, 1988; Lawton et al., 1991; Rosenheimer & Francis, 1992). Although institutional programs offer respite care at the cost of comparable amounts of in-home respite, caregivers still view it as a costly care alternative. Nursing homes and hospitals usually provide a supervised, professional setting equipped to handle emergencies, which seems to alleviate family anxiety about care. Caregivers, however, often try so hard to avoid nursing home placements that even a temporary placement evokes fear and guilt about future placement possibilities. In addition, although institutions typically can accept older individuals with a range of behavioral problems and functional disabilities, caregivers often fear that their elders will not receive proper, individual attention and care. The preparation required for a nursing home or hospital stay (e.g., filling out forms, preparing personal effects, explaining the situation to the care receiver, and transportation to and from the facility) and limitations on the number of days a person can stay in the program also discourage some caregivers from using this type of respite care.

Challenges for Respite Programs

Respite programs play an important role in maintaining and enhancing the psychological and physical well-being of older adults and their caregivers. We discuss a number of policy and programmatic challenges that must be addressed in the future.

Best Practice **Respite Program**

Persons living in rural South Carolina have had limited access to formal services. Social programs that do exist often do not consider the cultural norms and values of minority and rural populations. These problems are especially acute for caregivers of persons with Alzheimer's disease. In response to these problems, the South Carolina Commission on Aging established a statewide advisory committee on Alzheimer's disease. The committee identified the following as major barriers to services for persons with Alzheimer's and their caregivers:

- Inadequate access, use, and coordination for existing services, especially for minority, low-income, and rural individuals
- Lack of respite and supportive services
- Lack of diagnosis of memory impairment
- Lack of public knowledge about the disease, including awareness of available resources and services

To address these problems, project Care Options and Public Education (COPE) was created through a grant from the U.S. Public Health Service. The specific goals of the project are to expand the types of respite care and levels of service available; to develop a network of services, such as family support groups, care management, counseling, legal assistance, insurance counseling, and transportation; to improve public understanding and awareness of Alzheimer's disease; to improve access to and use of Alzheimer's services; and to enhance the skills related to the diagnostic and assessment capability of physicians and nurse practitioners, with a special focus on the rural areas.

Area agencies on aging in two regions will be chosen as demonstration sites. In each region, AAAs will develop and fund respite services, family support services, targeted outreach, and information and referral. The South Carolina Commission on Aging will also work with both medical schools in South Carolina to help with physician training. The program will use a sliding fee scale with fees charged on the basis of the individual's or family's ability to pay.

For more information about project COPE, contact the South Carolina Commission on Aging at 803-737-7500.

Increasing the Use of Respite Services

Researchers report that as a result of using respite services, caregivers enhance their well-being (Deimling, 1991), reduce their feelings of burden and stress (Conlin et al., 1992; Kosloski & Montgomery, 1993), and delay placing their loved one in a nursing home (Kosloski & Montgomery, 1995; Lawton et al., 1991). In addition, most caregivers who use respite services report being highly satisfied with the program and the care their family member receives (Buelow & Conrad, 1992; Henry & Capitman, 1995). Despite the potential for positive outcomes, and the growing availability of respite programs throughout the United States, caregivers are still reluctant to use any type of respite service. When caregivers do seek respite services, it is often at a time of crisis; their family situation escalates to a point at which they cannot continue providing care without some assistance. Even then, caregivers use respite services only in modest amounts.

To increase program use by family caregivers, providers must address both family-related and system-related variables. Family-related variables include caregivers' lack of awareness, apprehension, and attitudes about using respite services and the reactions of care receivers (Schmall & Webb, 1994). Many caregiving families have little or no contact with formal services and thus are often unaware of the availability of respite care in their communities. Even when caregivers are aware of such services, their fierce independence and personal beliefs about caregiving may hinder their use. It is not uncommon to hear caregivers say such things as "She's my mother, I am responsible for her care" or "No one can care for my wife better than I can." Just like William, whom we introduced at the beginning of the chapter, caregivers often feel guilty about leaving their care receivers and believe that using formal services is a sign of failure. They may be even more reluctant to use respite services if they see it as benefiting themselves, rather than their care receivers. In addition, some care receivers respond negatively to and resist respite care, thus reinforcing feelings of guilt often harbored by many caregivers.

System barriers related to the use of respite care services include lack of service availability when wanted or needed most and lack of control over who provides services (MaloneBeach, Zarit, & Shore, 1992). For in-home respite users, having different workers every time they request help is a deterrent to the use of such services. Caregivers generally want to have more control over which respite care workers provide care for their loved ones. The limited availability (e.g., only weekdays) and time schedules (e.g., 8:00 a.m. to 5:00 p.m.) of many respite programs prohibit their use by some caregivers, particularly those who are working outside the home. Transportation is another major barrier to the use of respite services, particularly for adult day care. Many family caregivers find it difficult to get their care receivers to a center, and many centers have limited means of providing transportation for their participants. Finally, the lack of reimbursement from Medicare and most private insurance carriers for respite care also is a significant barrier for many families who may otherwise wish to use this service.

Expanding Community Awareness and Education

The limited use experienced by some respite programs suggests the need for agencies and organizations to continually inform and educate people about their services. Caregivers are often unaware that respite services exist and do not understand the concept. They often see respite programs as a "last resort" or "end of the road" solution, rather than a preventive service. Respite services will be more effective in alleviating the stress and strains of caregiving if providers can get caregivers to enroll in their programs earlier in the caregiving career.

Providing Flexible and Alternate Formats

Needed are greater flexibility and expanded hours and days for all types of respite programs. Successful programs will adapt to the time needs of caregivers, particularly those who work outside the home. In recent years, the idea of the adult day center as the hub for an all-inclusive system of respite (e.g., weekend programs and overnight services) has emerged. Support for more inclusive programming has received strong endorsement, as evidenced by programs such as the Robert Wood Johnson Foundation's Dementia/Respite Services Program (1988-1992) and Partners in Caregiving Program (1993-1995). Although such programs are still in their infancy, advocates for providers of these programs assert the effectiveness and efficiency of delivering more comprehensive day programs ("The Extra Mile," 1996).

The idea of intergenerational day care centers deserves further consideration. Only about 9% of adult day centers in the United States share a common location with child care programs (Conrad et al., 1990). One such example is Stride Rite Intergenerational Center. In 1990, Stride Rite Company opened an intergenerational day care program in Cambridge, Massachusetts. The center provides to employees and members of the surrounding community an on-site day care for both children and adults. Although there are several intuitively positive sociocultural, organizational, and delivery aspects of providing care across generations (Stremmel, Travis, Kelly-Harrison, & Hensley, 1994), researchers need to assess the receptivity and feasibility of this model of care.

Reaching Underserved Populations

A frequent criticism of respite services is the lack of programs targeted to families of color or families in some other way identified as needing special programming because of their ethnic or cultural backgrounds (Petty, 1990). Senior programs must be marketed to all groups of individuals. They must employ professionals and volunteers who speak languages other than

English and have knowledge of and experience working with individuals from various backgrounds.

Providing respite services in rural areas can be especially challenging. Traveling distance for in-home respite providers and transportation for participants to attend out-of-home programs can prohibit the use of services in sparsely populated areas. Programs must consider nontraditional means of program delivery and develop public-private linkages to help expand services.

Enhancing the Quality of Care

Few systematic studies reported in the literature evaluate the outcomes of respite services. We have derived most of what we know about effectiveness of respite services on anecdotal or descriptive reports of small programs. In addition, few studies provide a comparison of respite users with nonusers or include baseline measures of caregivers' and care receivers' physical and emotional status before using respite care. Researchers need to consider these limitations and work with respite service providers in the development of more rigorous program evaluations. Tools such as the *Day Care Quality Assessment* are now available to assist programs in reviewing their operating, fiscal, and management practices (Capitman, Henry, & Yee, 1994).

Supporting the Future of Respite Programs

The 1995 White House Conference on Aging gave specific support for caregivers by passing a resolution that supported policies that expand availability, funding, and flexibility in the provision of respite care, including overnight and weekend services. In addition, delegates resolved to support policies that provide financial, including tax incentives, and other support services for caregiving spouses, adult children, and other family members providing long-term care. As with home care services discussed in the previous chapter, there will be an increased demand for respite services in the next 20 years. Sheer numbers of older adults, especially those over 85 years of age, will force the public and private sector to respond to the respite needs of older adults and their families.

 ## CASE STUDY

RESPITE FOR A DEVOTED CAREGIVER

Ben and Ethel have been married for 60 years. Both are 85 years old. They reside in a small apartment comparable with the size of an average high school classroom. They partially subsidize their rent through a Section 8 rental voucher program. Ben was a tenant farmer all his adult life. Ethel worked in the home. Both worked hard, but Ben's income was low, and he and Ethel were not able to accumulate any savings. Their only income is Ben's Social Security check of $475 per month. They barely can make ends meet.

Ben has some hearing loss and suffers from gout that interferes with his mobility. Ethel is bedridden with Parkinson's disease. She is totally incontinent, and someone must turn her three times per day to keep her from getting bedsores. Ethel communicates only by using eye signals and is on a liquid diet. Her condition warrants full-time, skilled nursing care. Ben's devotion to his wife of 60 years prohibits him from placing her in a nursing home. One of his few happy moments is when he is showing off their wedding picture.

Ben and Ethel have one daughter who is employed full-time. Their daughter does help her father prepare meals when she has time. The daughter is concerned about the tremendous caregiving load her father has assumed. Ben used to frequent the local senior center a couple days per week to play pool with "the guys." Occasionally, he would take a day trip on the senior center van. The daughter would like her father to "give in" and place Ethel in a nursing home so that he can have some time to himself. Her father simply will not consider it.

CASE STUDY QUESTIONS

1. On the basis of the information provided, what barriers are presented that would make it difficult to work with Ben to develop a respite care plan?

2. Despite the barriers that you have identified in the first question, what aspects of this situation lend itself to convincing Ben that respite care is an option for him to consider?

3. Given the financial situation of this couple, what type of respite options would you be looking for in this community?

4. Short of skilled nursing home care, what other community-based services might be appropriate for this couple to improve their quality of life?

5. Do you think the daughter should use legal means to force her father to place her mother in a nursing home? Why or why not?

LEARNING ACTIVITIES

1. Interview a director or staff member of a respite program. What services does the program provide and to whom? What is the cost of the services? What does the individual perceive to be the primary obstacles for caregivers in requesting or receiving respite services? What changes would the staff

member like to make to the legislative policy as it relates to respite care and to the program?

2. Interview someone who has received or is receiving respite services. How did the caregiver find out about the service? Why did the caregiver decide to use it? What does the caregiver see as the benefits to the service as well as what type of changes would be desirable? How has respite care affected the person's life? How has it affected the life of the care receiver?

3. Design a respite program that encompasses what you believe is necessary for an effective program. Include to whom the program would be directed and how you would fund it.

FOR MORE INFORMATION

National Resources

1. Alzheimer's Disease and Education and Referral Center, P.O. Box 8250, Silver Spring, MD 20907, 301-495-3311 or 800-438-4380 (e-mail: adear@alzheimers.org).

    This center, a service of the National Institute on Aging, offers information about diagnosis and treatment, research, and services available to patients and their families. Call for a list of publications.

2. American Health Assistance Foundation, 15825 Shady Grove Road, Suite 140, Rockville, MD 20850, 301-948-3244 or 800-437-2423.

    The American Health Assistance Foundation funds research and educates the public on age-related diseases. Its Alzheimer's Family Relief Program offers emergency grants of up to $500 to Alzheimer's patients and their caregivers in need.

3. National Council on the Aging, Adult Day Services Association, 409 Third Street SW, Washington, DC 20023, 202-479-1200 (Web site http://www.ncoa.org).

    The National Council on the Aging is a private nonprofit organization that serves as a national resource of information, training, technical assistance, advocacy, and research. The Adult Day Services Association promotes adult day care and acts as a resource center for information about standards and assessment of adult day care programs. The association has numerous professional and consumer publications about adult day care programs.

Web Resources

1. Virginia Tech Adult Day Services
    http://www.chre.vt.edu//fcd/center.adc.html

University of Missouri at Columbia
http://www.miaims.missouri.edu/shrp/docs/eldercar.html

At least two adult day care programs are affiliated with universities. The Virginia Tech Adult Day Services is in Blacksburg, Virginia. The Eldercare Center, University of Missouri at Columbia, is located within the School of Health Related Professions.

2. Administration on Aging, Family Caregiver Options
http://aoa.dhhs.gov/aoa/webres

This is a great place to start when looking for information about respite and caregiver support services. The Family Caregiver Options page is continually updated with links to national resources. Definitely worth the visit.

3. Caregiver's Handbook
http://www.acsu.buffalo.edu/drstall/hndbk0.html

This site contains a complete version of a handbook for caregivers originally published by the San Diego County Mental Health Services. In addition to 47 "chapters" (!) that cover every aspect of caregiving, there is also a guide for choosing a residential facility.

4. Caregiver Network, Inc.
http://www.caregiver.on.ca/

The Caregiver Network is a site maintained by Karen Henderson who dedicates her work to her mother. There are numerous links to information about financial and legal issues, social issues, care for the caregiver, day care programs, and other resources of interest to caregivers.

5. Eldercare WEB
http://www.elderweb.com

This site is similar to the Caregiver Network but is based in the United States. We think this is one of the first sites on caregiving to be established. It has lots of great information of value to caregivers and older adults. There are links to a library, a forum, and information about health (nutrition was the highlight topic when we visited last), aging, legal, and social issues.

6. Family Caregiver Alliance
http://www.caregiver.org/text/index.html

The Family Caregiver Alliance, a nonprofit organization with caregiver centers throughout California, provides assistance to caregivers of individuals with Alzheimer's, Parkinson's, and other brain disorders. The home page has links to resource centers, information about work and family, a newsletter published by the alliance, publications and fact sheets, and information on events.

19

Nursing Homes

As she approached her mother's room at Prairie View Manor, Sharon thought about the day she had had to come to grips with the reality that Eleanor, then 84 years old, needed nursing home care. She had promised her mother that she would never put her in a nursing home. This promise would nearly break Sharon mentally and physically, jeopardize her marriage, and drive a wedge between her and her children. At first, the extra work cleaning Grandma's house, caring for the yard, and taking her shopping and to the doctor was welcomed. The whole family pitched in to make it work. Eleanor went to the adult day program every day where the family knew she was safe while they were at work and at school. When Eleanor became more frail, her falls more frequent, and the incontinency too difficult to manage, Sharon brought her mother to live with her. Even with a leave of absence from her job, Sharon became exhausted trying to manage her mother's care. Her husband became more and more angry about all the time Sharon was spending caring for her mother, and her children resented their having to give up some of their activities to help care for Grandma. Why, thought Sharon, had it taken her so long to seek nursing home care? Eleanor was content. She loved her little room with a view across the countryside. Most happily for Sharon, her mother was still able to participate in limited activities and enjoy the company of a few new friends.

The words *nursing home* conjure up negative images, and most older adults and their families dread the thought of residing there. Sharon, like many other family members, goes to great lengths to avoid nursing home placement—even when such placement would be physically and psychologically beneficial for everyone. Despite the negative image nursing homes have, they are a critical part of the long-term care continuum in our communities and provide a wide range of vital services to those who live there.

Because nursing homes are a part of the long-term care continuum, many refer to nursing homes as long-term care facilities. Indeed, these facilities have evolved into more than *nursing* homes—they are places in which a wide range of restorative, rehabilitative, and medical services are delivered. The term *nursing home,* however, is still frequently used in the literature. Therefore, we will use the terms *long-term care facilities* and *nursing homes* interchangeably in our discussion. In this chapter, we review policies that have been instrumental in creating the existence of long-term care facilities and present a profile of users and programs. The chapter ends with a presentation of the many challenges that lie ahead for long-term care facilities.

Policy Background

The growth of the nursing home industry parallels the passage of federal policy that evolved in the first half of the 20th century (Waldman, 1985). Prior to the enactment of Social Security, Medicare, and Medicaid, many older adults had few options if they needed medical and personal care. In some communities, older adults were boarded out to families that agreed to provide care in their homes, many of which were in homes of retired nurses—thus the basis for the term *nursing home* (Crandall, 1991). In the early part of the century, almshouses or "poor farms" cared for many frail older adults, persons with mental illnesses, and those who were chronically ill. An estimated 60% to 90% of the persons living in almshouses were over age 65 (Fischer, 1978). Almshouses were deplorable places, and the few states that had old age assistance payments and, later, Social Security, would not send payments to almshouse residents (Small, 1988). Older adults who were financially well off had the option of living in old age homes run by ethnic or religious groups; German and Scandinavian immigrants built Lutheran Homes; and Jews and Methodists built their own facilities (Waldman, 1985). The 1950 amendments to the Social Security Act of 1935, allowing residents of institutions to receive benefits and health providers to directly receive payments for services, helped expand the creation of nursing homes. But the real impetus to the creation of the nursing home industry came with the enactment of Medicare and Medicaid. Both Medicare and Medicaid provide payments to nursing homes—Medicare for acute care and Medicaid for long-term care for those with low incomes (Crandall, 1991; Small, 1988). Since the enactment of Medicare and Medicaid, the rate of nursing home use doubled from 2.5% to 5% of persons 65 and older (Small, 1988). In 1995, there were 18,911 nursing facilities in the country (Administration on Aging, 1995b).

Payment of Nursing Home Care

The cost of nursing home care is approximately $30,000 per year (Spillman & Kemper, 1995). Thus, because of the high cost of nursing home care, many older adults and their families are concerned about having the resources to pay for care or are concerned about becoming impoverished while paying for care. Presently, there are four sources of payment of nursing home costs: Medicaid, Medicare, out-of-pocket, and long-term care insurance.

Most nursing homes are certified by the Health Care Finance Administration (HCFA) and are eligible to receive reimbursement for their services to persons qualified for Medicaid and Medicare. Annually, Medicaid pays approximately 47% of nursing home care for eligible individuals. Medicaid offers nursing home coverage to low-income individuals who meet income, asset, and medical guidelines. Medicare plays a limited role in covering nursing home costs because it pays only for *skilled nursing* services (24-hour care provided by a registered nurse, under a physician's supervision) and does not cover custodial care. Medicare pays 4.4% of nursing home costs (Spillman & Kemper, 1995).

Out-of-pocket payments made by older adults and their families amount to approximately 46% of nursing home care expenses (Spillman & Kemper, 1995). Because of the limited sources that help pay for long-term nursing home care costs, a small but growing number of adults have purchased long-term care insurance policies.

According to the Health Insurance Association of America, long-term care insurance policy sales have risen an average of 27% a year (or as many as half a million policies annually) since 1987, and approximately 3.4 million policies have been sold by 118 companies (Coronel & Fulton, 1995). Private insurance pays approximately 1% of nursing home costs (Wolf, Weisbrod, & Stearns, 1988). Older adults have been slow to purchase such policies because of the availability, cost, limited benefits, and a belief that Medicare will cover long-term care costs. The extent to which long-term care insurance will play a role in paying for long-term care costs in the future is unknown (see Zedlewski et al., 1990).

Users and Programs

Resident Characteristics

The decision to place an older adult in a nursing home is a difficult one for family and friends. Contrary to popular perception, families do not "dump" their older members in nursing homes at the first available opportunity. Like

---

For Your Files   **Long-Term Care Insurance**

The National Insurance Association of America has posted on their Web page a consumers' guide to long-term care insurance. Here is a summary of some key points. Visit their site to read the entire guide:

http://www.hiaa.org/library/iguides/ltc.html

Most long-term care insurance policies are indemnity policies that pay a fixed amount for each day of care received. Fixed amounts range from $40 to $200 per day, depending on the terms of the policy. Good policies will adjust the benefit amount each year (about 5%) to keep up with inflation.

The cost of long-term care insurance depends on the age of the beneficiary and the level of benefits and deductibles. For example, a policy offering $80 per day for 4 years, with a 20-day deductible, costs a 50-year-old approximately $50 per year, a 65-year-old about $855 per year, and a 79-year-old $3,641. The younger the age at purchase, the lower the cost; most companies, however, do not sell long-term care insurance to individuals under age 50.

Most policies cover skilled, intermediate, and custodial care as well as skilled and nonskilled home care, physical therapy, and care provided by homemaker home health aides. Some policies also cover adult day care and respite care. There are, however, exclusions for preexisting conditions and some types of disorders. Policies generally limit benefits to a maximum dollar amount or days of care.

Anyone interested in purchasing long-term care insurance should compare policies before they buy. Also check out *Consumer Reports,* which conducted in-depth reviews of long-term care insurance policies in 1988, 1991, and 1995. AARP also has resource materials available.

Sharon at the beginning of the chapter, they go to great lengths exploring other alternatives and often insist on providing caregiving activities at the expense of their personal well-being (Brody, 1985; Smallegan, 1985). Families provide an estimated 80% to 90% of long-term care to older adults while they are living in the community and continue providing assistance even after nursing home placement (Bowers, 1988; Stone et al., 1987). Nursing home placement is a community resource that is most often the last alternative used by families.

According to the U.S. Bureau of the Census (1996a), nearly 1.6 million older adults live in nursing homes, and the size of the nursing home population increased by 29% from 1980 to 1990. The increase in the percentage of oldest-old adults in nursing homes, however, is less than the increase in the size of the oldest-old population, suggesting that the rate of institutionalization of oldest-old persons might not increase as rapidly as the oldest-old population itself (65+). On the basis of past nursing home use rates, Kemper and Murtaugh (1991) estimated that the lifetime risk of institutionalization is 43% for those reaching age 65 in 1990 and that an estimated 52% of women and 33% of men would use a nursing home during their lifetimes.

Length of stay in a nursing home varies among different subpopulations as well. For example, length of stay for persons 65 years of age and older is longer for women than for men—26 months and 19 months, respectively (Freedman, 1993). Of older adults entering nursing homes for the first time, 42% die there (Dick, Garber, & McCurdy, 1994). Researchers have discovered several personal characteristics associated with the likelihood of living in a nursing home.

Age

Not surprisingly, the majority of nursing home residents are over age 75 (see Exhibit 19.1). Almost half (45%) of all nursing home residents were 85 years of age, whereas only 8% of community-dwelling older persons are 85 or older. The median age at first admission was 81 for men and 84 for women (Dick et al., 1994).

Sex

Mirroring the demographic characteristics of the older adult population, more nursing home residents are women. Seven of 10 residents are women; 34% of persons living in nursing homes are women over 85. Of women who died at 90 or older, 70% had lived in a nursing home (U.S. Bureau of the Census, 1996a).

Race

Older adults of color are underrepresented in nursing homes. As shown in Exhibit 19.2, smaller percentages of older persons of color 65 and older and 85 and older live in nursing homes compared with white elders. The differential use in nursing home care has been attributed to cost, discrimination, personal choice, and social and cultural differences (Moss & Halamandaris, 1977, cited in Yeo, 1993). According to testimony given by family members and professionals, Moss and Halamandaris concluded that all four reasons may be operating to different degrees in keeping older adults of color from

Exhibit 19.1   **Selected Characteristics of Nursing Home Residents and Community-Dwelling Residents**

Subject	Living in Nursing Homes	Living in the Community
Total Number (in thousands)	1,318	26,343
Age		
65 to 74	16.1%	61.7%
75 to 84	38.6%	30.7%
85+	45.3%	7.6%
Sex		
Women	74.6%	59.2%
Men	25.4%	40.8%
Race		
White	93.1%	90.4%
Black	6.2%	8.3%
Other	0.7%	1.3%
Marital Status		
Widowed	67.8%	34.1%
Married	12.8%	54.7%
Never married	13.5%	4.4%
Divorced/separated	5.9%	6.3%

SOURCE: U.S. Bureau of the Census, 1996a, Table 5-7.

receiving nursing home care. For example, among Pacific Asian elders, language differences and cultural differences were the most predominant explanations; among older blacks, cost and discrimination were the most important factors. Native American elders cited cost and personal choice as the most important. Older Hispanic adults identified more barriers to use than other groups—language and cultural differences, discrimination, and cost.

Marital Status and the Availability of a Caregiver

Widowed older adults represent the majority of those who live in nursing homes, followed by those who never married. Not surprisingly, the lack of an available caregiver, such as a spouse, adult child, or other relative, increases the likelihood of nursing home placement (Wingard, Jones, & Kaplan, 1987).

Exhibit 19.2 **Percentage of Long-Term Care Facility Residents by Race and Age**

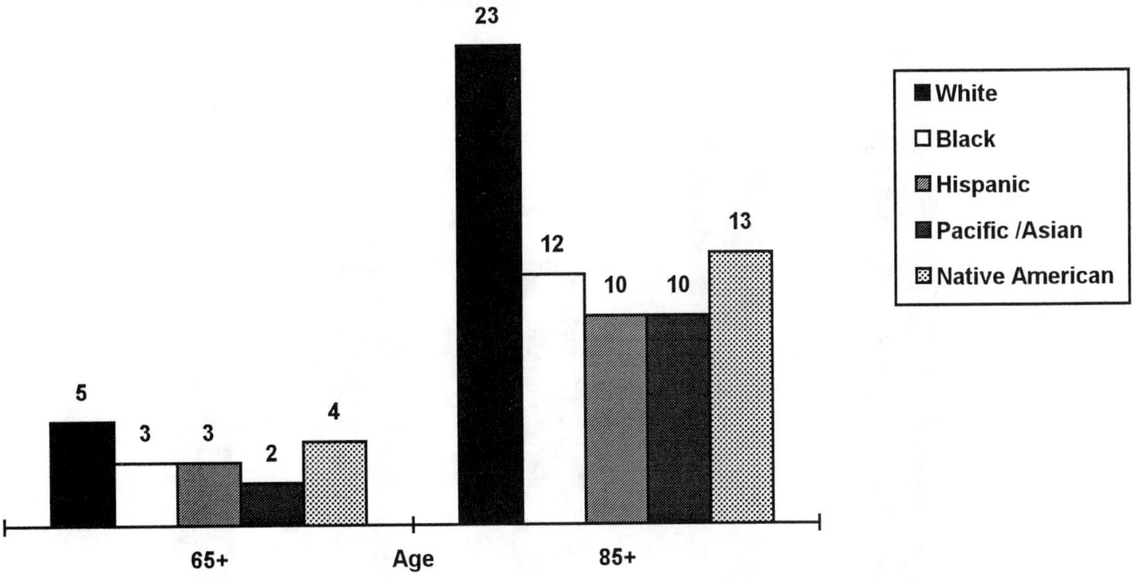

Legend:
- ■ White
- □ Black
- ▨ Hispanic
- ■ Pacific /Asian
- ▨ Native American

X-axis: 65+ / Age / 85+

Values at 65+: 5, 3, 3, 2, 4
Values at 85+: 23, 12, 10, 10, 13

SOURCE: American Association of Retired Persons Minority Affairs Initiative (1987).

Functional Status

A majority of residents of nursing homes have multiple impairments in ADLs for which they need assistance. Exhibit 19.3 shows the percentage of nursing home residents and community residents who need assistance in bathing, dressing, using the toilet, transferring, and eating. A large number of nursing home residents need assistance in all five ADLs, compared with community-dwelling older adults. More than 60% of nursing home residents need assistance in four of the five ADLs, whereas less than 7% of community-dwelling older adults need assistance in any of the five ADLs.

The percentage of residents needing assistance with ADLs increases with age. Higher percentages of residents 85 years of age and older need assistance with bathing, dressing, using the toilet, transferring, and eating and are incontinent, compared with younger residents. Thus, the majority of nursing home residents are quite old and in need of personal care assistance in a number of ADLs (see Exhibit 19.4).

Long-Term Care Facilities

Nursing home care is provided predominantly by for-profit enterprises. More than 40% are affiliated with a nursing home chain (Phillips & Hawes, 1996).

Exhibit 19.3 **Percentage of Nursing Home Residents and Community Residents Needing Assistance in Daily Activities**

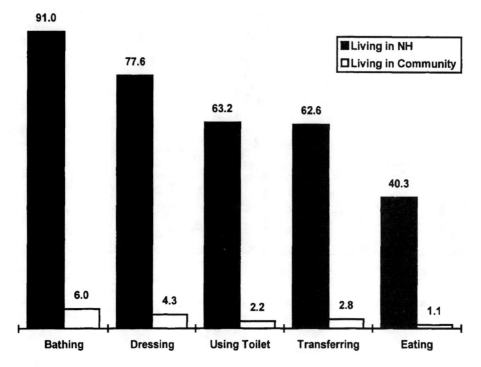

SOURCE: Compiled from U.S. Bureau of the Census, 1996a, Table 5-7.

Nonprofit nursing homes have an average of 101 beds, and for-profit homes average 87 beds; occupancy rates are, on average, around 95% (Sirrocco, 1988). The American Association of Homes and Services for the Aging (1988) reported that 2,108 of the more than 4,000 member agencies are associated with ethnic or denominational organizations. Such homes are sponsored by religious organizations including Baptist, Catholic, Mennonite, Jewish, and the United Church of Christ. Others are under national sponsorships, such as the British American Home; a few are racially specific such as the Eliza Bryant Center in Cleveland, which serves only older blacks (Kaplan & Shore, 1993).

Levels of Care

Prior to federal legislation passed in 1987, nursing homes had two levels of care on which reimbursement was based. Nursing homes were categorized as skilled nursing facilities or as intermediate care facilities. Skilled nursing facilities were designed to care for residents who needed skilled nursing care

Exhibit 19.4 **Percentage of Nursing Home Residents Who Need Assistance, by Age and Activity**

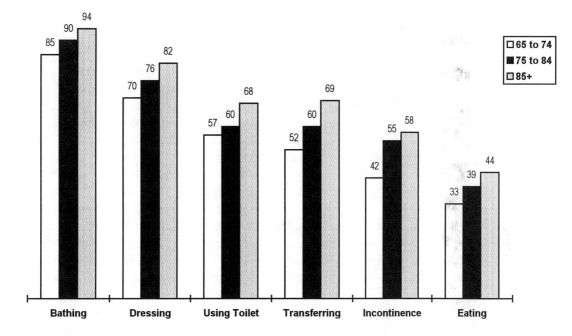

SOURCE: Hing (1987).

that was more medically oriented. Residents in intermediate care facilities required custodial, rather than skilled nursing, care. These classifications were based on Medicare and Medicaid payment criteria for nursing home care. Because the two levels of classification did not accurately reflect the variations in the functional abilities of nursing home residents, the federal government replaced the dichotomous classification with one designation—the nursing facility (Boondas, 1991). The HCFA, which administers Medicare and Medicaid, is in the process of designing a different classification system in six demonstration states. The nursing home case mix and quality demonstration project is testing a case mix classification system known as Resource Utilization Groups: Version III (RUG-III). Under the RUG classification system, nursing homes can use seven major classification groups for cost reimbursement—rehabilitation, extensive services, special care, clinically complex, impaired cognition, behavior problems, and reduced physical functions (Zbylot, Job, McCormick, Boulter, & Moore, 1995). The seven major groups are further divided into 44 case mix groups based on intensity of ADL needs. Such classification reflects the many types of residents in need of nursing home care. In part because of the increase in the number of residents with diverse health care needs, nursing homes are expanding the range of services they offer.

Subacute Care

Many long-term care facilities now offer a wide range of rehabilitative services to persons of all ages. Most notable of these services include subacute care units. *Subacute care* is provided to patients whose needs fall between acute hospital care and traditional nursing home care. Some subacute care units cater to a specific target population. For example, subacute units might specialize in serving rehabilitation patients who need help recovering from hip replacement or spinal cord injuries. Other subacute units are considered to be "medical subacute" units and serve patients who need intensive medical care, such as ventilator care, wound care, or IV therapy. Typically, subacute units require staff to be more highly trained, require more physician involvement, and use interdisciplinary teams to plan and monitor care. The growth of subacute care has been encouraged by Medicare's prospective payment system that pays hospitals a flat rate for care, resulting in a shorter length of stay (see Chapter 11). A shorter length of stay, in turn, encourages patient care in these "step-down" or subacute units. Studies of the effectiveness and efficiency of subacute care units are being conducted; it is generally thought that postacute care is a cost-effective alternative to inpatient acute hospital care (Office of the Assistant Secretary for Planning and Evaluation, 1995).

Specialized Alzheimer's Unit

In the last decade, increasing numbers of nursing homes have created specialized services to care for persons with Alzheimer's disease and other dementias. Included in these efforts are cluster settings, in which persons with dementia are grouped together on a floor or unit, and special care units (SCUs) that are housed in separate wings or buildings. SCUs have increased in part because of the special care needs of persons with various types of dementias. For example, persons with dementia are more likely to need assistance with ADLs, need help remaining continent, have psychiatric symptoms (delusions and hallucinations), and have behavioral problems (e.g., wandering and physically hurting self or others) than those without dementia (DHHS, 1991; U.S. Congress, Office of Technology Assessment, 1992). In response to a congressional request, OTA conducted a comprehensive review of the available research that exists about SCUs. The authors of the report concluded that because there is not a single agreed-on definition of SCU, it is difficult to determine the number of SCUs in existence across the country. Their best estimate, based on national data, is that 8% to 10% of nursing homes have SCUs for persons with Alzheimer's disease or dementia and that more facilities report having plans to create such units. Not surprisingly, larger nursing homes are more likely than smaller ones to have SCUs, and nursing homes in the West were more likely to report having SCUs than were homes located in other geographical areas. The majority of nursing homes indicated that residents of SCUs are charged more for their care than are residents in non-SCUs. Descriptive studies show that units vary greatly in their patient care philosophy, number of residents, physical design, staffing patterns and ratios, activity programs, and patient care practices. Patient care philosophies included goals such as to provide a safe, secure, and supportive environment for residents; reduce feelings of anxiety; maintain optimal levels of physical and cognitive functioning; and provide holistic care. The number of residents living in SCUs ranged from less than 10 to more than 40. Studies show that on average, SCU residents are younger, white, and male and are more likely to have a specific diagnosis, such as Alzheimer's disease, compared with other residents with or without dementia. SCU residents also were less likely than other nursing home residents with dementia to have impairments in ADLs but were more likely to exhibit behavioral problems.

According to the OTA (1992) report, most SCUs had some special environmental adaptations for residents, including alarm or locking systems, secured areas for wandering, and color coding of rooms and personal markers to help residents find their way around the unit. Many of the SCUs provided some type of specialized training for staff; these units had a higher staff-to-resident ratio than did non-SCUs. In addition, studies indicated that SCUs had activities designed to increase stimulation and reduce resident stress. Activities offered to residents in SCUs included singing, exercises, games, painting, field trips, reality orientation, and reminiscence therapy.

Some argue that segregating persons with dementias from other nursing home residents improves resident well-being, enhances family interaction and satisfaction, increases staff satisfaction, and improves the nursing home experience for residents who do not have dementia (Maas, 1988; Ronch, 1987). Others argue that there are no discernible differences in resident outcomes for those living in SCUs (Rabins, 1986; Ronch, 1987). Slone, Lindeman, Phillips, Moritz, and Koch (1995) evaluated studies of effectiveness of SCUs and concluded that existing studies are inconclusive because some investigators reported improvements in residents' ADL performance, mood, behavior, and cognition, whereas others found no differences in these outcomes. These seemingly contradictory findings are due to the difficulty in controlling for sampling variations and the differences in SCU care delivery, treatment, and outcome measurement.

For Your Files **Special Care Unit in Lynden, Washington**

The Christian Rest Home, a 150-bed nursing home in Lynden, Washington, has had a special care unit since 1988. The 15-bed special care unit was established because of staff concerns about the safety and well-being of residents with dementia who wander or have other behavioral symptoms that cannot be handled on the facility's regular units.

The special care unit consists of resident bedrooms, an activity/dining area, and an enclosed outdoor courtyard. Physical changes were made to the building to create the unit: (a) A set of doors was installed in an existing partition off the resident bedrooms and the activity/dining area; (b) a door was made in an exterior wall to give the residents access to the enclosed courtyard; and (c) keypad-operated locks were installed on the exit doors; the doors open when a number code is punched in on the keypad, and the doors open automatically when the alarm goes off. These physical changes cost less than $5,000.

Some residents of the special care unit have been transferred to the unit from other parts of the nursing home; other residents have been admitted directly from home. Although all the special care unit residents have dementia in the opinion of the facility staff, a few have not had a diagnosis of dementia in their medical records.

The objectives of the unit are to ensure the residents' safety, to reduce agitation and behavioral symptoms, to maintain independent functioning, and to improve the residents' quality of life. The staff members perceive resident agitation and behavioral symptoms as significant expressions of feelings and unmet needs. They attempt to understand and respond to those feelings and needs in the belief that by doing so, they will reduce agitation and behavioral symptoms and improve the residents' quality of life. Although many of the residents exhibited severe behavioral symptoms before coming to the unit, the unit staff reports that these symptoms are relatively easily managed on the special care unit.

Formal and informal activity programs are conducted on the unit. Each afternoon, there is a formal activity program, such as a weekly Bible study and music group, a weekly reminiscence group, a weekly "validation" group, and "high tea"—a Monday afternoon event with real china and lace tablecloths. Other activities, such as food preparation and singing, take place informally on the unit. One resident who likes to fold laundry is encouraged to do so. Family members are welcome on the unit at any time. Staff members know the residents' families and involve them in decisions about the residents' care. Staff members report that family members often thank them for the help they give the residents and the emotional support they give the family members.

During the day, the staff on the special care unit consists of one registered nurse, who functions as the unit coordinator, and two nurse aides. A licensed practical nurse and two other nurse aides take over for the evening shift. Because staff consistency is considered important for the unit, the unit staff members generally are not rotated to other units.

Special care unit residents are discharged from the unit when the staff considers that the residents can no longer benefit from the unit. Several spouses of former special care unit residents have created an informal support group that meets almost daily in the facility, presumably to replace the emotional support they previously received from the unit staff.

SOURCE: U.S. Congress, Office of Technology Assessment (1992).

Staffing Patterns

Nursing homes have a variety of professionals and paraprofessionals who provide care to their residents. The number of staff in each area depends on the number of beds; those certified by Medicare and Medicaid have to meet certain staffing requirements. Nursing homes generally have departments that are responsible for resident or social services, administrative services, rehabilitation, nursing, supportive services, and dietary services. Social services staff work with residents and their families to assist them in adjusting to the social and emotional aspects of living in the facility. In addition, social service staff offer medically related social and psychological treatment goals for residents. Nursing homes with 120 beds or more must employ a director of social services; smaller homes may employ a social service director on a consultant basis (Allen, 1987).

Mental health services may be provided by staff or contracted out with mental health professionals in the community. Facilities are also required to offer residents an activities program that enhances their physical, social, and psychological well-being. Staff in the activities department usually have training in recreational or therapeutic programming and are responsible for developing and implementing social and recreational activities for all residents. Activities staff also are responsible for recruiting, training, and using volunteers to assist with activities. Administrative services staff are responsible for processing admissions and financial accounting. Rehabilitation services such as physical, occupational, and speech therapies can be provided by qualified staff or contracted with outside companies. The goal of various therapies is to help the resident achieve the desired level of functioning in ADLs (Allen, 1987).

Support services staff tend to the cleanliness of the facility, laundry, and maintenance of the physical systems in the nursing home. Staff in the dietary department are responsible for the nutritional needs of the residents. Nursing departments are in charge of the delivery of nursing and personal care services to its residents. Nursing homes employ registered nurses and licensed practical nurses to deliver and oversee medical care, whereas certified nurse aides (CNAs) provide much of the personal care of the residents.

Staff retention has been a problem in many nursing homes across the country in part because of the stressful nature of the work and the low wages (Foner, 1994). Especially problematic are the turnover rates of CNAs. CNAs are responsible for approximately 80% of direct resident care, yet turnover rates in some facilities have been as high as 75% in a given year (Harrington, 1991). Factors associated with job satisfaction and turnover rates of CNAs include wage levels, job characteristics, interpersonal relationship with nursing staff, lack of involvement in care planning and assessment of residents, and lack of advancement opportunities (Banaszak-Holl & Hines, 1994; Foner, 1994; Wacker, 1996).

Activity Programs

As mentioned above, nursing homes are required to provide activity programs that enhance residents' physical and mental well-being. Indeed, researchers have shown that participation in activities is important to residents' quality of life (Lawton, 1989; Riddick & Keller, 1991). Nursing homes frequently offer discussion groups, religious groups and services, music programs, raised garden beds, pet visitation, exercise programs, and of course, bingo. One activity that fosters a helping relationship between nursing home residents and young adults are intergenerational learning programs. The purpose of these programs is to bring young people and older adults together in a way that allows both older and younger adults to assist one another. For example, an intergenerational learning program between one Illinois nursing home and a local elementary school provided both residents and students with positive interactions (Angelis, 1990). Students helped residents with letter writing and other activities, while residents often read to students and engaged in playing games. Students and residents exchanged cards and presents on birthday and participated in intergenerational group activities. In addition, several residents attended classes at the elementary school, and a school activity newsletter was sent to the residents every month. Intergenerational programs involving students and residents offer students an educational experience and improve resident well-being.

Resident Rights and the Ombudsman Program

As we discussed earlier in the chapter, older adults living in nursing homes suffer from multiple physical or cognitive impairments. By its very nature,

Best Practice **Community Certified Nurse Aide Training Program**

Many long-term care facilities and home health agencies struggle to recruit and retain CNAs. Training is done by most agencies on a continuing, as-needed basis. Professionals in Greeley, Colorado, decided to work together to improve the recruitment and retention rates of CNAs.

Representatives from four local nursing homes, three home health agencies, the local hospital, a residential care facility for persons with disabilities, AIMS Community College, and the gerontology program at the University of Northern Colorado came together to work on solving the CNA turnover problem in their community. With a grant from the Retirement Research Foundation, the group established the Community Certified Nurse Aide Training Program. Now all individuals who wish to become CNAs receive training through the program. The community training center offers continuity of training and a community focal point for CNA training needs.

The students receive more hours of training than required by law and, once hired, spend a week with a trained preceptor before working on their own. After they have been on the job for a month, they return to the training center for two follow-up sessions that cover topics such as teamwork, stress management, time management, and death and dying. The training program is also responsible for training the preceptors who work with the newly hired CNAs at their facilities. With the assistance of AIMS Community College, a CNA recruitment video was created, and recruitment efforts are conducted throughout the county.

For more information, contact Robbyn Wacker, Ph.D., University of Northern Colorado, 1000 Gunter Hall, Greeley, CO 80639, 970-351-1582, or e-mail (rwacker@hhs.univnorthco.edu).

institutional living tends to compromise individual choices. Thus, long-term care ombudsman programs were created to act as advocates for older adults living in nursing homes and board and care homes. In response to concerns raised about the quality of care provided in nursing homes, the federal government funded seven nursing home ombudsman demonstration projects in the early 1970s to establish a mechanism for receiving and resolving complaints regarding the delivery of nursing home care, to document problems in nursing homes, and to test the effectiveness of using volunteer ombudsmen (U.S. Senate Special Committee on Aging, 1993). By 1975, the AoA funded small resident rights programs in all 50 states, and in 1978, the ombudsman program was incorporated into the Older Americans Act. In 1981,

---

For Your Files **National Citizens' Coalition for Nursing Home Reform**

The National Citizens' Coalition for Nursing Home Reform, founded in 1975, is a nonprofit consumer advocacy group whose mission is to ensure quality of care for people in the long-term care system. There are more than 300 state and local member groups and approximately 1,000 members in 40 states. The coalition reviews and distributes information on legislative and regulatory issues; develops training and resource materials for those who act as advocates for nursing home residents; and connects local, state, and national organizations with long-term care experts and resources. The coalition also publishes a variety of resource materials and books, including the *Quality Care Advocate*, a bimonthly newsletter on issues relating to nursing home care and the use of restraints, and a recent book titled *Nursing Homes: Getting Good Care There*.

For more information, contact National Citizens' Coalition for Nursing Home Reform, 1424 16th Street NW, Suite 202, Washington, DC 20036-2211, 202-332-2275 (http://www.aginet.com/nccnhr).

---

ombudsmen were also directed to serve persons living in board and care homes. In 1995, there were 565 local ombudsman programs in the United States handling some 162,338 complaints (AoA, 1995b). Congress established separate authorization of $20 million for the ombudsman program in 1988; in 1992, Congress appropriated $8.3 million for ombudsman and elder abuse programs. In the reauthorization of the OAA in 1996, ombudsman services have been reorganized under Title III-B and have $4.449 million earmarked for such services (AoA, 1997a).

Under the OAA, each state must establish and operate a long-term care ombudsman program. Under the direction of a full-time state ombudsman, programs are directed to (a) identify, investigate, and resolve complaints regarding welfare of nursing home residents; (b) provide for the training of staff and volunteers working in ombudsman programs; (c) represent the interests of the residents before governmental agencies; (d) provide information to public agencies regarding the problems of nursing home residents; and (e) monitor the development of laws and regulations affecting the care of residents (U.S. Senate Special Committee on Aging, 1993).

One primary responsibility of ombudsmen is to protect the rights of residents. Resident rights are based on federal and state laws that are designed to protect the basic liberties of nursing home residents (see Exhibit 19.5). For

Exhibit 19.5   Summary of Nursing Home Residents' Rights

A. The right to be fully informed about
   - All services available and all charges
   - The facility's rules and regulations
   - How to contact the state ombudsman and other advocacy organizations
   - the state survey reports on the facility

B. The right to participate in their own care and to
   - Receive adequate or appropriate health care
   - Be informed of their medical condition, participate in treatment planning, and be invited to participate in care planning
   - Refuse medication and treatment
   - Participate in discharge planning and review their medical records
   - Have daily communication in their language
   - Have assistance if there is sensory impairment

C. The right to make independent choices, including the right to
   - Know that choices are available
   - Make independent personal decisions
   - Choose a physician
   - Participate in activities of the community inside and outside the facility and to participate in a resident council
   - Vote

D. The right to privacy and confidentiality, including the right to
   - Private and unrestricted communication with any person of their choice, including privacy for telephone calls, unopened mail, and privacy for meetings with family and friends and other residents
   - Privacy in treatment and care for personal needs
   - Have reasonable access to any entity or individual that provides health, social, legal, or other services
   - Confidentiality regarding medical, personal, and financial affairs

E. The right to security for possessions, including the right to
   - Manage financial affairs
   - File a complaint with the state agencies for abuse, neglect, or misappropriation of their property

F. The right to dignity, respect and freedom, including the right to
   - Be treated with consideration, respect, and dignity
   - Be free from mental and physical abuse
   - Be free from physical and chemical restraints
   - Have self-determination

G. The right to remain in the facility, including the right to
   - Be transferred or discharged only for medical reasons, if needs cannot be met in the facility, if the health and safety of other residents are endangered, or for nonpayment of stay
   - Receive notice of transfer: a 30-day notice for transfer out of the facility, including (a) reason for transfer, (b) effective date, (c) location to which the resident is discharged, (d) a statement of right to appeal, and (e) the name, address, and telephone number of the state long-term care ombudsman
   - Have sufficient preparation to ensure a safe transfer or discharge

H. The right to raise concerns or complaints, including the right to
   - Present grievances to the staff of the nursing home, or to any other person, without fear of reprisal
   - Prompt efforts by the facility to resolve grievances

I. The facility must maintain identical policies and practices regarding
   - Transfer, discharge, and provision of services for all residents regardless of payment source

SOURCE: Adapted from Burger, Fraser, Hunt, & Frank (1996).

Best Practice **Heart to Heart**

Heart to Heart, unveiled in February 1996 in Austin, Texas, has the ambitious goal of placing a volunteer ombudsman in every nursing home in Texas. Heart to Heart is a collaborative effort between the American Association of Retired Persons and the Texas Department on Aging. AARP will use its large, well-organized volunteer organization to recruit volunteer ombudsmen throughout the state. The Department on Aging will then train and certify the volunteers. The goal is to increase the number of volunteer ombudsmen from 700 to 1,200. This will enable volunteers to be placed in the 500 homes that the ombudsman program does not cover. The volunteer ombudsmen's duties will include helping residents, families, and friends identify, investigate, and resolve complaints. The ombudsmen will seek out and visit with the more isolated residents to make sure the residents' needs are being met. Without on-site ombudsmen and with more than 1,100 nursing homes in the state, many residents and their families have no outside person to listen to their concerns. Worse, many nursing home residents have no family or friends at all.

By joining forces, AARP, a private organization, and the Texas Department on Aging, a governmental organization, together have challenged the whole state to make quality of care in nursing homes a top priority. For more information, contact the Texas Department on Aging, P.O. Box 12786, Austin, TX 78711, 800-252-2412, or the AARP state office at 512-480-9797.

---

example, resident rights legislation includes the rights to receive information; participate in planning all types of care; make choices and independent personal decisions; enjoy privacy in care and confidentiality regarding medical, personal, and financial matters; be treated with dignity and respect; have personal possessions that are kept safe and secure; and have advance notice of transfer or change of rooms or roommates (Burger, Fraser, Hunt, & Frank, 1996).

Ombudsmen also deal with a wide range of other issues, including resolving problems that residents might have with their public benefits or guardianship procedures. Netting, Paton, and Huber (1992) examined ombudsman program reports sent to the AoA in 1990 to determine the nature of complaints received by long-term care ombudsman programs. They found that the largest number of complaints were related to resident care and included such things as not being dressed, physical abuse, neglect, and poorly trained staff. The next most frequent category of complaints was administrative complaints about understaffing, roommate conflict, and laundry procedures, followed by resident rights. In 1995, the complaints most frequently received by ombudsmen from residents in board and care homes were about menu quality, building disrepair, administration of medication, and staff respect and attitude (AoA, 1995b).

In their study of ombudsman programs, Monk, Kaye, and Litwin (1984) identified two models of ombudsman activities. The *patient rights model* is perceived as a watchdog approach designed to create systemic change in long-term care services. The *quality of life model* is based on resolving resident difficulties with staff on a more informal level. Of course, many programs may use both elements in delivering services. Regardless of the model selected by local programs, they all rely on well-trained staff to deliver program services. Some programs use paid staff, volunteers, or a combination of both to deliver its services. In a study of ombudsman programs in 46 states, 26 states reported that they used mostly volunteer staff, and 20 used primarily paid staff (U.S. Senate Special Committee on Aging, 1993). Although using volunteer ombudsmen has some drawbacks (see Monk et al., 1984), some programs have successfully relied on volunteers to provide services. For example, the East Tennessee Advocates for Elders Program has successfully used volunteer ombudsmen since 1978 and, in 1989, had 94 volunteers who were trained or being trained as ombudsmen (Netting & Hinds, 1989). The program covers a 16-county area and serves 104 nursing homes and board and care homes.

Resident Councils

In an attempt to give residents input in the quality of care that they receive, resident councils have emerged as a vehicle to voice residents' concerns. Meyer (1991) collected data about the activities of resident councils through participant observations and interviews with residents as well as statewide resident council members and staff. Resident councils usually meet once a month with the activities director facilitating the meetings; meetings are usually attended by 15 to 30 residents. On the basis of her observations, Meyer concluded that resident councils have at least four functions. First, they make modest changes in the care they receive and condition of the home. For example, specific items discussed at council meetings included acquiring shower chairs for frail residents, more frequent adjustment of window blinds by staff, and parking of carts and wheelchairs on only one side of the hallway. Their success in accomplishing these and other goals were mixed. Resident councils were more successful in obtaining products than they were in changing procedures or services. Second, resident councils provide services to residents and the needy living in their communities. Residents make and sell handcrafted items; the funds are used to assist residents who experienced a financial crisis or are given to charitable organizations. Third, they broaden the scope of social activities available to residents. These activities included feeding birds; planning ethnic and cultural menus and activities; and arranging social outings to nearby restaurants, zoos, and theaters. Finally, resident councils cooperate with resident councils at other nursing homes to lobby for improvements in quality of care.

Although resident councils were unsuccessful in changing procedures, participation in resident councils gave residents a sense of having some control over their lives and a chance to participate in beneficial activities. Meyer (1991) also identified barriers to participation in resident councils. Many residents have difficulty hearing, are entering nursing homes with more functional limitations, and have shorter average length of stays. Some residents did not participate because they felt that councils were ineffective in creating change, and others feared retaliation for voicing complaints. Overall, resident councils play an important role in improving the lives of nursing home residents. More research is needed, however, to determine ways to improve participation and outcomes.

Improving Quality of Life in Nursing Homes

The issue of quality of care has been a concern since nursing homes were formally established decades ago. Indeed, substandard resident care and resident abuse have led to nursing homes being one of the most regulated enterprises in the country. Quality of care includes a wide variety of indicators from the small details of accommodating personal preference to the delivery of personal and medical care.

Stop and consider for a moment how you begin a typical day. You get yourself up, shower and dress, and grab a bite to eat before you go on your way. You decide when to get up, what to wear, and what to eat. You also probably have routines built into your morning as well—perhaps enjoying a cup of coffee and reading the paper before having breakfast. The mere fact of residing in an institution compromises these types of personal freedoms to some extent. Higher-quality homes attempt to accommodate personal differences, employ well-trained staff, and deliver high-quality medical care.

A landmark work, *Improving Quality of Care in Nursing Homes* (Institute of Medicine, 1986), was instrumental in identifying key indicators of quality of care in nursing homes. Specific indicators that measured resident outcome and care process were identified. Negative indicators included excessive use of psychotropic drugs, high incidence of avoidable decubitus ulcers and urinary tract infections, dehydration, and considerable weight loss. Personal care indicators included whether residents' hair was neat and clean, whether they were dressed in their own clothing, whether they received daily oral care, and whether they received prompt response to resident call lights. Nutritional and dietary indicators included assisting residents who need help eating, serving food while it is still warm, and giving residents some choice in menu selections. Finally, overall quality of care indicators included living in a clean environment in which residents are allowed to have personal possessions and furnishings in their rooms, opportunities for personal choice, participation in social activities, and treatment by staff with dignity.

The extent to which nursing homes fail to provide good quality of care has been well documented. For example, in a survey of nursing home staff, Pillemer and Moore (1989) found that 36% of nursing home staff had seen at least one resident physically abused in the last year, and 10% admitted to physically abusing residents. Eighty-one percent reported seeing residents psychologically abused—most often in the form of being yelled at. In addition, treatment of residents has been found to be related to personal characteristics. Residents with higher incomes, more personal possessions, and visitors at least once a month and who were white received better overall quality of care (Pillemer, 1988).

Although much of what is reported in the popular press and to some extent in professional publications focuses on poor-quality care provided in some homes, researchers have identified positive outcomes for residents and family members after nursing home placement. For example, Smith and Bengston (1979) found in their 2-year study of nursing home residents and their families that 70% reported that the consequences of nursing home placement was positive. Families reported a renewed or continued closeness among family members as well as a reduction in caregiving stress, which in turn resulted in more time to focus on the emotional aspects of the relationship. Families also saw improvements in residents' physical and mental health and were pleased to see residents developing new relationships with other residents. For example, one resident stated a positive outcome, "I learned to walk when I got here." Another commented, "I've gained weight. You better believe it. I was going downhill rather rapidly before [moving into the nursing home]" (AARP, 1990, p. 13).

Challenges for Nursing Homes in the Future

For most of the general public, the nursing home stands as a symbol of all that is dreaded about old age—its residents are physically and mentally impaired, they have become dependent on others to accomplish the most basic tasks of daily living, and they appear lonely and discarded by society. Popular news programs report of the abuses that occur within its confines. These images are embedded in our collective consciousness. Nursing homes do care for those who are among the most frail and debilitated in our society; some facilities are better than others. But rather than view nursing homes with contempt, we must embrace them as necessary places within the continuum of care and work to enhance the quality of care provided to their residents. Improving quality of care is like putting together pieces of a puzzle. No one piece will solve the problems that exist in nursing homes because many pieces need to be addressed.

Reforming Reimbursement and Payment of Long-Term Care Facility Services

Having Medicaid as the largest third-party payer of nursing home care causes a number of problems. First, many have observed that Medicaid reimbursement rates are terribly inadequate, especially for those with high care needs (Swan & Benjamin, 1990). For example, in 1992, Arkansas's Medicaid program paid $49 per day, Mississippi's paid $58, and New York State's paid $125. The average per day rate across all Medicaid programs was $77.45 (Phillips & Hawes, 1996). This in turn has led, according to some scholars, to structural discrimination toward Medicaid residents in the form of long waiting lists and preferential treatment toward private-pay residents (Abend-Wein, 1991; Estes, Swan, & Associates, 1993; Grimaldi, 1982). Second, for middle-class families, the only alternative to paying for nursing home costs has been to impoverish themselves to qualify for nursing home care. How many older families, or their children, for that matter, who need to secure extended long-term care services can afford $100 per day—more than $30,000 per year—for nursing home care? Many health scholars have called for developing a more rational system for financing nursing home care—one that combines both public and private financing (Aiken, 1989; Estes et al., 1993). An increase in public support, either directly or through taxation, is needed, along with an increase in private sector insurance to help spread the risk of long-term care across different sectors of society and make nursing home care more affordable.

Attracting Qualified Staff and Improving Working Conditions

To increase the number of qualified staff applying for positions and working in nursing homes, we must endeavor to reduce the stigma associated with working in a nursing home among all professional and certified staff. Anecdotal evidence suggests that nursing homes are often the last employment choice of newly graduated nurses. Nursing programs can work to encourage the placement of their students into long-term care. Just as initiatives have been developed to increase the number of nurses placed in rural areas, so too should initiatives be implemented to increase the number of nurses placed in long-term care facilities. Of course, chances of attracting qualified staff are improved if working conditions and benefits are competitive. Salary and benefits must be competitive with both the medical and nonmedical employment sectors, opportunities for professional advancement must exist, and the organizational climate must convey a sense of respect and appreciation for its employees.

Increasing Family and Community Involvement

Researchers have discovered a link between increased volunteer and family visits and improved quality of care. Staff and those in the aging network must work together to improve the amount of community involvement in nursing homes. Something as simple as having the AAA advisory board meet every month in the nursing home's conference room could increase the amount of contact between "outsiders" and the nursing home community. One facility in Boston has started a "Love Is Ageless" program that encourages all nursing homes to display a banner proclaiming that love is ageless and inviting visitors from the community. They project that if only 3 new people visited each nursing home across the country, 15,000 new visitors would result.

Meeting the Care Needs of a Diverse Group of Residents

The changing nature of the health care delivery system means that the type of care provided in nursing homes will have to change as well. As more community-based alternatives emerge for persons who need custodial care, nursing homes will no doubt emerge as primary places for more therapeutic and rehabilitative care. Furthermore, the increased number of persons with AIDS who will need long-term nursing may have a hand in shaping the future of nursing homes (Aiken, 1989).

Supporting the Future of Long-Term Care Facilities

The 1995 White House Conference on Aging passed a resolution aimed at developing alternative options for funding long-term care. The delegates supported policies that establish (a) affordable public and private long-term care insurance plans, (b) uniform standards and consumer protection for long-term care insurance, and (c) the inclusion of payment for home care and community-based services in long-term care insurance policies. As the next century approaches, long-term care facilities will be faced with a myriad of social and organizational challenges.

 CASE STUDY

DEFENDING INDIVIDUAL RIGHTS: A NURSING HOME'S DILEMMA

Edna, an 83-year-old with mild dementia, has lived in a nursing home for the past 3 years. Her only remaining family is an estranged daughter. Although she can walk with assistance, she prefers to use a wheelchair. Edna has formed a strong attachment to George, a 90-year-old with moderate to severe dementia depending on the day and his stress level. George's chart also documents a diagnosis of transient ischemic attacks. George is quite handsome and is "the catch of the nursing home." Edna feels important when George is pushing her around in her wheelchair. Being with George has become a status symbol for Edna. George's roommate, Bud, has complained that he does not have any privacy. Edna and George neglect to pull the privacy curtain when they are lying in George's bed. Bud's family also has complained about how embarrassing it is, especially for younger family members, to find Edna and George in bed together when they visit. Edna's daughter called the nursing home and told the head nurse that the facility should stop this relationship because Edna and George were too old to have sex. She demanded that something be done immediately and indicated that if some measures were not taken, she would move her mother to another facility.

The staff of the facility have offered Edna and George the opportunity to room together. Some staff members are uncomfortable with this relationship because George is more confused than Edna, and they feel that she dominates the relationship. They suspect that she can be physically abusive to George if he refuses to spend time with her. They have observed such jealous behavior during group activities and in the dining room when other women try to sit next to George. Other staff members believe that to try to separate the couple would be a violation of their rights to choose their own companions. George's two sons are not adamantly opposed to George's being with Edna. They find it amusing and have joked about it in front of the staff.

Edna and George decide to be roommates. After 3 days together, George has many bruises on his arms and face. Staff members notice that he is attempting to avoid Edna. They ask George if he wants to move back into his old room, and he replies that he does. Staff members move George back to his room. Within a day, George is seeking Edna out and refuses to leave her. Staff decide to call the local long-term care ombudsman for technical assistance.

CASE STUDY QUESTIONS

1. As the long-term care ombudsman, what additional information would you like to know?

2. What resident rights are in question in this case scenario?

3. Whose interests must be considered? Do any of these interests take precedence over any of the others?

4. Do you believe it is a violation of George and Edna's rights to keep them separated? Why or why not?

5. Can you think of a creative compromise that would mostly satisfy all parties in this case? Are there any other community resources or agencies that could be called on to assist staff? Family members? George or Edna? Bud?

 ## LEARNING ACTIVITIES

1. Visit a resident council meeting at a local nursing home. What issues were discussed at the meeting? How many residents and staff attended? Interview the chair of the resident council. Have the chair reflect on the council's accomplishments during the last year.

2. Join the *Gerinet Listserv* discussion group. For instructions on how to log on, go to the *Community Resources for Older Adults* Web site (http://www.hhs.unco.edu/geron.htm). Monitor the discussion during a 2-week period. What issues are discussed by the group?

3. Obtain a map of your city and mark on the map the locations of the nursing homes in your community. On the same map, draw a line around what you believe are low-income or minority neighborhoods. Where are the nursing homes located in relation to these neighborhoods? If you live in a rural area, determine how far away these facilities are from smaller rural towns. What are the implications of the geographic location of these nursing homes?

 ## FOR MORE INFORMATION

National Resources

1. American Association of Homes and Services for the Aging, 901 E Street NW, Suite 500, Washington, DC 20004-2037, 202-783-2242.

   The American Association of Homes and Services for the Aging is the national association for nonprofit organizations involved in providing health, community, and related services to older adults. It distributes free information on a variety of issues including long-term care.

2. American Health Care Association, 1201 L Street NW, Washington, DC 20005, 202-842-4444.

   The American Health Care Association provides leadership in dealing with long-term care issues, offers continuing education programs for nursing home professionals, and publishes *Provider*, a monthly magazine for its members.

3. National Citizens' Coalition for Nursing Home Reform, 1424 16th Street NW, Suite 202, Washington, DC 20036-2211, 202-332-2275.

   The coalition works to achieve quality of care in nursing homes by conducting advocacy training, promotes best practices in care delivery, and provides publications on institutional-based long-term care. It also operates the National Long-Term Care Ombudsman Resource Center.

Web Resources

1. Health Insurance Association of America
   http://www.hiaa.org

   The Health Insurance Association of America has a number of consumer guides online, including one on long-term care insurance. The information about long-term care insurance is comprehensive and covers such topics as "Are you likely to need long-term care?" "What kind of insurance is available?" "What do policies cost?" and "What do long-term care insurance policies cover?" It is a good primer on long-term care insurance.

2. American Health Care Association Brochure on Long-Term Care Insurance
   http://www.napsnet.com/money/35400.html

   In contrast to the above Web information on long-term care insurance, this is an announcement of how to obtain a brochure for consumers about private long-term care insurance.

3. Nursing Facility Resource
   http://www.terranet.net/users/r/rbellora/

   A nursing home administrator in Kansas has put together his own home page to share information and news about nursing home facility operations. Even for those not interested in becoming nursing home administrators, the site has information about regulations and business practices that affect the quality and level of care given to residents.

4. Office of the Ombudsman
   http://www.ombud.gov.bc.ca/index.html

   This Web page does a good job of explaining what an ombudsman is and does and how to use one. The site also has links to other related resources.

5. MedAccess

   http://www.medaccess.com

   This site's stated goal is to be the premier provider of health and wellness information. On the basis of the amount of information it contains, it comes close to achieving this goal. Tucked away under its link called *Just for Seniors* is a guide to choosing a nursing home. Visitors may also take their health quiz.

6. Guide to Nursing Homes in Florida

   http://www-wane-leon.scri.fsu.edu/AHCA/NURSDAT/index-frame.html

   Even for nonresidents of Florida, this site is worth the visit. The Agency for Health Care Administration has created a home page with links to information about tips on finding a nursing home. Visitors can search the guide by region or by key word.

Part III

Preparing for the Future

20

Programs and Services in an Era of Change

In the previous chapters of this book, we have described the wide array of programs and services that exist to assist older adults. Yet to end without describing the important issues facing the nation with regard to service delivery of programs would present an incomplete picture. The programs and services we have described throughout this book exist within a social and political context that influences their existence, the nature of what they offer, and to whom they offer services. In this final chapter, we discuss the social forces that have brought us to a crossroads of aging policy and service delivery. We then discuss some key issues that will need to be addressed with subsequent reauthorizations of the Older Americans Act. We conclude with some thoughts about the changing nature of U.S. society and its implications for aging professionals.

Social and Political Influences on Aging Policies and Programs

Two key social and political factors that have emerged in the last decade are forcing a reexamination of aging policies, and in turn, the programs and services they fund. First, the number of people 65 and older is steadily increasing, and, concomitantly, there has been a steady increase in the percentage of the federal budget spent on older adults. Second, society's current image of older adults commonly portrays them as healthy, wealthy, and self-consumed. Such an image drives the opinion that programs and services for older adults are no longer needed. Thus, these social forces have influenced a discussion regarding possible solutions to "fix" Medicare, to stabilize Social Security in the 21st century, and to "protect" society from buckling under the weight of its burdensome older population. Many scholars have argued against the assumptions that older adults are a burden to society and that all older adults are financially and socially comfortable and have voiced the need for society to acknowledge the benefits, both direct and indirect, everyone experiences when society cares for its elders (see Kingston, Hirshorn, & Cornman, 1986; Marmor, Mashaw, & Harvey, 1990).

Because the OAA is the one of the key social policies created to serve older adults, it too has been the focus of much debate. Do we need an Older Americans Act? If so, what role should it play and who should its programs serve? We will examine some of the issues currently being debated that will shape the future of the OAA.

Challenges for the Older Americans Act

Policymakers and advocates of older adults are currently reexamining a number of issues associated with the OAA. The reauthorization of the act in 1997 has given professionals in the field of aging an opportunity to debate the role of the OAA, to think about new ways of increasing linkages with the private sector, and to reexamine who should be eligible for services.

The Role of the Older Americans Act

As numerous scholars have pointed out, the growth of the older adult population has exceeded the funding level for OAA programs for many years, and new amendments expanding the role of the aging network have been added in recent years without an increase in funding (Kutza, 1991). It is unlikely that an increase in funding will be forthcoming. Therefore, a reexamination of the role of the OAA has been called for by some. Kutza has suggested that the OAA be restructured to reflect its strengths: its advocacy role on behalf of older adults, its role in meeting the nutritional needs of older adults, and its role in providing information and referral services. A restructuring of this nature would allow area agencies on aging to concentrate its efforts on fewer services, rather than the multitude it now covers. Another possible change in the act could be to allow local AAAs more flexibility in determining what programs their communities need and, consequently, which are funded.

Reaching Out to the Private Sector

In the era of smaller budgets and greater needs, there has been a call for the aging network to expand its effort to work with the private sector to help meet the needs of older adults. A strong private sector presence currently exists in many areas of service delivery to older adults, including housing, long-term care, case management, transportation services, and recreational opportunities. With the increase in the number of older adults and an increase in the number of older adults who have adequate income, the role of the private sector in service delivery will become even greater. This increase in private sector involvement has several implications. First, the AAAs can increase their role in forging public-private partnerships to create employment opportunities and to create additional housing options (McConnel & Beitler, 1991). AAAs can also occupy leadership positions coordinating the services and programs offered by both the public and private sectors. Second, with the increase in the service options available because of private sector involvement, a central role of AAAs may be to act as a broker of services on behalf of older adults. As the choices for housing, health care, and other services become increasingly more complex, AAAs might become more actively involved in assisting older adults in making lifestyle choices that best fit their needs.

Who Should Be Eligible for Services?

There has been considerable debate about the universality of the OAA programs and services. As we discussed in Chapter 2, older adults 60 years of age and older may participate in OAA programs regardless of their income, although the act specifically targets low-income older adults and older adults of color. Again, because of the reduction in OAA funding and the need to extend its limited dollars to reach more people, the questions of who should be targeted to receive services and what cost, if any, participants should pay for those services have been posed.

Targeting Services

Through the years, the OAA has been amended so that it targets its services to those deemed to be most in need. The idea of redefining who should be targeted to receive services has once again emerged. Should the act be revised to raise the age of eligibility? Should additional classes of individuals be targeted, such as those living in public-assisted housing, those living alone, or those who are at risk when discharged from the hospital (AoA, 1997d)? Ideally, identifying and targeting services to those most in need make programs more effective in assisting the most needy. The outcome of expanding the number of targeted groups of older adults at the exclusion of those who do not occupy those statuses is unclear.

It also has been proposed that the OAA simply target its services to low-income individuals by developing financial eligibility standards for participation in its programs (see Gelfand & Bechill, 1991). Under the current provisions of the act, programs and services are meant to service those who have both economic and social need, but programs do not use specific income eligibility guidelines.

At first glance, establishing income eligibility guidelines seems to be a reasonable solution to shrinking funding levels. There are, however, many issues to consider. Using income as a criterion for eligibility undermines the "social insurance" principle that has provided broad-based support for universal programs from a wide variety of constituencies (Hudson & Kingson, 1991). The inclusion of the middle class along with the lower class broadens the power base that helps protect the program from complete elimination. Moreover, the exclusion of older adults who have more social and financial resources than their less well-off counterparts might have a negative impact on program delivery. Many of these older adults play a key role in volunteering and assisting their less well-off counterparts. In addition, a means-based program might keep older adults from attending to avoid the social stigma attached to "welfare" programs. More important, the development of the definition of need requires a great deal of thought. Clearly, the most convenient definition of need is based on income or asset level. Aside from the concern that collecting financial information from its participants would create an additional level of bureaucracy and a paperwork nightmare, how will programs measure "social need"? How will programs measure the social need of persons for whom attending a congregate meal is their only source of social interaction? If they do not meet the income guidelines developed, are they any less needy?

On the other hand, there are some arguments for implementing income eligibility criteria. First, insufficient resources force the need to target service to those least able to afford those services. Second, the collective plight of older adults was much worse when the OAA was enacted in 1965 than it is today. Thus, as social and economic conditions of older cohorts change, the OAA must respond in kind. Clearly, any change in whom the OAA serves would have to be carefully weighed against the advantages and disadvantages of changing the eligibility criteria.

Cost Sharing

Mandating cost sharing is another option that has been proposed as a way to make program dollars go farther. Requiring cost sharing also has some advantages and disadvantages. In addition to covering program costs, cost sharing might promote a sense of equity among participants (see Chapter 3) and reduce their feelings of dependency. Evidence shows that cost sharing can be successful. Participants at congregate meal sites are asked to make a suggested donation that helps cover programmatic expenses. As we discussed in Chapter 10, participant contributions play an important role in supporting the congregate meal program. On the other hand, if programs are required to implement cost sharing as a condition of participation, they will spend a great deal of time and money on the task of collecting and managing paperwork, determining the cost-sharing amount, and collecting the fee from participants. A cost-sharing requirement also may keep the most needy from receiving services.

The discussion about creating financial eligibility guidelines or cost-sharing provisions would benefit from research that collects demographic characteristics of all OAA participants, including measures of income and social support. If most OAA programs serve primarily older adults with middle to low incomes or those with minimal social support networks, as data suggest the congregate meal programs do, to what extent would eligibility criteria be needed? How much could participants contribute before the contribution becomes a barrier? The debate about providing services based on need rather than age will no doubt continue.

Serving a New Generation of Older Adults

We conclude with some final thoughts for readers. The challenge that aging professionals have always faced, and will continue to face, is how to change the way services are delivered to meet the needs of a new cohort in a new era. As we discussed in Chapter 1, the new cohort—the baby boomers—is different in a number of ways. But what about the new era in the next century? We will experience societal changes related to the way we interact with one another and the way we do business. Consider the influence that technology has had on our lives presently and will have in the future. Computer technology has made it possible to access information almost immediately, and through chat rooms and discussion lists, we now are able to make contact with people previously unknown to us. Assistive technology also holds great promise in helping people of all ages with various functional limitations to live more independently in our communities. The central role that technology now occupies in our lives will challenge professionals to consider ways to use technology in meeting the social, psychological, and physical needs of older adults. How can technology be used to deliver services? To provide information and referral? To reach those who are socially isolated?

A new era will also bring about changes in how we define and redefine what it means to be old. Former president George Bush, at age 73, jumped from an airplane (with a parachute, of course!). A 63-year-old woman gave birth to a child. These are not the activities that come to mind when thinking about the normative behaviors of older adults! Although these activities are not reflective of the behaviors of most older adults, perhaps the importance of these behaviors lies in their symbolism. They make us rethink what we can and cannot do in our old age.

A new era will also give us an opportunity to redefine the timing of our entry into life course transitions (Atchley, 1997). For example, the timing of entering and leaving the workforce, of entering into lifelong partnerships and having children, and of pursuing educational opportunities are all changing. How will the aging network respond to these changes? Our challenge will be to make sure that the programs and services we offer to older adults will evolve along with the social changes we encounter in the coming years.

Appendix 1

State Units on Aging

Alabama   Region IV

Martha Murphy Beck, Executive Director
Alabama Commission on Aging
RSA Plaza, Suite 470
770 Washington Avenue
Montgomery, AL 36130
phone 334-242-5743, fax 334-242-5594

Alaska   Region X

Connie Sipe, Director
Alaska Commission on Aging
Division of Senior Services, Department of Administration
P.O. Box 110209
Juneau, AK 99811-0209
phone 907-465-3250, fax 907-465-4716

American Samoa   Region IX

John E. Suisala, Director
Agency on Aging and Food and Nutrition Services
Government of American Samoa
Pago Pago, American Samoa 96799
phone 9-10-288-011-684-633-1251 or 633-7720
fax 9-10-288-011-684-633-2533 or 633-7723

Arizona Region IX

Art Olin, Administrator
Aging and Adult Administration, Department of Economic Security
1789 West Jefferson Street, 950A
Phoenix, AZ 85007
phone 602-542-4446, fax 602-542-6575

Arkansas Region VI

Herb Sanderson, Director
Division Aging and Adult Services, Arkansas Department of Human
Services
P.O. Box 1437, Slot 1412
1417 Donaghey Plaza South
Little Rock, AR 72203-1437
phone 501-682-2441, fax 501-682-8155

California Region IX

California Department of Aging
1600 K Street
Sacramento, CA 95814
phone 916-322-5290, fax 916-327-3661

Colorado Region VIII

Rita Barreras, Manager
Aging and Adult Services, Department of Social Services
110 16th Street, Suite 200
Denver, CO 80202-4147
phone 303-620-4147, fax 303-620-4191

Connecticut Region I

Christine M. Lewis, Director
Community Services, Division of Elderly Services
25 Sigourney Street
Hartford, CT 06106-5033
phone 203-424-5274, fax 203-424-4966

Delaware   Region III

Eleanor Cain, Director
Delaware Department of Health and Social Services
Division of Services for Aging and Adults with Physical Disabilities
1901 North DuPont Highway
New Castle, DE 19720
phone 302-577-4791, fax 302-577-4793

District of Columbia   Region III

Jearline Williams, Executive Director
District of Columbia Office on Aging
441 Fourth Street NW, Suite 900 South
Washington, DC 20001
phone 202-724-5622, fax 202-724-4979

Florida   Region IV

Bentley Lipscomb, Secretary
Department of Elder Affairs
4040 Esplanade Way
Tallahassee, FL 32399-7000
phone 904-414-2000, fax 904-414-6216

Georgia   Region IV

Judy Hagebak, Director
Division of Aging Services, Department of Human Resources
2 Peachtree Street NE, 18th Floor
Atlanta, GA 30303
phone 404-657-5258, fax 404-657-5285

Guam   Region IX

Arthur U. San Agustin, MHR, Acting Administrator
Division of Senior Citizens, Department of Public Health and Social
Services
P.O. Box 2816
Agana, Guam 96932
phone 671-475-0262/3, fax 671-477-2930

Hawaii Region IX

Marilyn Seely, Director
Hawaii Executive Office on Aging
335 Merchant Street, Room 241
Honolulu, HI 96813
phone 808-586-0100, fax 808-586-0185, modem 586-0184

Idaho Region X

Jesse Berain, Director
Idaho Commission on Aging
Statehouse, Room 108
Boise, ID 83720
phone 208-334-3833, fax 208-334-3033

Illinois Region V

Maralee Lindley, Director
Illinois Department on Aging
421 East Capitol Avenue, Suite 100
Springfield, IL 62701-1789
phone 217-785-2870
Chicago office: phone 312-814-2630, fax 217-785-4477

Indiana Region V

Bobby Conner, Director
Division of Disability, Aging and Rehabilitative Services
Family and Social Services Administration
Bureau of Aging and In-Home Services
402 W. Washington Street
Indianapolis, IN 46207-7083
phone 317-232-1147, fax 317-232-7867

Iowa Region VII

Betty Grandquist, Executive Director
Department of Elder Affairs
Jewett Building, Suite 236
914 Grand Avenue
Des Moines, IA 50319
phone 515-281-4646, fax 515-281-4036

Kansas   Region VII

Thelma Hunter Gordon, Secretary
Department on Aging
Docking State Office Building, Room 150
915 SW Harrison
Topeka, KS 66612-1505
phone 913-296-4986, fax 913-296-0256

Kentucky   Region IV

S. Jack Williams, Director
Kentucky Division of Aging Services, Department of Social Services
275 East Main Street, 6 West
Frankfort, KY 40621
phone 502-564-6930, fax 502-564-4595

Louisiana   Region VI

Robert Fontenot, Executive Director
Governor's Office of Elderly Affairs
P.O. Box 80374
Baton Rouge, LA 70898-0374
phone 504-925-1700, fax 504-925-1749

Maine   Region I

Christine Gianopoulos, Director
Bureau of Elder and Adult Services, Department of Human Services
35 Anthony Avenue
State House, Station #11
Augusta, ME 04333
phone 207-626-5335, fax 207-624-5361

Maryland   Region III

Sue Ward, Director
Maryland Office on Aging
State Office Building, Room 1004
301 West Preston Street
Baltimore, MD 21201-2374
phone 410-225-1102, fax 410-333-7943

Massachusetts   Region I

Franklin Ollivierre, Secretary
Massachusetts Executive Office of Elder Affairs
One Ashburton Place, 5th Floor
Boston, MA 02108
phone 617-727-7750, fax 617-727-9368

Michigan   Region V

Diane K. Braunstein, Director
Office of Services to the Aging
P.O. Box 30026
Lansing, MI 48909
phone 517-373-8230, director 517-373-7876, fax 517-373-4092

Minnesota   Region V

James G. Varpness, Executive Secretary
Minnesota Board on Aging
444 Lafayette Road
Saint Paul, MN 55155-3843
phone 612-296-2770, fax 612-297-7855

Mississippi   Region IV

Eddie Anderson, Director
Division of Aging and Adult Services
750 State Street
Jackson, MS 39202
phone 601-359-4925, fax 601-359-4370

Missouri   Region VII

Jerry Simon, Acting Director
Division on Aging, Department of Social Services
P.O. Box 1337
615 Howerton Court
Jefferson City, MO 65102-1337
phone 314-751-3082, fax 314-751-8493

Montana   Region VIII

Charles Rehbein, Aging Coordinator
Senior and Long Term Care Division, Public Health and Human Services
P.O. Box 4210
Helena, MT 59604
phone 406-444-5900, fax 406-444-7788

Nebraska   Region VII

Mark Intermil, Director
Department of Health and Human Services, Division on Aging
P.O. Box 95044
301 Centennial Mall South
Lincoln, NE 68509-5044
phone 402-471-2306, fax 402-471-4619

Nevada   Region IX

Carla Sloane, Administrator
Nevada Division for Aging Services, Department of Human Resources
340 North 11th Street, Suite 203
Las Vegas, NV 89101
phone 702-486-3545, fax 702-486-3572

New Hampshire   Region I

Ronald Adcock, Director
Division of Elderly and Adult Services
State Office Park South
115 Pleasant Street, Annex Bldg. #1
Concord, NH 03301-6501
phone 603-271-4680, fax 603-271-4643

New Jersey   Region II

Ruth Reader, Director
New Jersey Division on Aging, Department of Community Affairs
101 South Broad Street, CN 807
Trenton, New Jersey 08625-0807
phone 800-792-8820 or 609-292-3766, fax 609-633-6609

New Mexico   Region VI

Michelle Lujan Grisham, Director
State Agency on Aging
La Villa Rivera Building, Ground Floor
228 East Palace Avenue
Santa Fe, NM 87501
phone 505-827-7640, fax 505-827-7649

New York   Region II

Walter G. Hoefer, Executive Director
New York State Office for the Aging
2 Empire State Plaza
Albany, NY 12223-1251
phone 800-342-9871 or 518-474-5731, fax 518-474-0608

North Carolina   Region IV

Bonnie Cramer, Director
Division of Aging
CB 29531
693 Palmer Drive
Raleigh, NC 27626-0531
phone 919-733-3983, fax 919-733-0443

North Dakota   Region VIII

Linda Wright, Director
Department of Human Services, Aging Services Division
600 South 2nd Street, Suite 1C
Bismarck, ND 58504
phone 701-328-2577, fax 701-328-5466

Northern Mariana Islands   Region IX

Gregorio S. Delos Reyes, Administrator
Office on Aging, Department of Community and Cultural Affairs
Civic Center
Commonwealth of the Northern Mariana Islands
Saipan, MP 96950
phone 9-10-288-011-670-234-6011
fax 9-10-288-011-670-234-2565

Ohio   Region V

Judith V. Brachman, Director
Ohio Department of Aging
50 West Broad Street, 8th Floor
Columbus, OH 43266-0501
phone 614-466-5500, fax 614-466-5741

Oklahoma   Region VI

Roy R. Keen, Division Administrator
Services for the Aging, Department of Human Services
P.O. Box 25352
Oklahoma City, OK 73125
phone 405-521-2281 or 405-521-2327, fax 405-521-2086

Oregon   Region X

James C. Wilson, Administrator
Senior and Disabled Services Division
500 Summer Street NE, 2nd Floor
Salem, OR 97310-1015
phone 503-945-5811, fax 503-373-7823

Palau   Region X

Lillian Nakamura, Director
State Agency on Aging
Republic of Palau
Koror, Palau 96940
phone 9-10-288-011-680-488-2736
fax 9-10-288-680-488-1662

Pennsylvania   Region III

Richard Browdie, Secretary
Pennsylvania Department of Aging
Commonwealth of Pennsylvania
400 Market Street, 6th floor
Harrisburg, PA 17101-2301
phone 717-783-1550, fax 717-772-3382

Puerto Rico   Region II

Ruby Rodriguez Ramirez, M.H.S.A.. Executive Director
Commonwealth of Puerto Rico
Governor's Office of Elderly Affairs
Call Box 50063
Old San Juan Station, PR 00902
phone 809-721-5710, 809-721-4560, 809-721-6121, fax 809-721-6510

Rhode Island   Region I

Barbara Casey Ruffino, Director
Department of Elderly Affairs
160 Pine Street
Providence, RI 02903-3708
phone 401 277-2858, fax 401-277-3664

South Carolina   Region IV

Constance C. Rinehart, Executive Director
South Carolina Division on Aging
202 Arbor Lake Drive, Suite 301
Columbia, SC 29223-4535
phone 803-737-7500, fax 803-737-7501

South Dakota   Region VIII

Gail Ferris, Administrator
Office of Adult Services and Aging
Richard F. Kneip Building
700 Governors Drive
Pierre, SD 57501-2291
phone 605-773-3656, fax 605-773-6843

Tennessee   Region IV

Emily Wiseman, Executive Director
Commission on Aging
706 Church Street, Suite 201
Nashville, TN 37243-0860
phone 615-741-2056, fax 615-741-3309

Texas   Region VI

Mary Sapp, Executive Director
Texas Department on Aging
P.O. Box 12786 Capitol Station
Austin, TX 78711
phone 512-444-2727, fax 512-440-5290

Utah   Region VIII

Helen Goddard
Division of Aging and Adult Services
Box 45500, 120 North 200 West
Salt Lake City, UT 84145-0500
phone 801-538-3910, fax 801-534-4395

Vermont   Region I

Lawrence G. Crist, Commissioner
Vermont Department of Aging and Disabilities
Waterbury Complex
103 South Main Street
Waterbury, VT 05676
phone 802-241-2400, fax 802-241-2325

Virginia   Region III

Thelma Bland Watson, Commissioner
Virginia Department for the Aging
1600 Forest Avenue, Preston Building, Suite 102
Richmond, VA 23229
phone 804-662-9333, fax 804-662-9354

Virgin Islands   Region II

Juel Rhymer Molloy, Commissioner
Virgin Islands Department of Human Services
Knud Hansen Complex, Building A
1303 Hospital Ground
Charlotte Amalie, VI 00840
phone 212-264-2976

Washington   Region X

Charles Reed, Assistant Secretary
Aging and Adult Services Administration
Department of Social and Health Services
P.O. Box 45050
Olympia, WA 98504-5050
phone 360-493-2500, fax 360-438-8633

West Virginia   Region III

William E. Lytton Jr., Interim Executive Director
West Virginia Commission on Aging
1900 Kanawha Blvd. East
Charleston, WV 25305-0160
phone 304-558-3317, fax 304-558-0004

Wisconsin   Region V

Donna McDowell, Director
Bureau on Aging, Department of Health and Social Services
P.O. Box 7851
Madison, WI 53707
phone 608-266-2536, fax 608-267-3203

Wyoming   Region VIII

Deborah Fleming, Administrator
Division on Aging, Department of Health
117 Hathaway Building, Room 139
Cheyenne, WY 82002-0480
phone 307-777-7986, fax 307-777-5340

SOURCE: Administration on Aging (1997c).

Legal Services Developers

Alabama

Derek Lee
Legal Services Developer
Alabama Commission on Aging
P.O. Box 301851
Montgomery, AL 36130-1851
phone 334-242-5743, fax 334-242-5594

Alaska   (Duties shared)

Fran Purdy
Long-Term Care Ombudsman
Office of the Long-Term Care Ombudsman
3601 C Street, Frontier Bldg., Suite 380
Anchorage, AK 99503-5209
phone 907-563-5654, fax 907-562-3040

Alaska   Also send information to

Connie Sipe
Executive Director, Division of Senior Services
Department of Administration
3601 C Street, Frontier Bldg., Suite 380
Anchorage, AK 99503-5209
phone 907-563-5654, fax 907-562-3040

This mailing list is a courtesy of the Center for Social Gerontology and the National Association of Legal Services Developers. If you know of any changes, please contact the Center for Social Gerontology at 2307 Shelby Avenue, Ann Arbor, MI 48103-3895; phone 313-665-1126.

Arizona

Ray De La Rosa
Legal Services Developer
Arizona Aging and Adult Administration, Department of Economic Security
1789 West Jefferson, 950A
Phoenix, AZ 85007
phone 602-542-6440, fax 602-542-6575

Arkansas

Beau Murray
Legal Services Developer
Arkansas Department of Human Services, Division of Aging and Adult
Services
P.O. Box 1473, Slot 1412
Little Rock, AR 72203-1437
phone 501-682-2441 or 800-950-5871 ext. 118, fax 501-682-8155

California

Chisorom U. Okwuosa
Legal Services Developer
California Department of Aging
1600 K Street, 4th Floor
Sacramento, CA 95670
phone 916-327-6849, fax 916-324-1903
e-mail: cda.cokwuosa@hwi.cahwnet.gov

Colorado

Jan Myers
Legal Services Developer for the Elderly
The Legal Center
455 Sherman Street, Suite 130
Denver, CO 80203
phone 303-722-0300 or 800-288-1376, fax 303-722-0720

Connecticut

Mimi Peck-Llewellyn
Legal Services Developer
Connecticut Elderly Services Division, Department of Social Services
25 Sigourney Street, 10th Floor
Hartford, CT 06106
phone 203-424-5244, fax 203-424-4966

Delaware

Christine Frysziacki
Deputy Director and Legal Services Development Specialist
Delaware Division on Aging
CT Building
1901 N. DuPont Highway
New Castle, DE 19720
phone 302-577-4791, fax 302-577-4793

District of Columbia

Jan May
Legal Services Developer
Legal Counsel for the Elderly/AARP
601 E Street NW
Washington, DC 20049
phone 202-434-2164, fax 202-434-6464

Florida

Karen Campbell
Senior Attorney
Florida Department of Elder Affairs
4040 Esplanade Way, Building B, Suite 152
Tallahassee, FL 32399-7000
phone 904-414-2000, fax 904-414-2006

Georgia

Natalle Thomas
Legal Services Developer
Georgia Division of Aging Services, Department of Human Resources
2 Peachtree Street, 36th Floor
Atlanta, GA 30303-3176
phone 404-657-5328, fax 404-657-5285

Hawaii

Gail Robertson
Legal Services Developer
Executive Office on Aging
1 Capital District, 250 South Hotel Street
Honolulu, HI 96813
phone 808-586-7309, fax 808-586-0185

Idaho

Omar R. Valverde
Legal Services Developer, State Adult Protection Coordinator
Idaho Commission on Aging
P.O. Box 83720
Boise, ID 83720-0007
phone 208-334-2220, fax 208-334-3033

Illinois

Lee Beneze
Legal Services Developer
Illinois Department on Aging
421 E. Capitol Avenue, Suite 100
Springfield, IL 62701-1789
phone 217-524-7945, fax 217-232-7867

Indiana

Tom Chambley
Legal Services developer
Family and Social Services Administration
Division of Disability, Aging and Rehabilitation Services
402 W. Washington, P.O. Box 7083
Indianapolis, IN 46207-7083
phone 317-232-7148, fax 317-232-7867

Iowa

Deanna Clingan-Fischer
Legal Services Developer
Iowa Department of Elder Affairs
200 Tenth Street, Clemens Building, 3rd Floor
Des Moines, IA 50309-3609
phone 515-281-4657, fax 515-281-4036

Kansas

Vern Norwood
Legal Services Developer
Kansas Department on Aging
915 SW Harrison, Docking State Office Building, Room 150
Topeka, KS 66612-1500
phone 913-296-4986 or 913-296-2717, fax 913-296-0256

Kentucky

Gary Hammonds
Legal Services Developer
Kentucky Cabinet for Human Resources
275 East Main Street, Sixth Floor West
Frankfort, KY 40621
phone 502-564-5920, fax 502-564-4595

Louisiana

Jane Thomas
Legal Services Developer
Louisiana Governor's Office of Elderly Affairs
4550 North Blvd., 2nd Floor
Baton Rouge, LA 70898-0374
phone 504-925-1700, fax 504-925-1745

Maine

Sally Wagley
Maine Bureau of Elder and Adult Services
State House, Station 11
35 Anthony Avenue
Augusta, ME 04333
phone 207-624-5335, fax 207-624-5361

Maryland

Marjorie Richmond
Legal Assistance Developer
Maryland Office on Aging
301 W. Preston Street, Room 1007
Baltimore, MD 21201-2374
phone 410-225-1074 or 800-243-3425, fax 410-333-7943

Massachusetts

Joel Samuels
Legal Services Developer
Executive Office of Elder Affairs
One Ashburton Place, Fifth Floor
Boston, MA 02108
phone 617-727-7750, fax 617-727-9368

Michigan

Mark Manrique
Legal Services Developer
Michigan Office of Services to the Aging
P.O. Box 30026
Lansing, MI 48909
phone 517-373-4076, fax 517-373-4092

Minnesota

Betty A. Berger
Legal Assistance Developer
Minnesota Board on Aging
Human Services Building, Fourth Floor
444 Lafayette Road
Saint Paul, MN 55155-3843
phone 612-296-0378, fax 612-297-7855
e-mail: betty.berger@state.mn.us

Mississippi

Tom Coward
Legal Assistance Developer
Mississippi Division of Aging and Adult Services, Department of Human
Services
750 N. State Street
Jackson, MS 39202
phone 601-359-4929, fax 601-359-4370

Missouri

Rita Summers
Aging Program Specialist
Missouri Division on Aging, Department of Social Services
P.O. Box 1337, 615 Howerton Court
Jefferson City, MO 65102-1337
phone 573-751-3082, fax 573-751-8493

Montana

Rick Bartos
Aging Coordinator/Legal Services Developer
Montana Department of Family Services
48 N. Last Chance Gulch, P.O. Box 1051
Helena, MT 59620
phone 406-444-5900, fax 406-444-5956

Nebraska

Janet Claassen
Legal Services Developer
Nebraska Department on Aging
301 Centennial Mall South, Box 95044
Lincoln, NE 68509-5044
phone 402-471-2306, fax 402-471-4619

Nevada

Elizabeth Kolkoski
Elder Rights Attorney
Division for Aging Services, Nevada Department of Human Resources
340 N. 11th Street, Suite 114
Las Vegas, NV 89101
phone 702-486-3545, fax 702-486-3572

New Hampshire

Charles H. Weatherill, Esq.
Elderly Legal Services Developer
Division of Elderly and Adult Services
6 Hazen Drive, Building 3
Concord, NH 03301
phone 603-271-4690, fax 603-271-4643

New Jersey

Alexandria Bonsa
Legal Services Developer
State of New Jersey Department of Health and Senior Services, Division of
Senior Affairs
CN 807, 101 South Broad Street
Trenton, NJ 08625-0807
phone 609-292-0921, fax 609-663-6609

New Mexico

Mary H. Smith
Legal Services Developer
State Agency on Aging
La Villa Rivera Building, 228 East Palace Avenue
Santa Fe, NM 87501
phone 505-827-7642, fax 505-827-7649

New York

William T. Graham
Assistant Counsel/Legal Services Developer
New York State Office for the Aging
Two Empire State Plaza
Albany, NY 12223-0001
phone 518-474-0388, fax 518-474-0608

North Carolina

Gary Cyrus
Chief Field Operations and Legal Services Developer
North Carolina Division of Aging, Department of Human Resources
693 Palmer Drive, CB 29531
Raleigh, NC 27626-0531
phone 919-733-8400, fax 919-733-0443

North Dakota

Larry Wagner
Legal Services Developer
Aging Services Division, North Dakota Department of Human Services
600 South Second Street, Suite 1C
Bismarck, ND 58504-5729
phone 701-328-8906, fax 701-328-8989

Ohio

Jim Fultz
Legal Services Developer
Ohio Department of Aging
50 West Broad Street, 9th Floor
Columbus, OH 43215-5928
phone 614-466-0466, fax 614-466-5741

Oklahoma

Richard Ingham
Legal Services Developer
Aging Services Division, Oklahoma Department of Human Services
312 NE 28th Street
Oklahoma City, OK 73105
phone 405-522-3069, fax 405-521-2086

Oregon

Cinda Conroyd and Marcie McMinimee
Legal Services Developers
528 Cottage NE, P.O. Box 469
Salem, OR 97308-0459
phone 503-364-7000, fax 503-585-0699

Pennsylvania

James L. Bubb Jr.
Legal Services Developer
Pennsylvania Department of Aging
400 Market Street
Harrisburg, PA 17101-2301
phone 717-772-2934, fax 717-772-3382

Puerto Rico

Igor Ortiz
Acting Legal Services Developer
Vameo Central Elsplano Building, Suite 1501
Ponce de Leon Avenue, #221
Hato Rey, PR 00917
phone 787-763-8989, fax 809-751-8641

Puerto Rico   Also send information to

Ruby Rodriguez Ramirez
Director, Governor's Office of Elderly Affairs
P.O. Box 50063
Old San Juan Station
San Juan, PR 00902
phone 809-721-5710, fax 809-721-6510

Rhode Island

John Smollins
Legal Services Developer
Division of Elderly Affairs
160 Pine Street
Providence, RI 02903
phone 401-277-2894, fax 401-277-2130

South Carolina

Dale Watson
Elder Rights Specialist
Governor's Office Division on Aging
202 Arbor Lake Drive, Suite 301
Columbia, SC 29223
phone 803-737-7500, fax 803-737-7501

South Dakota

Michael Parker
Legal Services Developer
Office of Adult Services and Aging, Department of Social Services
700 Governor's Drive
Pierre, SD 57501
phone 605-773-3656, fax 605-773-4855

Tennessee

Colleen MacLean and Susan Cope
Legal Services Developers
Tennessee Commission on Aging
500 Deadrick Street, Andrew Jackson Building, Ninth Floor
Nashville, TN 37243-0860
phone 615-741-2056, fax 615-741-3309

Texas

Christy Fair
Legal Services Developer
Texas Department on Aging
P.O. Box 12786
Austin, TX 78711
phone 512-424-6850, fax 512-424-6890

Utah

Judith Mayorga
Legal Services Developer
Utah Legal Services
254 West, 400 South, 2nd Floor
Salt Lake City, UT 84111
phone 801-328-8891, fax 801-328-8901

Utah Also contact

Sally Brown
Program Coordinator
Utah Division on Aging
120 North, 200 West
Salt Lake City, UT 84103
phone 801-538-3910, fax 801-534-4395

Vermont

John Hall
Vermont Legal Services Developer
RFD 1, Box 80A
East Burke, VT 05832
phone 802-467-3037, fax 802-467-8381

Virginia

William Peterson
Legal Services Developer/Policy Analyst
Virginia Department for the Aging
1600 Forest Avenue, Preston Building, Suite 102
Richmond, VA 23229
phone 804-662-9333, fax 804-662-9354

Washington

Hank Hubbard
Legal Services Developer
DSHS, Aging and Adult Services, State Unit on Aging
P.O. Box 45600
Olympia, WA 98504-5600
phone 360-493-2543, fax 360-438-8633

West Virginia

Sheree Knotts
Legal Services Developer
Commission on Aging
State Capitol
1900 Kanawha Blvd. East
Charleston, WV 25305
phone 304-558-3317, fax 304-558-0004

West Virginia Also send information to

Bob Bianchinotti
Commission on Aging
State Capitol
1900 Kanawha Blvd. E
Charleston, WV 25305
phone 304-558-2241, ext. 17, fax 304-558-0004

Wisconsin

Glen Silverberg
Legal Services Developer
Wisconsin Bureau on Aging
217 S. Hamilton Street, Suite 300
Madison, WI 53703
phone 608-267-3201, fax 608-267-3203

Wyoming

Janet Mallard
Legal Services Developer
Wind River Legal Services
P.O. Box 247
Fort Washakie, WY 82514
phone 307-332-6626

References

Abend-Wein, M. (1991). Medicaid's effect on the elderly: How reimbursement policy affects priority in the nursing home. *Journal of Applied Gerontology, 10*(1), 71-87.

Abrahams, R., Nonnenkamp, L., Dunn, S., Mehta, S., & Woodard, P. (1988). Case management in the social/health maintenance organization. *Generations, 12*(5), 39-43.

Achenbaum, W. A., & Morrison, M. H. (1993). Is unretirement unprecedented? In S. Bass, F. Caro, & Y. Chen (Eds.), *Achieving a productive aging society* (pp. 97-116). Westport, CT: Auburn House.

ACTION. (1990a). *Foster Grandparent Program 25th anniversary 1965-1990: Bridging the generations of need*. Washington, DC: Author.

ACTION. (1990b). *Senior Companion Program: Serving with compassion, caring as friends*. Washington, DC: Author.

ACTION. (1992). *Retired Senior Volunteer Program: A part of ACTION*. Washington, DC: Author.

Adams, J. S. (1965). Inequity in social exchange. In L. Berkowitz (Ed.), *Advances in experimental social psychology* (Vol. 2, pp. 267-300). New York: Academic Press.

Administration on Aging. (1983). *An evaluation of the nutritional services for the elderly: Volume 3. Descriptive report* (OHDS Publication No. 83-20917). Washington, DC: Government Printing Office.

Administration on Aging. (1994a). *Infrastructure of home and community based services for the functionally impaired elderly: State source book*. Washington, DC: Author.

Administration on Aging. (1994b). *National summary of program activities as authorized under titles III and VII of the Older Americans Act*. Washington, DC: Author.

Administration on Aging. (1995a, January). *Elder facts: The Administration on Aging*. Washington, DC: Author.

Administration on Aging. (1995b). *Long-term care ombudsman annual report: Fiscal year 1995*. Washington, DC: Author.

Administration on Aging. (1997a). *Older Americans Act appropriation information* [Online]. Available: http://www.aoa.dhss.gov/aoa/pages/97oaaapp.html

Administration on Aging. (1997b). *Resource centers* [Online]. Available: http:www.aoa.dhhs.gov

Administration on Aging. (1997c). *State units on aging* [Online]. Available: http://www.aoa.dhhs.gov/aoa/pages/state.html

Administration on Aging. (1997d). *Targeting of Older Americans Act services: Issues for reauthorization*. Washington, DC: Author.

Adult Education Act of 1988, 20 U.S.C. § 1201 *et seq.*

Advisory Council on Social Security. (1996). *The findings and recommendations of the 1994-1996 Advisory Council: Vol. I* [Online]. Available: http://www.ssa.gov/adcouncil/toc.htm

Age Discrimination in Employment Act of 1967, Pub. L. No. 90-202, 29 U.S.C. § 621 *et seq.* (1967), as amended 1986.

Aiken, L. H. (1989). An agenda for the year 2000. In M. D. Mezey, J. E. Lynaugh, & M. M. Cartier (Eds.), *Nursing homes and nursing care: Lessons from the teaching nursing homes* (pp. 145-156). New York: Springer.

Ailinger, R., & Causey, M. (1993). Home health service utilization by Hispanic elderly immigrants: A longitudinal study. *Home Health Care Quarterly, 14,* 85-96.

Alegria, F. (1992). *A guide to state-level policies, practices, and procedures: Enhancing employment opportunities for older workers*. Washington, DC: National Governors' Association.

Alexander, G. J. (1991). Time for a new law on health care advanced directives. *Hastings Law Journal, 42,* 755-778.

Allen, J. E. (1987). *Nursing home administration*. New York: Springer.

Altman, B., & Walden, D. (1993). *Home health care: Use, expenditures, and sources of payment* (AHCPR Publication No. 93-0040: National Medical Expenditures Survey Research Findings No. 15). Rockville, MD: Public Health Service.

Amborgi, D. M., & Leonard, F. (1988). The impact of nursing home admission agreements on resident autonomy. *The Gerontologist, 28*(Suppl.), 82-89.

American Association of Homes and Services for the Aging. (1988). *Directory of members*. Washington, DC: Author.

American Association of Homes for the Aging. (1987). *Continuing care retirement communities: An industry in action: Analysis and developing trends 1987*. Washington, DC: Author.

American Association of Retired Persons. (1985). *The right place at the right time: A guide to long-term care choices*. Washington, DC: Author.

American Association of Retired Persons. (1989). *Business and older workers: Current perceptions and directions for the 1990s*. Washington, DC: Author.

American Association of Retired Persons. (1990). *Nursing home life: A guide for residents and family.* Washington, DC: Author.

American Association of Retired Persons. (1992). *Understanding senior housing for the 1990's: An American Association of Retired Persons survey of consumer preferences, concerns, and needs.* Washington, DC: Author.

American Association of Retired Persons. (1994a). *Activating ideas: Promoting physical activity among older adults.* Washington, DC: Author.

American Association of Retired Persons. (1994b). *Connecting the generations: A guide to intergenerational resources.* Washington, DC: Author.

American Association of Retired Persons. (1996). Program highlights. *Perspectives in Health Promotion and Aging, 11*(2), 5.

American Association of Retired Persons Minority Affairs Initiative. (1987). *A portrait of older minorities.* Washington, DC: Author.

American Public Welfare Association. (1997). What are health care waivers and how are states opting to use them? [Online]. Available: http://www.apwa.org/faq/quest6a.htm

Americans With Disabilities Act, 42 U.S.C. § 12101 *et seq.* (1990).

Anderson, R. (1995). Revisiting the behavioral model and access to medical care: Does it matter? *Journal of Health and Social Behavior, 36,* 1-10.

Anderson, R., & Newman, J. (1973). Societal and individual determinants of medical care utilization in the United States. *Milbank Memorial Fund Quarterly, 51,* 95-124.

Angelis, J. (1990). *Intergenerational service learning: Strategies for the future.* Carbondale, IL: Author.

Angelis, J. (1992). The genesis of an intergenerational program. *Educational Gerontology, 18,* 317-327.

Ansak, M. L. (1990). The On Lok model: Consolidating care and financing. *Generations, 14*(2), 73-74.

Applebaum, R., & Wilson, N. (1988). Training needs for providing case management for the long-term care client: Lessons learned from the National Channeling Demonstration. *The Gerontologist, 28,* 172-176.

Arneson, B. (1994). State and federal legislation: Nonmedical homecare services. In J. Handy & C. Schuerman (Eds.), *Challenges and innovations in homecare* (pp. 53-55). San Francisco: American Society on Aging.

Arora, N. S., & Rochester, D. V. (1982). Respiratory muscle strength and maximal voluntary ventilation in undernourished patients. *American Review of Respiratory Diseases, 126,* 5-8.

Ashford, N., Bell, W. G., & Rich, T. A. (1982). *Mobility and transport for elderly and handicapped persons: Proceedings of a conference held at Churchill College, Cambridge, UK, July 1981.* New York: Gordon & Breach Science.

Atchley, R. (1971). Retirement and leisure participation: Continuity or crisis? *The Gerontologist, 11,* 13-17.

Atchley, R. (1989). A continuity theory of normal aging. *The Gerontologist, 29,* 183-190.

Atchley, R. (1997). *Social forces and aging: An introduction to social gerontology* (8th ed.). Belmont, CA: Wadsworth.

Atkinson, V., & Stuck, B. (1991). Mental health services for the rural elderly: The SAGE experience. *The Gerontologist, 31,* 548-551.

Austin, C. (1996). Aging and long-term care. In C. Austin & R. McClelland (Eds.), *Perspectives on case management practice* (pp. 73-98). Milwaukee, WI: Families International.

Axel, H. (1989). *Job banks for retirees.* New York: Conference Board.

Baker, B., & Murowski, K. (1986). A method for measuring paid staff support for volunteer involvement. *Journal of Voluntary Action Research, 15,* 60-64.

Balsam, A., & Osteraas, G. (1987). Instituting a continuum of community nutrition services: Massachusetts elderly nutrition programs. *Journal of Nutrition for the Elderly, 6*(4), 51-67.

Balsam, A. L., & Rogers, B. L. (1988). *Service innovations in the elderly nutrition program: Strategies for meeting unmet needs.* Medford, MA: Tufts University School of Nutrition.

Balsam, A. L., & Rogers, B. L. (1991). Serving elders in greatest social and economic need: The challenge to the elderly nutrition program. *Journal of Aging and Social Policy, 3*(1/2), 41-55.

Banaszak-Holl, J., & Hines, M. A. (1994, November). *Organizational antecedents of nursing home staff turnover.* Paper presented at the annual meeting of the Gerontological Society of America, Atlanta, GA.

Bane, S. (1992). Rural caregiving. *Rural Elderly Networker, 3,* 1-6.

Bane, S. D., Rathbone-McCuan, E., & Galliher, J. (1994). Mental health services for the elderly in rural America. In J. Krout (Ed.), *Providing community-based services to the rural elderly* (pp. 243-266). Thousand Oaks, CA: Sage.

Barker, P., Manderscheild, R., Hendershot, G., Jack, S., Schoenborn, C., & Goldstrom, I. (1992). *Serious mental illness and disability in the adult household population: United States, 1989* (Advanced Data From Vital and Health Statistics, No. 218). Hyattsville, MD: National Center for Health Statistics.

Barocas, V. (1994). *Rethinking retirement income.* New York: Conference Board.

Barresi, C. M., & Stull, D. E. (1993). Ethnicity and long-term care: An overview. In C. M. Barresi & D. E. Stull (Eds.), *Ethnic elderly and long-term care* (pp. 3-21). New York: Springer.

Barrow, G. M. (1996). *Aging, the individual and society* (6th ed.). Minneapolis, MN: West.

Bartholomew, A. M., Young, E. A., Martin, H. W., & Hazuda, H. P. (1990). Food frequency intakes and sociodemographic factors of elderly Mexican Americans and non-Hispanic whites. *Journal of the American Dietetic Association, 90*(12), 1693-1696.

Bass, S. (1992). Gerontology program succeeds in Boston. *Adult Learning, 3,* 22-23.

Bechill, W. (1992, December). At age 27, the Older Americans Act needs spirited advocacy, understanding. *Perspective on Aging, 21,* 9-11.

Bedford, V. H. (1989). Understanding the value of siblings in old age: A proposed model. *American Behavioral Scientist, 33,* 33-44.

Bedient, D., Snyder, V., & Simon, M. (1992). Retirees mentoring at-risk college students. *Phi Delta Kappan, 73,* 462-463, 466.

Belloc, N., & Breslow, L. (1972). Relationship of physical health status and health practices. *Preventive Medicine, 1,* 409-421.

Benett, J. (1992, October 10). Hidden malnutrition worsens health of elderly. *New York Times,* pp. A1, A4.

Benjamin, A. (1992). An overview of in-home health and supportive services for older people. In M. Ory & A. Dunker (Eds.), *In-home health care for older people* (pp. 9-52). Newbury Park, CA: Sage.

Berry, G., Zarit, S., & Rabatin, V. (1991). Caregiver activity on respite and nonrespite days: A comparison of two service approaches. *The Gerontologist, 31,* 830-835.

Biegel, D., Sales, E., & Schultz, R. (1991). *Family caregiving in chronic illness.* Newbury Park, CA: Sage.

Biegel, D., Schultz, R., Shore, B., & Morycz, R. (1988). Economic supports for family caregivers of the elderly: Public sector policies. In M. Z. Goldstein (Ed.), *Family involvement in the treatment of the frail elderly* (pp. 157-201). Washington, DC: American Psychiatric Press.

Bild, B. R., & Havingurst, R. J. (1976). Senior citizens in great cities: The case of Chicago. *The Gerontologist, 16*(1, Pt. 2), 3-88.

Binney, E., Estes, C., & Ingman, S. (1990). Medicalization, public policy and the elderly: Social services in jeopardy? *Social Science and Medicine, 30,* 761-771.

Bird, C. (1992). *Second careers: New ways to work after 50.* Boston: Little, Brown.

Blank, T. O. (1988). *Older persons and their housing, today and tomorrow.* Springfield, IL: Charles C Thomas.

Blazer, D. G. (1989). The epidemiology of psychiatric disorders in later life. In E. W. Busse & D. G. Blazer (Eds.), *Geriatric psychiatry* (pp. 235-262). Washington, DC: American Psychiatric Press.

B'nai B'rith. (1997). *B'nai B'rith senior housing: An overview* [Online]. Available: http://www.bnaibrith.org/sch/over.html

Bocian, K., & Newman, S. (1989). Evaluation of intergenerational programs: Why and how? In S. Newman & S. Brummel (Eds.), *Intergenerational programs: Imperatives, strategies, impacts, trends* (pp. 147-163). New York: Haworth.

Bogren, S., & Hyman, G. (1994). Medicaid transportation's future uncertain. *Community Transportation Reporter, 12*(3), 20-22.

Boondas, J. (1991). Nursing home resident assessment classification and focused care. *Nursing and Health Care, 12*(6), 308-312.

Bouvier, L. F., & De Vita, C. J. (1991, November). The baby boom: Entering midlife. *Population Bulletin, 46*(3), 1-34.

Bowers, B. (1987). Intergenerational caregiving: Adult caregivers and their aging parents. *Advanced Nursing Science, 9,* 20-31.

Bowers, B. J. (1988). Family perceptions of care in a nursing home. *The Gerontologist, 27,* 4-8.

Bratter, B., & Freeman, E. (1990). The maturing of peer counseling. *Generations, 14*(1), 49-52.

Brehm, J. W. (1966). *A theory of psychological reactance.* New York: Academic Press.

Brehm, S. S., & Brehm, J. W. (1981). *Psychological reactance: A theory of freedom and control.* New York: Academic Press.

Briggs, E. (1992). *Nutrition and the black elderly.* San Diego, CA: San Diego State University, National Resource Center on Minority Aging Populations.

Brody, E. M. (1981). Women in the middle and family help to older people. *The Gerontologist, 21,* 471-480.

Brody, E. M. (1985). Parent care as a normative family stress. *The Gerontologist, 25,* 19-29.

Brown, R. (1989). *The rights of older persons* (2nd ed.). Carbondale: Southern Illinois University Press.

Brubaker, T., & Roberto, K. A. (1993). Family life education for the later years. *Family Relations, 42,* 212-221.

Buchner, D. M., & Pearson, D. C. (1989). Factors associated with participation in a community senior health promotion program: A pilot study. *American Journal of Public Health, 79,* 775-777.

Buckwalter, K., Smith, M., & Caston, C. (1994). Mental and social health of the rural elderly. In R. Coward, C. N. Bull, G. Kukulka, & J. Galliher (Eds.), *Health services for rural elders* (pp. 203-232). New York: Springer.

Buckwalter, K., Smith, M., Zevenbergen, P., & Russell, D. (1991). Mental health services of the rural elderly outreach program. *The Gerontologist, 31,* 408-412.

Buelow, J., & Conrad, K. (1992). Assessing the influence of adult day care on client satisfaction. *Journal of Health and Aging, 4,* 303-321.

Burger, S. G., Fraser, V., Hunt, S., & Frank, B. (1996). *Nursing homes: Getting good care there*. San Luis Obispo, CA: Impact.

Burns, B., Wagner, H. R., Taube, C., Magaziner, J., Permutt, T., & Landerman, L. R. (1993). Mental health service use by the elderly in nursing homes. *American Journal of Public Health, 83,* 331-337.

Cahn, E. S. (n.d.). *The time dollar* [Brochure]. Washington, DC: Author.

Cain, M. (1996). Health maintenance organizations. In L. A. Vitt, J. K. Siegenthaler, N. E. Culter, & S. Golant (Eds.), *Encyclopedia of financial gerontology* (pp. 243-248). Westport, CT: Greenwood Press.

Canan, M., & Mitchell, W. (1991). *Employee fringe and welfare benefits plans*. Saint Paul, MN: West.

Cantor, M. H. (1979). Neighbors and friends: An overlooked resource in the informal support system. *Research on Aging, 1,* 434-463.

Cantor, M. H. (1983). Strain among caregivers: A study of experience in the United States. *The Gerontologist, 23,* 597-604.

Cantor, M. H. (1991). Family and community: Changing roles in an aging society. *The Gerontologist, 31,* 337-346.

Capitman, J., Henry, M., & Yee, L. (1994). *Day care quality assessment (DCQA): A guide for adult day program review and planning*. Waltham, MA: Brandeis University National Resource Center on Diversity and Long-Term Care.

Carlton-LaNey, I. (1991). Some considerations of the rural elderly black's underuse of social services. *Journal of Gerontological Social Work, 16,* 3-16.

Caro, F., & Bass, S. (1995). Increasing volunteering among older people. In S. Bass (Ed.), *Older and active: How Americans over 55 are contributing to society* (pp. 71-96). New Haven, CT: Yale University Press.

Carter, W. B., Elward, E., Malmgren, J., Martin, M., & Larson, E. (1991). Participation in health promotion programs and research: A critical review of the literature. *The Gerontologist, 31,* 584-592.

Centaur Associates. (1986). *Report on the 502(e) experimental projects funded under Title V of the Older Americans Act*. Washington, DC: Author.

Chandra, R. K. (1992). Effect of vitamin and trace-element supplementation on immune responses and infection in elderly subjects. *Lancet, 340,* 1124-1127.

Chappell, N. L., & Blandford, A. A. (1987). Health service utilization by elderly persons. *Canadian Journal of Sociology, 12*(3), 195-215.

Chelimsky, E. (1991). *Older Americans Act: Promising practice in information and referral services*. Washington, DC: Government Printing Office.

Chellis, R., & Grayson, P. (1990). *Life care: A longterm solution?* Lexington, MA: Lexington Books.

Cherry, R., Prebis, J., & Pick, V. (1995). Service directories: Reinvigorating community resource for self-care. *The Gerontologist, 35,* 560-563.

Chicago Department on Aging, National Council on the Aging, and Washington Business Group on Health. (1992, December). *Public/private partnerships: Examples from the aging network.* Washington, DC: National Eldercare Institute on Business and Aging.

Christianson, J. B., Warrick, L. H., Netting, F. E., Williams, F. G., Read, W., & Murphy, J. (1991). Hospital case management: Bridging acute and long-term care. *Health Affairs, 10*(2), 173-184.

Civil Rights Act of 1964, Pub. L. No. 88-352, 78 Stat. 241.

Civil Service Retirement Act of 1920, 5 U.S.C. § 8331 *et seq.* (1990).

Cohen, E. (1991). Nursing case management: Does it pay? *Journal of Nursing Administration, 21,* 20-25.

Cohen, E., & Cesta, T. (1994). Case management in the acute care setting: A model for health care reform. *Journal of Case Management, 3,* 110-116.

Coleman, B. (1989). *Primer on employee retirement income security act* (3rd ed.). Washington, DC: Bureau of National Affairs.

Coleman, D., & Iso-Ahola, S. (1993). The role of social support and self-determination. *Journal of Leisure Research, 25,* 111-128.

Coleman, N., Wood, E. F., Sabatino, C. P., Nelson, B., & Baker, C. D. (1986). *Assisting the aging network with private bar involvement and selected legal issues: Final report on a model project.* Washington, DC: American Bar Association.

Coles, R. (1991). Midlife and older women: Valuable resources for today's workforce. In *Resourceful aging: Today and tomorrow: Vol. 4. Work/second careers* (pp. 27-42). Washington, DC: American Association of Retired Persons.

Colston, L., Harper, S., & Mitchener-Colston, W. (1995). Volunteering to promote fitness and caring: A motive for linking college students with mature adults. *Activities, Adaptation, & Aging, 20,* 79-90.

Committee for the Study on Improving Mobility and Safety for Older Persons. (1988). *Transportation in an aging society: Improving mobility and safety for older persons* (Vol. 1). Washington, DC: National Research Council, Transportation Research Board.

Committee on Personnel for Health Needs of the Elderly Through the Year 2020. (1988). *Report.* Washington, DC: Government Printing Office.

Commonwealth Fund. (1993). *The untapped resource: The final report of the Americans Over 55 at Work Program.* New York: Author.

Community Mental Health Act of 1963, 42 U.S.C. § 2689 *et seq.,* as amended.

Community service is key. (1994). *Community Transportation Reporter, 13*(4), 5. [Editorial]

Community Transportation Association of America. (1995, December). Transportation access technologies developed under project ACTION. *Community Transportation Reporter, 13,* 2-4.

Comprehensive Health Planning and Public Health Service Amendments of 1966, 42 U.S.C. §§ 243, 246.

Conlin, M., Caranasos, G., & Davidson, R. (1992). Reduction of caregiver stress by respite care: A pilot study. *Southern Medical Journal, 85,* 1096-1100.

Connecticut Continuing Care. (1994). *Guidelines for long-term care case management practices.* Bristol, CT: Author.

Conrad, K., Hanrahan, P., & Hughes, S. (1990). Survey of adult day care in the United States: National and regional findings. *Research on Aging, 12,* 36-56.

Conrad, K., Hughes, S., Hanrahan, P., & Wang, S. (1993). Classification of adult day care: Cluster analysis of services and activities. *Journal of Gerontology: Social Sciences, 48,* S112-S122.

Corder, R. (1991). Getting volunteers involved: San Clemente PD's retired senior volunteers. *Western City, 67,* 21-23.

Coronel, S., & Fulton, D. (1995). *Long term care insurance in 1993.* Washington, DC: Health Insurance Association of America.

Corporation for National Service. (1995). *Senior volunteer programs* [Online]. Available: http://www.cns.gov\senior.html

Coulton, C., & Frost, A. K. (1982). Use of social and health services by the elderly. *Journal of Health and Social Behavior, 23,* 330-339.

Courson, F., & Heward, W. (1989). Using senior citizen volunteers in the special education classroom. *Academic Therapy, 24,* 525-532.

Courtenay, B. (1990). Community education for older adults. In M. Galbraith (Ed.), *Education through community organizations* (pp. 37-44). San Francisco: Jossey-Bass.

Covey, H. C., & Menard, S. (1988). Trends in elderly criminal victimization from 1973 to 1984. *Research on Aging, 10,* 329-341.

Cox, C., & Monk, A. (1990). Integrating the frail and well elderly: The experience of senior centers. *Journal of Gerontological Social Work, 15,* 131-147.

Cox, C., & Monk, A. (1993). Black and Hispanic caregivers of dementia victims: Their needs and implications for service. In C. M. Barresi & D. E. Stull (Eds.), *Ethnic elderly and long-term care* (pp. 57-67). New York: Springer.

Coyne, A. C. (1991). Information and referral service usage among caregivers for dementia patients. *The Gerontologist, 31,* 384-388.

Crandall, R. C. (1991). *Gerontology: A behavioral science approach.* New York: McGraw-Hill.

Craven, S. (1992). Membership: Marketing, recruitment, and retention. In R. Fischer, M. Blazey, & H. Lipman (Eds.), *Students of the third age* (pp. 67-83). New York: Macmillan.

Cruzan v. Director, Missouri Department of Health, 497 U.S. 261 (1990).

Cruzan v. Harmon, 760 S.W.2d 408 (1988).

Crystal, S., & Beck, P. (1992). A room of one's own: The SRO and the single elderly. *The Gerontologist, 32,* 684-692.

Cuellar, J. (1990). Hispanic American aging: Geriatric education curriculum development for selected health professions. In M. S. Harper (Ed.), *Minority aging* (DHHS Publication No. HRS P-DV-90-4). Washington, DC: Government Printing Office.

Cushing, M., & Long, N. (1974). *Information and referral services: Reaching out* (DHEW Publication No. OHD 75-20110). Washington, DC: Government Printing Office.

Davis, M. A., Murphy, S. P., Neuhaus, J. M., & Lein, D. (1990). Living arrangements and dietary quality of older U.S. adults. *Journal of the American Dietetic Association, 90*(12), 1667-1672.

Davis, M. A., Randall, E., Forthofer, R. N., Lee, E. S., & Margen, S. (1985). Living arrangements and dietary patterns of older adults in the United States. *Journal of Gerontology, 40*(4), 434-442.

Deimling, G. (1991). Respite use and caregiver well-being in families caring for stable and declining AD patients. *Journal of Gerontological Social Work, 18,* 117-134.

Delfosse R. (1995). *Hospice and home health agency characteristics: United States, 1991.* Hyattsville, MD: National Center for Health Statistics.

Dellasega, C., & Stricklin, M. L. (1993). Cognitive impairment in elderly home health clients. *Home Health Care Services Quarterly, 14,* 81-92.

DelTogno-Armanasco, V., Olives, G., & Harter, S. (1989). Developing an integrated nursing case management model. *Nursing Management, 20,* 26-29.

DePaulo, B. M. (1978). Help seeking from the recipient's point of view. *JSAS Catalogue of Selected Documents in Psychology, 8,* 62. (Ms. No. 1721b)

DePaulo, B. M., & Fisher, J. D. (1980). The cost of asking for help. *Basic and Applied Social Psychology, 1,* 23-35.

DeRenzo, E., Byer, V., Grady, H. S., Matricardi, E., Lehmann, S., & Gradet, B. (1991). Comprehensive community-based mental health outreach services for suburban seniors. *The Gerontologist, 31,* 836-840.

Dick, A., Garber, A. M., & McCurdy, T. A. (1994). Forecasting nursing home utilization of elderly Americans. In D. A. Wise (Ed.), *Studies in the economics of aging.* Chicago: University of Chicago Press.

Dickerson, B., Myers, D., Seelbach, W., & Johnson-Dietz, S. (1991). A 21st century challenge to higher education: Integrating the older person into academia. In R. Sherron & D. B. Lumsden (Eds.), *Introduction to educational gerontology* (3rd ed., pp. 297-331). New York: Hemisphere.

Dispute Resolution Center. (1997). *Dispute Resolution Center* [Online]. Saint Paul, MN: Author. Available: http://www.spacestar.net/users/tkhedeen/drc.htm

Doolin, J. (1985). America's untouchables: The elderly homeless. *Perspective on Aging, 9*(2), 8-12.

Doty, P. (1986). Family care of the elderly: The role of public policy. *Milbank Memorial Fund Quarterly, 64,* 34-75.

Downing, R. (1985). The elderly and their families. In M. Weil, J. Karls, & Associates (Eds.), *Case management in human service practice: A systematic approach to mobilizing resources for clients* (pp. 145-169). San Francisco: Jossey-Bass.

Drenning, S., & Getz, L. (1992). Computer ease. *Phi Delta Kappan, 74,* 471-472.

Dumazadier, J. (1967). *Towards a society of leisure.* New York: Free Press.

Dwyer, J. (1991). *Screening older Americans' nutritional health: Current practices and future possibilities.* Washington, DC: Nutrition Screening Initiative.

Dwyer, J. (1994). Nutritional problems of elderly minorities. *Nutrition Reviews, 52*(8), S24-S27.

Eckert, J., & Murrey, M. (1987). Alternative housing modes. In J. Hancock (Ed.), *Housing the elderly* (pp. 57-80). New Brunswick, NJ: Center for Urban Policy Research.

Edelstein, S. (1996). *Legal issues and resources: An introduction for professionals in aging.* Unpublished manuscript.

Edelstein, S., & May, J. (1993). Senior attorney volunteers: A resource for legal services programs. *Clearinghouse Review, 27,* 619-621.

Eldeman, T. S. (1990). The nursing home reform law: Issues for litigation. *Clearinghouse Review, 24,* 545-550.

Eldercare locator gets high marks. (1996, March). *Information and Referral Reporter, 5*(1), 1-2.

Emlet, C., & Hall, A. M. (1991). Integrating the community into geriatric case management: Public health interventions. *The Gerontologist, 31,* 556-560.

Employee Benefit Research Institute. (1994a, March). Changes in defined benefit and defined contribution plans occurring mainly among small plans. *Employee Benefit Notes, 15,* 1-3.

Employee Benefit Research Institute. (1994b). *Characteristics of the part-time work force* (Special Rep. No. 149). Washington, DC: Author.

Employee Benefit Research Institute. (1994c). *Employee Benefit Research Institute* (3rd ed.). Washington, DC: Author.

Employee Retirement Income Security Act of 1974, 29 U.S.C. §§ 1001-1461 (1974), as amended.

Epstein, B., & Koenig, V. (1990). Education for elderly caregiving. *Journal of Extension, 28,* 8-10.

Erickson, R., & Eckert, J. K. (1977). The elderly poor in downtown San Diego hotels. *The Gerontologist, 17,* 440-446.

Ernst & Young (for American Association of Homes for the Aging). (1989). *Continuing care retirement communities: An industry in action*. Washington, DC: American Association of Homes for the Aging.

Estes, C. (1979). *The aging enterprise*. San Francisco: Jossey-Bass.

Estes, C. L., Swan, J. H., & Associates (1993). *The long term care crisis: Elders trapped in the no-care zone*. Newbury Park, CA: Sage.

Eubank, W., & Snodgrass, P. L. (1993). *Retirement: A place to live, choices and options* [Online]. Available: http://etcs.ext.missouri.edu/publications/xplor/hesguide/intdes/gh2003.htm

Evans, M. (1994). Seniors housing finally scores. *Journal of Property Management, 59*(3), 28-32.

The extra mile: Overnight and weekend care. (1996, Fall/Winter). *Respite Report*, 1-2, 6.

Factor, A. (1993). Translating policy into practice. In E. Sutton, A. Factor, B. Hawkins, T. Heller, & G. Seltzer (Eds.), *Older adults with developmental disabilities: Optimizing choices and change* (pp. 257-275). Baltimore: P. H. Brookes.

FallCreek, S. J., Allen, B. P., & Halls, D. M. (1986). *Health promotion and aging: A national directory of selected programs* (DHHS Publication No. OHDS 86-20950). Washington, DC: U.S. Department of Health and Human Services, Office of Human Development Services, Administration on Aging.

FallCreek, S. J., & Franks, P. (1984). *Health promotion and aging: Strategies for action* (DHHS Publication No. OHDS 84-20818). Washington, DC: U.S. Department of Health and Human Services, Office of Human Development Services, Administration on Aging.

FallCreek, S. J., & Mettler, M. (1982). *A healthy old age: A sourcebook for health promotion with older adults* (DHHS Publication No. 447-a-1). Washington, DC: U.S. Department of Health and Human Services, Office of Human Development Services, Administration on Aging.

Family and Medical Leave Act of 1993, 5 U.S.C. § 6381 *et seq.*, 29 U.S.C. §§ 2601 *et seq.*, 2631 *et seq.* (1993).

Farkas, K., & Milligan, S. (1991, November/December). Volunteers tell of benefits from service to others. *Perspective on Aging, 20*(20), 26-29.

Federal funding resources. (1995, January). *Community Transportation Reporter, 13*, 21-30.

Federal Transit Act of 1988, 49 U.S.C. § 1601 *et seq.* (1988).

Feldman, N. S. (1991). Lifelong education: The challenge of change. In *Resourceful aging: Today and tomorrow: Vol. 5. Lifelong education* (pp. 17-31). Washington, DC: American Association of Retired Persons.

Feldman, P. (1993). Work life improvements for home care workers: Impact and feasibility. *The Gerontologist, 33*, 47-54.

Fellin, P., & Powell, T. (1988). Mental health services and older adult minorities: An assessment. *The Gerontologist, 28,* 442-447.

Ficke, S. C. (1985). *Older Americans Act 1965-1985: 20th anniversary: An orientation to the Older Americans Act.* Washington, DC: National Association of State Units on Aging.

Finkel, S. (1993). Mental health and aging: A decade of progress. *Generations, 17*(1), 25-30.

Fischer, C. A., Crockett, S. J., Heller, K. E., & Skauge, L. H. (1991). Nutrition knowledge, attitudes and practices of older and younger elderly in rural areas. *Journal of the American Dietetic Association, 91*(11), 1398-1401.

Fischer, D. L. (1978). *Growing old in America.* New York: Oxford University Press.

Fischer, K., Rapkin, B., & Rappaport, J. (1991). Gender and work history in the placement and perceptions of older community volunteers. *Psychology of Women Quarterly, 15,* 261-279.

Fischer, L. (1993). Recruiting older volunteers. *Journal of Volunteer Administration, 11*(2), 13-17.

Fischer, L., Mueller, D., & Cooper, P. (1991). Older volunteers: A discussion of the Minnesota senior study. *The Gerontologist, 31,* 183-194.

Fischer, L. R., & Schaffer, K. B. (1993). *Older volunteers: A guide to research and practice.* Newbury Park, CA: Sage.

Fischer, R. (1992). Post-retirement learning. In R. Fischer, M. Blazey, & H. Lipman (Eds.), *Students of the third age* (pp. 13-21). New York: Macmillan.

Fisher, J., & Carstensen, L. (1990). Behavioral management of the dementias. *Clinical Psychology Review, 10,* 611-629.

Fisher, J. D., & Nadler, A. (1976). The effect of donor resources on recipient self-esteem and self-help. *Journal of Experimental Social Psychology, 12,* 139-150.

Fisher, J. D., Nadler, A., & Whitcher-Alagna, S. (1983). Four conceptualizations of reactions to aid. In J. D. Fisher, A. Nadler, & B. M. DePaulo (Eds.), *New directions in helping* (Vol. 1, pp. 51-84). New York: Academic Press.

Fiske, S. T., & Taylor, S. E. (1991). *Social cognition* (2nd ed.). New York: McGraw-Hill.

Floyd, M. D. (1993). Should government regulate the financial management of continuing care retirement communities? *Elder Law Journal, 1*(1), 29-74.

Foner, N. (1994). *The caregiving dilemma.* Los Angeles: University of California Press.

Food Stamp Act of 1964, 7 U.S.C. § 2011 *et seq.* (1995).

Ford, M. (1996). *Medicaid reform and FY 1996 budget* (Congressional Research Service IB95099). Washington, DC: Library of Congress.

Freedman, M. (1994). *Seniors in national and community service: A report prepared for the Commonwealth Fund's Americans Over 55 at Work Program*. Philadelphia: Public/Private Ventures.

Freedman, V. A. (1993). Kin and nursing home lengths of stay: A backward recurrence time approach. *Journal of Health and Social Behavior, 34,* 138-152.

Freiman, M., Cunningham, P., & Cornelius, L. (1993). The demand for health care for the treatment of mental problems among the elderly. *Advances in Health Economics and Health Services Research, 14,* 17-36.

Gallagher, D., Wrabetz, A., Lovett, S., Maestro, S., & Rose, J. (1988). Depression and other negative affects in family caregivers. In E. Light & B. Lebowitz (Eds.), *Alzheimer's disease treatment and family stress: Directions for research* (pp. 218-244). Washington, DC: Government Printing Office.

Gallagher-Thompson, D. (1994). Direct services and interventions for caregivers. In M. H. Cantor (Ed.), *Family caregiving: Agenda for the future* (pp. 102-122). San Francisco: American Society on Aging.

Garson, A. (1994, September). RSVP International: Putting seniors to work as volunteers. *Transitions Abroad, 18,* 53.

Gelfand, D. E., & Bechill, W. (1991). The evolution of the Older Americans Act: A 25-year review of the legislative changes. *Generations, 15*(3), 19-22.

Geller, P. (1994). Taking the next steps in adult day care. *Perspective on Aging, 23,* 13-15.

George, L. (1987). Respite care. In G. Maddox (Ed.), *The encyclopedia of aging* (pp. 576-577). New York: Springer.

George, L. (1992). Community and home care for mentally ill older adults. In J. Birren, R. B. Sloane, & G. Cohen, *Handbook of mental health and aging* (2nd ed., pp. 793-813). New York: Academic Press.

George, L. K., Blazer, D. G., Winfield-Laird, I., Leaf, P. J., & Fischbach, R. L. (1988). Psychiatric disorders and mental health service use in later life: Evidence from the epidemiologic catchment area program. In J. A. Brody & G. L. Maddox (Eds.), *Epidemiology and aging: An international perspective* (pp. 189-219). New York: Springer.

Gerber, I. (1969). Bereavement and the acceptance of professional service. *Community Mental Health Journal, 5,* 487-495.

Gerber, J., Wolff, J., Klores, W., & Brown, G. (1989). *Life trends: The future of baby boomers and other aging Americans*. New York: Macmillan.

Gergen, K. J., Morse, S. J., & Kristeller, J. L. (1973). The manner of giving: Cross-national continuities in reactions to aid. *Psychologia, 16,* 121-131.

Geron, S., & Chassler, D. (1994). *Guidelines for case management practice across the long-term care continuum*. Bristol: Connecticut Community Care.

Geron, S., & Chassler, D. (1995). Advancing the state of the art: Establishing guidelines for long-term care case management. *Journal of Case Management, 4,* 9-13.

Golant, S. M., & LaGreca, A. J. (1994). Housing quality of U.S. elderly households: Does aging or place matter? *The Gerontologist, 34,* 803-814.

Gonyea, J. (1988). Acceptance of hospital-based respite care by families and elders. *Health and Social Work, 3,* 201-208.

Goodwin, J. S. (1989). Social, psychological and physical factors affecting the nutritional status of elderly subjects: Separating cause and effect. *American Journal of Clinical Nutrition, 50,* 1201-1209.

Gottlieb, G. (1990). Market segmentation. In B. Fogel, A. Furino, & G. Gottlieb (Eds.), *Mental health policy for older Americans: Protecting minds at risk* (pp. 135-155). Washington, DC: American Psychiatric Press.

Grabbe, L., Demi, A., Whittington, F., Jones, J., Branch, L., & Lambert, R. (1995). Functional status and the use of formal home care in the year before death. *Journal of Aging and Health, 7,* 339-364.

Grad, S. (1990). *Income of the population 55 or over, 1988* (Social Security Publication No. 13-11871). Washington, DC: Government Printing Office.

Grady, S. (1990). Senior centers: An environment for counseling. *Generations, 14*(1), 15-18.

Green, L., Fitzhugh, E., Wang, M. Q., Perko, J., Eddy, J., & Westerfield, C. (1993). Influence of living arrangements on dietary adequacy for U.S. elderly: 1987-1988 nationwide food consumption survey. *Wellness Perspectives: Research, Theory and Practice, 10*(1), 32-40.

Greenberg, M. S., & Shapiro, S. P. (1971). Indebtedness: An adverse aspect of asking for and receiving help. *Sociometry, 34,* 290-301.

Greenberg, M. S., & Westcott, D. R. (1983). Indebtedness as a mediator of reactions to aid. In J. D. Fisher, A. Nadler, & B. M. DePaulo (Eds.), *New directions in helping* (Vol. 1, pp. 85-112). New York: Academic Press.

Green Thumb, Inc. (1995). *The 1995 senior community service employment program calendar/handbook.* Arlington, VA: Author.

Grimaldi, P. L. (1982). *Medicaid reimbursement of nursing home care.* Washington, DC: American Enterprise Institute.

Guttman, D. (1980). *Perspective on equitable shares in public benefits by minority elderly: Executive summary.* Washington, DC: Catholic University of America.

Guttman, R. (1991). *Adult day care for Alzheimer's patients: Impact on family caregivers.* New York: Garland.

Hale, N. (1990). *The older worker.* San Francisco: Jossey-Bass.

Halpert, B., & Sharp, T. (1989). A model to nationally replicate a locally successful rural family caregiver program: The volunteer information provider program. *The Gerontologist, 29,* 561-563.

Hamburg, D., Elliot, G., & Parron, D. (1982). *Health behavior: Frontiers of research in the biobehavioral sciences*. Washington, DC: National Academy Press.

Hanley, R., & Wiener, J. (1990). *Use of paid home care by the chronically disabled elderly*. Washington, DC: Brookings Institution.

Hanssen, A., Meima, N., Buckspan, L., Henderson, B., Helbig, T., & Zarit, S. (1978). Correlates of senior center participation. *The Gerontologist, 18,* 193-199.

Hare, P. (1991). An increasing source of affordable housing. *Public Management, 73*(9), 5-9.

Hare, P. H. (1990). The echo housing/granny flat experience in the US. *Journal of Housing for the Elderly, 7*(2), 57-70.

Harper, B. (1995). Report from the national task force on access to hospice care by minority groups. *Hospice Journal, 10,* 1-9.

Harper, M. S. (1991). Delivery of mental health services in the home, and other community-based health services. In M. S. Harper (Ed.), *Management and care of the elderly* (pp. 320-331). Newbury Park, CA: Sage.

Harper, N., McDowell, D., Turner, J., & Sharma, A. (1988). Planned short-stay admissions to a geriatric unit: One aspect of respite care. *Age and Ageing, 3,* 199-203.

Harrington, C. (1991). The nursing home industry: A structural analysis. In M. Minkler & C. L. Estes (Eds.), *Critical perspectives on aging: The political and moral economy of growing old*. Amityville, MD: Baywood.

Harris, M. (1988). *Home health care administration*. Owings Mills, MD: National Health Publishing.

Harris & Associates. (1975). *The myth and reality of aging in America*. Washington, DC: National Council on the Aging.

Hasler, B. S. (1990). *Reporting of minority participation under Title III of the Older Americans Act*. Washington, DC: Public Policy Institute/American Association of Retired Persons.

Hatfield, E., & Sprecher, S. (1983). Equity theory and recipient reactions to aid. In J. D. Fisher, A. Nadler, & B. M. DePaulo (Eds.), *New directions in helping* (Vol. 1, pp. 113-141). New York: Academic Press.

Haupt, B. (1997). *Characteristics of patients receiving hospice care services: United States: 1994* (Advance Data From Vital and Health Statistics, No. 282). Hyattsville, MD: National Center for Health Statistics.

Hawes, C., Wildfire, J. B., & Lux, L. J. (1993). *The regulation of board and care homes: Results of a survey in the 50 states and the District of Columbia: National summary*. Washington, DC: American Association of Retired Persons.

Health Care Finance Administration. (1996a). *Medicaid eligibility* [Online]. Available: http://www.hcfa.gov/medicaid/medmed.htm.

Health Care Finance Administration. (1996b). *Medicaid services* [Online]. Available: http://www.hcfa.gov/medicaid/mservice.htm

Health Care Finance Administration. (1996c). *Medicaid under welfare reform: An overview* [Online]. Available: http://www.hcfa.gov/medicaid/welrefrm.htm

Health Care Finance Administration. (1996d). *Medicare and medicaid: Brief summaries of Title XVIII and Title XIX of the Social Security Act* [Online]. Available: http://www.hcfa.gov/medicare/medmed.htm

Health Care Finance Administration. (1997a). *Medicaid vendor payments by type of service* [Online]. Available: http://www.hcfa.gov/medicaid/595.htm

Health Care Finance Administration. (1997b). *Medicare handbook* [Online]. Available: www.hcfa.gov/pubforms/mhbkc05.htm and www.hcfa.gov/pubforms/mhbkc04.htm

Heath, A. (1993). *ElderTransit facts: Increasing minority participation in transportation programs* [Brochure]. Washington, DC: National Eldercare Institute on Transportation.

Henkin, N., & Weinstein-Shr, G. (1989). College students tutor older refugees in English. *Aging, 359,* 17-19.

Henry, M. E., & Capitman, J. (1995). Finding satisfaction in adult day care: Analysis of a national demonstration of dementia care and respite services. *Journal of Applied Gerontology, 14,* 302-320.

Herman, C. J., & Wadsworth, N. (1992). *Action for health: Older women's project.* Cleveland, OH: Case Western Reserve University School of Medicine.

Heumann, L. F. (1990). The housing and support costs of elderly with comparable support needs living in long-term care and congregate housing. *Journal of Housing for the Elderly, 6*(1/2), 45-71.

Hickey, T., & Stilwell, D. L. (1991). Health promotion for older people: All is not well. *The Gerontologist, 31,* 822-829.

High, D. M. (1988). All in the family: Extended autonomy and expectations in surrogate health care decision making. *The Gerontologist, 28*(Suppl.), 46-52.

Higher Education Act, 20 U.S.C. § 1001 *et seq.* (1965).

Hing, E. (1987, May 14). *Use of nursing homes by the elderly: Preliminary data from the 1985 National Nursing Home Survey* (Advance Data From Vital and Health Statistics, No. 135, DHHS Publication No. PHS 87-1250). Hyattsville, MD: National Center for Health Statistics.

Hing, E. (1994). *Characteristics of elderly home health patients: Preliminary data from the 1992 National Home and Hospice Care Survey* (Advance Data From Vital and Health Statistics, No. 247). Hyattsville, MD: National Center for Health Statistics.

Hing, E., & Bloom, B. (1990). *Long-term care for the functionally dependent elderly* (Vital and Health Statistics, Series 13, No. 104, DHHS Publication No. PHS 90-1765). Hyattsville, MD: Public Health Service.

Hirshorn, B., & Hoyer, D. (1994). Private sector hiring and use of retirees: The firm's perspective. *The Gerontologist, 34,* 50-58.

Hodgson, L. G. (1995). Adult grandchildren and their grandparents: The enduring bond. *International Journal of Aging and Human Development, 34,* 209-225.

Hooper, K., & Hamberg, J. (1986). The making of America's homeless: From skid row to the new poor, 1945-1984. In R. Bratt, C. Hartman, & A. Meyerson (Eds.), *Critical perspectives in housing.* Philadelphia: Temple University Press.

Hooyman, N. R., & Kiyak, H. A. (1996). *Social gerontology: A multidisciplinary perspective.* Needham Heights, MA: Simon & Schuster.

Horowitz, A. (1985). Family caregiving to the frail elderly. In C. Eisdorfer (Ed.), *Annual review of gerontology and geriatrics* (Vol. 5, pp. 194-246). New York: Springer.

Hospice fact sheet. (1995, October). Arlington, VA: National Hospice Organization.

House calls. (1989). *ABA Banking Journal, 81,* 79-80.

Howe, R. (1994). A framework for case management. In R. Howe (Ed.), *Case management for health care professionals* (pp. 3-12). Chicago: Precept.

Hudson, R. B., & Kingson, E. R. (1991). Inclusive and fair: The case for universality in social programs. *Generations, 15*(3), 51-56.

Hushbeck, J. (1990). American business, public policy, and the older worker. *Virginia Journal of Science, 41,* 169-181.

Huttman, E. D. (1985). *Social services for the elderly.* New York: Free Press.

Iams, H. (1987). Jobs of persons working after receiving retired-worker benefits. *Social Security Bulletin, 50,* 5-12.

Independent Sector. (1988). Giving and volunteering in the United States: Findings from a national survey. Washington, DC: Author.

Institute of Medicine. (1986). *Improving the quality of care in nursing homes.* Washington, DC: National Academy Press.

Institute of Medicine. (1991). *Disability in America: Toward a national agenda for prevention.* Washington, DC: National Academy Press.

Intermodal Surface Transportation Efficiency Act of 1991, Pub. L. No. 102-240, 105 Stat. 1914.

Jaffe, D. J., & Howe, E. (1988). Agency-assisted shared housing: The nature of programs and matches. *The Gerontologist, 28,* 318-324.

Jette, A., & Branch, L. (1992). A ten-year follow-up of driving patterns among the community-dwelling elderly. *Human Factors, 34*(1), 25-31.

Jirovec, R. L., Erich, J. A., & Sanders, L. J. (1989). Patterns of senior center participation among low income urban elderly. *Journal of Gerontological Social Work, 13,* 115-132.

Job Training Partnership Act of 1982, Pub. L. No. 97-300, 96 Stat. 1322 (1982).

Jones, A. (1994). *Hospice and home health agencies: Data from the 1991 National Health Provider Inventory* (Advance Data From Vital and Health Statistics, No. 257). Hyattsville, MD: National Center for Health Statistics.

Jones, D. C., & Vaughan, K. (1990). Close friendships among senior adults. *Psychology and Aging, 3,* 451-457.

Justice, D. (1993). *Case management standards in state community based long-term care programs.* Washington, DC: Congressional Research Service.

Kane, N. (1989). The home care crisis of the nineties. *The Gerontologist, 29,* 24-31.

Kane, R., & Caplan, A. (Eds.). (1993). *Ethical conflict in the management of home care: Case manager's dilemma.* New York: Springer.

Kane, R., & Frytak, J. (1994). *Models for case management in long-term care: Interactions of case managers and home care providers.* Minneapolis, MN: National Long-Term Care Resource Center.

Kane, R., Illston, L., & Miller, N. (1992). Qualitative analysis of the program of all-inclusive care for the elderly (PACE). *The Gerontologist, 32,* 771-780.

Kane, R., & Kane, R. (1981). *Assessing the elderly: A practical guide for measurement.* Lexington, MA: Lexington Books.

Kane, R., Kane, R., Kaye, N., Mollica, R., Riley, T., Saucier, P., Snow, K., & Starr, L. (1996). *Managed care: Handbook for the aging network.* Minneapolis, MN: National Long-Term Care Resource Center.

Kane, R. A., & Wilson, K. B. (1993). *Assisted living in the United States: A new paradigm for residential care for frail older persons?* Washington, DC: American Association of Retired Persons.

Kannel, W. B. (1986). Nutritional contributors to cardiovascular disease in the elderly. *Journal of the American Geriatrics Society, 34,* 27-36.

Kansas Department of Commerce and Housing. (1997). *Sunflower supportive services program.* [Online]. Available: http://kicin.cecase.ukans.edu/kdoch/html/ssp.html

Kaplan, J., & Shore, H. (1993). The Jewish nursing home: Innovations in practice and policy. In C. M. Barresi & D. E. Stull (Eds.), *Ethnic elderly and long-term care* (pp. 115-129). New York: Springer.

Kart, C. S. (1997). *The realities of aging: An introduction to gerontology* (5th ed.). Needham Heights, MA: Allyn & Bacon.

Kaye, L. (1992). *Home health care.* Newbury Park, CA: Sage.

Kaye, L., & Applegate, J. (1990). *Men as caregivers to the elderly: Understanding and aiding unrecognized family support.* Lexington, MA: Lexington Books.

Keith, P. M., & Wacker, R. R. (1994). *Older wards and their guardians*. New York: Praeger.

Kelley, H. H. (1967). Attribution theory in social psychology. In D. Levin (Ed.), *Nebraska Symposium on Motivation* (pp. 151-174). Lincoln: University of Nebraska Press.

Kelley, T. (1991). Volunteerism legislation. In *Resourceful aging: Today and tomorrow: Vol. 2. Volunteerism* (pp. 77-81). Washington, DC: American Association of Retired Persons.

Kelly, J. R., Steinkamp, M. W., & Kelly, J. R. (1986). Later life leisure: How they play in Peoria. *The Gerontologist, 26,* 531-537.

Kelly, J. R., Steinkamp, M. W., & Kelly, J. R. (1987). Later life satisfaction: Does leisure contribute? *Leisure Sciences, 9,* 189-200.

Kemper, P. (1988). The evaluation of the National Long Term Care Demonstration: Overview of the findings. *Health Services Research, 23,* 161-174.

Kemper, P., & Murtaugh, C. (1991). Lifetime use of nursing home care. *New England Journal of Medicine, 324*(9), 595-600.

Kenney, G., & Dubay, L. (1992). Examining area variation in the use of Medicare home health services. *Medical Care, 30,* 43-57.

Kent, D. (1978, May/June). The how and why of senior centers. *Aging,* 2-6.

Kent, K. (1990). Elders and community mental health centers. *Generations, 14*(1), 19-21.

Kingston, E. R. (1996). Ways of thinking about the long-term care of the baby-boom cohort. *Journal of Aging and Social Policy, 7*(3/4), 3-23.

Kingston, E. R., Hirshorn, B. A., & Cornman, J. M. (1986). *Ties that bind: The interdependence of generations*. Cabin John, MD: Seven Locks.

Kirschner Associates, Inc. (1983). *An evaluation of the nutritional services for the elderly* (Vols. 1-5). Washington, DC: U.S. Department of Health and Human Services, Administration on Aging.

Kirwin, P., & Kaye, L. (1991). Service consumption patterns over time among adult day care program participants. *Home Health Care Services Quarterly, 12,* 45-58.

Klein, S. (1989). Respite program gives care givers a break. *Health Progress, 70,* 64-68.

Klein, S. (Ed.). (1986). *In-home respite care for older adults: A practical guide from program planners, administrators, and clinicians*. Springfield, IL: Charles C Thomas.

Kochhar, S. (1992, Summer). Denial of SSI applicants because of excess resources. *Social Security Bulletin, 55,* 52-56.

Korim, A. (1974). *Older Americans and community colleges: A guide for program implementation*. Washington, DC: American Association of Community and Junior Colleges.

Kosloski, K., & Montgomery, R. (1993). The effects of respite on caregivers of Alzheimer's patients: One year evaluation of the Michigan model of respite programs. *Journal of Applied Gerontology, 12,* 4-17.

Kosloski, K., & Montgomery, R. (1995). The impact of respite use on nursing home placement. *The Gerontologist, 35,* 67-74.

Kotlikoff, L. J., & Wise, D. A. (1989). *The wage carrot and the pension stick.* Kalamazoo, MI: W. E. Upjohn Institute.

Krout, J. (1981). *Service utilization patterns of the rural elderly: Final report to the Administration on Aging.* Fredonia, NY: Author.

Krout, J. (1982). *Determinants of service use by the aged: Final report to the AARP Andrus Foundation.* Fredonia, NY: Author.

Krout, J. (1983a). Correlates of senior center utilization. *Research on Aging, 5,* 339-352.

Krout, J. (1983b). Knowledge and use of services by the elderly: A critical review of the literature. *International Journal of Aging and Human Development, 17,* 153-167.

Krout, J. (1984). Knowledge of senior center activities among the elderly. *Journal of Applied Gerontology, 3,* 71-81.

Krout, J. (1985a). Senior center activities and services. *Research on Aging, 7,* 455-471.

Krout, J. (1985b). Service awareness among the elderly. *Journal of Gerontological Social Work, 9,* 7-19.

Krout, J. (1987a). Rural verses urban differences in senior center activities and services. *The Gerontologist, 27,* 92-97.

Krout, J. (1987b). *Senior center linkages and the provision of services to the elderly: Final report to the AARP Andrus Foundation.* Fredonia, NY: Author.

Krout, J. (1988). *The frequency, duration, stability, and discontinuation of senior center participation: Causes and consequences: Final report to the AARP Andrus Foundation.* Fredonia, NY: Author.

Krout, J. (1989a). *Area agencies on aging: Service planning and provision for the rural elderly: Final report to the Retirement Research Foundation.* Fredonia, NY: Author.

Krout, J. (1989b). *Senior centers in America.* Westport, CT: Greenwood.

Krout, J. (1990). *The organization, operation, and programming of senior centers in America: A seven-year follow-up: Final report to the AARP Andrus Foundation.* Fredonia, NY: Author.

Krout, J. (1993a). Case management activities for the rural elderly: Findings from a national study. *Journal of Case Management, 2,* 137-146.

Krout, J. (1993b). *Senior centers and at-risk older persons: A national agenda.* Washington, DC: National Institute on the Aging.

Krout, J. (1995). Senior centers and services for the frail elderly. *Journal of Aging and Social Policy, 7*(2), 59-76.

Krout, J., Cutler, S. J., & Coward, R. T. (1990). Correlates of senior center participation: A national analysis. *The Gerontologist, 30,* 72-79.

Kuhn, B. A., Dunn, P. A., Smallwood, D., Hanson, K., Blaylock, J., & Vogel, S. (1996). Policy watch: The food stamp program and welfare reform. *Journal of Economic Perspectives, 10*(2), 189-198.

Kutza, E. A. (1991). The Older Americans Act of 2000: What should it be? *Generations, 15*(3), 65-68.

Lalonde, B., Hooyman, N., & Blumhagen, J. (1988). Long-term outcome effectiveness of a health promotion program for the elderly: The Wallingford Wellness Project. *Journal of Gerontological Social Work, 13,* 95-112.

Lattanzi-Licht, M. (1989). Bereavement services: Practice and problems. In M. Lattanzi-Licht, J. Kirschling, & S. Flemming (Eds.), *Bereavement care: A new look at hospice and community based services* (pp. 1-28). New York: Haworth.

Lawton, M. P. (1980). Housing elderly: Residential quality and residential satisfaction. *Research on Aging, 2,* 309-328.

Lawton, M. P. (1982). Competence, environmental press, and the adaptation of older people. In M. P. Lawton, P. G. Windley, & T. O. Byerts (Eds.), *Aging and the environment: Theoretical approaches* (pp. 33-59). New York: Springer.

Lawton, M. P. (1989). Three functions of the residential environment. In L. A. Pastalan & M. E. Cowart (Eds.), *Lifestyles and housing of older adults* (pp. 35-50). New York: Haworth.

Lawton, M. P., Brody, E., & Saperstein, A. (1991). *Respite for caregivers of Alzheimer's patients: Research and practice.* New York: Springer.

Lawton, M. P., Moss, M., & Fulcomer, M. (1982). Determinants of the leisure activities of older people. Philadelphia: Philadelphia Geriatrics Center.

Lawton, M. P., & Nahemow, L. (1973). Ecology and the aging process. In C. Eisdorfer & M. P. Lawton (Eds.), *Psychology of adult development and aging* (pp. 619-674). Washington, DC: American Psychological Association.

Leanse, J., Tiven, M., & Robb, T. B. (1977). *Senior center operation.* Washington, DC: National Council on the Aging.

Leanse, J., & Wagner, L. (1975). *Senior centers: A report of senior group programs in America.* Washington, DC: National Council on the Aging.

Lebowitz, B., Light, E., & Bailey, F. (1987). Mental health services for the elderly: The impact of coordination with area agencies on aging. *The Gerontologist, 27,* 699-702.

Lebowitz, B., & Niederehe, G. (1992). Concepts and issues in mental health and aging. In J. Birren, R. B. Sloane, & G. Cohen (Eds.), *Handbook of mental health and aging* (2nd ed., pp. 3-26). New York: Academic Press.

Lee, G. R. (1983). Social integration and fear of crime among older persons. *Journal of Gerontology, 38*(6), 745-750.

Lee, J. (1991). *Development, delivery, and utilization of services under the Older Americans Act: A perspective of Asian American elderly.* New York: Garland.

Lee, J. (1993, April). *ElderTransit facts: Analysis of area agency on aging transportation survey* [Brochure]. Washington, DC: National Eldercare Institute on Transportation.

Lefebvre, R. C., Harden, E. A., Rawkowski, W., Lasater, T. M., & Careton, R. A. (1987). Characteristics of participants in community health programs: Four-year results. *American Journal of Public Health, 77,* 1342-1344.

Legal Services Corporation Act, 42 U.S.C. § 2996 *et seq.* (1974).

Legal Services Corporation (1997). LSC Acts/Regulations. [Online]. Available at http://www.ltsi.net/lsc/acts.html

Lemke, S., & Moos, R. (1989). Personal and environmental determinants of activity involvement among elderly residents of congregate facilities. *Journal of Gerontology, 44,* S139-S148.

Levinson, R. W. (1988). *Information and referral networks.* New York: Springer.

Lichtenberg, P. (1994). *A guide to psychological practice in geriatric long-term care.* New York: Haworth.

Liebson, C., Naessons, J., Krishan, I., Campion, M., & Ballard, D. (1990). Disposition at discharge and 60 day mortality among elderly people following shorter hospital stays: A population based comparison. *The Gerontologist, 30,* 316-322.

Liess, D. (1996). *Healthwise for Life: Evaluative report.* Greeley: Colorado State University Cooperative Extension.

Lifelong Learning Act, Pub. L. No. 94-482 (1976).

Lindquist, J. H., & Duke, J. M. (1982). The elderly victim at risk: Explaining the fear-victimization paradox. *Criminology, 20*(1), 115-126.

Lipman, A., & Longino, C. F., Jr. (1982). Formal and informal support: A conceptual clarification. *Journal of Applied Gerontology, 1,* 141-146.

Lipman, A., & Sterne, R. (1962). Aging in the United States: Ascription of a terminal sick role. *Sociology and Social Research, 53,* 194-203.

Lipsky, M., & Thibodeau, M. A. (1990). Domestic food policy in the United States. *Journal of Health Politics, Policy and Law, 15*(2), 319-339.

Litwak, E. (1985). *Helping the elderly: The complementary roles of informal networks and formal systems.* New York: Guilford.

Litwak, E., & Misseri, P. (1989). Organizational theory, social supports, and mortality rates: A theoretical convergence. *American Sociological Review, 54,* 49-66.

Long, N. (1975). *Information and referral services: Research findings* (DHEW Publication No. OHDS 77-20410). Washington, DC: Government Printing Office.

Long, N., Anderson, J., Burd, R., Mathis, M. E., & Todd, S. P. (1971). *Information and referral centers: A functional analysis* (DHEW Publication No. OHD 75-20235). Washington, DC: Government Printing Office.

Loomis, L. M., Sorce, P., & Tyler, P. R. (1989). A lifestyle analysis of healthy retirees and their interest in moving to a retirement community. In L. A. Pastalan (Ed.), *The retirement community movement: Contemporary issues* (pp. 19-35). New York: Haworth.

Looney, K. (1987). The respite care alternative. *Journal of Gerontological Nursing, 13,* 18-21.

Lowenthal, B., & Egan, R. (1991). Senior citizen volunteers in a university day-care center. *Educational Gerontology, 17,* 363-378.

Lowy, L. (1980). *Social policies and programs on aging.* Lexington, MA: Lexington Books.

Lowy, L., & Doolin, J. (1985). Multipurpose and senior centers. In A. Monk (Ed.), *Handbook of gerontological services* (pp. 342-376). New York: Van Nostrand Reinhold.

Maas, M. (1988). Management of patients with Alzheimer's disease in long term care facilities. *Nursing Clinics of North America, 23,* 57-68.

MacAdam, M., Capitman, J., Yee, D., Prottas, J., Leutz, W., & Westwater, D. (1989). Case management for frail elders: The Robert Wood Johnson Foundation's program for hospital initiatives in long-term care. *The Gerontologist, 29,* 737-744.

MacDonald, D. (1992). Hospice patients without primary caregivers: A critique of prevailing intervention strategies. *Home Healthcare Nurse, 10,* 24-26.

MaloneBeach, E., Zarit, S., & Shore, D. (1992). Caregivers' perceptions of case management and community-based services: Barriers to service use. *Journal of Applied Gerontology, 11,* 145-159.

Mangum, W. (1985). But not in my neighborhood: Community resistance to housing for the elderly. *Journal of Housing for the Elderly, 3,* 101-119.

Manheimer, R. (1992). Creative retirement in an aging society. In R. Fischer, M. Blazey, & H. Lipman (Eds.), *Students of the third age* (pp. 122-131). New York: Macmillan.

Manheimer, R., Snodgrass, D., & Moskow-McKenzie, D. (1995). *Older adult education: A guide to research, programs, and policies.* Westport, CT: Greenwood.

Mantell, J., & Gildea, M. (1989). Elderly shared housing in the United States. In D. J. Jaffe (Ed.), *Shared housing for the elderly* (pp. 13-23). New York: Greenwood.

Manton, K. I. (1987). Patterns and psychological correlates of material support within a religious setting: The bidirectional support hypothesis. *American Journal of Community Psychology, 15,* 185-207.

Mark Battle Associates. (1977). *Evaluation of information and referral services for the elderly: Final report* (DHEW Publication No. OHDS 77-20109). Washington, DC: Government Printing Office.

Marmor, T. R., Mashaw, J. L., & Harvey, P. L. (1990). *America's misunderstood welfare state: Persistent myths, enduring realities.* New York: Basic Books.

Marriott Senior Living Services. (1991). *Marriott seniors volunteerism study.* Washington, DC: Author.

Marsden, A. (1990). Education for support of nursing home residents. *Journal of Extension, 28,* 10-12.

Matthews, D. H., & Sprey, J. (1984). The impact of divorce on grandparenthood: An exploratory study. *The Gerontologist, 24,* 41-47.

Matthews, J. (1992). *Social Security, Medicare, and pensions: A sourcebook for Older Americans* (5th ed.). Berkeley, CA: Nolo.

Matthews, J., & Berman, D. M. (1990). *Social Security, Medicare and pensions* (3rd ed.). Berkeley, CA: Nolo.

Matthews, J., & Berman, D. M. (1996). *Social Security, Medicare, and pensions* (6th ed.). Berkeley, CA: Nolo.

Matthews, S. H., & Rosner, T. T. (1988). Shared filial responsibility: The family as the primary caregiver. *Journal of Marriage and the Family, 50,* 185-195.

Mauser, T. (1994). *Colorado transit overview.* Denver: Colorado Department of Transportation.

Maves, P., & Bock, K. (Eds.). (1990). *Organizational manual for Shepherd's Center.* Kansas City, MO: Shepherd's Center of America.

Maxwell, J. (1962). *Centers for older people: Guide for programs and facilities.* Washington, DC: National Council on the Aging.

McCaslin, R. (1981). Next steps in information and referral for the elderly. *The Gerontologist, 21,* 184-193.

McCaslin, R. (1989). Service utilization by the elderly: The importance of orientation to the formal system. *Journal of Gerontological Social Work, 14,* 153-174.

McClusky, H. (1974). Education for aging: The scope of the field and perspectives for the future. In S. M. Grabowski & W. D. Mason (Eds.), *Learning for aging* (pp. 324-355). Washington, DC: Adult Education Association of the USA.

McConnel, S., & Beitler, D. (1991). The Older Americans Act after 25 years: An overview. *Generations, 15*(3), 5-10.

McDaniel, S. A. (1986). *Canada's aging population.* Toronto, Ontario, Canada: Butterworths.

McGinnis, J. (1988). *Year 2000 health objectives for the nation: Proceedings of the surgeon general's workshop: Health promotion and aging*. Washington, DC: Government Printing Office.

McKee, P. (1995). Gardening: An equal opportunity joy. *Activities, Adaptation, & Aging, 20,* 71-78.

McNaught, W., & Barth, M. (1992). Are older workers "good buys"? A case study of Days Inns of America. *Sloan Management Review, 33,* 53-63.

Meals on Wheels America: A history of success. (1996, Spring). *Meals on Wheels America,* 1-2.

Meeks, S., Carstensen, L., Stafford, P., Brenner, L., Weathers, F., Welch, R., & Oltmanns, T. (1990). Mental health needs of the chronically ill elderly. *Psychology and Aging, 5,* 163-171.

Mettler, M., & Kemper, D. W. (1995, January/February). Healthwise study shows rural self-care training pays off. *Aging Today,* 5.

Meyer, M. D. (1991). Assuring quality of care: Nursing home resident councils. *Journal of Applied Gerontology, 10*(1), 103-116.

Mikelsons, J., & Turner, M. (1991). *Housing conditions of the elderly in the 1980's: A data book*. Washington, DC: Urban Institute.

Miko, P. S., & Sanchez, M. A. (1993). Hispanic elderly, Orgullo Communal, and recreation. *Journal of Physical Education, Recreation, and Dance, 64,* 45-47.

Miller, D., & Goldman, L. (1989). Perceptions of caregivers about special respite services for the elderly. *The Gerontologist, 29,* 408-410.

Miller, D., Gulle, N., & McCue, F. (1986). The realities of respite for families, clients, and sponsors. *The Gerontologist, 26,* 467-470.

Miller, J. A. (1991). *Community-based long-term care: Innovative models*. Newbury Park, CA: Sage.

Miller, P. A. (1992). Introduction: Negotiating the retirement rite. In R. Fischer, M. Blazey, & H. Lipman (Eds.), *Students of the third age* (pp. 1-9). New York: Macmillan.

Mills, E. (1993). *The story of Elderhostel*. Hanover, NH: University Press of New England.

Milne, K. (1994). The evolution of case management to care management. In R. Howe (Ed.), *Case management for health care professionals* (pp. 179-190). Chicago: Precept.

Miner, S., Logan, J. R., & Spitz, G. (1993). Predicting the frequency of senior center attendance. *The Gerontologist, 33,* 650-657.

Minkler, M., & Pasick, R. J. (1985). Health promotion and the elderly: A critical perspective on the past and future. In K. Dychtwald (Ed.), *Wellness and health promotion for the elderly* (pp. 39-51). Rockville, MD: Aspen.

Minkler, M., & Roe, K. M. (1996). Grandparents as surrogate parents. *Generations, 20*(1), 34-37.

Miranda, M. (1988, November). The older worker. *Aging Network News, 5,* 12.

Mitchell, J. (1995). Service awareness and use among older North Carolinians. *Journal of Applied Gerontology, 14*(2), 193-209.

Mitchell, O. (Ed.). (1993). *As the work force ages: Costs, benefits, and policy challenges.* Ithaca, NY: ILR.

Moen, E. (1978). The reluctance of the elderly to accept help. *Social Problems, 25,* 293-303.

Monahan, D. (1993). Utilization of dementia-specific respite day care for clients and their caregivers in a social model program. *Journal of Gerontological Social Work, 20,* 57-70.

Monk, A., & Kaye, L. W. (1991). Congregate housing for the elderly: Its need, function, and perspective. *Journal of Housing for the Elderly, 9*(1/2), 5-20.

Monk, A., Kaye, L. W., & Litwin, H. (1984). *Resolving grievances in the nursing home: A study of the ombudsman program.* New York: Columbia University Press.

Montgomery, R. (1992). Examining respite: Its promise and limits. In M. Ory & A. Dunker (Eds.), *In-home care for older people: Health and supportive services* (pp. 75-96). Newbury Park, CA: Sage.

Montgomery, R. J., & Kamo, Y. (1989). Parent care by sons and daughters. In J. A. Mancini (Ed.), *Aging parents and adult children* (pp. 213-228). Lexington, MA: Lexington Books.

Moody, H. R. (1976). Philosophical presuppositions of education for older adults. *Educational Gerontology, 2,* 1-16.

Moody, H. R. (1988). *Abundance of life: Human development policies for an aging society.* New York: Columbia University Press.

Moon, M., & Ruggles, P. (1994). The needy or the greedy? Assessing the income support of an aging population. In T. Marmor, T. Smeeding, & V. Greene (Eds.), *Economic security and intergenerational justice: A look at North America* (pp. 207-226). Washington, DC: Urban Institute.

Moore, M., & Piland, W. (1994). Impact of campus physical environment on older adult learners. *Community College Journal of Research and Practice, 18,* 307-317.

Moore, W. (1989, March/April). Assessing the unmet legal needs of older persons: What will it cost to meet that need? *Elder Law Forum, 1*(2), 4.

Moore, W. (1992). Improving the delivery of legal services for the elderly: A comprehensive approach. *Emory Law Journal, 41,* 805-861.

Mor, V., & Allen, S. (1995). Hospice. In G. Maddox (Ed.), *The encyclopedia of aging* (2nd ed., pp. 475-477). New York: Springer.

Morrow-Howell, N., Lott, L., & Ozawa, M. (1990). The impact of race on volunteer helping relationships among the elderly. *Social Work, 35,* 395-402.

Morrow-Howell, N., & Mui, A. (1989). Elderly volunteers: Reasons for initiating and terminating service. *Journal of Gerontological Social Work, 13*(3/4), 21-34.

Mosher-Ashley, P. (1993). Referral patterns of elderly clients to a community mental health center. *Journal of Gerontological Social Work, 20* 3/4, 5-23.

Mosher-Ashley, P., & Allard, J. (1993). Problems facing chronically mentally ill elders receiving community-based psychiatric services: Need for residential services. *Adult Residential Care Journal, 7,* 23-30.

Moss, F. E., & Halamandaris, V. J. (1977). *Too old, too sick, too bad.* Germantown, MD: Aspen.

Motenko, A. (1988). Respite care and pride in caregiving: The experience of six older men caring for their disabled wives. In S. Reinharz & G. Rowles (Eds.), *Qualitative gerontology* (pp. 104-127). New York: Springer.

Motenko, A. (1989). The frustrations, gratifications, and well-being of dementia caregivers. *The Gerontologist, 29,* 166-172.

Mullins, L. C., Cook, C., Mushel, M., Machin, G., & Georgas, J. (1993). A comparative examination of the characteristics of participants of a senior citizens nutrition and activities program. *Activities, Adaptation, & Aging, 17*(3), 15-37.

Murakami, E. (1994, November). *ElderTransit facts: Improving travel for the elderly* [Brochure]. Washington, DC: National Eldercare Institute on Transportation.

Murtaugh, C., Kemper, P., & Spillman, B. (1990). The risk of nursing home use in later life. *Medical Care, 28,* 952-962.

Nadler, A., Fisher, J. D., & Streufest, S. (1976). The donor's dilemma: Recipient's reactions to aid from friend or foe. *Journal of Personality, 44,* 392-409.

Nadler, A., & Mayseless, O. (1983). Recipient self-esteem and reactions to help. In J. D. Fisher, A. Nadler, & B. M. DePaulo (Eds.), *New directions in helping* (Vol. 1, pp. 167-188). New York: Academic Press.

Nadler, A., Sheinberg, L., & Jaffe, Y. (1981). Coping with stress by help seeking: Help seeking and receiving behavior in male paraplegics. In C. Spielberger, I. Sarason, & N. Milgram (Eds.), *Stress and anxiety* (Vol. 8, pp. 375-386). Washington, DC: Hemisphere.

Naifeh, M. L. (1993). *Housing of the elderly: 1991* (U.S. Bureau of the Census, Current Housing Reports, Series H-123, No. 93-1). Washington, DC: Government Printing Office.

National Academy on Aging. (1995, August). *Facts on the Older Americans Act.* Washington, DC: Author.

National and Community Service Trust Act of 1993, 42 U.S.C. § 12571 *et seq.* (1996).

National Association of Area Agencies on Aging. (1996). *Legislative briefing: Advocate's guide to 1996 national policy priorities.* Washington, DC: Author.

National Association for Home Care. (1995). *Basic statistics about home care 1995.* Washington, DC: Author.

National Association for Home Care. (1997). *Home care on-line* [Online]. Available: http://www.nahc.org

National Center for Educational Statistics. (1991). *Integrated postsecondary education data system: Fall enrollment, 1987 survey.* Washington, DC: U.S. Department of Education.

National Center for Health Statistics. (1990, October). *Current estimates from the National Health Interview Survey: 1989* (Vital and Health Statistics, Series 10, No. 176). Washington, DC: Government Printing Office.

National Center for Health Statistics. (1993). *Health: United States.* Hyattsville, MD: Public Health Service.

National Eldercare Institute on Health Promotion. (1995). Telephone links reduce isolation. *Perspectives in Health Promotion and Aging, 10*(1), 2.

National Eldercare Institute on Transportation. (1992, September). *Focus group report.* Washington, DC: Author.

National Eldercare Institute on Transportation. (1994). *Meeting the challenge: Mobility for elders* (Prepared for the Administration on Aging). Washington, DC: Author.

National Institute of Senior Centers. (1978). *Senior center standards: Guidelines for practice.* Washington, DC: National Council on the Aging.

National Institute on Adult Day Care. (1990). *Standards and guidelines for adult day care.* Washington, DC: National Council on the Aging.

National Institute on Aging and Administration on Aging. (1996). *Resource directory for older people* (NIH Publication No. 95-738). Washington, DC: Government Printing Office.

National Policy and Resource Center on Nutrition and Aging. (1996). *Use of medical food and food for special dietary uses in elderly nutrition programs.* Miami: Florida International University.

National Senior Service Corps. (1994a). *Foster grandparent program fact sheet.* Washington, DC: Author.

National Senior Service Corps. (1994b). *RSVP fact sheet.* Washington, DC: Author.

Neal, M., Chapman, N., Ingersoll-Dayton, B., & Emlen, A. (1993). *Balancing work and caregiving for children, adults, and elders.* Newbury Park, CA: Sage.

Netting, F. E., & Hinds, H. (1989). Rural volunteer ombudsman programs. *Journal of Applied Gerontology, 8*(4), 419-427.

Netting, F. E., Paton, R. N., & Huber, R. (1992). The long-term care ombudsman program: What does the complaint reporting system tell us? *The Gerontologist, 32,* 843-848.

Newman, S., & Riess, J. (1992). Older workers in intergenerational child care settings. *Journal of Gerontological Social Work, 19,* 45-66.

Noggle, B. (1995). Identifying and meeting needs of ethnic minority patients. *Hospice Journal, 10,* 85-93.

Norry, L. J., & Williams, B. T. (1994). *Homeowners, home maintenance, and home improvements: 1991.* (U.S. Bureau of the Census, Current Housing Reports, Series H-121, No. 93-4). Washington, DC: Government Printing Office.

Northeast Midwest Institute. (1997, February). *Weatherization Assistance Program: Fiscal 1996 and fiscal 1997* [Online]. Available: http://www.nemw.org/weath96.htm

Office of the Assistant Secretary for Planning and Evaluation. (1995). *Sub-acute care: Policy synthesis and market area analysis* [Online]. Available: http://aspe.os.dhhs.gov/daltcp/ltc/xsubacut.htm

O'Hare, W. P. (1996). A new look at poverty in America. *Population Bulletin, 51*(2), 1-48.

Older Adult Service and Information System. (1991). *Older adult service and information system: OASIS fact sheet and brochure.* St. Louis, MO: Author.

Older Americans Act of 1965, Pub. L. No. 89-73, 42 U.S.C. § 3001 *et seq.,* as amended or reauthorized 1967, 1968, 1972, 1973, 1974, 1975, 1977, 1978, 1984, 1987, 1992, 1997.

Older Workers Benefit Protection Act of 1990, 29 U.S.C. §§ 623, 626, 630 (1990).

Omnibus Budget Reconciliation Act of 1980, 5 U.S.C. § 8340 *et seq.,* as amended.

Omnibus Budget Reconciliation Act of 1981, Pub. L. No. 97-35, 95 Stat. 357, 5 U.S.C. § 8340 *et seq.,* as amended.

Omnibus Budget Reconciliation Act of 1987, 5 U.S.C. § 8340 *et seq.,* as amended.

Omnibus Budget Reconciliation Act of 1989, 5 U.S.C. § 8340 *et seq.,* as amended.

Omnibus Budget Reconciliation Act of 1990, 5 U.S.C. § 8340 *et seq.,* as amended.

O'Neill, C., & Sorensen, E. (1991). Home care of the elderly: A family perspective. *Advances in Nursing Sciences, 13,* 28-37.

Ostrander, N. (1992, February/March). Alcoholism and aging: A rural community's response. *Aging Today, 19.*

Ovrebo, B., Minkler, M., & Liljestrand, P. (1991). No room in the inn: The disappearance of SRO housing in the United States. *Journal of Housing for the Elderly, 8*(1), 77-92.

Palley, H. A., & Oktay, J. S. (1983). *The chronically limited elderly: The case for a national policy for in-home and supportive community based services*. New York: Haworth.

Parmelee, P. A., & Lawton, M. P. (1990). The design of special environments for the aged. In J. E. Birren & K. W. Schaie (Eds.), *Handbook of the psychology of aging* (3rd ed., pp. 464-487). San Diego, CA: Academic Press.

Pascucci, M. (1992). Measuring incentives to health promotion in older adults: Understanding neglected health promotion in older adults. *Journal of Gerontological Nursing, 18,* 16-23.

Patterson, A. H. (1985). Fear of crime and other barriers to use of public transportation by the elderly. *Journal of Architectural Planning and Research, 2,* 277-288.

Pearson, M. A., & Deitrick, E. (1989). A volunteer program for in-home respite care. *Caring, 8,* 18-22.

Penning, M., & Wasyliw, D. (1992). Homebound learning opportunities: Reaching out to older shut-ins and their caregivers. *The Gerontologist, 32,* 704-707.

Personal Responsibility and Work Opportunity Reconciliation Act of 1996, Pub. L. No. 104-193, H.R. 3734, 104th Cong., 1st Sess., Cong. Rec. H8831 (1996).

Perspective on Aging. (1993). The first half-century of senior centers charts the way for decades to come. *Perspective on Aging, 22*(3), 16-25.

Peterson, D. (1985). A history of education for older learners. In D. Lumsden (Ed.), *The older adult as learner* (pp. 1-23). New York: Hemisphere.

Peterson, D. (1990). A history of the education of older learners. In R. Sherron & D. Lumsden (Ed.), *Introduction to educational gerontology* (3rd ed., pp. 1-21). New York: Hemisphere.

Peterson, J. (1995). The faces of community transportation. *Community Transportation Reporter, 13*(3), 10-12.

Peterson, S. A. (1989). Elderly women and program encounters: A rural study. *Journal of Women and Aging, 1*(4), 41-56.

Peterson, S. A., & Maiden, R. (1991). Older Americans' use of nutrition programs. *Journal of Nutrition for the Elderly, 11*(1/2), 49-67.

Petty, D. (1990). Respite care: A flexible response to service fragmentation. In N. Mace (Ed.), *Dementia care: Patient, family, and community* (pp. 243-269). Baltimore: Johns Hopkins University Press.

Phillips, C. D., & Hawes, C. (1996). Nursing homes. In L. A. Vitt, J. K. Siegenthaler, N. E. Culter, & S. Golant (Eds.), *Encyclopedia of financial gerontology* (pp. 385-390). Westport, CT: Greenwood.

Phillips, K. (1992). State and local government pension benefits. In J. A. Turner & D. J. Beller (Eds.), *Trends in pensions: 1992.* Washington, DC: Government Printing Office.

Pierce, D. (1993). Edu-tourism. *Winds of Change, 8,* 62-65.

Pillemer, K. (1988). Maltreatment of patients in nursing homes: Overview and research agenda. *Journal of Health and Social Behavior, 29*(3), 227-238.

Pillemer, K., & Finkelhor, D. (1989). The prevalence of elder abuse: A random sample survey. *The Gerontologist, 28,* 51-57.

Pillemer, K., & Moore, D. W. (1989). Abuse of patients in nursing homes: Findings from a survey of staff. *The Gerontologist, 29,* 132-135.

Pirie, P. L., Elias, W. S., Wackman, D. B., Jacobs, D. R., Murray, D. M., Mittelmark, M. B., Luipker, R. V., & Blackburn, H. (1986). Characteristics of participants and non-participants in a community cardiovascular disease risk factor screening: The Minnesota Heart Health Program. *American Journal of Preventive Medicine, 2,* 20-25.

Ponza, M., Ohls, J. C., & Millen, B. E. (1996). *Serving elders at risk: The Older Americans Act nutrition programs national evaluation of the elderly nutrition program, 1993-1995.* Washington, DC: U.S. Department of Health and Human Services.

Posner, B. M. (1979). *Nutrition and the elderly.* Lexington, MA: Lexington Books.

Powers, E., & Bultena, G. (1974). Correspondence between anticipated and actual uses of public services by the aged. *Social Service Review, 48,* 245-254.

Pynoos, J. (1992). Strategies for home modification and repair. *Generations, 16*(2), 21-25.

Quinn, J. (1993). *Successful case management in long-term care.* New York: Springer.

Quinn, J., Burkhauser, R., & Myers, D. (1990). *Passing the torch: The influence of economic incentives on work and retirement.* Kalamazoo, MI: W. E. Upjohn Institution for Employment Research.

Quirk, D. A., Whaley, J. S., & Hutchinson, A. B. (1994). *Enhancing the capacity of state aging information and referral systems to meet the future needs of an aging society.* Washington, DC: National Association of State Units on Aging.

Rabins, P. V. (1986). Establishing Alzheimer's units in nursing homes: Pros and cons. *Hospital and Community Psychiatry, 37,* 120-121.

Raiff, N., & Shore, B. (1993). *Advanced case management: New strategies for the nineties.* Newbury Park, CA: Sage.

Railroad Retirement Act of 1937, 45 U.S.C. § 201 *et seq.* (1995).

Ralston, P. (1982). Perceptions of senior centers by the black elderly: A comparative study. *Journal of Gerontological Social Work, 4,* 127-137.

Ralston, P. (1985, November). *Determinants of senior center attendance.* Paper presented at the Annual Scientific Meeting of the Gerontological Society of America, New Orleans, LA.

Ralston, P. (1991). Senior centers and minority elderly: A critical review. *The Gerontologist, 31,* 325-331.

Ralston, P. (1993). Health promotion for rural black elderly: A comprehensive review. *Journal of Gerontological Social Work, 20,* 53-78.

Ralston, P., & Cohen, N. L. (1994). Nutrition and the rural elderly. In J. Krout (Ed.), *Providing community-based services to the rural elderly* (pp. 202-220). Thousand Oaks, CA: Sage.

Rasmussen, W. (1989). *Taking the university to the people: Seventy-five years of cooperative extension.* Ames: Iowa State University Press.

Rayman, P., Allshouse, K., & Allen, J. (1993). Resiliency amidst inequity: Older women workers in an aging United States. In J. Allen & A. Pifer (Eds.), *Women on the front lines: Meeting the challenges of an aging America* (pp. 133-166). Washington, DC: Urban Institute.

Redford, L., & Severns, A. (1994). Home health services in rural America. In J. Krout (Ed.), *Providing community-based services to the rural elderly* (pp. 221-242). Thousand Oaks, CA: Sage.

Regan, J. (1990). Home care and the government regulations and reimbursement. In C. Zuckerman, N. Dubler, & B. Collopy (Eds.), *Home health care options: A guide for older persons and concerned families* (pp. 59-88). New York: Plenum.

Region VIII Office, Administration on Aging. (n.d.). *Title IV research and development: History of making a difference.* Denver, CO: Author.

Regnier, V. (1988). Sensitive environments that overcome barriers. *Architecture California, 10,* 18-26.

Regnier, V., & Culver, J. (1994, February). Single room occupancy: SRO-type housing for older people. *The Supportive Housing Connection: A Technical Assistance Quarterly From the National Eldercare Institute on Housing and Supportive Services,* 1-3.

Rehabilitation Act of 1973, 29 U.S.C. § 701 *et seq.*

Reschovsky, J. D., & Newman, S. J. (1991). Home upkeep and housing quality of older homeowners. *Journal of Gerontology, 46,* S288-S297.

Revenue Act of 1921, Pub. L. No. 136, 42 Stat. 227 (1921).

Rich, B. M., & Baum, M. (1984). *The aging: A guide to public policy.* Pittsburgh, PA: University of Pittsburgh Press.

Richardson, V. (1990). Gender differences in retirement planning among educators: Implications for practice with older women. *Journal of Women and Aging, 2,* 27-40.

Richardson, V. (1993). *Retirement counseling.* New York: Springer.

Riddick, C., & Keller, J. (1991). The benefits of therapeutic recreation in gerontology. In C. P. Coyle, W. B. Kinney, B. Riley, & J. Shank (Eds.), *Benefits of therapeutic recreation: A consensus view* (pp. 151-204). Philadelphia: Temple University Press.

Riddick, C. C., & Stewart, D. G. (1994). An examination of the life satisfaction and importance of leisure in the lives of older female retirees: A comparison of blacks to whites. *Journal of Leisure Research, 26*(1), 75-87.

Rife, J. (1992). Case manager's perceptions of case management practice: Implications for educational preparation. *Journal of Applied Social Sciences, 16,* 161-176.

Riley, T. (1989). *Quality assurance in home care.* Washington, DC: AARP Public Policy Institute.

Rix, S. (1994). *Older workers: How do they measure up? An overview of age differences in employee cost and performance.* Washington, DC: American Association of Retired Persons.

Roberto, K. A. (1990, April). *Education and training of family caregivers in rural areas.* Paper presented at the meeting of the National Council on the Aging, Washington, DC.

Roberto, K. A., & Scott, J. (1986). Equity considerations in the friendships of older adults. *Journal of Gerontology, 41,* 241-247.

Roberto, K. A., & Stroes, J. (1992). Grandchildren and grandparents: Roles, influences, and relationships. *International Journal of Aging and Human Development, 34,* 227-239.

Robins, B., & Howe, E. (1989). Patterns of homesharing in the United States. In D. J. Jaffe (Ed.), *Shared housing for the elderly* (pp. 25-36). New York: Greenwood.

Rogers, C. R. (1991). Health and social characteristics of the nonmetro elderly. *Agriculture Outlook, 92*(4), 21-29.

Rollinson, P. A. (1990). The story of Edward: The everyday geography of elderly single room occupancy (SRO) hotel tenants. *Journal of Contemporary Ethnography, 19*(2), 188-206.

Rollinson, P. A. (1991a). Elderly single room occupancy (SRO) hotel tenants: Still alone. *Social Work, 36,* 303-308.

Rollinson, P. A. (1991b). The spatial isolation of elderly single-room-occupancy hotel tenants. *The Professional Geographer, 43,* 457-464.

Ronch, J. (1987). Specialized Alzheimer's units in nursing homes: Pros and cons. *American Journal of Alzheimer's Care and Research, 2,* 10-19.

Rook, K. S. (1987). Reciprocity of social exchange and social satisfaction among older women. *Journal of Personality and Social Psychology, 52,* 145-154.

Ropes, J. (1991). Senior environmental employment program. In *Resourceful aging: Today and tomorrow: Vol. 4. Work/second careers* (pp. 93-94). Washington, DC: American Association of Retired Persons.

Rose, J., & DelMaestro, S. (1990), Separation-individuation conflict as a model for understanding distressed caregivers: Psychodynamic and cognitive case studies. *The Gerontologist, 30,* 693-697.

Rosenbloom, S. (1993a). *ElderTransit facts: Issues of concern in aging and transportation* [Brochure]. Washington, DC: National Eldercare Institute on Transportation.

Rosenbloom, S. (1993b). *ElderTransit facts: What you should know about the Americans With Disabilities Act* [Brochure]. Washington, DC: National Eldercare Institute on Transportation.

Rosenbloom, S. (1993c). *Will older persons lose mobility?* Washington, DC: American Association of Retired Persons.

Rosenheimer, L., & Francis, E. (1992). Feasible with subsidy: Overnight respite for Alzheimer's. *Journal of Gerontological Nursing, 18,* 21-29.

Rosenzwieg, E. (1995). Trends in home care entitlements and benefits. *Journal of Gerontological Social Work, 24,* 9-29.

Rowland, D., & Lyons, B. (1991). A proposal to expand home care benefits. In D. Rowland & B. Lyons (Eds.), *Financing home care: Improving protection for disabled elderly people* (pp. 229-247). Baltimore: Johns Hopkins University Press.

Ruchlin, H. S., Morris, S., & Morris, J. N. (1993). Resident medical care utilization patterns in continuing care retirement communities. *Health Care Finance Review, 14*(4), 151-168.

Rucker, G. (1994). *Status report on public transportation in rural America.* Washington, DC: Community Transportation Association of America.

Rucker, G. (1995a). *ElderTransit facts: Legislation of interest to community transportation: Intermodal Surface Transportation Efficiency Act (ISTEA)* [Brochure]. Washington, DC: National Eldercare Institute on Transportation.

Rucker, G. (1995b). *Rural transit: Stretching to meet the needs of the neediest* (National Transit Resource Center Fact Sheet 9). Washington, DC: National Transit Resource Center.

Ryan, V. C., & Bower, M. E. (1989). Relationship of socioeconomic status and living arrangements to nutritional intake of the older persons. *Journal of the American Dietetic Association, 89,* 1805-1807.

Salamon, M., & Rosenthal, G. (1990). *Home or nursing home: Making the right choices.* New York: Springer.

Sangl, J. (1985). The family support system of the elderly. In R. J. Vogel & H. C. Palmer (Eds.), *Long-term care: Perspectives from research and demonstration* (pp. 307-336). Rockville, MD: Aspen.

Saxton, S. V., & Etten, M. J. (1994). *Physical change and aging: A guide for the helping professions* (3rd ed.). New York: Tiresias.

Schafer, R. B., & Keith, P. M. (1982). Social-psychological factors in the dietary quality of married and single elderly. *Journal of the American Dietetic Association, 81,* 30-34.

Schaie, K. W. (1994). The course of adult intellectual development. *American Psychologist, 49*(4), 304-313.

Scharlach, A., & Boyd, S. C. (1989). Caregiving and employment: Results of an employee survey. *The Gerontologist, 29,* 382-387.

Scharlach, A., & Frenzel, C. (1986). An evaluation of institutional-based respite care. *The Gerontologist, 26,* 77-82.

Scharlach, A., Lowe, B., & Schneider, E. (1991). *Elder care and the work force: Blueprint for action.* Lexington, MA: Lexington Books.

Schauer, P. M., & Weaver, P. (1994). Rural elder transportation. In J. A. Krout (Ed.), *Providing community-based services to the rural elderly,* pp. 42-64. Thousand Oaks, CA: Sage.

Schlenker, R. E., Shaughnessy, P. W., & Crisler, K. S. (1995). Outcome-based continuous quality of improvement as a financial strategy for home health care agencies. *Journal of Home Health Care, 7*(4), 1-15.

Schmall, V., & Webb, L. (1994). Respite and adult day care for rural elders. In J. Krout (Ed.), *Providing community-based services to the rural elderly* (pp. 156-178). Thousand Oaks, CA: Sage.

Schmid, H. (1993). Home care workers' assessment of differences between nonprofit and for-profit organizations delivering home care services to the Israeli elderly. *Home Health Care Services Quarterly, 14,* 127-147.

Schoeffler, R. W. (1995). Senior centers as brokers of home and community-based long term care. In D. Shollenberger (Ed.), *Senior centers in America: A blueprint for the future: Outcomes of a national meeting convened to develop recommendations for programs, policies, and funding of senior center programs of the future.* Washington, DC: National Council on the Aging.

Scholen, K. (1990). *Home-made money: A consumer's guide to home equity conversion.* Washington, DC: American Association of Retired Persons.

Schraeder, C., Fraser, C., Bruno, C., & Dworak, D. (1990). *Case management in primary care: A manual.* Englewood, CO: Center for Research in Ambulatory Health Care Administration.

Schultz, J. (1992). *The economics of aging* (5th ed.). Westport, CT: Auburn House.

Schultz, J. (1995). *The economics of aging* (6th ed.). Westport, CT: Auburn House.

Schwenk, F. N. (1992). Economic status of rural older adults. *Agriculture Outlook, 92*(4), 3-14.

Second, L. (1987). *Private case management for older persons and their families: Practice, policy, potential.* Excelsior, MN: Interstudy Center for Aging and Long-Term Care.

Seltzer, B., Rheaume, Y., Volicer, L., Fabiszewski, K., Lyon, P., Brown, J., & Volicer, B. (1988). The short-term effects of in-hospital respite on the patient with Alzheimer's disease. *The Gerontologist, 28,* 121-124.

SeniorNet. (1997). *Inside SeniorNet* [Online]. Available: http://www.seniornet. org/inside/about.html

Shanas, E. (1979). Older people and their families: The new pioneers. *Journal of Marriage and the Family, 42,* 9-15.

Shapiro, E. (1995). Case management in long-term care: Exploring its status, trends, and issues. *Journal of Case Management, 4,* 43-47.

Shapiro, E. G. (1983). Embarrassment and help-seeking. In J. D. Fisher, A. Nadler, & B. M. DePaulo (Eds.), *New directions in helping* (Vol. 2). New York: Academic Press.

Shawn, K. (1994). *American Indian transportation: Issues and successful models* (Tech. Assistance Brief No. 14). Washington, DC: National Transit Resource Center.

Shelton, P., Schraeder, C., Britt, T., & Kirby, R. (1994). A generalist physician-based model for a rural geriatric collaborative practice. *Journal of Case Management, 3,* 98-104.

Sherman, S. R., & Newman, E. S. (1988). *Foster families for adults: A community alternative in long-term care.* New York: Columbia University Press.

Sherwood, S., Ruchlin, H. S., & Sherwood, C. (1989). CCRCs: An option for aging in place. In D. Tilson (Ed.), *Aging in place: Supporting the frail elderly in residential environments.* Glenview, IL: Scott, Foresman.

Siegel, P. M. (1989). *Educational attainment in the United States: March 1982 to 1985* (U.S. Bureau of the Census, Current Population Reports, Series P-20, No. 415). Washington, DC: Government Printing Office.

Silvey, R. (1962). Participation in a senior citizen day center. In J. Kaplan & G. J. Aldridge (Eds.), *Social welfare of the aging.* New York: Columbia University Press.

Sinnen, M., & Schifalacqua, M. (1991). Coordinated care in a community hospital. *Nursing Administration, 22,* 38-42.

Sirrocco, A. (1988). *Nursing and related care homes as reported from the 1986 inventory of long-term care places.* Hyattsville, MD: National Center for Health Statistics.

Slone, P. D., Lindeman, D. A., Phillips, C., Moritz, D. J., & Koch, G. (1995). Evaluating Alzheimer's special care units: Reviewing the evidence and identifying potential sources of study bias. *The Gerontologist, 35,* 103-111.

Smale, B. J. A., & Dupuis, S. L. (1993). The relationship between leisure activity participation and psychological well-being across the lifespan. *Journal of Applied Recreation Research, 18,* 281-300.

Small, N. R. (1988). Evolution of nursing homes. In N. R. Small & M. B. Walsh (Eds.), *Teaching nursing homes: The nursing perspective* (pp. 31-46). Owings Mills, MD: National Health Publishing.

Smallegan, M. (1985). There was nothing else to do: Needs for care before nursing home admission. *The Gerontologist, 25,* 364-369.

Smith, G., Smith, M., & Toseland, R. (1991). Problems identified by family caregivers in counseling. *The Gerontologist, 31,* 15-22.

Smith, K. F., & Bengston, V. L. (1979). The positive consequences of institutionalization: Solidarity between elderly parents and their middle-aged children. *The Gerontologist, 19,* 438-447.

Smith, L. (1992, January 13). The tyranny of America's old. *Fortune, 125,* 68-72.

Smith, T., & Newman, S. (1992). Older adults in Head Start. *National Head Start Association Journal, 10,* 33-35.

Smith, T., & Newman, S. (1993). Older adults in early childhood programs: Why and how. *Young Children, 48,* 32-35.

Social Security Act of 1935, 42 U.S.C. § 301 *et seq.* (1935), as amended 1939, 1950, 1956, 1961, 1965, 1972, 1974.

Social Security Administration. (1996a). *Social Security beneficiaries* [Online]. Available: http://www.ssa.gov/statistics/chart.html

Social Security Administration. (1996b). *Social Security: You may be able to get benefits.* Washington, DC: Author.

Social Security Administration. (1997a). *History of Social Security* [Online]. Available: http://www.ssa.gov/history/history6.html

Social Security Administration. (1997b). *Social Security benefits* [Online]. Available: http://www.ssa.gov/OACT/ProgData/benefits.html and www.ssa.gov/pubs/10080.html

Southwestern Indiana Regional Council on Aging. (1997). *First call for help* [Online information and referral home page]. Available: http://www.accessevansville.org

Spangenberg Group. (1991). *Wisconsin elder legal needs study: Final report of the American Bar Association Commission on legal problems of the elderly.* Madison, WI: Author.

Special Committee on Aging. (1963). *A compilation of materials relevant to the message of the president of the United States on our nation's senior citizens.* Washington, DC: Government Printing Office.

Spense, S. A. (1992). Use of community-based social services by older rural and urban blacks: An exploratory study. *Human Services in the Rural Environment, 15*(4), 16-19.

Spillman, B. C., & Kemper, P. (1995). Lifetime patterns for nursing home care. *Medical Care, 35*(3), 280-296.

Spitz, B., & Abramson, J. (1987). Competition, capitation, and case management: Barriers to strategic reform. *Millbank Quarterly, 65,* 348-370.

Stanford, P., & Bois, B. (1992). Gender and ethnicity patterns. In J. Birren, R. B. Sloane, & G. Cohen (Eds.), *Handbook of mental health and aging* (2nd ed., pp. 99-117). New York: Academic Press.

Stanley, D., & Freysinger, V. J. (1995). The impact of age, health, and sex on the frequency of older adults' leisure activity participation: A longitudinal study. *Activities, Adaptation, & Aging, 19,* 31-42.

Starret, R. A., Wright, R., Mindle, C. H., & Van Tran, T. (1989). The use of social services by Hispanic elderly: A comparison of Mexican American, Puerto Rican and Cuban elderly. *Journal of Social Service Research, 13*(1), 1-25.

Steele, M. F., & Bryan, J. D. (1986). Dietary intake of homebound elderly recipients and nonrecipients of home-delivered meals. *Journal of Nutrition and the Elderly, 5,* 23-35.

Stentzel, C., & Steenland, S. (1987). *Women, work, and age: A report on older women and employment.* Washington, DC: National Commission on Working Women.

Sterns, H., & McDaniel, M. (1994). Job performance and the older worker. In S. Rix (Ed.), *Older workers: How do they measure up?* Washington, DC: American Association of Retired Persons.

Steuerle, C. E., & Bakija, J. M. (1994). *Retooling social security for the 21st century: Right and wrong approaches to reform.* Washington, DC: Urban Institute.

Stevens, D. A., Grivetti, L. E., & McDonald, R. B. (1992). Nutrient intake of urban and rural elderly receiving home-delivered meals. *Journal of the American Dietetic Association, 92*(6), 714-718.

Stevens, E. (1991). Toward satisfaction and retention of senior volunteers. *Journal of Gerontological Social Work, 16*(3/4), 33-41.

Stevens, E. (1993). Older women who volunteer: Tapping a valuable woman resource. *Journal of Volunteer Administration, 11*(4), 9-13.

Stoller, E. P. (1989). Formal services and informal helping: The myth of service substitution. *Journal of Applied Gerontology, 8,* 37-52.

Stoller, E. P., & Pugliesi, K. (1988). Informal networks of community based elderly: Changes in composition over time. *Research on Aging, 10,* 499-516.

Stone, R., Cafferata, G., & Sangl, J. (1987). Caregivers of the frail elderly: A national profile. *The Gerontologist, 27,* 616-626.

Storey, R. (1962). Who attends a senior activity center? A comparison of Little House members with non-members in the same community. *The Gerontologist, 2,* 216-222.

Strauss, P. J., Wolf, R., & Schilling, D. (1990). *Aging and the law.* Chicago: Commerce Clearing House.

Strawbridge, W., & Wallhagen, M. (1991). Impact of family conflict on adult child caregivers. *The Gerontologist, 31,* 770-777.

Stremmel, A., Travis, S., Kelly-Harrison, P., & Hensley, A. D. (1994). The perceived benefits and problems associated with intergenerational exchanges in day care settings. *The Gerontologist, 34,* 513-519.

Struntz, K. A., & Reville, S. (1985). *Growing together: An intergenerational sourcebook.* Washington, DC: American Association of Retired Persons.

Sugerman, D. (1989). A "wild idea: Adventure programs help seniors "age successfully." *Camping Magazine, 61,* 18-21.

Suitor, J. J., & Pillemer, K. (1990). Transitions to the status of family caregiver: A new framework for studying social support and well-being. In S. M. Stahl (Ed.), *The legacy of longevity* (pp. 310-320). Newbury Park, CA: Sage.

Swan, J. H., & Benjamin, A. E. (1990). Nursing costs of skilled nursing care for AIDS. *AIDS and Public Policy Journal, 5,* 64-67.

Taietz, P. (1976). Two conceptual models of the senior center. *Journal of Gerontology, 31,* 219-222.

Takamura, J. C. (1991). Dana is joy: A volunteer caregivers' program in the Buddhist tradition. *Generations, 15*(4), 79.

Taube, C., Goldman, H., & Salkever, D. (1990). Medicaid coverage for mental illness: Balancing access and costs. *Health Affairs, 9,* 5-18.

Tax Equity and Fiscal Responsibility Act of 1982, Pub. L. No. 97-248, 96 Stat. 324 (1982).

Teague, M. L. (1987). *Health promotion programs: Achieving high-level wellness in the later years.* Indianapolis, IN: Benchmark.

Tessler, R. C., & Schwartz, S. H. (1972). Help seeking, self-esteem, and achievement motivation: An attributional analysis. *Journal of Personality and Social Psychology, 21*(3), 318-326.

Tokarek, J. (1996). Keeping frail seniors independent through money management. *Aging, 367,* 84-86.

Toseland, R., & Rossiter, C. (1989). Group interventions to support family caregivers: A review and analysis. *The Gerontologist, 29,* 438-448.

Toseland, R., & Smith, G. (1990). Effectiveness of individual counseling by professional and peer helpers for family caregivers of the elderly. *Psychology and Aging, 5,* 256-263.

Travis, S. S. (1995). Families and formal networks. In R. Blieszner & V. H. Bedford (Eds.), *Handbook of aging and the family,* pp. 459-473. Westport, CT: Greenwood.

Urban Institute. (1993). *Hunger and food insecurity among the elderly.* Washington, DC: Author.

Urban Mass Transportation Act of 1964, 49 U.S.C. § 1601 *et seq.* (1964).

Urv-Wong, E., & McDowell, D. (1994). Case management in a rural setting. In J. Krout (Ed.), *Providing community-based services to the rural elderly* (pp. 65-89). Thousand Oaks, CA: Sage.

U.S. Bureau of the Census. (1990a). *Census of population: General population characteristics: United States* (CP-1-1). Washington, DC: Government Printing Office.

U.S. Bureau of the Census. (1990b). *Money income and poverty in the United States: 1989* (Current Population Reports, Series P-60, No. 168). Washington, DC: Government Printing Office.

U.S. Bureau of the Census. (1992). *Sixty-five plus in America* (Current Population Reports, Series P-23, No. 178). Washington, DC: Government Printing Office.

U.S. Bureau of the Census. (1993). *Population projections of the United States by age, sex, race, and Hispanic origin: 1993 to 2050* (Current Population Reports, Series P-25-1104). Washington, DC: Government Printing Office.

U.S. Bureau of the Census. (1994a). *Educational attainment in the United States: March 1993 and 1992* (Current Population Reports, Series P-20, No. 476). Washington, DC: Government Printing Office.

U.S. Bureau of the Census. (1994b). *Education in the United States* (CP-3-4). Washington, DC: Government Printing Office.

U.S. Bureau of the Census. (1994c). *Statistical abstract of the United States*. Washington, DC: Government Printing Office.

U.S. Bureau of the Census. (1996a). *65+ in the United States* (Current Population Reports, Special Studies, Series P-23, No. 190). Washington, DC: Goverment Printing Office.

U.S. Bureau of the Census. (1996b). *Statistical abstract of the United States* (116th ed.). Washington, DC: Author.

U.S. Commission on Civil Rights. (1982). *Minority elderly services: New programs, old problems: A report of the United States Commission on Civil Rights*. Washington, DC: Author.

U.S. Congress, Office of Technology Assessment. (1987). *Losing a million minds: Confronting the tragedy of Alzheimer's disease and other dementias*. Washington, DC: Government Printing Office.

U.S. Congress, Office of Technology Assessment. (1990). *Health care in rural American* (Publication No. OTA-H-434). Washington, DC: Government Printing Office.

U.S. Congress, Office of Technology Assessment. (1992). *Special care units for people with Alzheimer's and other dementias: Consumer education, research, regulatory, and reimbursement issues* (Publication No. OTA-H-543). Washington, DC: Government Printing Office.

U.S. Department of Education. (1990, June). *National goals for education 2000*. Washington, DC: Author.

U.S. Department of Health and Human Services. (1990). *Healthy people 2000: National health promotion and disease prevention objectives*. Washington, DC: Government Printing Office.

U.S. Department of Health and Human Services. (1991). *Mental illness in nursing homes: United States, 1985* (DHHS Publication No. PHS 91-1766). Washington, DC: Government Printing Office.

U.S. Department of Health and Human Services. (1993). *Growing older: Healthy black lifestyles: The health promotion programs in historically black colleges and universities* (DHHS Publication No. MF 0447-A-01). Washington, DC: Government Printing Office.

U.S. Department of Health and Human Services. (1997). *Low-Income Home Energy Assistance Program: Funding 1997* [Online]. Available: http://www.acf.dhhs.gov/programs/liheap/funding.htm#fy97

U.S. Department of Health, Education and Welfare. (1964, August). Foster care. *Aging, 16,* 1-3.

U.S. Department of Health, Education and Welfare. (1979). *Healthy people: The surgeon general's report on health promotion and disease prevention* (PHS Publication No. 79-55071). Washington, DC: Government Printing Office.

U.S. Department of Labor. (1989). *Trends in pensions.* Washington, DC: Pensions and Welfare Benefits Administration.

U.S. Department of Labor. (1990a, January). *Employment and earnings* (Vol. 37, No. 1). Washington, DC: Bureau of Statistics.

U.S. Department of Labor, Bureau of Labor Statistics. (1990b, March 29). *Thirty-eight million persons do volunteer work* (Press Release 90-154). Washington, DC: Author.

U.S. Department of Labor. (1993, Summer). *Private pension plan bulletin.* Washington, DC: Author.

U.S. Department of Labor. (1994). *1993 handbook on women workers: Trends and issues.* Washington, DC: Women's Bureau.

U.S. Department of Transportation. (1980). *Elderly market for urban mass transit.* Washington, DC: Government Printing Office.

U.S. General Accounting Office. (1991a). *Longstanding transportation problems need more federal attention* (Publication No. HRD-91-117). Washington, DC: Government Printing Office.

U.S. General Accounting Office. (1991b). *Older Americans Act: Promising practice in information and referral services* (GAO Publication No. PEMD-91-31). Washington, DC: Government Printing Office.

U.S. General Accounting Office. (1993). *Long-term care case management: State experiences and implication for federal policy.* Washington, DC: Author.

U.S. General Accounting Office. (1995). *Supplemental Security Income: Growth and changes in recipient population call for re-examining program* (GAO Publication No. HEHS-95-137). Washington, DC: Government Printing Office.

U.S. General Accounting Office. (1996a). *Medicaid long-term care: State use of assessment instruments in care planning.* Washington, DC: Author.

U.S. General Accounting Office. (1996b). *Medicare HMO's: Rapid enrollment growth concentrated in selected states* (GAO Publication No. HEHS-96-63). Washington, DC: Government Printing Office.

U.S. House Select Committee on Aging. (1984). *Quackery: A $10 billion scandal* (Comm. Publication No. 98-435). Washington, DC: Government Printing Office.

U.S. House Select Committee on Aging. (1992a). *Elderly households: A profile* (Comm. Publication No. 102-912). Washington, DC: Government Printing Office.

U.S. House Select Committee on Aging. (1992b). *Hunger and nutrition: Challenges to older Americans' health* (Comm. Publication No. 102-872). Washington, DC: Government Printing Office.

U.S. House Select Committee on Aging. (1992c). *Older workers in the labor market* (Comm. Publication No. 102-839). Washington, DC: Government Printing Office.

U.S. Housing Act, 12 U.S.C. §§ 24, 371, 1422, 1423, 1430 *et seq.* (1975).

U.S. Library of Congress. (1995a). *H.R. 2076: Payments to the Legal Services Corporation* (104th Cong., 1st Sess.). Available via WWW. Server: rs9.loc.gov. Directory: cgi-bin/query/3?c104:./temp. File: 104ZrhX:e149049: legal+services+corporation

U.S. Library of Congress. (1995b). *H.R. 4603: Payment to the Legal Services Corporation* (103d Cong., 2d Sess.). Available via WWW. Server: rs9.loc. gov. Directory: cgi-bin/query/3?c103:./temp. File: c103h7Ut:e108477: legal+services+corporation

U.S. Senate Special Committee on Aging. (1990). *Developments in aging: 1989* (Vol. 1). Washington, DC: Government Printing Office.

U.S. Senate Special Committee on Aging. (1991a). *Aging America: Trends and projections* (DHHS Publication No. FCoA 91-28001). Washington, DC: Department of Health and Human Services.

U.S. Senate Special Committee on Aging. (1991b). *Developments in aging: 1990* (Vol. 1). Washington, DC: Government Printing Office.

U.S. Senate Special Committee on Aging. (1991c). *Lifelong learning for an aging society* (No. 102-J). Washington, DC: Author.

U.S. Senate Special Committee on Aging. (1992). *Developments in aging: 1991* (Vol. 1). Washington, DC: Government Printing Office.

U.S. Senate Special Committee on Aging. (1993). *Developments in aging: 1992* (Vol. 1). Washington, DC: Government Printing Office.

U.S. Small Business Administration. (1995). *SCORE: Service Corps of Retired Executives* [Online]. Available: http://www.wings.usps.gov/Federal/SBA/score.html

Varady, D. P. (1990). Which elderly home owners are interested in accessory apartment conversion and home-sharing? *Journal of Housing for the Elderly, 6*(1/2), 87-99.

Ventura-Merkel, C. (1991). Community colleges in an aging society. In *Resourceful aging: Today and tomorrow: Vol. 5. Lifelong education* (pp. 49-56). Washington, DC: American Association of Retired Persons.

Wachs, M. (1979). *Transportation for the elderly.* Berkeley: University of California Press.

Wacker, R. R. (1985). *Long term care admission agreements in Colorado: A review.* Denver, CO: Advocacy Assistance Program.

Wacker, R. R. (1992). *What do you think? An evaluation of the Weld County senior nutrition program*. Greeley: University of Northern Colorado.

Wacker, R. R. (1996). *Improving quality of care for nursing home residents: An innovative community program to enhance certified nurse aide training: Final report to the Retirement Research Foundation*. Greeley: University of Northern Colorado.

Wacker, R. R., & Blanding, C. (1994). *Comprehensive leisure and aging study: Final report*. Washington, DC: National Recreation and Park Association.

Waggoner, G. (1995). Adopt an elder: Linking youth and the elderly. *Activities, Adaptation, & Aging, 20,* 41-52.

Wagner, D. L. (1995a). Senior center research in America: An overview of what we know. In D. Shollenberger (Ed.), *Senior centers in America: A blueprint for the future: Outcomes of a national meeting convened to develop recommendations for programs, policies, and funding of senior center programs of the future*. Washington, DC: National Council on the Aging.

Wagner, D. L. (1995b). Senior centers and the "new" elderly cohorts of tomorrow. In D. Shollenberger (Ed.), *Senior centers in America: A blueprint for the future: Outcomes of a national meeting convened to develop recommendations for programs, policies, and funding of senior center programs of the future*. Washington, DC: National Council on the Aging.

Wagner, E. H., Grothaus, L. C., Hecht, J. A., & LaCroix, A. Z. (1991). Factors associated with participation in a senior health promotion program. *The Gerontologist, 31,* 598-602.

Wagnild, G., & Grupp, K. (1991). Major stressors among elderly home care clients. *Home Healthcare Nurse, 9,* 15-21.

Waldman, S. (1985). A legislative history of nursing home care. In R. J. Vogel & H. C. Palmer (Eds.), *Long-term care: Perspectives from research and demonstrations* (pp. 507-535). Rockville, MD: Aspen.

Walker, D., & Beauchene, R. E. (1991). The relationship of loneliness, social isolation, and physical health to dietary adequacy of independently living elderly. *Journal of the American Dietetic Association, 91*(3), 300-305.

Walker, S. N. (1889). Health promotion for older adults: Directions for research. *American Journal of Health Promotion, 3,* 47-52.

Walster, E., Berscheid, E., & Walster, G. W. (1973). New directions in equity research. *Journal of Personality and Social Psychology, 25,* 176-184.

Warrick, L., Netting, E., Christianson, J., & Williams, F. (1992). Hospital-based case management: Results from a demonstration. *The Gerontologist, 32,* 781-788.

Warshaw, G. (1988). Health promotion and aging: Preventive health services. *Surgeon general's workshop: Health promotion and aging*. Washington, DC: Government Printing Office.

Webb, L., & Heide, J. (1991). *Day care programs and services for elders in rural America.* Kansas City, MO: National Center for Rural Elderly.

Webber, P. A., Fox, P., & Burnette, D. (1994). Living alone with Alzheimer's disease: Effects on health and social service utilization patterns. *The Gerontolgist, 34,* 8-14.

Weiner, J., Illston, L., & Hanley, R. (1994). *Sharing the burden: Strategies for public and private long-term care insurance.* Washington, DC: Brookings Institution.

Weinstock, R. (1978). *The graying of the campus.* New York: Educational Facilities Laboratory.

Weissert, W. (1977). Adult day care programs in the United States: Current research projects and a survey of ten centers. *Public Health Reports, 92,* 49-56.

Weissert, W., Elston, J., Bolda, E., Cready, C., Zelman, W., Sloane, P., Kalsbeek, W., Murtrun, E., Rice, T., & Koch, G. (1989). Models of adult day care: Findings from a national survey. *The Gerontologist, 29,* 640-649.

Wellman, B., & Wortley, S. (1989). Brothers' keepers: Situating kinship relations in broader networks of social support. *Sociological Perspectives, 32,* 273-306.

Wellman, N. S. (1994). The nutrition screening initiative. *Nutrition Reviews, 52*(8), S44-S47.

West, G. E., Delisle, M.-A. Simard, C., & Drouin, D. (1996). Leisure activities and service knowledge and use among the rural elderly. *Journal of Aging and Health, 8,* 254-279.

Whaley, J. S., & Hutchinson, A. B. (1993a). *Assessment guide for Older Americans Act information and referral services.* Washington, DC: National Information and Referral Support Center.

Whaley, J. S., & Hutchinson, A. B. (1993b). *Implementation guide for Older Americans Act information and referral services.* Washington, DC: National Information and Referral Support Center.

Whaley, J. S., & Hutchinson, A. B. (1993c). *National standards for Older Americans Act information and referral services.* Washington, DC: National Information and Referral Support Center.

White House Conference on Aging. (1995). *The road to an aging policy for the 21st century: Final report of the 1995 White House Conference on Aging.* Washington, DC: Author.

White, J. V., Ham, R. J., & Lipschitz, D. A. (1991). *Report of nutritional screening: Vol. 1. Toward a common view.* Washington, DC: Nutrition Screening Initiative.

White, M., Gundrum, G., Shearer, S., & Simmons, J. (1994). A role for case managers in the physician office. *Journal of Case Management, 3,* 62-68.

Wiencek, T. (1991). How the Older Workers' Benefit Protection Act affects employers. *The Practice Lawyer, 37,* 69-76.

Wiener, J. M., Hanley, R. J., Clark, R., & Van Norstrand, J. F. (1990). Measuring activities of daily living: Comparisons across national surveys. *Journal of Gerontology, 45*(6), S229-S237.

Wilhite, B. C., Sheldon, K., & Jekubovich-Fenton, N. (1994). Leisure in daily life: Older widows living alone. *Journal of Park and Recreation Administration, 12,* 64-78.

Wilke, H., & Lazette, J. T. (1970). The obligation to help: The effects of amount of prior help on subsequent helping behavior. *Journal of Experimental Social Psychology, 6,* 488-493.

Williamson, J. B. (1974). The stigma of public dependency: A comparison of alternative forms of public aid to the poor. *Social Problems, 22,* 213-238.

Wilson, L., & Simson, S. (1993). Senior volunteerism policies at the local level: Adaptation and leadership in the 21st century. *Journal of Volunteer Administration, 11*(4), 15-23.

Wingard, D. L., Jones, D. W., & Kaplan, R. M. (1987). Institutional care utilization by the elderly: A critical review. *The Gerontologist, 27,* 156-163.

Wolf, N., Weisbrod, B. A., & Stearns, S. (1988). Summary proceedings long-term care for the elderly: Issues and options. *Journal of Aging Studies, 2*(1), 83-94.

Wolf, R. S. (1996). Understanding elder abuse and neglect. *Aging, 367,* 4-9.

Wurtman, J. J., Lieberman, H., Tsay, R., Nader, T., & Chew, B. (1988). Calorie and nutrient intakes of elderly and young subjects measured under identical conditions. *Journal of Gerontology, 79,* 117-131.

Wykle, M., Segall, M., & Nagley, S. (1992). Mental health and aging: Hospital care: A nursing perspective. In J. Birren, R. B. Sloane, & G. Cohen (Eds.), *Handbook of mental health and aging* (2nd ed., pp. 815-831). New York: Academic Press.

Yeo, G. (1993). Ethnicity and nursing homes: Factors affecting use and successful components for culturally sensitive care. In C. M. Barresi & D. E. Stull (Eds.), *Ethnic elderly and long term care* (pp. 161-177). New York: Springer.

Young, K. (1992). LIR program and organizational models. In R. Fischer, M. Blazey, & H. Lipman (Eds.), *Students of the third age* (pp. 25-37). New York: Macmillan.

Zbylot, S., Job, C., McCormick, E., Boulter, C., & Moore, A. (1995). A case-mix classification system for long-term care facilities. *Nursing Management, 26*(4), 49-54.

Zedlewski, S., Barnes, R., Burt, M., McBride, T., & Meyer, J. (1990). *The needs of the elderly in the 21st century* (Urban Institute Report No. 90-5). Washington, DC: Urban Institute.

Zeilinger, C. (1994). *Rural transit in the age of ISTEA* (National Transit Resource Center Info. Brief No. 3). Washington, DC: Community Transportation Association of America.

Index